SPORT AND INTERNATIONAL POLITICS

SPORT AND INTERNATIONAL POLITICS

BARRIE HOULIHAN

New York London Toronto Sydney Tokyo Singapore

First published 1994 by
Harvester Wheatsheaf
Campus 400, Maylands Avenue
Hemel Hempstead
Hertfordshire HP2 7EZ
A division of
Simon & Schuster International Group

Typeset in 10/12pt Ehrhardt
by Inforum, Rowlands Castle, Hants

Printed and bound in Great Britain by
Biddles Ltd, Guildford and King's Lynn

British Library Cataloguing in Publication Data

A catalogue record for this book is available from
the British Library

ISBN 0-7450-1342-2

1 2 3 4 5 98 97 96 95 94

For my mother and father

Contents

Preface

The immediate origins of this book lie in an earlier study of the policy process for sport in Britain. As I explored the policy process for issues such as drug abuse by athletes and football spectator violence I became acutely aware of the extent to which influences on sports policy lay outside the control of national governmental and non-governmental organisations. The longer-term origins of this study lie in a course in 'Sport and World Politics' to which I have contributed for a number of years at Staffordshire University. This book is the outcome of the overlap of interest in sports policy and international politics.

As with all research I have accumulated a number of debts which I am happy to acknowledge. Iain Reddish, Head of the International Unit at the Sports Council, deserves first mention. Not only was he a stimulating source of ideas and information but he also gave me a long list of contacts in the world of international sport. Derek Casey, also at the Sports Council as Director of National Services, provided a number of sharp insights into the relationship of governments to sports organisations and particularly the role of the Council of Europe. George Walker, Head of the CDDS at the Council of Europe, was generous with his time and provided me with invaluable material on the work of the CDDS. John Tomlinson, MEP for Walsall and chair of the EC Intergroup on Sport, provided much useful information on the work of the Intergroup and much stimulating comment on the role of the EC in sports policy. David Dixon, Honorary Secretary to the Commonwealth Games Federation, provided many thoughtful insights into the operation and future of the Commonwealth Games. At the IAAF Jane Pearce and Brian Wootton were always willing to give me some of their time, even during particularly hectic periods. I would also like to take this opportunity to record my thanks to Donald Macintosh, for giving me access to his forthcoming study of sport and Canadian foreign policy, and to David Jary for his comments on Chapter 8.

Finally, I would like to thank Kevin Ellard and his staff at Staffordshire University library who helped me track down a large number of elusive references.

List of abbreviations

AAU	American Athletic Union
ACP	African, Caribbean and Pacific (States)
AENOC	Association of European National Olympic Committees
AIWF	Association of Winter Sports Federations
ANOC	Association of National Olympic Committees
ASOIF	Association of Summer Olympic International Federations
ATP	Association of Tennis Professionals
CCC	Council for Cultural Co-operation
CDDS	Committee for the Development of Sport
CGF	Commonwealth Games Federation
CHOG	Commonwealth Heads of Government
CIGEPS	Intergovernmental Committee for Physical Education and Sport
CONI	National Olympic Committee of Italy
DLV	Deutscher Leichtathletik Verband (German Athletic Federation)
EC	European Community
ECU	European Currency Unit
ENGSO	European Non-governmental Sports Organisations
ESC	European Sports Conference
FIDE	International Chess Federation
FIDEPS	Fund Internationale pour le Développement du Education Physique et Sport
FIFA	International Federation of Football Associations
FINA	International Swimming Federation

FISU	International Federation of University Sport
FRG	Federal Republic of Germany
GAA	Gaelic Athletic Association
GAISF	General Association of International Sports Federations
GANEFO	Games of the New Emerging Forces
GATT	General Agreement on Tariffs and Trading
GDR	German Democratic Republic
IAAF	International Amateur Athletic Federation
IAAR	International Association of Athlete's Representatives
ICC	International Cricket Conference
ICSPE	International Council for Sport and Physical Education
ICSSPE	International Council for Sport Science and Physical Education
IF	International (Sports) Federation
IGO	International Governmental Organisation
IMF	International Monetary Fund
(I)NGO	(International) Non-governmental organisation
IOA	International Olympic Academy
IOC	International Olympic Committee
ITF	International Tennis Federation
MEP	Member of the European Parliament
MNC	Multi-national Corporation
NATO	North Atlantic Treaty Organisation
NIEO	New International Economic Order
NOC	National Olympic Committee
OCA	Olympic Council for Asia
OECD	Organisation for Economic Co-operation and Development
PASO	Pan American Sports Association
PE	Physical education
PRC	People's Republic of China
SAN-ROC	South African Non-Racial Olympic Committee
SCSA	Supreme Council for Sport in Africa
SED	Sozialistische Einheitspartei (Communist Party of the GDR)
TAC	The Athletic Congress
TOP	The Olympic Programme
UEFA	Union of European Football Associations

UNESCO	United Nations Educational, Scientific and Cultural Organisation
USOC	United States Olympic Committee
WPBSA	World Professional Billiards and Snooker Association

Note

Acronyms derived from foreign languages have been given their conventional English expression where possible.

1

Politics and sport

It (sport) is always serious. It is organised: it is an industry; it is business, money, vested interests: it is a medium of and for ideology, prestige, status, nationalism, internationalism, diplomacy and war. (Tatz 1986: 47)

Sport is a political process based on play, game, and posture. If the activity is not serious, neither can be the positions, political or otherwise, of the national players. (Kanin 1980: 3)

Introduction

The 1972 Olympic Games were held in Munich, West Germany. For Lord Killanin, then one of the vice-presidents of the International Olympic Committee (IOC), holding the Games in Munich was significant for two reasons: first, because it took the Games 'to the place where Nazism festered' (1983: 89); and second, because it showed 'the world that its [West Germany's] youth could take part in wholesome sporting competitions and that Germany had risen from the ashes of war' (1983: 89). However, it was not just Lord Killanin who recognised the political opportunities that the Olympic Games provided. During the Games, on 5 September, eight Palestinian terrorists stormed into the Israeli living quarters in the Olympic village, killing one Israeli in the process and taking nine athletes and two of their bodyguards hostage. In return for the safe release of the hostages the terrorists demanded the release by the Israeli government of over 250 imprisoned Palestinians. The Israeli government refused to negotiate and stated that the safety of its athletes was the responsibility of the West German government. The West German authorities decided to storm the building in which the athletes were being held. Together with a number of the terrorists all the Israelis died. The executive of the IOC resolved that after a one-day period of mourning the Games should continue.

The tragedy brought into sharp relief the extent to which sport and politics intertwine. The incident raised a number of questions about the relationship between sport and politics. The foremost question was whether the Olympic Games were merely a convenient arena for the action of the terrorists or whether sport and sporting events are preferable targets for political action. Put another way, were Israeli athletes attending the Games a more desirable target than Israeli businessmen attending a conference or Israeli musicians performing in a concert abroad? If we accept that sport provides an easily accessible platform for political exploitation then we need to explore why it has this distinction. Is it only because of the high media coverage that sporting events generate or is it something inherent in the nature of sport that makes it vulnerable to political manipulation? A comment from a Palestinian terrorist suggests that the Olympic Games were chosen not only because they were a major international media event, but also because they were a sporting event. 'We recognise that sport is the religion of the western world . . . So we decided to use the Olympics, the most sacred ceremony of this religion, to make the world pay attention to us' (quoted in Killanin 1983: 98). Finally, we may ask whether the Olympic Games are more vulnerable than other major sporting events such as the soccer World Cup. Wren-Lewis and Clarke argue that the World Cup has been 'able to resist too great a politicisation' (1983: 124), even in 1982 when four of the qualifying countries were at war over the Falkland Islands.[1]

The Munich incident raised a number of important questions about the relationship between sport and politics, and an examination of two other occasions when they have overlapped will help to add to and refine the main themes of this study. In the early 1970s the Canadian government decided to inject a substantial amount of public money into sport. The decision came after a series of poor performances by Canadian athletes during the 1960s and a growing realisation that Canada's sporting prowess was in decline. There then followed a rapid rise in the investment by the Canadian federal and provincial governments. For many Canadians the return on their government's investment was reflected in the steady increase in the number of medals won in major championships. The pinnacle of achievement was reached during the

Seoul Olympics in 1988 when Ben Johnson became the fastest man on Earth by breaking the world record for the 100m with a run of 9.79 seconds. Unfortunately for Johnson and for his fellow Canadians the euphoria was short-lived as his routine urine sample was tested positive for anabolic steroids.

The dramatic removal of Johnson's Olympic title was the result of a test conducted under the auspices of the IOC which was responsible for overseeing drug testing during the Games. However, the routine drug tests carried out at Olympic events are only one part of an extremely complex anti-doping policy aimed at eliminating drug abuse in sport. If the campaign is to be successful then random unannounced tests must also be carried out throughout the competitive season of the particular sport and also during the pre-season training period. Anabolic steroids, for example, are a group of drugs that are most effective as aids to a training programme rather than being of use on the day of a competition. In order to enforce an anti-doping policy sports organisations have to achieve a high level of cooperation between international sports federations (IFs) and domestic governing bodies of sport, and between sports organisations and governments.

The IOC has provided a powerful lead to other sports organisations, but it is the IFs that have to make the anti-doping policy work outside the period of the Olympic Games. The International Amateur Athletic Federation (IAAF), the IF for athletics and one of the most prominent anti-doping campaigners, operates its drugs policy through its domestic governing bodies in each member country and through the operation of a 'flying squad' of drug testers who travel to athletes' out-of-season training bases to carry out random tests. The evolution of the present anti-doping policy is the result of a series of international negotiations and agreements involving not just the IOC, a number of IFs and their respective domestic governing bodies, but also a range of international governmental organisations. For example, the Council of Europe began discussion of the development and harmonisation of anti-doping policy for sport in the late 1970s and produced, in 1989, a European Anti-Doping Convention which gave member states clear guidance on policy and implementation. A less formal international governmental forum for policy development is the European Sports Conference (ESC) whose membership is drawn largely from government departments responsible for sport or from government-sponsored agencies for sport, such as the British Sports Council. The ESC draws its membership from all European countries irrespective of politics and has played an important part, through its Anti-doping Working Party, in harmonising policy between western and eastern Europe.

Among the most significant aspects of the present policy are the agreements between the IAAF and a large number of governments to waive, or at least speed, visa requirements to enable the 'flying squad' of testers to operate quickly and to retain an element of surprise. In addition, a number of countries have concluded reciprocal agreements so that each will carry out random, out-of-season tests on foreign athletes who may be training in their country.

The development of a policy at international level to combat drug abuse by athletes highlights the network of links that have developed between governments and international non-governmental organisations and also the significance of the latter in the process of negotiating policy on international issues. Transnational organisations, such as the IOC and the major IFs, have close links with governments and a range of international governmental organisations which combine to produce an extremely complex pattern of interaction on policy.

This brief outline of the development and implementation of anti-doping policy suggests a number of important questions about the role and significance of transnational sporting organisations. Among the most important are the extent to which the organisations involved constitute independent actors in the international policy process; the extent to which they provide arenas for states to pursue national interests; the resources they possess and how they deploy them; and their effectiveness in shaping policy. Although the IOC is the most prominent transnational sporting organisation, there are a number of other bodies, including the Commonwealth Games Federation (CGF), which have a potentially significant role in the fabric of international relations.

The third example of the relationship between sport and politics concerns the defection of Hu Na from the People's Republic of China (PRC) to the United States of America in July 1982 (see Pendleton 1986 for a more detailed account of the repercussions of Hu Na's defection). Hu Na, a national star within China and promising international tennis player, defected during a visit by a PRC tennis team to California. The visit by the team was part of the slow process of improving relations between the two countries. Sport has frequently been an element in the progress towards 'normal' relations between two previously hostile states. With regard to the relationship between the USA and the PRC, the dispatch of a table tennis team to the People's Republic by the Nixon administration in 1971 marked one of the first steps in the process of *rapprochement*. Between 1971 and 1982 a broad range of largely cultural and artistic exchanges between the two countries had taken place, reflecting the steady improvement in the relationship.

The defection of Hu Na threatened to jeopardise the progress made so painstakingly. Indeed, while the United States was still considering Hu Na's application for asylum nine cultural bilateral exchanges scheduled for 1983 were cancelled and the PRC withdrew from ten international sports events due to be held in the USA. The cancellations were accompanied by warnings from Beijing that the granting of asylum would constitute a 'grave political incident' (Pendleton 1986: 16). To compound matters the defection took place against a background of intense and highly sensitive negotiations between the two countries over a number of important issues, including trade relations and the transfer of high technology to the PRC. Given the delicacy of these particular issues and the Sino-American relationship in general it would not have been surprising if Hu Na's defection had precipitated a serious deterioration in relations. However, Sino-American relations were soured for only a relatively short period of time and within eighteen months discussions on cultural exchanges began; by 1984 these were once again increasing in number.

Hu Na's defection is interesting because, even though China was not a major sporting nation and Hu Na was not an established international athlete, her defection generated considerable diplomatic activity and seriously affected Sino-American relations, albeit for a relatively short time. Yet Hu Na was not an exception as defections by athletes are generally treated as politically significant by governments and by the media. The defection of a number of West German athletes, including Emil Reinicke and Wolfgang Rupe, to East Germany in the early 1950s was heralded as a significant political coup by the East Germans. The defection of fifty Hungarians at the 1956 Melbourne Olympics was greeted in the west as further evidence of the repressive rather than liberating motives for the Soviet invasion of Hungary. The defection, in 1976, of Viktor Korchnoi, the Soviet chess grandmaster, was also applauded in the west. His subsequent world championship match against the Soviet champion, Anatoly Karpov, proved a profound embarrassment for the Soviet Union. More recently the defection of the Romanian Olympic gymnast Nadia Comeneci gained as much if not more media coverage than the migration of the hundreds of Romanians who took advantage of Hungary's decision to open its border with Austria in November 1989.

Why are defections by sportsmen and women, such as Hu Na, perceived as significant by politicians and the media? Part of the answer, one might suggest, lies in the symbolic value of the athlete and of sporting success. For many, or indeed most, countries athletes are seen as personifying certain characteristics of the state or the people that inhabit it. In the German Democratic Republic (GDR), the USSR and the PRC, for example, it was possible to find many comments by sports administrators and politicians which praised sporting success as reflecting and demonstrating the virtues of the socialist organisation of society. Yet it is not just the communist states that saw sportsmen and women as symbolising the characteristics of a particular state or race. Hitler used the 1936 Olympic Games to attempt to demonstrate the superiority of the 'aryan race' and, in a less sinister fashion, the Americans, Australians and Canadians have all elevated athletes to the status of national heroes. Given the status that many athletes are accorded it is not surprising that they have a considerable capacity to embarrass their governments.

Sport, policy and international politics

The three episodes outlined above illustrate a number of the ways in which politics and sport intertwine and the variety of questions that such intertwining generates. The aim of this book is to examine these and other questions that arise from a study of sport and international politics. However, in order to explore the relationship between sport and international politics it is necessary to establish some agreement about the use of these terms. Definition is frequently a soul-destroying exercise as the more one attempts to capture the essence of meaning of a human activity, the more one becomes aware of the ambiguities and the compromises necessary to arrive at a plausible definition. However, it is important to establish a common language if political science investigation is to take place.

Coakley provides a comprehensive definition of sport as 'an institutionalised competitive activity that involves vigorous physical exertion or the use of relatively complex physical skills by individuals whose participation is motivated by a combination of intrinsic and extrinsic factors' (1986: 17). Coakley is at pains to distinguish sport from recreation, play and spectacle. All attempts at definition have grey edges and it would be possible to idle away considerable time debating whether professional wrestling, chess, synchronised swimming and ice dancing qualified as sports. For our purposes Coakley's definition is sufficient to indicate the field of policy that is the concern of this book (see Edwards 1973: 57–8 and Allison 1986: 5 for other examples of definitions of sport).

Politics, and especially international politics, is equally difficult to define. For Millar politics is an activity that 'arises out of disagreement, and it is concerned with the use of government to resolve conflict in the direction of change or in the prevention of change' (1962: 16). The stimulus to political activity is therefore disagreement and conflict. Crick shares Millar's definition of politics as a process for resolving disputes. He refers to politics as 'the activity by which differing interests within a given unit of rule are conciliated' (1964: 21). It might be argued with some justification that the definitions provided by Millar and Crick, while being valuable because of their precision, are rather too narrow. The emphasis is not just on recognised political institutions but also on what one might call 'high' politics involving political parties, governments, international governmental institutions, and major pressure groups.

A different emphasis is one that sees the defining characteristic of politics as the use of power at varying levels in international society. According to this view power is derived from the use or control of resources. Resources may be tangible such as money, military might, raw materials, and the location of a country, or they may be intangible such as moral authority (for example, of some religious groups and leaders such as the Pope, or of some countries such as Sweden and Switzerland) and political legitimacy (of an elected politician). These resources are sources of power to influence the choices of decision-makers. Decisions which affect our 'life chances' are not taken just by governments or supra-governmental organisations such as the European Community (EC), but may be taken by a wide range of organisations including the parochial (schools, the workplace and the family) or the international (multi-national corporations). For the athlete this range may, in addition, include local clubs, governing bodies of sport and international organising bodies. According to this definition politics is a ubiquitous phenomenon in our lives and cannot be seen as a separate activity. As Leftwich claims, 'politics is at the heart of *all* collective social activity, formal and informal, public and private, in *all* human groups, institutions and societies, not just some of them, and that it always has been and always will be' (1984: 63). According to this view politics is closely woven into the patterns of decision-making in a society, its ideologies and its distribution of power. It is proposed to adopt this broader definition of politics for the purposes of this study as it will enable an examination not just of the political relationship between governmental institutions and sport, but also of the internal politics of non-governmental institutions and sporting bodies themselves.

The utilisation of resources to generate power is stimulated by the desire to influence policy. However, policy is, like politics, open to a number of differing definitions. The term may be used quite loosely to include what Hogwood refers to as 'policy as aspiration' (1987: 4) as well as more precisely to describe the 'deliberate choice of action or inaction' (Smith 1979: 13). But it is not just governments that can have policies: supra-national organisations; international sports federations; domestic governing bodies of sport, physical education bodies and individual clubs, for example, may all have policies which they seek to advance. A distinction may be made between public policy, which Dye (1975: 1) defines as 'whatever governments choose to do or not to do', and private policy, which refers to the policy procedures and objectives of non-governmental organisations. The basis of such a distinction is that states or supra-national institutions have a legitimacy based on control of the government or based on representative links with government. However, in practice such a distinction is frequently artificial and not an indicator of greater influence on policy matters. There are many instances where the terrorist organisation, the multi-national corporation or religious group has been able to mobilise greater resources on some issues than many governments or inter-governmental organisations.

Themes for discussion

Armed with definitions of sport, politics and policy we can now return to the issues and questions raised in the first section of this chapter. In order to explore these and other issues and questions that arise from any examination of the relationship between sport and politics it is necessary to find some way of organising our discussion. While the questions of theory and conceptual language appropriate for the study of sport and international politics are presented in the next chapter the following discussion of the variety of ways in which sport and politics overlap will establish the major themes which recur throughout the book.

McIntosh notes that there are 'very few governments in the world which do not accept the political importance of success in international sport' (1963: 187). Yet, as will be demonstrated, governments intervene in sport policy for a wide variety of reasons: some are concerned to achieve objectives that are primarily internal, such as fostering the development of sport as a sector of the leisure industry, or to improve the nation's health. By contrast there are instances where a government's intention in intervening is directed at the achievement of foreign policy objectives, such as improving relations with other states. Unfortunately distinctions between domestic and international functions of sport are by no means watertight. For example, the emphasis given by many European countries on improving the physical fitness of their populations in the 1920s and 1930s was intended to enhance the quality of their armed forces and can therefore be seen as an element of foreign, rather than domestic, policy. Similarly, it is possible to argue that a number of countries that participated in the boycott of South Africa did so partly for domestic policy reasons, such as to placate national pressure groups or to enhance national unity. It is not always clear therefore whether the focus or objective of government intervention is internal or external. Another area of ambiguity is the difficulty in distinguishing between the overt and covert intentions or motives of government. As will be shown a policy that is overtly directed at one objective, for example fostering goodwill with another state, may have the covert objective of demonstrating superiority. The discussion of themes that follows explores and highlights these and other ambiguities in the analysis of government involvement in sport, and particularly international sport.

However, it is not just governments that have policy objectives or who see international sport as a suitable vehicle for their realisation. International sports organisations will also have policy objectives, for example related to the development of their sport, the payment of athletes, or the health of athletes. There is also a wide range of non-sporting national and international organisations, some of which are governmental organisations such as the EC and UNESCO, while others are businesses possibly involved in the marketing of sporting events, the selling of sportswear and equipment, or the broadcasting of sports events. All these organisations will be involved in a complex set of relationships in their bid to influence policy so as to achieve their own objectives.

The following themes overlap and interweave with one another and therefore care needs to be exercised in identifying a particular action or event, for example boycotts of the Olympic Games, as illustrative or typical of a particular theme. The purpose of identifying distinct themes is to indicate the variety of ways in which actions and events may be seen and as an attempt to impose some order on a complex field of study.

Sport and diplomacy

For many governments the development of international sporting contact has provided them with a low-cost, but high-profile resource for publicising their policy on international issues or towards specific states. Mention has already been made of the well-known use to which sport was put in the early 1970s when attempts were being made to improve relations between the USA and the PRC. Following an invitation from the Chinese in 1971 the United States sent a table tennis team to the PRC, followed, a year later, by a basketball team. The sports were carefully chosen for their diplomatic value. The USA was not a highly ranked table tennis nation, whereas the PRC was renowned for the quality of its players. As the USA was not expected to win its defeat would not result in any loss of prestige. Similarly, basketball is a minority sport in China and no loss of dignity would be attached to a Chinese defeat (Kropke 1974). These sporting exchanges were an acceptable means for building contacts between the two countries, a process which led, in 1972, to the visit by President Nixon (Nafziger 1978).

A more common use of sport is as a means of registering disapproval of a state's actions. In 1979 the Soviet Union sent troops into Afghanistan and prompted a chorus of international criticism, mainly because Afghanistan was considered to be outside the Soviet Union's traditional sphere of influence. The dilemma facing the USA, the Soviet Union's main critic, was how to demonstrate its disapproval while not disrupting, too seriously, the delicate relationship between the two superpowers. According to Kanin, 'Sport, that most peripheral and most publicised form of international relations, provided the perfect answer' (1980: 6). The boycott of the Moscow Olympic Games was seen by the American government as a suitably high-profile response. The decision, by President Carter, in early 1980 to boycott the Games was followed by a period of intense diplomatic activity as the USA attempted to generate support for its stand. It is this period of intensive diplomacy that demonstrated how important sport is as a cypher for the underlying pattern of relations between states. In Europe, for example, France, traditionally suspicious of US motives, opposed the boycott, as did traditionally neutral Ireland; Finland, probably due to its close proximity to the Soviet Union and its delicate relationship with the superpower, also opposed the boycott; Greece hoping to become the permanent host of the Games, was also opposed; while the British government strongly supported the Americans, but could not convince its athletes who, with some exceptions, decided to attend. Outside Europe, in South America for example, the boycott call was also interpreted with regard to foreign policy priorities. For most South American states it was the superpower to the north rather than the Soviet Union that was the cause of greatest concern.

Consequently, apart from Chile, all other countries accepted the Soviet invitation to Moscow, some, no doubt, desiring to demonstrate their independence from the USA and others with an eye on their standing in the non-aligned movement.

In practical terms the boycott by over fifty countries had little effect on Soviet foreign policy, as its troops stayed in Afghanistan.[2] Nevertheless President Carter clearly felt that the boycott had been successful, arguing, that 'The fact that the troops are still in Afghanistan indicates that we generated enough international reaction to make their takeover more difficult. . . . It could be argued that without it, they would have also sent troops into Poland.'[3] Carter's attempt to identify some tangible gain from the boycott is understandable, if somewhat implausible. An alternative view is given by Kanin who observes that the main purpose of the boycott was as a 'medium for appropriate public expression of the deterioration of superpower relations' (1980: 23).

It is not just sporting events that have been subject to boycotts; there have also been attempts to isolate particular countries from sporting contact. Both South Africa and Israel have been faced with concerted attempts to exclude them from world sport. The development of the boycott and South Africa's attempts to overcome it will be discussed in more detail in Chapter 5 and so only Israel's experience will be explored here. Israel has much in common with South Africa: both are faced with hostile neighbours; both are relatively powerful in their region, and in Israel's case have powerful allies; and both have had to contend with sustained campaigns to exclude them from international sport.

In the early years of Israel's existence it sent athletes and teams to a number of international sports competitions including the regional Asian Games which take place under the auspices of the IOC (Simri 1983). In 1962, however, the Games were awarded to the predominantly Muslim country of Indonesia, which despite expressions of goodwill failed to allow Israel to participate. Israel attended the next two Asian Games (both in Bangkok) but the earlier problems recurred when the Games were awarded to Iran in 1974. Although Israeli athletes did attend they were faced with some boycotts by individual athletes, but more worrying for Israel was the emergence of a concerted attempt to exclude them from future competitions. Between 1974 and 1976 Israel was excluded from the Asian Football Confederation (soccer) and from participation in future Asian Games. Israel's experience highlights the particular role of the international sports organisations such as the IOC and FIFA. Both these organisations expressed their opposition to Israel's exclusion but backed away from expelling the countries supporting the boycott, thus avoiding a direct confrontation with Asian sports organisations.

Reviewing the use of sport in diplomatic relations one is tempted to agree with Kanin and those who see sport as part of the ephemera of international relations. According to this view sport may be dismissed as a low-cost, low-threat resource to be used casually by governments. Such a view would be to misinterpret the utility and significance of sporting contacts. Taking the boycott episodes as an example, they were important in providing an opportunity for a large number of states to send diplomatic signals to each other on a very public stage. States used the episode to demonstrate independence and/or solidarity, to build stronger links with particular states or groups of states or to loosen ties with particular power blocs, and to demonstrate commitment to causes. The call for a Moscow boycott provided a major arena for the exchange of diplomatic information within a low-risk context. In other words one could argue that the lead-up to the 1980 Olympic Games enabled states to try out developments in foreign policy when the stakes were relatively low.

Sport and ideology

It is all too easy for discussions of the relationship between sport and ideology to confuse more than enlighten. Accepting that the concept is problematic (McLellan 1986) I will use the term 'ideology' to refer to 'a set of closely related beliefs or ideas, or even attitudes, characteristic of a group or community' (Plamenatz 1970: 15). One might add to this definition that an ideology gives meaning to actions and in that sense provides a rationale or justification for a chosen course of action.

The following discussion identifies three aspects of the relationship between sport and ideology: sport as an element in a repressive ideology, sport as a reflection of the prevailing ideology, and sport as a source of counter-ideology. The three aspects are by no means distinct as it is, for example, not uncommon for sport to be used as an element in a policy of social control yet for it to become a rallying point for opposition. In any review of the uses of sport by governments there is a long list of examples which indicate the malleability of sport for political ends. The first aspect of the relationship therefore is one where sport may be seen simply as a tool for ideological manipulation at the disposal of a government, much in the same way as the media are used in many states.[4] Sport can and has been used to achieve a number of differing political purposes including the manipulation of the international image of the state, as a means of establishing leadership within the international community, or acting as an agent of socialisation within a state.

Possibly the most common use to which sport is put is as a vehicle for projecting an image of the state and its political and ideological priorities. According to McIntosh 'Sportsmen and women . . . are under pressure to vindicate not merely their own prowess but the ideology of their country' (1987: 204). Sometimes openly, but frequently more discreetly, athletes are projected as symbolic of the virtues of their country. This role for athletes was clearly apparent in the organisation of the 1936 Olympic Games hosted by Germany. Hitler and the Nazi government showed just how pliable sport was during the Berlin Games where almost every aspect of the Games was manipulated to enhance the prestige of the Third Reich and national socialism (Mandell 1971; Hart-Davis 1986). Other examples are easy to find. The Mexican government, which hosted the 1968 Olympic Games, sought to use the event to project an image of the state as modern, North American and stable. In order to achieve this Mexico City was cleared of the homeless and the vigorous student movement was effectively destroyed when soldiers opened fire on a student meeting in Tlatelolco Plaza in October 1968, killing over 300. Unfortunately pre-Olympic repression is not unusual and also took place in 1936, Berlin; 1980, Moscow; and 1988, Seoul (Hoberman 1986).

A number of states have found sport a valuable tool for attempting to establish international leadership, of which the organisation of the Games of the New Emerging Forces (GANEFO) in 1964 by President Sukarno of Indonesia is a good illustration. In 1962 Sukarno had prevented Israel from taking part in the Asian Games as an act of solidarity with other Muslim states and as a snub to the USA. In consequence the IOC banned Indonesia from participating in the 1964 Olympics. Sukarno retaliated by hosting, with the support of the PRC, GANEFO as an anti-imperialist Asian Olympics. GANEFO served a number of functions for the Sukarno government: first, it diverted attention away from Indonesia's internal problems (Kropke 1974) and second, it provided Indonesia with a platform from which to bid for leadership of the third world/non-aligned countries (Sie 1978). Cuba, in much the same way, used its international sporting success to enhance its claims to leadership in the non-aligned movement. Cuba has provided sports advice, coaches and facilities to a number of countries including Angola, Ethiopia and Nicaragua (Sugden *et al.* 1990).

A third purpose to which sport may be put by governments is that of a focus of socialisation. Sport has frequently been fostered within states because it is seen as inculcating desirable attitudes and values. In Victorian England there was a strong feeling among the middle class that too much undisciplined leisure time for the poor was a danger to social stability (Bailey 1979). As a result a mix of political and religious interests fostered the development of 'rational recreation' in preference to the unruly games of the street and waste ground. The ideas underlying this blend of middle-class patronage and 'muscular Christianity' were reflected in the legislation of the time, particularly the 1870 and 1902 Education Acts. These Acts emphasised the need for fitness and obedience among the lower classes, to be achieved through a programme of physical drill and training. In contrast, sport for the children of the wealthy in the public schools centred on the development of leadership and loyalty through the playing of team games (Holt 1989).

Others have drawn attention to the sport's potential as a means of inculcating values appropriate to a capitalist economy. Taking Weber's analysis of the relationship of protestantism and capitalism as a starting point Galliher and Hessler, for example, argue that 'The competitiveness of sport is ideally suited to the spirit of capitalism' (1979: 11). As well as instilling and reinforcing capitalist values there are those who also see sport as an important element in a state's repressive armoury. Brohm refers to the 'essentially repressive nature of sport' (1978: 38) and sees the development of a policy towards sport by the French government as being aimed at 'keeping control over young people' (p. 39). Not only is sport seen as a distraction from the reality of exploitation and a useful source of value reinforcement in capitalist states, it is also suggested that within capitalist economies sport itself and athletes become mere commodities to be traded and exploited for profit (Rigauer 1981; Klein 1991b).

It is not just capitalist states that have recognised the utility of sport as a vehicle for socialisation, however. In the post-war period a number of communist states acknowledged the value of sport as an ideological support to the regime. Cuba (Sugden *et al.* 1990), the Soviet Union (Riorden 1978; Hardman 1987; Carr 1976), the GDR and Romania (Vinokur 1988), the PRC (Kolatch 1972) have all used sport as 'a vehicle for the inculcation of the ideals of the revolution and the development of socialist and communist values' (Sugden *et al.* 1990: 105). The value of sport as an agent of socialisation is also discussed in a later section when its role in nation-building is assessed.

The second aspect of the relationship between sport and ideology is where sport is seen as a reflection of the underlying political and economic substructure of society. For Hoberman 'sport, like the arts, is a political sub-culture that expresses prevailing ideological trends' (1987a: 156). In his examination of the relationship between sport and political ideology in pre- and post-Maoist China Hoberman identifies the shifting pattern of attitudes towards competitive sport. He shows how an ideology that rejected individualism and was highly suspicious of the technical expert (and hence the elite athlete) led to the rejection of 'medal and trophyism'. However, even during the height of the Cultural Revolution an accommodation between Maoism and competition was achieved and high performance remained a 'recessive ideological priority' (p. 165) that was to be given greater prominence after Mao's death. This accommodation was achieved in a number of ingenious ways, for example in singing competitions in praise of Mao and in contests designed to determine who could read Mao's quotations fastest! But more orthodox sporting competitions also existed and were justified, first, on the grounds that any record-setting by the individual was a product of striving for 'collective excellence' by the mass (Galliher and Hessler 1979: 14), and, second, on the grounds that individual success was a demonstration of the effectiveness of 'ideological discipline'. Hoberman shows how, as the dominance of Maoism declined, attitudes towards competitive and elite sport changed to reflect the revised ideology which gave greater emphasis to the need to modernise China in order to catch up with the western world.

According to this view sport is a mirror of society and consequently it is a reasonably accurate reflection of the prevailing ideology found within a particular state at a particular time. Such a view tends to deny sport any serious degree of autonomy within the culture of a society. In opposition to this analysis it is possible to argue that competitive sport may be seen as possessing its own value system which therefore needs to be reconciled with or incorporated into the dominant ideology of the state. It is often claimed that sport and particularly international sport is supported by a set of values that is at odds with many of the ideologies found in the political sphere. Many would identify fairness, excellence, merit and mutual respect as key values of the international sport community. The more naïve participants in international sport derive from these core values a belief that sport and politics should not mix. There were those in the IOC, for example, who felt that South Africa's internal policy of apartheid was of no concern to the Olympic movement as it was essentially, if not exclusively, a political rather than a sporting issue. Similarly, in the wake of the terrorist attack at the Munich Games there was a strong feeling among the IOC executive that any attempt to politicise the Games had to be resisted. A less naïve interpretation and application of the core values of sport has led a number of those involved in international sport to claim that sporting contact between states is an important contribution to global peace and stability. There is some disagreement as to whether peace is a product of the greater mutual understanding and respect that international sporting contact generates or whether it results from a displacement of interstate rivalry from markets and the battlefield to the sports arena (see, for example, Heinila 1985; Luschen 1982; Illmarinen 1982).

The contention that sport as a cultural form possesses a degree of autonomy suggests that sport and sporting events may, and frequently do, prove to be less amenable to ideological manipulation than governments would wish. As we have seen, the attempt to use sport to demonstrate the superiority of a state's political and social system is seriously undermined if, for example, athletes defect, take drugs or fail to be successful. Sport may therefore be seen as ideologically contested terrain and a potential source of tension and opposition within a state.

This conclusion leads to the third aspect of the relationship between sport and ideology, which sees the former as a potential source of counter-ideology. From among Marxist scholars Mandle and Mandle (1990) identify a school of 'liberatory' analysis which suggests that the area of popular culture is one aspect of existence in a capitalist economy where the working class has potential for a degree of autonomy. According to Mandle and Mandle 'Marxists . . . argue that by using sport to create their own popular cultural activities, the lower classes can emphasise their own values, thereby posing an alternative to, and highlighting the oppressive nature of, life under capitalism' (1990: 69). This argument has its extension into the field of international relations when it is applied to the relationship between imperial powers and their (ex-)colonies. Whether cricket and basketball in the Caribbean, for example, constitute the basis for cultural dependency or the basis for cultural resistance is explored below.

Sport and nation-building

During the twentieth century nearly sixty new states have been established; many as a result of the process of decolonialisation or of the redrawing of the world map in the wake of two world wars. Many of these new states were faced with the acute problem of establishing a sense of national identity. For former colonies the unity of the immediate pre-independence period was built around a common colonial enemy. When that enemy withdrew or was expelled, previously subsumed divisions of race, tribe or wealth commonly surfaced. These divisions had either to be allowed an expression that did not challenge the state's fragile stability or subsumed under a stronger loyalty to the new state. Sport was seen as a potential contributor to both strategies. For Mazrui (1976) sport could act as a source of displacement for the stress and tensions arising from inter-tribal friction, while for Uwechue (1978) sport was seen as one way in which a sense of national identity could be fostered. As Monnington observes, 'success in international sport is highly visible and offers quick returns for relatively minimal expense' (1986: 155).

The clear attraction of sport as a vehicle for nation-building has led, in most states, to close control of sport by governments. However, this has not always been easy to achieve for, as Monnington, who is generally sceptical about the efficacy of sport as a contribution to nation-building, points out (1986: 154), some sports, such as soccer in Tanzania, have steadfastly resisted attempts at manipulation for political ends. In addition there are also examples of sport resulting in a sharpening of social divisions in a number of newly independent countries. Igbinovia (1985), for example, points to the association between soccer and inter-ethnic violence in west Africa. The relationship between sport and nation-building is therefore far from uniform.

Many colonies were exposed to the sporting traditions of the imperial power often with the intention of undermining traditional sports or with the aim of 'civilising' the colony. While some ex-colonies rejected the imperial culture most sought an accommodation with it. In his study of the strong cricketing tradition in the West Indies Patterson argues that the persistence of cricket in the Caribbean is a result of the self-denigration of black culture. In exploring the political symbolism of cricket he argues that 'Cricket is the game we love for it is the only game we can play well, the only activity which gives us some international prestige. But it is the game, deep down, which we must hate – the game of the master.' (1969: 23–4) By contrast James (1963; 1977) sees cricket in a more positive light, drawing attention to its capacity to provide a focus for West Indian identity. St Pierre goes even further and argues that cricket 'has been re-shaped in sympathy with the cultural ethos of the West Indies [and] has been used as a tool to foster and further nationalist sentiment and racial pride' (1990: 23). Tiffin, while accepting James' view that cricket offered 'the colonial a chance to strike back' (1981: 190), nonetheless argues that being successful at cricket is still being successful at a British, not a Caribbean, sport. Thus, while James and St Pierre view cricket as a focus for West Indian pride, Patterson and Tiffin both see cricket as perpetuating a colonial mentality and cultural dependence.

A somewhat different situation existed in the British ex-colonies of Australia and Canada where the indigenous population was both small and systematically marginalised by the late nineteenth century. The problem for these states was similar to African ex-colonies insofar as, by the middle of the twentieth century, they wished to build a separate identity from the imperial power, but different in the sense that they clearly shared a common sporting and cultural heritage with Britain. Caldwell (1982) argues persuasively that sport has been a key force in the emergence of an Australian national identity. In particular he makes claims very similar to those of James in terms of the symbolic importance of cricket and particularly matches against England. Echoing Mandle's (1973) hypothesis that success at cricket was a necessary stimulus for the development of a sense of nationhood, Caldwell suggests that 'there is little doubt that Australians shared in a culture that was all too ready to see in sport, and especially in cricket, the test of a country's real worth' (1982: 176). Beating England was an important means of asserting Australian equality and demonstrating its vitality. Indeed, so important is sport to Australian identity that the poor performance of its athletes in the 1976 Montreal Olympics prompted a government inquiry. Similar claims may be made for the importance of sport in Canada. In the early 1970s sport was recognised by the federal government of Pierre Trudeau as a partial means of overcoming the problems arising from Canada's strong provinces, small dispersed population and cultural divisions between English and French speakers. From a situation in the 1960s where Canada was involved in little international sport the government invested considerable sums through the Sport Canada programme and was rewarded with a steady rise in sporting achievement measured by Olympic and Commonwealth medals.

It is not just British ex-colonies that have to come to terms with the sporting traditions of hegemonic cultures. A number of states within the cultural sphere of the USA have inspired analyses similar to those relating to the experience of British ex-colonies. Klein, for example, discusses the significance of baseball in the relationship between the Dominican Republic and the United States (1989; 1991a; 1991b). He argues that baseball mirrors the political economy of other commercial businesses in poor countries which leads to systematic underdevelopment. He demonstrates how Dominican baseball talent is fostered, traded and discarded by the large US clubs, simultaneously undermining the development of a strong baseball league in the Republic. However, he also argues, in a similar fashion to James and St Pierre, that baseball has also provided the basis for cultural resistance: 'The American game has, in a sense, been metamorphosed from an index of American cultural superiority to a demonstration of Dominican excellence' (1989: 109). Constantino raises similar issues regarding the relationship of economic and cultural dependence between the Philippines and the USA. For Constantino 'Filipino consciousness under the Americans was a further deepening of the colonial consciousness that the Spaniards had implanted' (1978: 79). Sport, such as basketball, was seen as part of the apparatus that helped to instil and support an 'Americanised' culture (for further discussion see Hoch 1972; Brohm 1978; Eichberg 1984; Mandle and Mandle 1990).

Perhaps the most dramatic use of sport as a contribution to developing a sense of national identity occurred in the communist states of eastern Europe. The German Democratic Republic (GDR) and the Soviet Union, in particular, systematically used sport to develop a form of socialist nationalism. For the GDR the objective was not only to foster a sense of national identity distinct from West Germany, but also to eradicate any lingering association between sport and Nazism. For Manfred Ewald, president of the Deutscher Turn und Sportsbund, athletes were seen as the 'conscious builders of the socialist GDR' and for the State Council Chairman, Walter Ulbricht, sport played an important role in the development of the 'socialist personality', demonstrating the superiority of socialist democracy over its bourgeois rival.[5]

The structure of sport's organisation in the GDR mirrored closely the structure found in the Soviet Union. For a brief period after the 1917 revolution sport was abandoned as a bourgeois diversion. However, by the mid-1930s sport had been reintroduced into Soviet society as the leadership became aware of the political potential to be derived from sporting success, particularly in the areas of nation-building and international public relations. As Morton notes:

> At home foreign sports triumphs, officially presented as proof of socialism's superiority over capitalism, are primarily used to stimulate feelings of national pride and Soviet patriotism to aid in preserving national unity in a polyglot society which has over 100 nationalities, and in which the ruling Russians no

> longer hold a majority. Abroad, USSR athletes competing frequently and winning games, medals and championships project a positive, vibrant image of success and strength which can be transferred to the Soviet Union. Athletes and coaches competing and offering clinics are valuable assets as citizen diplomats, generating good will with foreign publics who might have had no previous interaction with Soviets. (1982: 210)

The recent collapse of the Soviet economy and empire, and the reunification of Germany should not lead us to dismiss the communist experiments with the diplomatic use of sport. For both countries sporting achievement was, from the mid-1950s to 1990, one of the few areas where their excellence was internationally acknowledged and respected. However, one has to question the effectiveness of sport as a contribution to nation-building when the reappearance of militant ethnic nationalism followed so promptly on the end of the Cold War. The eagerness of the East Germans for reunification and the development of nationalist movements in the Baltic states, Russia and Georgia, and also in Yugoslavia are indications of the superficiality of the sense of East German, Soviet and Yugoslav nationhood.

For many of the 'states' attempting to gain international recognition of their sovereignty, in the wake of the Soviet collapse, the journey towards a seat at the United Nations begins with an application for membership of the IOC or one of the main international sports federations. Establishing a nation's claim to sovereignty depends, in part, on the ability of its representatives to gain access to forums where it may make its case and which have a degree of status, legitimacy and publicity value.

Sport and access

The main governmental transnational organisations are, with some limited exceptions, dominated by a very small number of states. The United States is the leading member of NATO; the permanent members of the Security Council of the United Nations wield considerable influence within the General Assembly; GATT discussions, the IMF, the World Bank and the Group of Seven are dominated by a similarly small cluster of predominantly western, industrialised democracies. As states seek to pursue their foreign policy interests on a range of issues, access to these organisations becomes more important. However, a major and persistent problem for most states is their inability to gain direct access to these prestigious world stages. The response of many smaller and weaker states in recent years has been to operate within cultural and sporting organisations with the aim of using them as a point of entry to major international bodies. Most cultural and sporting bodies provide greater opportunities for access because they possess some or all of the following qualities: they are less prestigious and therefore less likely to be dominated by the major powers; they are concerned with policy issues where overt political interference by major powers is perceived as inappropriate; or are organised on a basis that ensures a greater equality of voice for member states (Cameron 1989; Sharp 1987; DeWitt and Kirton 1983; East 1980). Thus FIFA, the IOC or the Commonwealth Games Federation are significant avenues of access to the world stage for many countries (Monnington 1986). For example, the attempt to impose sporting isolation on South Africa, discussed in more detail in Chapter 9, not only provided black Africa with a cause around which to rally and thereby project an image of African unity, but more importantly it also gave a lever to use at the more powerful arenas such as the United Nations, the Commonwealth and the EC.

Many transnational sports organisations, for example international federations, possess some if not all three of these qualities. Consequently, in the post-war period the organisation and operation of many such organisations have become increasingly politicised. The IOC, for example, has been the focus for intense political activity particularly over the issue of the recognition of states. The IOC, while not permitting full equality between states, does work on a basis which provides a voice for states in eastern Europe, the Far East and the southern hemisphere. A number of states have therefore used it, and the major IFs, as arenas to conduct battles over diplomatic recognition as a means of establishing a base from which to approach the more prestigious international forums.

This was the strategy of the GDR which conducted a highly successful campaign for recognition as a sovereign state following the end of the Second World War. Strenk (1978) shows how, as a result of the GDR's inability to press its claims for recognition by more orthodox means, such as trade, diplomacy or war, it turned to international sport as a vehicle for its foreign policy ambitions. This decision obviously depended on the ability of the GDR to produce sufficient high-class athletes to merit competition at international level. In this they succeeded dramatically. The strategy adopted by the GDR involved a number of distinct stages: first, the GDR sought invitations for its athletes to compete on foreign soil, hoping that this *de facto* recognition would lead to *de jure* recognition; second, it would attempt to gain representation on a number of IFs, with membership of the IOC being the prime target; and third, it would apply to IFs for the right to host major international competitions. It is hard to disagree with Strenk's observation that the results of the strategy were 'phenomenal' as within ten years the GDR was a major force in international sport and within twenty-five years it had achieved widespread diplomatic recognition even from some of its most implacable opponents including Britain and the USA (1978; 36). In a similar fashion the PRC and Taiwan (nationalist China) used the IOC and major sporting events as arenas for discrediting each other's claims to represent all China (Espy 1979; Pendleton 1983; Guttmann 1984). More recently the IOC received applications for membership or the reactivation of past membership of the Olympic movement from the Ukraine, Estonia, Lithuania and Latvia as initial steps in their wider bid for independence from the Soviet Union.

Sport and money

For most sports the distinction between amateur and professional has disappeared, as with athletics, or is under considerable challenge, as in rugby union. Many athletes may now make a living at their sport, while an increasing number are able to earn sums beyond the wildest dreams of sportsmen and women a generation earlier. Sport has not merely become an accepted source of income, it has become a means of accumulating considerable wealth and consequently agents, players' unions and managers increasingly mediate between the athlete and the sport.

Business has become more involved in sport in a number of ways. For some sports the involvement of business has been as a result of the marketing opportunities that the sport presents for particular products such as insurance services, cigarettes, television advertising or food products. Other sports have proved attractive to businesses operating in the sports goods industry. In tennis, soccer and athletics sports goods manufacturers vie with one another to arrange contracts with the major stars and teams. Some sports, such as American football and road cycling, and many soccer clubs are businesses themselves, where athletes are viewed as assets to be quantified and disposed of as one would a parcel of land or a piece of machinery. To a great extent the increased involvement of business in sport has grown with the expansion of television coverage of sport. Television companies themselves have done much to inject money into sport through their bidding for the right to cover particular prestigious events such as the Olympic Games or the soccer World Cup.

There is much interesting analysis of the process of commercialisation and commodification of sport and athletes. On the one hand this process may be an indication of the capacity of business to 'invade' social activities such as sport. Hargreaves, for example, suggests that 'Market pressure imposes an instrumental rationality on sporting institutions' (1986: 114). On the other hand one might argue that there are attributes within most sports that invite commercialisation and commodification. Pearson (1979), for example, in his study of surfing in Australia and New Zealand, argues that even those involved in the more spontaneous and unstructured sports such as surfing are constantly having to resist pressures to bureaucratise, rationalise and commercialise.

The significance of business in sport in the late twentieth century is undeniable and given that an increasing number of companies involved with sport are transnational operations such as Adidas, Kodak, American Express and Coca-Cola, the question of the impact that their involvement has on sport must be addressed. A number of studies have pointed to the ability of business to influence the rules of many sports in order to make them a more attractive marketing vehicle, for example introducing the tie-break in tennis and the altering of the scoring system in squash. Similarly a number of new versions of sports have been created especially for the media, for example pro-celebrity golf and 'Pot Black' snooker (Hargreaves 1986). There was even some discussion within FIFA, soccer's international sports federation, about how to adjust the rules for the 1994 World Cup to make the game more palatable to a US television audience and therefore attractive to advertisers.

Beyond the ability to influence the development of specific sports a much broader question arises of the ability of business to affect the world-wide development of sport. It is not being suggested that business will consciously seek to mould world sport to a predetermined pattern but rather the question focuses on the cumulative impact of business priorities and values becoming more prominent in international sport. For example, one might ask whether certain types of sport or athletes, and indeed certain types of countries, are preferred. One might hypothesise that in track and field events, for example, male events are more popular with sponsors than female, that track are more popular than field, that 'east–west' matches were preferred to 'north–south'. Further one might hypothesise that business favours the dramatic, aggressive and explosive events and sports, and also that business sees some states and athletes, especially those that are poor and black, as less marketable than others.

In addition, one might hypothesise that the long-term involvement of business in sport will weaken the ability of governments to manipulate and exploit sport for diplomatic purposes. Already a number of athletes, in cycling and motor-racing for example, are more closely associated with their business sponsors than their countries, while in other sports, such as golf and tennis, nationality seems relatively unimportant in their marketing. Finally, a number of nationally based sports competitions such as the Davis Cup in tennis and the Commonwealth Games are being undermined by commercial priorities. For example, the 1994 Commonwealth Games are proving difficult to organise as finding a gap in the programme of more lucrative (and prestigious) commercially sponsored events is increasingly difficult.

As the interaction between sport, particularly international sport, and multi-national business has intensified some have explored the consequences in terms of Americanisation, commodification, commercialisation, and cultural imperialism (Hargreaves 1975; Shinnick 1978; Schiller 1985; Schlesinger 1987). An often explicit assumption is that cultural domination follows from the global economic hegemony of the United States or capitalism, and has the effect of undermining resistance to capitalist values. As Piccone (1978) argues, 'the Marines give way to Coca-Cola and Xerox machines; cultural hegemony displaces political domination in a society where the victims yearn for their own form of oppression'. However, this is a strongly contested hypothesis as there is a highly plausible argument that while the cultural stimulus might be increasingly homogeneous, the way in which different cultural groups respond to and interpret the stimulus is heterogeneous (Featherstone 1987; Wernick 1991; Robertson 1990a).

An important dimension to the debate on the significance of business for international sport and international relations is provided by the growing interest in the notion of globalisation of culture. Globalisation offers a more sophisticated conceptual framework for the analysis of the role of international business. Globalisation is best seen as a process arising from the 'increase in the numbers of international agencies and institutions, the increasing global forms of communication, the acceptance of unified global time, and the development of global competitions and prizes' (Featherstone 1990: 6). Both business and sport are an intimate part of the process of extending global cultural interrelatedness which according to Featherstone results, ironically, in a sharper sense of cultural identity, but also results in the emergence of transnational cultures oriented beyond national boundaries. Thus societies may retain, with renewed vigour, elements of their traditional culture (for example as reflected in the rise of religious fundamentalism and ethnic nationalism), while at the same time assimilating aspects of a transnational, global culture. Transnational organisations, including sports organisations and businesses, will endeavour to manipulate the direction in which the global culture develops according to their own interests. For example, the United Nations and Amnesty International are both committed to promoting respect for human rights as an element in global culture; the Coca-Cola corporation will attempt to insert its products into the global cultural fabric; and the IOC and the major IFs will hope to globalise a cultural rejection of doping in sport. For Robertson (1990b) there are three major forces contributing to globalisation, namely the spread of capitalism, western imperialism and the development of a global media system. Sport and sports-related businesses are intimately connected with these three factors and must therefore form a central theme of this book.

The structure of the book

In recent years there has been a steady growth in the number of studies which have set out to explore the relationship between sport and politics. Some of these studies have focused on specific policy problems, such as football hooliganism, drug abuse or the commercialisation of sport (see, for example, Dunning *et al.* 1988; Williams *et al.* 1984; Donohoe and Johnson 1986; Goldlust 1987; N. Wilson 1988); other studies have focused on the interpenetration of sport and politics in one country (see, for example, Lawrence and Rowe 1986; Macintosh *et al.* 1987; Riordan 1978; Coghlan 1990; Houlihan 1991); while a substantial number have examined the politics of the Olympic Games (Tomlinson and Whannel 1984; Hoberman 1986; Kanin 1981; Espy 1979). Although many of the studies of the Olympic Games deal with a range of issues in international relations there are few studies which aspire to a more comprehensive exploration of the significance of sport for international politics (Allison 1986; Lowe *et al.* 1978 are two important exceptions).

The aim of this book is to explore the relationship between sport and international politics. The book not only considers the dominant contours of the post-war relationship, but also seeks to identify the direction that the relationship will take in the future. For much of the recent period the relationship has been shaped by the major international cleavages between the communist and capitalist blocs, between South Africa and black Africa, and between the industrialised and wealthy northern and western states and the poorer southern states. With the ending of the Cold War and the imminent collapse of apartheid two of the main reference points of government involvement in sport have gone and it is now an appropriate time to ask what shape the relationship between sport and international politics will take in the coming decades.

The next chapter provides an introduction to the conceptual language and models of international relations and identifies the role of international sports organisations within the overall pattern of interaction. The chapter also identifies the different ways in which the policy process for sport at international level may be examined. Chapter 3 explores the organisation and role of the major international non-governmental sports organisations. A distinction is made between IFs and international organising bodies such as the IOC and the CGF. The discussion focuses on the pattern of links between these bodies, between them and their national organisations, and between them and national governments. Three issues have been selected to illustrate the politics and interrelationship of these bodies, namely the enforcement of anti-doping policy, the recognition of states and the location of major championships. These issues are intended to enable an examination of the themes associated with the diplomatic use of sport, access to international arenas, and the value of sport as an aid to nation-building.

Chapter 4 explores the growing significance of international governmental bodies for sport. UNESCO and, particularly, the Council of Europe and the EC are all important actors in the global policy process for sport. This chapter considers how they interact with international sports bodies, the resources they control and the influence they exert. Most of the main themes of the book are explored in this chapter but of particular importance is the interaction between governmental and non-governmental bodies with an interest in sport. Chapter 5 examines the most important sports organisation and event of the twentieth century, the Olympic Games. The general history and politics of the Games are already well researched; therefore this chapter focuses on an analysis of three of the most significant aspects of the Olympic movement, namely the attraction of the Olympics to governmental and non-governmental political interests, the way in which political interests seek to exploit the

Olympic movement, and why the movement is seemingly so vulnerable to political manipulation. The chapter concludes with an examination of contemporary Olympic values and how they are promoted globally.

Chapter 6 examines the political significance of sport within the Commonwealth. Particular consideration is given to the relationship between the Commonwealth Games and the contemporary Commonwealth as a major international political institution in the light of the changing significance of the Commonwealth and of Britain's role within it. Among the themes that are dealt with explicitly in this chapter are the Games as an opportunity for access to the international stage, as a diplomatic resource, and their significance for nation-building. Chapter 7 investigates the relationship between sport and business, looking specifically at the growing importance of sponsorship, the particular role of the media and the role of corporate patrons in sport. The chapter also considers the implications of the increasing commercialisation of sport for the autonomy of sports organisations and the influence of government.

Chapter 8 explores a range of issues associated with the significance of sport for poorer states. It also explores the consequences of the unequal distribution of resources for the spread of sport and the dependence of some states on the wealth and administrative capacity of others. More specifically the chapter examines the role of the IOC and the major IFs in developing sport on a world-wide basis and addresses the series of related analyses and critiques of the sport development process in terms of notions of 'Americanisation', cultural imperialism, and globalisation. The final chapter returns to the five themes identified in this chapter. The aim is to explore how the themes will develop in the coming years and how their changing salience to sport and governments will affect sport and its development into the next century.

Notes

1 While the World Cup has been free of overt politics by comparison to the Olympic Games it has not been able to avoid the intrusion of politics completely. For example in November 1973 the Soviet Union was scheduled to play Chile in a World Cup qualifying match. The match was due to be played in the National Stadium in Santiago just two months after the military coup that ousted the elected government of Salvador Allende. The Soviet Union refused to play in Chile and asked for the venue to be altered. FIFA refused and the Soviet Union was expelled from the 1974 World Cup.

2 Indeed there is considerable evidence that suggests that boycotts and other sanctions, such as trade boycotts, are rarely effective. See for example Nossal (1989); Daoudi and Dajani (1983); Hufbauer and Schott (1985).

3 From an interview with P. Axthelm, 'The Olympics: Boycotts can work', *Newsweek*, 10 October 1983, quoted in Toohey (1986).

4 See Cantelon and Gruneau (1982) for a stimulating discussion of a range of critical and Marxist views of the relationship between sport, ideology and the state.

5 Both quoted in Hardman (1987: 20).

2

International relations theory and sport

The first chapter identified a number of illustrations of the overlap between sport and international politics and suggested a number of questions that these illustrations prompted. Five broad themes were identified: diplomacy, ideology, nation-building, access, and money. A thematic approach has some value: it is often a useful way of ordering material as it enables similarities to be identified and provides a basis for comparison. However, what it does not do is help to explain why particular incidents took place nor why particular themes emerge. In order to move from the level of description to the level of explanation it is necessary to set empirical data within a theoretical context and to identify a conceptual language that can facilitate analysis. The purpose of this chapter is to outline and review a number of alternative theoretical perspectives on international politics and evaluate them in terms of their utility in explaining the role and significance of sport in international politics.

Within the study of international politics there are three major perspectives: realism, pluralism, and a looser cluster of perspectives that are referred to as 'globalism' or 'dependence'. Each has its subspecies, its internal disputes and a history of debate and evolution. Thus what at first appears to be a trio of discrete perspectives is in fact a cluster of overlapping approaches to the study of international relations. The same authors are frequently referred to by advocates of different perspectives, and authors will often object to the location of their work within a particular perspective. Yet, even though the literature on international relations theory is large and contains a number of competing theories, its focus is generally narrow. Any casual glance along the library shelves will reveal

Table 2.1 A typology of international interactions

	Resources involved			
Level of interaction	Finances	People	Knowledge/culture	Territory
Government & transnational governmental organisations	Aid (civil & military, trade; focus on e.g. World Bank, IMF & NATO).	Ambassadors, armed forces, delegations, conferences; focus on e.g. EC, GATT, UN, Council of Europe, NATO	E.g. sovereignty, human rights, security, trade conditions, consumerism	Alterations to borders, invasion, reunification, occupation; consulates
Formal non-governmental organisations	Aid and trade in goods and finance	Aid workers, business people, specialists, cosmopolitans	E.g. religions, consumerism, capitalism, dependency	Purchase of land for development, environmental protection
Informal/personal	Repatriation of earnings; tourist spending	Migrants, tourists, refugees, students	Language and customs	Holiday homes, settling by migrants, refugees

the primary concerns of international relations theory namely security and war, trade, diplomatic relations and foreign policy. At first sight it seems difficult to identify a branch of theory where sport might be accommodated. Table 2.1 illustrates the problem. The table suggests a typology of international interactions in terms of the level of interaction and the particular resources involved.

The table indicates the extent of variation in level and focus of international interaction and is not intended to present an exhaustive overview of the range of possible interactions. However, as an heuristic device it has two functions: first, to enable a consideration of the nature of international sporting contact and, second, to aid an assessment of the explanatory power of the various theoretical models that will be discussed. In summary, it will be suggested that current theories of international relations overconcentrate on the governmental level and, while paying some attention to the activities of non-governmental organisations, seriously neglect the informal and personal level of contact. In addition current theories also overconcentrate on issues concerning territory and finance.

Using the typology in Table 2.1 as a framework it is possible to construct a second table that illustrates the pattern of international interactions through sport (Table 2.2).

As Table 2.2 suggests, while sports-based interactions take place at all three levels they are more significant at the levels of formal non-governmental organisations and at the informal and personal levels. In addition the basis for interaction tends to be culture/knowledge and people. At the heart of sport interaction is the cultural diffusion of sport, both in terms of the organisational rationality that underpins sports activity in northern/industrialised countries and also in terms of specific sports and their associated rules and procedures. Such a focus highlights the importance of the wide range of non-governmental bodies that have facilitated the codification and rationalisation of sport. It is their endeavours that have enabled the diffusion of sport and the development of international sporting contact, and thereby enabled governments to utilise international sporting contact as an element in diplomacy.

Table 2.2 indicates the range of interactions between states which deliberately or unwittingly use sport as a medium. In order to answer questions concerning the significance of sport in international relations this pattern of interaction can best be explored by relating it, initially at least, to the established body of international relations theory. Placing the observable patterns within a variety of theoretical frameworks will not only enable a sharper understanding of empirical data, but should also

Table 2.2 Examples of sport-based international relations

Level of interaction	Finance	People	Knowledge/culture	Territory
Government and transnational governmental organisations	Generally slight volume: some sports development aid direct from governments (e.g. Canada & Sweden) and some via agencies such as UNESCO	Moderate volume: some provision of coaches and administrators as part of overseas aid work; some examples of governments using athletes as 'goodwill' ambassadors; government permission for access to sporting events hosted by ideological opponents, e.g. Moscow, Seoul Olympic Games; some examples of prevention of athletes travelling to overseas events, e.g. to South Africa, Moscow Olympic Games	Moderate volume: transfer of cultural values (the hegemonic concerns of governments) through sport and games; imperialism; boycotts and imposition of games/sports; role of Council of Europe in promoting 'Sport for All' and supporting anti-doping campaign	Zero
Formal large non-governmental organisations	Moderate to high volume: transfer of funds to support sports development projects, e.g. through Olympic Solidarity, Commonwealth Games Federation, major international sports federations; sale/purchase/sponsorship of major events by TV and other businesses	High volume: much sports aid and development is in the form of coaching and administrative personnel; organisation of teams for international competition	High volume: western values reflected in sports values, competition, consumerism and organisational rationality	Zero

Table 2.2 *Continued*

Level of interaction	Finance	People	Knowledge/culture	Territory
Informal/personal/local organisation	Moderate volume: repatriation of earnings; transfer fees between clubs; sports scholarships (e.g. to North America)	High volume: sports scholarships to North America; the export and import of human capital by clubs; recruitment of athletes for western/northern hemisphere teams and events; sports tourism; travelling fans; defection	High volume: sports values and rules shared and learned through migration, quartering of soldiers in war/ occupation/imperialism	Low volume: establishing sports training camps in poorer countries

allow an evaluation of the adequacy of existing international relations theory to explore issues beyond its traditional preoccupations.

A review of international relations perspectives

The aim of theory is to help the researcher understand the social phenomenon that is being observed. While it is possible simply to describe a sequence of events, for example the boycotts, whether threatened or actual, associated with recent Olympic Games, such an exercise would do little to explain why sporting events in general are vulnerable to boycotts and why the Olympic Games in particular are so frequently targeted. Theory, then, should enhance description by identifying underlying social processes and help the researcher look beyond surface appearance. However, exploring and evaluating social science theory and particularly that associated most closely with the study of international relations is not a task for the faint-hearted. The study of international relations may be approached through theories which seek explanation at the global level, while other, partial theories seek to explain aspects of global politics, for example the causes of war or how decisions are taken in crises. In addition some theories aim to explain patterns found among phenomena while other theoretical approaches are concerned to indicate how international relations *ought* to be conducted.

A study which is concerned to explore sport as a global phenomenon requires theories with a similarly broad scope. What follows is an examination of three well-established perspectives on international relations – realism, pluralism and globalism. Each will be outlined briefly and then assessed in terms of its utility for generating theory capable of aiding the study of the role and significance of sport in international relations. For the reader who is unfamiliar with these major perspectives it is possible to distinguish between them in terms of four key assumptions: the unit of analysis; the central characteristics of the unit of analysis; the nature of the process that the actors are involved in; and the issues that tend to dominate. Table 2.3 provides a summary of the three perspectives.

The simplification required to fit the perspectives into the summary in Table 2.3 should not be taken as an indication that the three perspectives do not possess areas of overlap, nor that authors have not taken elements from more than one perspective. Indeed much of the most incisive analysis of international politics comes from those scholars who have been willing to incorporate elements of one perspective with the strengths of another.

Table 2.3 Major assumptions of the realist, pluralist and globalist perspectives

	Realism	Pluralism	Globalism
Units of analysis	The state	The state and non-state actors	Classes and class-based organisations including the state and non-state actors
Central characteristics of the unit of analysis	The state is a unitary actor	The state and non-state actors are often fragmented, with subunits possessing objectives different from each other and from the publicly stated goals of the organisation	Classes are the product of economic tensions
Process	The state seeks to maximise its interests in competition with other states	Using a variety of tangible and intangible resources actors bargain and negotiate, and seek to establish advantageous coalitions	Establishment of domination/hegemony
Dominant issues	National security	Broad range of issues but trade is frequently a key issue along with national security	Preservation of class dominance; trading relations and values supportive of open trade

Source: Adapted from Viotti and Kauppi (1987), p. 11.

Realism

Within the realist perspective the state is the primary unit of analysis. Other transnational organisations such as the United Nations, NATO, the Council of Europe, and the International Olympic Committee are seen as having much lower significance. In the case of the first three organisations their lower significance is due to their actions being seen as determined by sovereign states; for the IOC its weakness is even greater and is seen as the result of its lack of direct links with state power.

Power is a key concept within the realist perspective. For the realist power is derived from the control over key resources such as military force, wealth, technology and diplomatic capability (Organski 1968; Knorr 1970; Singer *et al.* 1972). For many subscribing to the realist perspective power can be quantified and confidently used to account for the outcome of interstate conflict (Bueno de Mesquita 1981). The focus is on the quantification of power for each state in a vacuum rather than focusing on the relationship between states. Consequently it is rare in the realist school for power to be distinguished from authority or hegemony. A focus on authority lessens the importance of the quantity of power possessed by a state and draws attention to the perception of states held by others as non-aligned or champions of human rights, for example. These (positive) perceptions will give a capacity to lead greater than a quantification of power resources would suggest.

The emphasis given to power rather than authority in the realist perspective is based on the belief that anarchy is the defining characteristic of the international system; and anarchy is the absence of authority. Sovereign states in such an unstable system, it is argued, will aim to maximise short-term self-interest and particularly reduce their exposure to the actions of other states. One qualification of this description of unfettered self-interest is the notion of hegemonic stability (Keohane 1980). The concept of hegemony has been partly developed by those seeking to broaden realist theory to enable it to take account of economic interactions (Hollis and Smith 1991). According to this (neo-realist) view, temporary stability can be achieved through the assumption of global leadership by the dominant power or hegemon. 'The hegemon influences states to cohere and establish the rules by which international relations are to be conducted in various issue areas, such as the exchange of money, trade, finance, health, communications, air transport, and navigation on the high seas' (Viotti and Kauppi 1987: 58). Britain in the nineteenth century and the USA from 1945 are seen as classic examples of hegemonic domination. Central to the notion of hegemony is the ability of the dominant power to establish a regime or set of international norms to which other states will willingly subscribe. Cox describes the period of *pax britannica* as follows: 'The norms of liberal economics (free trade, the gold standard, free movement of capital and persons) gained widespread acceptance with the spread of British prestige, providing a universalistic ideology which represented these norms as the basis of a harmony of interests. . . . (T)he ideological separation of economics from politics meant that the City [of London] could appear as administrator and regulator according to these universal rules, with British sea power remaining in the background as potential enforcer.' (1981: 142) Hegemony for some realists is consequently seen as a source of stability in the international system and as a means of overcoming the risks of interdependence. For the realist the term 'interdependence' refers to the vulnerability of states to the actions of others and is considered a potentially destabilising relationship. Gramsci, writing from within a Marxist perspective, also used the concept of hegemony in which emphasis was given to the willing cooperation of the dominated in their own subordination. While the realist use of the concept retains the clear assumption that the development of normative hegemony is based directly on military power, Gramsci's use of the concept allows a greater autonomy to ideological hegemony.

The realist conception of interdependence is very different from that adopted by pluralists who see it largely as a source of stability. Similarly, the concept of hegemony is also used by the globalists who incorporate it into a view of world politics which results in the attempted perpetuation of dependency among developing states.

Realists' greatest difficulty is in explaining the dynamic of the international system. Given the assertion of the rational self-interest of states and the incipient anarchy of the international system, it is understandable that the focus for much theorising is on sources of stability rather than on seeking to uncover the dynamic of change. The result is a concern to understand (and maintain) the balance of power, not in order to maintain peace but in order to maintain the system itself (Bull 1977). Underlying much realist discussion is the assumption that the international system will tend towards equilibrium and that, even if war occurs and the pattern of major power relationships is altered, the integrity of the system will be maintained. Leaving aside the potential problems in reconciling the notion of hegemonic stability with the balance of power, the latter idea is of only limited value in explaining why change occurs in the system.

Explaining change is probably the most unsatisfactory aspect of the realist perspective. At an extreme there is the view that change is substantially the outcome of a process of systemic determinism (Waltz 1979). While most realists would acknowledge that change is the outcome of an interaction between systemic factors and the actions of states, the sources of change that they consider are generally limited. For example, for Gilpin (1981) the source of change is aggressive self-interest and the pursuit of dominance (or more accurately the escape from dependence). In somewhat contradictory fashion Jervis (1976) suggests that the source of change is a spiral of insecurity that results in 'arms races' or competition for colonies. For Modelski (1978) and Kennedy (1988) the source of change is the pursuit of hegemony and the inevitable decay in the strength of dominant powers. For all these authors war is central to change. Realists in general have considerable difficulty in incorporating sources of change that may lie within the domestic politics of states or in the global political economy.

Other weaknesses of the realist perspective include its normative preoccupation; the vagueness of the central concept of 'balance of power'; and the oversimplification of international relations (Der Derian and Shapiro 1989). It is hard not to agree with Rothstein (1972: 349) when he suggests that realism 'simply constitutes belief in the wisdom of certain "eternal verities" about politics'. Possibly the greatest weakness of the realist perspective is that once one moves beyond an acknowledgement of the significance of states and their concern with national security one still has a rich pattern of international interaction in trade, telecommunications and culture, etc. which is either ignored or at best assumed to be a reflection of security priorities. Finally, the nature of explanation offered by realist theorists is often at a high level of generality and of limited value in casting light on the events that constitute much international activity.

Realism and international sport

At first sight the realist perspective would seem to have little to contribute to an understanding of the role and significance of international sport in world politics. Issues of national security, balance of power and interdependence seem remote from the activities of the IOC, international soccer fixtures and World Cup cricket. However, it is possible to argue that realism may prove useful in understanding some aspects of international sport.

Within the realist perspective a fundamental prerequisite for participation in the international system as an independent actor is recognition of national sovereignty. The emergence of Pakistan and Israel, for example, as sovereign states was based on a mix of military and diplomatic effort, but the emergence and recognition of the German Democratic Republic and the People's Republic of China was based on a broader mix of foreign policy tools of which sport was one. The use of sport and international sports organisations as vehicles for the pursuit of recognition is best exemplified by the GDR where, as both Strenk (1978) and Guttmann (1984) show, intense political activity through sports organisations was an important element in securing international recognition. However, while concern with recognition and sovereignty are important to the realist perspective the means by which the GDR and the PRC achieved recognition highlights the significance of non-state organisations. It is doubtful whether realism is sufficiently flexible to be able to take account of the role of the IOC, for example, as a forum for diplomatic activity.

Closely intertwined with the pursuit of 'the legal institution of sovereignty' (Stoessinger 1973: 13) is the development of other objective and subjective requisites of nationhood. Among the ingredients of nationhood is a common culture and what Stoessinger calls the 'psychological phenomenon of nationalism' (1973: 13). In both these areas domestic and international sport have a potentially important contribution to make, as was suggested in the opening chapter. Domestic sport and international sporting contact are often used explicitly by governments to foster and sustain a nascent sense of national identity (Taylor 1988). While many realist theorists will acknowledge that resources beyond military power are important in determining the pattern of international relations they rarely give non-military resources, such as cultural influences and religion, the depth of analysis or weight that they give to the military dimension.

A second area where realism might be able to provide an insight is on those occasions where sport has been used as a tool of foreign policy, particularly where international sport is seen as a safety valve for international tension or where it is seen as a means of improving relations between states. International sport can therefore be seen as a resource available to states to enable them to manage their interdependent relationships. In the previous chapter reference was made to the use of 'ping-pong' diplomacy between the USA and China. Many other examples of the use of sporting contact as an explicit tool of diplomacy exist. For example, goodwill baseball tours of Latin America were common in the inter-war period. The relationships between the USA and Panama and Mexico were improved by baseball diplomacy, according to Crepeau (1980) and Sinclair (1985). During the 1920s and 1930s, when the relationship between the USA and Japan was often extremely tense, the strong baseball links between the two countries was seen, by President Harding, as being of significant diplomatic value in bringing about 'exactly the right kind of emulation and of promoting of good feeling that make better understanding possible' (quoted in Sinclair 1985: 47). Unfortunately, baseball's diplomatic success did not survive beyond the mid-1930s and was of uneven value in Latin America. What makes realist theory unattractive for the exploration of the diplomatic value of sport is the scant attention it gives to the role of non-governmental organisations such as governing bodies of sport that are central to the utilisation of sport for diplomatic purposes.

The final area of realist theory which might be of value in casting light on the role of sport is its use of the concept of hegemony. For the realist hegemony is seen as the augmentation of the military might of the dominant state with the willing acknowledgement of its authority and rights by the dependent state. Sport, as part of a broader cultural package, can be viewed as an important non-military ingredient in the establishment and maintenance of hegemony. For many nineteenth- and twentieth-century imperial powers, such as Britain, France and the USA, sport was seen in precisely this way. However, within realist theory most uses of the concept place greater emphasis on the possession of military power than on the non-military bases of hegemony. In addition where non-military aspects of hegemony are discussed they are invariably considered as elements of a state strategy. Such a state-centred approach is limiting as it reduces the scope for an exploration of the potential for multi-national corporations to seek hegemonic status. Given that the struggle for resources is the primary basis of global politics then all organisations which have resource demands and are capable of acting on the international stage will seek to achieve hegemony. It is important therefore that a perspective is adopted which accepts that hegemony is an aspiration of both non-state and state actors. As we will see below the globalist notion of hegemony is more accommodating to such a view.

In conclusion, it is tempting to dismiss realist theory as being a 'rationalisation of cold war politics' (Hoffman 1977: 48), preoccupied with normative prescriptions, based on a priori assumptions about human nature (Snyder *et al.* 1962), and overly focused on the state and its military capacity. Tempting though this might be, the realist perspective is a necessary corrective to those who would prefer to downgrade the significance of the state as an actor in the international system and marginalise the significance of national security as a central policy priority.

Moreover, realist theorists have made attempts to respond to their critics, particularly by focusing on areas of international cooperation and by taking greater account of the activities of international organisations (see, for example, Keohane 1984; Krasner 1983). However, the conclusion must be that the capacity of realist theory to provide a satisfying explanation of an international cultural phenomenon such as sport is limited. In terms of the variety of interactions described in Table 2.2 it would be difficult to utilise a realist perspective beyond the interests of government in the areas of territorial and financial matters.

Pluralism

As described in Table 2.3 pluralism adopts as its units of analysis both state and non-state actors; regards these actors as pursuing policies which are the product, not of rational self-interest, but of a process of bargaining and negotiation based on sectional definitions of both problems and solutions; and gives weight to a range of issues beyond national security. In particular, pluralists consider the growth of multi-national corporations, and other transnational organisations, such as the Commonwealth Games Federation and the various international sports federations, to be a major post-war development in the international system forcing a necessary reconsideration of state-centric theories. Pluralists also challenge the assumption of the state as a unitary actor, and prefer to conceptualise it as a bureaucratic organisation comprising many subunits each possessing its own interests and perspective on issues and its own responses. In addition, pluralists also emphasise the possibility of the misperception of issues by actors which may compound the variation in response due to the protection of bureaucratic interest. Finally, for the pluralist the range of issues that is deemed worthy of examination is broader than for the realist. Whereas the latter is generally reluctant to move the focus much beyond national security, the former argues that the foreign policy agenda contains a number of other issues, such as economic, social, cultural and environmental, which are often of major international significance and therefore capable of casting light on the international system.

Pluralism developed partly as a reaction to realism and partly as an extension of the dominant perspective within American political science. The assumptions of 'interest group liberalism' (Viotti and Kauppi 1987: 196) at the heart of pluralism are exemplified in the work of Robert Dahl (1961; 1963) and Nelson Polsby (1963) in their analyses of domestic politics in the USA. In summary, they described a political system in which power is dispersed among a politically active citizenry and among a multiplicity of elites, institutions and organisations. The underlying assumption is that policy is the outcome of a process of competition and bargaining between these interests. Access to the political agenda is relatively open and it is assumed that no particular interest will be excluded permanently. The state in the pluralist model is neutral and fulfils the function of adjudicating between interests and has no inherent bias toward any one set of interests.

Extending this model to an analysis of international relations resulted in a research focus on a series of middle-range issues concerned with how individuals and groups perceive problems, particularly when under pressure. What these approaches tended to highlight was the potential for cognitive distortion in crisis situations, thus challenging the realist assumptions of rationality (see Jervis 1976; Janis 1972). The pluralist perspective also stimulated a concern with the internal policy processes of the government bureaucracy. The analysis of the 1962 Cuban missile crisis by Allison stressed the significance of organisational routines and procedures as determining, at least some, foreign policy decisions and particularly their implementation (1969; 1971; Allison and Halperin 1972). Keohane and Nye (1974) extended the pluralist perspective to suggest that elements of the government bureaucracy and non-state organisations may transcend the boundaries of the state and form links with organisations in other states. The formation of transnational coalitions may operate at cross-purposes to those of individual governments.

The emphasis given to the development of transnationalism is central to the pluralist perspective. For the pluralist the modernisation of the international system is reflected in the increasingly porous nature of territorial boundaries. A familiar simile used to convey an impression of this model of the international system is to liken it to a cobweb, with its multiplicity of connections. The connections would link not only states, but also multi-national corporations and international organisations such as the European Community and the United Nations, and take account of interactions based on trade, tourism, media communications, and migration. The primary consequence of the growth in number and diversity of linkages is interdependence within the international system. Thus, if interdependence suggests 'vulnerability' to the realist then it suggests 'sensitivity' to the pluralist and opens the way for a positive-sum outcome to international political interaction (Viotti and Kauppi 1987: 209–10).

The capacity of pluralism to take account of the less formal non-governmental forms of transnational interaction is important in a study of international sport and as, Table 2.2 showed, there is much interaction of this type that needs to be evaluated. However, there are few examples of the empirical study of the significance of informal transnational participation. Agnell's study of the influence of transnational participation on progress towards international peace, is one important exception. He defines transnational participation as 'All types of residence abroad . . . including study, teaching and research, business, military duty, technical assistance or peace corps assignments, and missionary duty. In all these situations the visitors take lasting roles in institutions that bring them into contact with members of the host society. Both the visitors and the hosts with whom they are in contact are transnational participants' (1969: 25). In addition, Agnell treats as significant the visiting of relatives and friends due to the intensity of the contact, and also the first years of residence of migrants. Agnell claimed that his studies demonstrated support for the hypothesis that American foreign policy-makers were being subjected to a stream of influence from a series of elite groups aimed at promoting an accommodation between nations.

Other studies to explore similar ground include that by Coombs who also argues for the significance of personal transnational contact in influencing the direction of foreign policy. However, for Coombs the primary purpose of these exchanges is the fostering of solidarity within the anti-communist coalition led by the USA. He argues that this coalition must be 'steadily nurtured by a broad and fruitful interchange, at all levels, of intellectual, scientific, and cultural activity. In the last analysis it is this interchange which is the lifeblood of the democratic community, and always has been' (1964: 114). Bennett (1991: 255) best sums up the difficulties in assessing the value of studies such as those by Agnell and Coombs. He suggests that the impact of personal contact should be acknowledged, but he also points out the problems in quantifying its significance and in distinguishing it from the role and significance of the organisations in which the individuals participate.

Overall the pluralist model of international politics has many attractions it allows the consideration of multi-national corporations as independent actors; it acknowledges the multiplicity of interactions in the international system; its emphasis on negotiation of policy is more convincing than assumptions of the rational and unified state; and its voluntarism allows organisations involved in international politics to influence change in contrast to the determinism implicit in the theory of balance of power. Unfortunately, it also has some serious weaknesses. A central weakness is that in contrast to the realist (and as we shall see the globalist theorists) pluralism offers insights into aspects of individual and organisational behaviour without basing them securely in an overarching theory of society. As Viotti and Kauppi note, 'Islands of theory are constructed rather than building such general theory as is offered by realist proponents of balance of power theory' (1987: 212). Thus pluralists run the risk of putting aspects of organisational behaviour under such a sharp focus that they lose the capacity to understand the broader pattern of relations within the international system and the impact of organisational behaviour. By insisting on a detailed recording of the complexity of international politics the pluralist finds it difficult to move from description to analysis and explanation. Indeed some writers such as Sklair argue that the focus on transnational relations is best seen as an 'injunction to researchers to pay more attention to non-governmental entities' rather than a theory (1991: 3).

A second criticism is that while the pluralist theorists accuse realists of over-emphasising the existence of 'national interests' and the concern of states with security, they themselves are guilty of exaggerating the extent of fragmentation within government, the scope for misperception of issues and the significance of non-security issues. A further criticism of the pluralist perspective is that its utility is diminished due to its development within the context of American domestic politics. Realists consequently doubt the applicability of pluralism to the policy process in totalitarian states.

Pluralism and international sport

The three episodes related at the start of the last chapter all involved a range of organisations beyond the domestic state machinery. The decisions of the IOC were important in the handling of the terrorist attack at Munich; the IOC, a range of other international sports federations, and the Council of Europe all played crucial parts in developing and implementing the anti-doping policy; and various domestic governing bodies of sport were important in facilitating the sporting exchanges between the USA and the PRC. Given this diversity of organisational participation the pluralist perspective appears very attractive. In particular it would allow an examination of the role of transnational organisations in mediating the relations between states and also of their potential to participate as independent actors in international politics. For example, the decisions by the IOC to award the Olympic Games to West Germany in 1972 and to Japan in 1964 were important in aiding the rehabilitation and readmission of both these countries to the international community. A pluralist perspective would allow us to enquire into the decision processes of the IOC and the interaction between the IOC and states with membership of the Olympic movement. Similarly, a pluralist perspective would also accommodate an examination of the IOC decisions about the eligibility of nationalist China and East Germany for membership of the Olympic movement which involved IOC officers in considerable negotiation and consultation with governments. Other examples highlighting the need to analyse the role and significance of non-state actors would include the relationship between the CGF and the Commonwealth over the question of the status of South Africa, the influence of television companies on the location and organisation of international sports events, and the contribution of the Council of Europe to the development of 'sport for all' and anti-hooliganism policies. Adopting a perspective which encourages a focus on a broad range of actors in the international system has clear attractions.

In addition, a pluralist perspective, and the emphasis that it gives to bureaucratic politics and the significance of issue and policy perception, would also support an examination of the pattern of influence and interaction between domestic sports governing bodies and their international counterparts. For example, over the issue of sporting links with South Africa the contact between rugby union governing bodies in Britain, New Zealand and South Africa was frequently at odds with the policy preferences of their respective governments. Similarly, the decision by the British Olympic Association to ignore the British government's demand for a boycott of the 1980 Moscow Olympic Games contrasts with acquiescence of the national Olympic committees of Canada and the USA. An exploration of these issues would reveal much about the autonomy of sport as a political resource and the capacity of sports organisations to function as independent actors on the international stage.

The pluralist perspective is also more accommodating to a focus on sport/cultural policy than the realist perspective: rather than having to justify a concern with international sport as an adjunct to concerns with sovereignty or security it could be analysed and evaluated, in its own right, as part of the 'cobweb' of international interactions. Thus there would be more support from the pluralist perspective for an exploration of hypotheses concerning the value of sport as an independent resource in international politics. In terms of the characterisation of sport-based international relations given in Table 2.2 a pluralist perspective is able to accommodate a focus on a broader range of bases for interaction and at the level of both governmental organisations and large-scale non-governmental organisations. However, pluralism has difficulty in taking account of interaction at the informal and personal level.

Globalism

The final cluster of theories is derived from a broad perspective generally referred to as 'globalism'. As the title suggests the level of analysis is the international system rather than individual states or transnational organisations within it. The latter two sets of actors are constrained by the nature of the international system. For the globalist it is economic factors rather than security concerns which are the dominant focus for international activity and which are central to an understanding of the development and present character of world politics. In contrast to the pluralist perspective, but similarly to the realist, the globalist emphasises the need to analyse the system as a whole. However, in common with the pluralist the globalist accepts the significance of non-security issues and the role of non-state actors. The common themes found in globalist literature are the relationship between Third World countries and the richer states and particularly the role of multi-national corporations in contributing to the dependency of poorer states, at the periphery of the world system, on the richer, central, states.

Within the globalist perspective one may find both Marxist and non-Marxist theories, but one of the most important strands of theorising concerned the development of a global system of imperialism. From a non-Marxist position Hobson (1965) outlined a theory of imperialism at the heart of which lay an analysis of capitalism which suggested that as capitalism developed it would encounter crises arising from over-production and underconsumption resulting from the severity with which the domestic proletariat is exploited. Low wages in the domestic market would result in high output but low effective demand, hence over-production and underconsumption. Imperialism, according to Hobson, provided the solution because it created new markets (and new sources of raw materials) through conquest. Adopting much of Hobson's theory, Lenin argued that the development of imperialism was an inevitable consequence of the underlying forces of capitalist accumulation (1966). Of particular importance to the evolution of the globalist perspective was the emphasis placed by Hobson and Lenin on the global nature of capitalism and its inherent tendency to distribute the benefits of the global economy to the disadvantage of the poorer states.

This view of the global economy contrasted with the more optimistic analyses of (predominantly American) social scientists who posited a developmental process of modernisation (see Harrison 1988 for a summary of the literature). At its simplest modernisation theory suggested that industrial development followed a uniform and coherent pattern of growth which in turn would produce similar social and political structures and practices across a range of different states and cultures (Fukuyama 1992; Lerner 1958; Parsons 1964; Weiner and Huntington 1987; Binder 1986). Thus studying Britain, Germany or the USA – the countries that industrialised first – would show the route that others were destined to follow. Although there was some disagreement on the details of the direction of modernisation there was general agreement that the process was clearly directional and that greater prosperity and a version of liberal democracy lay at the end. The failure of many South American and Third World countries to behave as the theory predicted stimulated a debate on the adequacy of modernisation theory and also on the cause of their economic stagnation. Some explanations were offered in terms of the cultural values found in some states which, it was argued, were not conducive to an acceptance of capitalist values (Weber 1958). Other explanations were offered in terms that stressed the context in which states were attempting to develop. Development, it was suggested, is not purely or even primarily an internal process, but rather one that is strongly influenced, if not determined, by the advanced capitalist economies. The relationship between the advanced northern states and the poorer southern states was one of dependency of the latter on the former (see Sklair 1988 and 1991, and Fukuyama 1992 for reviews of the dependency literature). Third World countries are attempting to develop in a very different context from that within which the advanced countries developed. As Sunkel put it the underdevelopment of Third World countries must be seen in the context of 'the development of an international capitalist system, whose dynamic has a determining influence on the local processes' (1972: 520). However, as Sklair (1991) points out, 'underdevelopment' is only one possible outcome of the relationship between First and Third World countries in a global capitalist system. If underdevelopment represents the systematic crippling of the potential for economic modernisation then 'dependent development' is a relationship where a degree of economic modernisation is allowed but only under the strict control of the First World power.

An important element in both variations on dependency theory is the link between the capitalist elites in developed (centre) states and in underdeveloped (peripheral) states. This analysis of class alliances suggests that the capitalist elite (comprador class) in a peripheral country will play an important role in the exploitation of its own countrymen due to the 'coincidence of interests between local dominant classes and international ones' (Cardoso and Faletto 1979: xvi). A central role in maintaining dependency is played by the multi-national corporations.

There have been a number of attempts to extend and develop the globalist perspective. Wallerstein, for example, extended the dependency theories in an attempt to theorise global economic, political and social processes and construct an explanation of the functioning and dynamics of the 'world system'. Where most dependency theorists sought to explain Third World underdevelopment Wallerstein aimed to explain both development and underdevelopment and at different historical periods (see, for example, Wallerstein 1974; 1979). A second interesting development within the globalist perspective comes from Galtung. For him imperialism is not confined to an economic relationship between states; rather, it is a structural relationship which facilitates dominance in the spheres of culture, politics, military matters and communications as well as in the economic sphere. Galtung's contribution to theory development within the globalist perspective is discussed more fully below.

A key issue for globalists is how change occurs in the world system. For some (Alker 1981) change arises out of the clash between power blocs, for example between states and multi-national corporations or between capitalist and socialist blocs. This view is in contrast to Marxist analyses of change which stress the vulnerability of the world system to revolutionary action. But the failure of many Marxist-inspired revolutionary movements in the Third World, the rapid expansion of Pacific Rim economies, and the collapse of the socialist bloc are three factors used by critics of globalism to challenge its conception of change (see, for example, Fukuyama 1992: chapter 9). Further criticism is directed at the alleged over-reliance on systemic factors to explain the lack of development in the Third World. The critics suggest that account must be taken of the internal politics, culture and economic structure of Third World countries. Finally, realist critics accuse globalists of an over-reliance on the explanatory power of economic factors and of ignoring other factors such as security.

Globalism and sport

Globalists, like realists, rely heavily on the explanatory power of one factor within the international system. Economic relations – as the central dynamic of the global system – suggests, initially at least, only limited scope for addressing the role and significance of international sport. In addition, the central concern with 'dependency' and its establishment and maintenance would seem to contrast with the apparent democracy and autonomy of national sports organisations within the international sphere. Most international sports federations and the CGF operate, at the public level at least, on a basis of equality among affiliated organisations. The narrowness of the focus of much globalist theory, like that of the realists, indicates that its explanatory capacity in relation to international sport is limited. However, even if the perspective is defined in narrow terms it still retains some explanatory value.

For globalists the primary agents for the maintenance of the system of dependency are the multi-national corporations (MNCs). Significant among MNCs are those with interests in international sport through marketing, television and other media, leisure wear, and sports equipment. These corporations share the concerns of other MNCs to achieve the most advantageous balance between costs of production, profitability and market share. Thus even though these commercial concerns are only peripheral to international sporting competition it is possible to argue that they will, nonetheless, affect the development of sport as it too is shaped to fulfil the priorities of international capitalism.

It is also possible to argue that dependency relations affect sport in a much more direct fashion. The classic dependency relation is where a Third World country is exploited for its raw materials or its supply of cheap labour. In this respect there is a direct equivalence where the sporting talent of Third World countries is systematically exploited for the profit of rich nations. The relationship between the USA and the Dominican Republic in baseball is a prime example, but so too is the export of talented soccer players from Africa to Europe, the movement of cricketers from the Caribbean to English clubs, and the movement of talented athletes from Africa to US colleges.

Both the location of sports-related corporations within the circle of MNCs and the dependency relationship in the trade in human sporting talent are important factors in helping to shape the role and significance of sport in international relations. Globalism is a broad perspective and there are clearly strands within it that would aid a sharper focus on sport. Of particular interest are those global theorists, Galtung in particular, who have widened their focus beyond a concern with economic relations. For example, there has been substantial interest in using the concept of cultural imperialism to explore the non-economic aspects of the relationship between dominant and dependent states and, in more recent years, the related notion of cultural globalisation has emerged as an important focus for exploring the relations between states and one that clearly encompasses international sport.

Cultural imperialism and globalisation

For Lenin the economic penetration of underexploited regions produced higher rates of profit not only because of the cheapness of labour and the lower composition of capital, but also because the mechanics of imperial rule ensured that the preconditions for monopolistic privileges were maintained. Integral to this analysis was the argument that in order to maximise the benefits of the imperial relationship, control over the internal politics of the poorer region must be achieved. The most common form of control was through the establishment of colonies administered and policed either directly by the imperial power or by its local agents. As O'Connor (1970) shows, by the middle years of this century direct colonial domination had been augmented and more frequently replaced by a variety of forms of economic domination and control over assets. These 'informal modes of political control [including] economic, political and cultural missions, labour union delegations, joint military training programs, military grants, bribes to local ruling classes in the form of economic "aid", substitute for direct colonial rule' (p. 147).

Galtung in his discussion of the relationship between dominant and subordinate classes in, and between, centre and periphery states creates an opportunity to move even further away from the classic formulations of imperialism. For Galtung the key to understanding the persistence of imperialism is the harmony of interests between the large dominant class in the centre state and the smaller dominant class within the peripheral state. This harmony of interests is in marked contrast to the disharmony of interests experienced by the dominated classes in the centre and periphery states. The third ingredient in Galtung's model of imperialism is that the degree of disharmony of interest between the dominant and dominated classes in the peripheral state is greater than that found in the centre state due to the dominated class in the centre state receiving some small share of the benefits of the imperial relation. The final element in Galtung's model of imperialism is that periphery states tend to be tied into the orbit of particular centre states with the consequences that periphery states have only limited contact with other periphery states and that the contact that they do have is frequently mediated by the centre state. The commonality of interests between dominant classes and the inability of dominated classes in peripheral states to link with similar classes in other peripheral states are the two aspects of the structure by which the imperial relationship is maintained. As Galtung notes, 'Only imperfect, amateurish imperialism needs weapons: professional imperialism is based on structure rather than direct violence' (1971: 90).

Building upon this model Galtung outlines a series of different dimensions of imperialism, namely economic, political, military, communication and cultural, and suggests that imperialism can be established on any of these dimensions. Of particular interest is Galtung's suggestion that culture and communication can be seen as central elements in an imperialist relationship. Accepting that dominance can be achieved, or at least substantially contributed to, through cultural means opens up a whole series of complex questions concerning the nature of the exported culture, the process of imposition/absorption, and the impact on the target/recipient culture. These questions will be considered more fully in Chapter 8, and it is sufficient here to note that an acknowledgement of the potential importance of culture in shaping the pattern of international relations suggests a number of interesting avenues for research. Agnell (1969), for example, highlights the effects on attitudes and values concerning foreign policy issues of residence abroad and involvement in transnational organisations. There is also a growing body of research into the impact of world-wide tourism on the cultures of poorer countries. Erisman (1983), for example, suggests that local cultures, such as in the West Indies, are undermined due to the demands for a standardised, commodified tourist experience (see also Matthews 1978; Cohen 1977; Nash 1978).

However, the bulk of research in this area has focused on the role and significance of the media in facilitating the diffusion of dominant culture. The most common argument is that the peripheral state may provide the 'event' but it will be the central state that will provide the means of disseminating (and interpreting) information about that event. More importantly it is also the case that many peripheral states gain information about events in their own territory primarily through media owned and controlled by the central state. Locksley, commenting on the 'electronic imperialism' of the developed world's media, sees the impact as being pernicious due to the effect on 'the self-image of poor countries generated by Northern news and information providers . . . [which] stigmatises poor countries as earthquakes, disasters and human zoos' (1986: 93).

Finally, Galtung argues that, in general, peripheral states will be presented with more information about 'their' central state than about either themselves or other peripheral states. Cultural imperialism clearly has much in common with this aspect of communication imperialism, as both are concerned with the ability of the central state to determine what is worth knowing. Furthermore, as Galtung argues, 'in accepting cultural transmission the periphery also, implicitly, validates for the centre the culture developed in the centre [and also] reinforces the centre as a centre' (1971: 93).

Without wishing to undermine the significance of trade, politics and military power as elements in the relationship between rich and poor states a focus on communication and culture provides a valuable context for an evaluation of international sport. Sport, as both a cultural product and as an important concern of the international media, provides rich scope for exploring the extent to which the media is fostering the spread of a global sporting culture and also the significance of globalisation for the relationship between states in general and the rich and poor states in particular.

Conclusion

Sport as a major twentieth-century cultural phenomenon, as an element in the globalisation of culture, as a foreign policy resource, and as an arena in which international relations take place, provides a rich variety of contexts within which to explore the significance of sport in world politics. The perspectives explored above provide a number of frameworks within which to explore sport and while theoretical issues will be more fully explored in Chapter 8, preliminary observations relating to the explanatory capacity of the three major perspectives will be presented now. The dominant perspective in international relations – realism – has, in many respects, a compelling logic. Its assumptions about the primacy of security to states and its emphasis on military power as a determining variable in international relations cannot be ignored. But it is this narrowness of focus that also makes it less useful. At its simplest it may be argued that military power is a resource that can be activated on only rare occasions. States, including dominant/hegemonic states, need to have a wider repertoire of resources to project and protect their interests. Within that repertoire there need to be resources that are more subtle than force and also less costly. The need for a broader range of policy instruments is further justified by the fact that within international relations states will have a hierarchy of interests, some of which will be so central that military action will be triggered, others where lower tariff sanctions will be employed, and still others where the issues are of only peripheral interest to the state and therefore warrant a low tariff and definitely non-military response.

In addition, the problem, faced by those adopting a realist perspective, of theorising the role of non-governmental organisations (NGOs) is a clear weakness. While the resources controlled by multi-national corporations cannot hope to match those of the major world powers they must be considered as significant when their relationship is with a poorer state. However, even if one is sceptical about according the status of an independent actor in world politics to NGOs one must at least accept that they are frequently a significant medium through which state power is articulated. Consequently, it remains to be established the extent to which NGOs act merely as conduits for state interests or as interpreters of state interests on the world political stage.

The necessity to look beyond the narrow range of resources considered by realist theorists and the need to pay greater attention to the role of NGOs diminishes the overall utility of this perspective for the study of sport. By contrast the pluralist perspective offers a much more accommodating framework for analysis, particularly as regards its explicit recognition of the importance of NGOs and its concern with policy processes. A view of the international system which stresses a multiplicity of interests and resources and which acknowledges the salience to states of issues beyond those that impinge directly on security matters is a much more persuasive context for analysis. The danger that the pluralist perspective downplays too sharply the significance of the state is a real one, but is also one that can be overcome. That some organisations, such as the state, play an authoritative role in a pattern of interorganisational relations is clearly acknowledged and can be accommodated within a pluralist perspective (Theonig 1978).

What is generally lacking from the pluralist perspective is an acknowledgement of the importance of ideology as a factor shaping the pattern of international relations. The significance of ideology as the 'mobilisation of bias' or as the 'deep structure' (Benson 1979) of the international system needs to be addressed. Benson, for example, argues persuasively, with regard to interorganisational relations, that it is necessary to locate relationships in a 'deep structure' of power relations found in wider society. Applying his argument to the international system it is suggested that the nature and character of the system configuration and the distribution of power within it is not just the outcome of effective strategy development in the competition for resources, but is the product of biases fundamental to the global structure. These biases are manifest not simply as power constellations (classes, military alliances, trade agreements, etc.), but also as the taken-for-granted rules of structure formation. In other words the assumption is that the solution to international political problems must be consistent with the fundamental features of the international system. In summary, what is suggested is a bounded pluralism in which the limits of pluralist activity are constructed in terms of the interests of dominant states and powerful NGOs but expressed or presented as a set of neutral values.

This framework brings pluralism much closer to the concerns found within the global perspective. The concern of globalists with the exploitative relationship between rich and poor states and the acceptance by some working within this perspective that, while trade and military relations are central, cultural relations may also be important, provide rich opportunities for research into the significance of international sport. Thus the emergence of sport as a global phenomenon raises questions regarding the interests that benefit most from this development and the extent to which the globalisation of sport is supported and manipulated to serve particular interests.

A recognition that most international sporting contact takes place within a highly nationalistic context, albeit against a background of universalistic rhetoric, suggests that a central role in the manipulation of sport is filled by states. However, not only does this assertion need to be explored and demonstrated but, more importantly, the role of international sports organisations and international business (particularly the media) needs to be examined.

The chapters that follow explore the significance of sport for international politics from within a broadly pluralist framework which acknowledges the central and often authoritative role of the state within the international system, but which also accepts that other actors have organisational objectives that, while not likely to thwart those of major states, at least have the potential to distort state goals. The pluralist analysis takes place, however, within a context that acknowledges that sport is a global cultural phenomenon and in that sense is a resource to be used in the conduct of international politics.

3

International sport organisations and international politics

The role of international organisations in world politics

In the previous chapter attention was drawn to the differing weight and attention given to the state in studies of international relations. For some, particularly those working within the realist perspective, the state was considered to be so dominant that there was little to be gained by exploring the activities of non-state actors. However, for others, from both pluralist and globalist perspectives, a full understanding of international politics was not possible without acknowledging and exploring the significance of non-state actors. Accepting that to focus solely on the state provides only a partial insight into world politics, there are two important types of non-state actor that require discussion: international governmental organisations (IGOs) and international non-governmental organisations (INGOs).

The former refer to voluntary groupings of states in, for example, military alliances (NATO), financial/economic/trade organisations (GATT, World Bank, European Community, IMF), and diplomatic forums (Council of Europe, United Nations). According to Bennett (1991: 2) IGOs and non-profit-making INGOs normally share the following common characteristics: '(1) a permanent organisation to carry on a continuing set of functions, (2) voluntary membership of eligible parties, (3) a basic instrument stating goals, structure, and methods of operation, (4) a broadly representative consultative conference organ, and (5) a permanent secretariat to carry on continuous administrative, research, and information functions.'

Intergovernmental organisations have played, and continue to play, an important role in the relationship between sport and world politics and will be examined in more detail in the next chapter. The focus for this chapter is on international non-governmental organisations. These bodies, sometimes referred to as transnational actors, characteristically have a headquarters in one country but operate across national boundaries and seek access to a number of sovereign states. In attempting to capture the essential distinction between IGOs and INGOs it can be suggested that for IGOs nationality and national interest are primary concerns while for INGOs they are at best secondary considerations or even seen as impediments to the achievement of objectives. Unfortunately it is easier to distinguish between IGOs and INGOs in theory than in practice. A number of major international organisations operate in a 'grey area' which straddles the two categories. Groom gives the example of the International Labour Organisation which, while being formed of states, is represented by three distinct sets of delegates from government, management and business (Groom 1988: 7).

INGOs cover the whole range of human activity and most do not aspire (publicly at least) to exert influence over international political issues. However, there are others which are much more likely to acknowledge an explicit interest in global issues. Some of the most prominent are to be found among multi-national corporations (MNCs), such as General Motors, Exxon, Hilton Hotels and British Petroleum; religions, such as the Roman Catholic Church; humanitarian and environmental organisations, such as Oxfam, the International Red Cross, and Greenpeace; and political organisations, including the Palestine Liberation Organisation. What these highly varied organisations have in common is 'a desire to accomplish their goals by acting transnationally as well as working within the confines of geographically defined national units' (Kegley and Wittkopf 1989: 131).

INGOs can be categorised in a number of different ways including their geographical spread; whether they have general or specific purposes; and whether they deliver a service or provide a forum for debate. Categorisation is of little utility in itself but does serve the valuable purpose of demonstrating the range and differentiation among sport organisations. Table 3.1 categorises sport INGOs by purpose and geographical scope.

As can be seen sport organisations feature strongly in each category as a result of the development of a hierarchy of national, regional and global organisations and the extensive specialism produced over the last hundred years. The growth in sports INGOs parallels the general expansion in the number of international organisations in the last fifty years.

A particularly important theme running through the literature on INGOs is a concern to identify their role and significance within the

Table 3.1 Sport international non-governmental organisations

	Global	National, regional, subregional, interregional
Single sport	International Amateur Athletic Federation (IAAF) International Federation of Football Associations (FIFA)	European Union of Football Association (UEFA) European Hockey Federation (EHF)
Multi-sport	International Olympic Committee (IOC) Commonwealth Games Federation (CGF) International Paralympic Committee (IPC) International Federation for University Sport (FISU)	Pan American Sports Association (PASO) Le Comité International des Jeux de la Francophonic (CIJF) National Olympic committees

Source: Adapted from Kegley and Wittkopf (1989).

international system. The four most frequently voiced views are first, that INGOs undermine the sovereign state; second, that they provide the state with other points of access to the international system; third, that they mediate and modify state influence; and fourth, that they achieve a degree of relative autonomy from states.

The suggestion that INGOs undermine the sovereign state is an accusation that is levelled most frequently at MNCs who have traditionally been viewed with considerable suspicion by many, particularly poor, states. The financial resources of major international manufacturing firms and their ability to move capital around the globe are both attractive to developing countries as a potential catalyst for development but also a source of concern due to the capacity of MNCs to act as potential sources of instability should that investment be withdrawn. Concern is not limited to the role of the multi-national manufacturing industries. Of equal concern to poorer states are the multi-national media corporations which exert considerable control over the flow of information into and out of poorer states. Apart from the MNCs, concern is also expressed about the effect of international missionary organisations and the activities of some aid agencies which are seen as interfering in the internal affairs of the host state (Cutler 1978; Kurdle 1987; Spero 1985).

These arguments about the capacity of international organisations to undermine sovereign states are, not surprisingly, voiced by poorer states: for the rich states, INGOs are rarely perceived as a threat. A number of studies suggest that although the state is the key actor within international systems non-state actors are important as a means by which one state becomes sensitive to the interests of another (Keohane and Nye 1975) and as vehicles for policy implementation (Young 1980). Both these views imply that INGOs are largely neutral vessels for the communication of state interests. While it is indeed likely that under many circumstances INGOs provide states with lines of access to other states or to international forums it is also likely that the communications between states are modified as a result of this mediating process. For Pentland international organisations 'become an institutional manifestation of the general set of restraints placed on states by the international system' (1976: 641). This view is elaborated by Keohane and Nye (1989) who argue that state actions depend to a great extent on prevailing institutional arrangements. According to this view international institutions are 'persistent and connected sets of rules (formal and informal) that prescribe behavioural roles, constrain activity, and shape expectations' (1989: 3). Consequently, INGOs help to interpret interests, shape the perception of issues and define solutions. The capacity of INGOs to modify state behaviour is greatest at times of multi-polarity, wide distribution of resources, and growing transnational interdependence.

Many INGOs will be able to claim that rather than possessing the modest degree of autonomy suggested by a mere mediating role they are in fact influential actors within the international system and possess a considerable degree of discretion over their actions and have the capacity to affect the behaviour of others. The capacity to affect others and withstand pressure from others is a product of control over resources such as expertise, finance, legitimacy, decision-making capacity, popular support, etc. Quite clearly INGOs will vary greatly in terms of the range and depth of resources that they possess, but equally clearly an increasing number of organisations are now sufficiently resource-rich to be able to act with greater confidence on the international stage and affect the decisions of governments. To the familiar example of the Catholic Church may be added aid agencies, such as Oxfam and Save the Children Fund, and sport organisations, such as the International Olympic Committee, IAAF and FIFA.

Support for this view comes from a wide variety of sources. Keohane (1989), for example, has argued strongly that INGOs may well be capable of pursuing their own interests, and that their pursuit of self-interest will have an effect upon the character of the regimes of which they are part. Lindblom, though exploring the politics of national political systems, also provides the basis for challenging the assumption that INGOs, particularly business INGOs, are peripheral actors or simply mediators in the international system. In his analysis of the relationship between business and the state, Lindblom suggests that while the state may be formally independent of business it is heavily reliant on it for achieving publicly accepted goals. Business is capable of exercising a degree of hegemonic influence such that 'citizens' volitions serve not their own interests but the interests of business' and that 'when a government official asks himself whether business needs a tax reduction, he knows that he is asking a question about the welfare of the whole society and not simply about a favour to a segment of the population' (Lindblom 1977: 176, 175). The correspondence of interests between business and the state in industrialised countries suggests that rather than business INGOs being perceived as either second-order actors to the state or rival actors they are seen as complementary and mutually supportive, and ideologically dominant.

To analyse the global pattern of relationships between states and INGOs with the expectation of being able to produce reliable generalisations is foolhardy. Common sense would suggest that the characteristics of an international regime will differ from one policy area to another as well as varying over time. However, it should be possible to examine a particular policy area, such as sport, and produce an assessment of the role of relevant INGOs. The primary concern of the remainder of this chapter is to assess the capacity of sport INGOs to function effectively within the international system. Two questions are central: first, do these organisations, either individually or collectively, possess the resources necessary to influence the policy process and second, is it possible to provide evidence of actual influence? If examples of influence can be identified then a number of additional questions arise concerning the scope of influence and the conditions under which influence is greatest. The discussion that follows focuses primarily on the role in sport policy of the IOC and the major international federation, the IAAF.

International non-governmental organisations in sport

International organisations involved in sport can be divided into two major groups: on the one hand those organisations associated with the

Table 3.2 The relationship between the international federations and the Olympic movement

Organisation	Linked to
ASOIF	IOC, GAISF
AIWF	IOC, GAISF
IOC	ANOC
ANOC	Individual NOCs; Continental groupings of NOCs
GAISF	IFs
IFs	National governing bodies

international sports federations and on the other those associated with the Olympic movement (Table 3.2). While these two groups may be seen as constituting the heart of the international sports community they also represent two distinct sets of interests which are frequently in conflict. It is also possible to identify a third emerging international grouping, namely the athletes themselves, acting either individually via agents and managers or collectively through representative organisations such as the Association of Tennis Professionals and the International Association of Athlete's Representatives (representing track and field athletes). While this group is not a powerful force at present it is beginning to make demands for access to the policy agenda of international sport.

Within most countries each major sport is organised by a specialist governing body whose main functions are to agree and apply rules of the sport; organise events; and select teams and manage international fixtures. As international competition became more common in the early part of this century international federations began to be established to coordinate competition and to ensure the necessary uniformity in rules. It is the hundred or so international federations (IFs), and within this group the 25 IFs of Olympic sports, that constitute one of the major clusters of INGOs within sport. Yet few individual IFs have sufficient resources to be influential beyond a narrow range of issues (rules and competition) concerning their own sport. Among the few exceptions is the IAAF which has played an important part in shaping the debate and policy on issues such as doping, recognition of states and sport development.

As a consequence of the weakness of individual IFs a series of representative bodies have developed in recent years. Three are particularly important, namely the General Association of International Sports Federations (GAISF), the Association of Summer Olympic International Federations (ASOIF), and the Association of Winter Sports Federations (AIWF). GAISF was established in 1967 and like the IOC has its headquarters in Lausanne, Switzerland. It comprises 75 members and includes nearly all IFs holding regular competitions at world level. Among the specific aims of GAISF are the promotion of closer links between members and other sports organisations, and collaboration with the IOC concerning the global promotion of sport. However, other aims include the maintenance of the authority and autonomy of its members, and the protection of their common interests. The inclusion of aims that promote cooperation alongside those that stress the protection of independence reflects the tension that exists between the IFs and the Olympic movement. GAISF grew out of an increasing desire among the federations to increase their share of the revenue from the sale of television rights. However, as Espy (1979: 113) points out the concern was not purely financial and was as much to do with a fear of a decline in the status of the federations which would leave them at a permanent disadvantage in their relationship with the increasingly powerful Olympic movement. Despite initial hostility from the IOC and some reluctance from the IAAF, who feared that they might lose their privileged access to the IOC, GAISF rapidly became an established part of the cluster of key sports INGOs. The IOC soon adjusted to the presence of the General Association in its orbit and through a process of modest concessions (for example, allowing IFs to hold world championships outside the Olympics) and co-option of key IF leaders (most recently, Primo Nebiolo, President of the IAAF) it has managed to maintain federation support and compliance. As Hill notes, the maintenance by the IOC of its pre-eminent position in international sport is the result of a shrewd distribution of financial resources for sport development to Third World countries, 'an understanding of human motivation, and the prudent manipulation of power' (1992: 66).

The Association of Summer Olympic International Federations was formed in 1983 by the then 21 IFs whose sports made up the Olympic programme. Among the aims of ASOIF are to aid the IOC in the organisation of the Games, to inspect the facilities offered by candidate cities, and to decide the division of income from TV rights among IFs. In addition, the Association aims to maintain the authority, independence and autonomy of its members. As with GAISF the Association's aims reflect an ambivalent attitude towards the IOC, seeking to cooperate in its success, but wary of being overwhelmed by it. Much the same may be said of the Association of Winter Sports Federations. Although an older organisation, founded in 1970, it shares similar aims and concerns with its summer equivalent.

The position of the federations is undoubtedly weakened by the existence of three representative organisations and as a result there have been periodic attempts to develop closer ties between GAISF, AWIF and ASOIF. At present there are discussions taking place between GAISF and ASOIF with the aim of merging. Yet if the merger is to take place a number of interests need to be reconciled as the non-Olympic IFs have different concerns from those already in the Olympic programme, and the large IFs face problems very different from those of the smaller federations. Finally, a merger, if it can be engineered, would not be to the liking of the IOC whose strategy of 'divide and rule' would be undermined.

Turning to the Olympic organisations it is the International Olympic Committee which is located at the pinnacle of the movement and at the centre of a complex network of international sports organisations. The primary function of the IOC is to oversee Olympic sport and any competitions permitted by the IOC to use the Olympic name, such as the Pan-American Games and the Asian Games. However, given the stature of the Games, the financial resources of the Committee and, not least, the IOC's moral authority the Committee plays a key role in influencing the direction and pace of development of sport at international and national levels. This pre-eminent role has increased considerably in the last decade.

Since the breakup of the Soviet Union the Olympic movement now has links with over 200 countries, 92 of which, in 1989, had 'members' on the IOC, who reported back to their individual national Olympic committee (NOC). The word 'member' is preferred to 'representative' because the IOC Charter treats IOC members not as representatives of their respective NOCs to the IOC but rather as members *of the IOC in their country*. The IOC is at the heart of what Scherer refers to as the last empire of this century (Scherer, quoted in *Sport Intern*, 10 May 1989). He notes that there are, in addition to the IFs whose sports are part of the Olympic programme, 16 federations recognised by the IOC and waiting to be included in the Olympic programme, three organising committees for forthcoming Games as well as 36 organisations with special objectives recognised by the IOC, such as World Disabled Sports Federation. In addition to the IOC and the various NOCs there is a world Association of National Olympic Committees (ANOC) and a number of continental associations of NOCs such as the Pan American Sports Association (PASO).

The IOC comprises two organisations: the first is the Session, or General Assembly, comprising the 92 IOC members, which elects the second organisation, the nine-person Executive Board. The Board is at the heart of Olympic decision-making and management and is supported by a series of Commissions which provide advice and also help run the movement. Among the 23 current Commissions or working groups are those responsible for developing policy regarding drugs, television contract negotiation, and world-wide sport development.

Much of the IOC's claim to autonomy in international politics is based, in large part, on its considerable financial resources. In recent years the Committee has operated with an annual budget in excess of $15m and boasts reserves of over $72m and aims to raise its reserves to over $100m thus enabling it to meet its annual running costs out of the interest. The bulk of IOC income comes from its current 7% share of the television rights for the Games.

One problem that the IOC clearly faces is that of balancing the increasingly complex and intense political pressures that confront it. Part of this problem concerns the difficulties involved in maintaining the maximum independence of the national Olympic committees from their respective governments and part concerns the prevention of the IOC becoming simply another forum for international politics. As regards the independence of NOCs the IOC asserts that it alone can decide who the NOC representative on the IOC will be. But this assertion is balanced by a pragmatic acceptance that in many, if not most, countries NOCs are heavily dependent on government finance, goodwill and administrative support (Guttmann 1984: 134–5). In general the IOC is more alarmed at the prospect of a growth of NOC influence than a growth in the influence of the federations. While the latter may pressure the IOC for a greater say in Olympic decision-making their primary motive is to extract maximum benefit for their individual sports; in contrast the IOC is deeply suspicious of the motives of many of the NOCs and their continental representative bodies. The focus of the IOC's concern is the belief that the central motivation of the majority of NOCs is ideological or sectional, as many of the proposals for membership reform were formulated by the Soviet Union and supported by its communist allies and the African bloc.

As a result, the key demand by the NOCs that they should have more extensive representation on the IOC has been strongly resisted by the IOC on the grounds that such a move would result in a further consolidation of political camps within the Olympic movement along the lines of the United Nations General Assembly. It was in a largely successful attempt to divide the Third World bloc from the communist bloc that the IOC established a major sports development programme, Olympic Solidarity, directed primarily at the needs of poorer countries.

When attempting to assess the ability of INGOs to operate effectively in the international system a valuable starting point is to explore their organisational capacity. In simple organisational terms the major sports INGOs possess considerable resources which should enable them to achieve substantially the goal of any international organisation, namely a leadership role on policy issues that are central to their activities, and a capacity to voice and protect their interests when sports-related issues are being discussed in non-sport policy arenas. In organisational terms the sports INGOs have a number of clear strengths. Of particular importance is the legitimacy that is derived from the global coverage of the major sports organisations, and for most (the IOC being an important exception), the 'one country – one vote' basis of decision-making. In addition, sports INGOs are seen, by sports organisations, as retaining considerable autonomy from national governments. Finally, an increasing number of sports INGOs are now both wealthy bodies in their own right and, possibly more importantly, bodies capable of generating wealth, for example through the choice of venue for championships. However, it may be argued that the price of greater independence from governments is a greater dependence on the media.

Consequently, on many issues the sports INGOs are able to combine to make a formidable force within international sport and politics. The capacity of sports INGOs to shape the agenda on sport issues of international concern is best illustrated by the development and implementation of a policy towards drug abuse by athletes (Houlihan 1991). One can also point to the decisions surrounding the location of major championships where, despite periodic complaints from northern European (especially British) sports administrators that there is a conspiracy among the leaders of FIFA, IAAF and the IOC to give preference to Latin countries, the evidence suggests that the primary factors influencing the choice of venue are sports development opportunities, marketing, the availability of suitable facilities, and the willingness of the host city or government to meet the requirements of the organising committee. For example, Montreal was selected to host the 1976 Games in preference to Los Angeles and Moscow. Among the reasons offered for Montreal's selection were its neutral stance on the war in Vietnam, the quality of the security on offer and, according to the IOC itself, the importance of demonstrating that smaller cities could host the Games 'completely self-financed' (Espy 1979: 133). Unfortunately, the fact that the 1976 Games eventually left the people of Montreal with a substantial debt did not send the desired message to other smaller cities, let alone those in the developing world. Four years later the Games were hosted by Moscow in preference to Los Angeles, thus realising the long-expressed wish within the IOC to take the Games into new areas of the world. The selection of Seoul, despite the opposition of the Soviet Union, for the 1988 Games can be seen as part of the same policy. More recently, the choice of Lillehammer in Norway for the 1994 Winter Olympics illustrates the extent to which the IOC delegates jealously guard their independence. In choosing this small town the IOC rejected Sofia (and the influence of the socialist bloc vote), Ostersund, Sweden (where even King Carl Gustav lobbied on its behalf) and Anchorage (and the lure of American dollars).

A positive assessment of the influence to be derived from the organisational capacity of the major sports INGOs needs to be tempered by an acknowledgement that there are substantial divisions between the Olympic movement and the international federations. For the federations the primary concern is that they are rapidly losing control over their sports to the IOC. This fear is not focused on the possibility of a loss of control over the rules of particular sports but rather on a loss of control over the development of the sport. In other words there is a fear that the Olympic event is becoming more important than the component sports. A secondary concern among federations is that the sheer size and wealth of the Olympic movement has distorted the established relationship between it and the federations.

As already noted these underlying tensions are reflected in a number of specific issues including the role of federations in influencing the selection of a venue for the Games; the division of television income; the terms on which sports will be included in the Games; and the management of events at the Games. It is partly as a response to these concerns of the federations that the suggestion was made that the GAISF and ASOIF should merge (possibly including FISU, the world student sport body). The aim is to strengthen the federation lobby and thereby restore the previous balance in the relationship with the IOC. In the past there have also been suggestions that the leaders of the major Olympic federations should be *ex-officio* members of the IOC, or even of its Executive Board.

To a large extent the IOC has accommodated the wishes of the federations by agreeing to give them a major say in the choice of Games venue and by accepting the need to incorporate major federation leaders within the ambit of the IOC. However, tensions still remain and may be illustrated by the continuing dispute between the soccer federation, FIFA, and the IOC over the terms on which soccer is included in the Olympic programme. IOC President, Samaranch, has always insisted that the ideal of the Olympic Games is to provide a showcase for the highest-quality competition in the world's most popular sports. Given that few sports can claim the global participation levels of soccer it is not surprising that Samaranch has been keen to develop the role of soccer in the Games. Unfortunately, FIFA sees this move as a threat to its own world championships, the World Cup, and has consistently resisted pressure to allow senior national teams to participate, preferring to impose an age limit (currently 23) on team selection.

A second source of tension concerns the distribution of the huge sums of money generated by the Games through the sale of television rights and through sponsorship. At present the Olympic IFs gain a share of the income from the sale of broadcasting rights, while the IOC retains the income from its sponsorship programme known as TOP (The Olympic Programme). The federations have recently suggested that not only should TOP income be shared with them but that advertising should be allowed on participants' clothing and also in the stadium.

In summary, one can argue that there are a number of sports INGOs that possess the necessary resources to enable them actively to protect their interests within the international system. When acting in a concerted fashion the major federations and the IOC have the potential to form a powerful lobby. However, this capacity is certainly weakened by the tensions between the federations and the Olympic movement and the degree of mutual suspicion that is frequently apparent. The following sections examine two issues in order to explore the extent to which the sports INGOs are able to utilise their resources to translate potential influence into effective participation in the international system.

The international enforcement of sport's anti-doping policy

One of the most persistent problems in modern sport is drug abuse. While there has always been some attempt to gain an advantage through the use of drugs it is only in the last twenty years that the problem has been recognised as widespread, persistent and, more importantly, a threat to the future popularity and financial security of competitive sport. While the problem of eliminating drug abuse from sport has been the subject of concern and action in a number of countries for many years the focus for policy-making and enforcement has been the IFs, particularly the IAAF, and the IOC.

The IOC outlawed doping in 1962 and then proceeded to establish a Medical Commission in 1967 to oversee the Committee's development of a policy to combat drug abuse. This activity was paralleled by discussions within a number of governing bodies including the IAAF, who formed a Medical Committee in 1972, also with the responsibility of formulating an anti-doping policy. Individual countries, including Sweden and Britain, were also taking action to research the issues and problems. Testing began, if in a somewhat limited fashion, in the late 1960s and early 1970s with tests being carried out at the 1968 Winter Olympics, the 1966 World Cup, the 1970 Commonwealth Games, and the 1974 European Athletics Championships.

Three issues have dominated the agendas of governing bodies, their IFs and the IOC, namely agreement on the list of banned substances and practices, the implementation of the testing procedure, and finally the penalties to be imposed on transgressors. Each of these issues, but particularly the testing procedure, raised problems concerning the relationship between the Olympic movement, the IFs and governments. In general there has been little disagreement over the drugs and practices to be prohibited. Most IFs have been content to follow the lead given by the IOC and the IAAF. Increasingly the IOC list is being seen as the international standard and there are only relatively minor differences between the lists produced by the IOC, the IFs and domestic governing bodies. For example, the modern pentathlon IF (Union Internationale de Pentathlon Moderne et de Biathlon) has added sedatives, such as valium, to its list; the International Rugby Board has added lignocaine, a local anaesthetic, to its list; and the World Professional Billiards and Snooker Association (WPBSA) allows selective use of cardio-beta-blockers if permission is applied for in advance. Cycling, through the International Federation of Professional Cycling, bans a broader range of steroids than other sports but also wants a revision of the list to allow some mild painkillers such as codeine. The International Cycling Union has recently removed beta-blockers from its list of proscribed drugs.

It is undoubtedly in the area of implementing the testing regime that the most significant problems remain. The IOC and the IAAF quickly acknowledged that to implement the anti-doping policy via the activities of domestic governing bodies or solely at international competitions was still allowing scope for considerable drug abuse. In the first place many countries could not be relied upon to undertake rigorous testing either due to a lack of commitment, as in East Germany, or in poorer countries due to a lack of resources and particularly laboratories. Second, many of the newer drugs were designed to enhance training and as such were used during out-of-competition preparation. As a result individual domestic governing bodies and one or two state-funded organisations, such as the British Sports Council, began to introduce random out-of-competition testing.

In Britain out-of-competition random testing was piloted by the British Amateur Athletics Board in 1985 and later in 1988 widened, by the Sports Council, to include all governing bodies. However, given the frequency with which top-flight athletes train abroad out-of-competition testing had to be organised on an international basis. To this end GAISF lent its weight to the extension of testing at its 1988 conference, as did the European Sports Conference when it met in Sofia in 1989. Later, in April 1989, the IAAF council decided to impose random testing on all international athletes thereby bypassing those remaining countries where random out-of-competition testing did not take place. In May 1990, in one of the first examples of random testing by an international governing body, an IAAF 'flying squad' of drug testers visited the Soviet Union and tested sixteen athletes; all tests were negative. Similar 'flying squad' teams were subsequently sent to Italy and France.

Two recent cases illustrate some of the difficulties that the IFs face in attempting to implement their anti-doping policy. The first concerns a routine sample taken at an IAAF-approved event while the other concerns an out-of-competition test on German athletes training in South Africa. On 12 August 1990 Harry 'Butch' Reynolds was found to have traces of nandrolone in his urine sample. Reynolds was suspended by The Athletic Congress (TAC), the United States track and field governing body. However, TAC announced in June 1991 that it was to permit Reynolds to take part in competitions within the US as a result of an appeal by Reynolds to the American Arbitration Association. Part of Reynolds' motive to compete was a desire to participate in the US qualifying events in preparation for the Barcelona Olympic Games. Reynolds took part in the TAC/Mobil National Championships in June much to the annoyance of the IAAF who threatened an increased ban on Reynolds and the possibility that TAC's action might put at risk the participation of other US athletes in IAAF-approved events. In addition, the IAAF informed the US Olympic Committee and the IOC of its concern. Finally, after much fruitless correspondence with TAC the IAAF compromised and agreed to a review of the case by its Arbitration Panel which took place in May 1992. The function of the Arbitration Panel is to settle disputes between the IAAF and its member federations. The Panel confirmed the original decision of the IAAF and further declared that any athlete competing with Reynolds would be ineligible for participation in IAAF-approved events (the 'contamination' rule). Despite this confirmation Reynolds competed in two events during the early part of June. The IAAF stood by its decision and suspended the five American athletes who had run against Reynolds. By this time Reynolds was seeking support from the court in the form of a restraining order against the Federation to enable him to participate in the Olympic trials. The initial grant of a temporary restraining order was made by the District Court, only to be overturned by the Cincinnati Appeals Court. Finally, the US Supreme Court ordered TAC to allow Reynolds to take part in the trials. The response of the Federation was to retreat and waive its 'contamination' rule for the 400m trial while still asserting that even if Reynolds was successful in the trials he could not participate in the Olympic Games. Meanwhile Reynolds successfully sued the IAAF for damages and was awarded $28m against the Federation.

At about the same time the IAAF was dealing with an equally awkward problem concerning one of the most successful and famous women athletes. In January 1992 an out-of-competition testing team visited the South African training base of three German athletes, Silke Moller, Grit Breuer and Katrin Krabbe (IAAF world champion at 100m and 200m in 1991). A urine sample was taken from each of the three athletes but was found on analysis to have come from the same person. All were suspended for alleged doping sample manipulation and at a meeting of the Board of the Deutscher Leichtathletik Verband (DLV), the German governing body for track and field, the suspension was confirmed. However, the decision was subsequently reviewed by the DLV legal committee and the suspension lifted. The basis for the reversal of the initial decision was that while it was accepted that the urine samples had been manipulated it was a requirement of the IAAF rules that the method of manipulation be identified and this, according to DLV officials, could not be done. As a result the IAAF Arbitration Panel felt obliged to accept the DLV decision, stating that 'it was not empowered to interpret the National Legislation of jurisdictions or the rules of National Federations'

(*IAAF News*, May 1992). However, the Arbitration Panel added that 'we have serious reservations of the correctness of the DLV legal committee's decision as to whether the athletes committed doping offences' (*IAAF News*, May 1992).

In August 1992 the IAAF announced that Krabbe had tested positive for clenbuterol in the previous month, but even with this second offence there were problems of implementing the IAAF anti-doping policy. On this occasion there was a dispute over the scientific nature of clenbuterol whether it was an anabolic steroid or whether it was a stimulant (some of which are allowed in training). A second problem concerned the capacity of the DLV to impose a four-year ban due to advice which suggested that if an appeal were made to the German courts the penalty would be overturned on the grounds that it was too severe. As a result the penalty on Krabbe was cut by the DLV arbitration panel to a one-year ban.

The problems that the IOC and the IAAF face in successfully implementing an anti-doping policy are considerable and are amply illustrated by the Reynolds and Krabbe cases. Both cases highlight the number of policy actors involved and the number of clearance points required for the construction of a successful policy. Although the IOC and the IAAF lead is well established the key problem lies in achieving compliance at national level from the governmental and non-governmental organisations involved. In the USA and Germany there were suggestions that the governing bodies were less than wholehearted in their pursuit of drug abusers. Both examples also draw attention to the problems of achieving compliance from the domestic state and the vulnerability of their policy to challenge from rich athletes in the law courts. However, the Reynolds and Krabbe cases should not be taken as signs of failure on the part of the sport INGOs. The problems posed by these two cases need to be set against the changing nature of the problem and the fact that implementation is still in its early stages. When compared to other international problems such as copyright infringement or the dumping of waste at sea, the progress in this IOC-led policy must be judged as good.

Issues of recognition

The recognition by IFs of states is one area where sports INGOs are directly involved in matters of primary importance to the international political community and consequently provides a major opportunity to assess the capacity of sport INGOs to operate as independent actors in international politics. In the post-war period two conflicts over recognition have dominated international politics, namely the two Germanies and the two Chinas. However, these are not the only examples. Disputes over the recognition of Palestine, Israel, Rhodesia, the Baltic states and the ex-Yugoslav states have all featured on the agenda of international sports organisations.

The issue of German membership of federations and the IOC has its origins in the immediate post-war period when Germany was divided into four sectors, each under the control of one of the Allied powers. The failure of the Allied powers to reach agreement over the future political structure for Germany resulted in the establishment of the Federal Republic of Germany in 1949 which comprised the territories administered by Britain, France and the United States, and which claimed to represent all Germans. Diplomatic recognition followed swiftly and within a few years it had diplomatic relations with over one hundred states (Strenk 1978: 348). Provisional recognition by the IOC was granted in 1950, but full recognition was delayed until 1951 because the IOC wished to have a unified team and because of the attempts by the German Democratic Republic (GDR) to gain recognition both as an independent state and as an independent NOC.

As Strenk (1978; 1980) shows, West Germany's progress from three occupied military zones to an independent state was both rapid and relatively uncomplicated. West Germany's recognition was accompanied by a policy, strongly supported by the three Allied powers, designed to promote the FRG's membership of major international organisations and the systematic isolation of the GDR. Consequently, East Germany's progress to international recognition, beyond a small group of socialist states, was protracted and tortuous. For a state in such a situation there are a limited number of options: it can alter its internal structures to conform to pressures from its environment (compliance); it can attempt to alter its environment (intransigence); or it can attempt to restructure its relationship with its environment so as to minimise the negative consequences (management).[1] The policy of the East German Communist Party (Sozialistische Einheitspartei (SED)) was clearly one of intransigence. However, so great was the level of international opposition to the GDR that its foreign policy had to be not only uncompromising, but also innovative (Strenk 1978: 348).

Sport provided a foreign policy tool which was certainly innovative and which was also undeniably highly successful. International sporting contact provided the opportunity to demonstrate the existence of the East

German state and would force the issue of *de facto* recognition which, according to the East German leadership, would lead to *de jure* recognition. In addition, sport would enable access to be gained to international sports organisations which could be used as a springboard for membership of related international forums. During the early 1950s the GDR hosted a number of sports events involving foreign teams or athletes; took part in a number of unofficial or disguised 'international' competitions; and even encouraged a number of West German athletes to move to the east.

International sports organisations were in an extremely difficult position. On the one hand there was the Federal Republic already widely recognised and sponsored by major sporting and diplomatic powers. On the other hand there was the GDR seeking to end its diplomatic isolation and backed by a smaller, but no less committed, group of sponsoring states. The key target for GDR efforts was membership of the IOC. However, the Committee had a clear policy position which allowed recognition of only one NOC for each country. The preference of the IOC was to support the West German claim to represent all Germans and to prevaricate over recognition of the GDR. The motives for its actions were complex and included an intense conservatism coupled with a loyalty to the existing West German IOC member Von Halt; a general anti-communism; and a resistence to attempts at political manipulation.

For much of the 1950s and 1960s the IOC was able to maintain its formal policy position for, despite granting provisional recognition to the GDR in 1955, it was conditional upon an all-German team participating in the Olympic Games. Indeed all-German teams did participate in the Games of 1956, 1960 and 1964 (Winter Games). Nevertheless, in 1968 the IOC conceded the East German demand for recognition and in 1972 the GDR participated as a second German state, ironically at the Munich Olympic Games. IOC recognition coincided with a period of rapid progress by the GDR in gaining full diplomatic recognition within the broader international community.

Interpretations of the IOC's action differ, with Hill painting a picture of the IOC taking 'a strong line with East Germany' (1992: 39) and generally acting as a shrewd judge of the prevailing pattern of diplomatic relations between the GDR and the most influential states in the international community. As Hill argues, the IOC's primary concern was to preserve the integrity of the Olympic movement. Thus, the IOC's decision neither to isolate the GDR nor to acquiesce fully to its demands, but to develop a response which maximised participation in Olympic sport may be seen as a reflection of the IOC's independence in international relations even at the peak of the Cold War.

Hoberman (1986: 54–5) shares the view that the IOC's main concern was to protect Olympic interests but assesses the IOC, and Avery Brundage in particular, as largely naïve, lacking in the sophistication required to defend successfully Olympic interests and ultimately unable to reconcile the contradiction between the anti-communism of the majority of the IOC and their awe at communist achievements in sport. Consequently, Brundage's boast that by negotiating an all-German team in 1956 the Olympic movement had succeeded where the United Nations had failed, has a hollow ring. Indeed it is possible to argue that while full recognition was the ultimate goal of the GDR the 'all-German team' solution was a very acceptable alternative. Not only did the solution require the West German NOC to compromise but it also provided the GDR with an opportunity to probe the scope for asserting its claims to independence and, coincidentally, the limits of the IOC's tolerance.

The East German episode is especially interesting because of the light it casts on the complex of relationships involving the IOC, the major IFs and states. For example, the IOC was not simply concerned to preserve its autonomy in relation to individual states and major power blocs; it was also extremely sensitive to the effect of its actions on its leadership of the international sports community, and particularly in relation to the major international federations. The IFs were aware that strong sporting states, such as the GDR, had the potential to ignore the federations and sponsor athletes and host events independently. Consequently, in order to prevent this erosion of authority a number of IFs chose to recognise the GDR (Guttmann 1984: 156). As Hill (1992: 36) makes clear, this course of action presented the IOC with a dilemma as its leadership would be undermined if the IFs were seen to be shaping the policy response of international sport. Unfortunately, the IOC's authority would also be weakened if it contravened its declared policy of one NOC for each state. Fortunately for the IOC, Olympic recognition of the GDR was rapidly followed by diplomatic recognition by the main western powers. However, it is hard to avoid the conclusion that the East German episode demonstrated not the capacity of the IOC to maintain its own policy objectives but rather the tensions within the international sports community and the vulnerability of the IOC's leadership within it.

At the same time as international sports organisations were attempting to decide between the contesting claims for recognition of the two Germanies they were also attempting to resolve a similar dispute concerning the People's Republic of China and (Nationalist) China. The roots of the dispute lay in the collapse of Chiang Kai-shek's Nationalist government in 1949 and the flight of the remnants of the government to the island of Taiwan. Mainland China now came under the control of the victorious Communist Party led by Mao Tse-tung. The existing Chinese members of the IOC were closely associated with the defeated Nationalists and the PRC was keen to have them replaced with members more closely allied with the new government.

In the thirty years from 1950 both states used the IOC as a forum to promote claims to represent all China and to undermine the international recognition of the other. During this turbulent time the IOC's objectives remained reasonably clear. After some initial indecision the IOC adopted a policy of accommodation with the PRC primarily because of the commitment of the Olympic movement to the universalism of sport. In addition, the IOC was willing to accept a 'two Chinas' formula which would enable Nationalist China to retain its right to send athletes to Olympic competitions. (The IOC was prepared to ignore its expressed policy of 'one NOC for each country' on the grounds that the PRC and Taiwan were demonstrably two distinct territories.)

For much of the 1950s the IOC successfully resisted pressure from the United States and the Soviet Union to favour their respective Chinese allies. However, during the PRC's withdrawal from mainstream international sport in the 1960s at the height of the Cultural Revolution the IOC, not surprisingly, 'edged back toward recognition of Taiwan' (Kanin 1978: 268). Until the early 1970s Taiwan was able to hold unchallenged the title of 'Olympic Committee of the Republic of China'. Taiwan's prominence within the IOC was relatively short-lived for by the early 1970s the PRC was seeking to re-establish its relations with the wider international community and consequently in 1975 applied for membership of the Olympic movement.

The application for recognition by the IOC came after a period of *rapprochement* dating from 1970 during which the PRC used the development of sporting links as a vehicle for the rebuilding of its international relations (Chan 1985). Sporting contact took place with Britain, Japan and, most importantly, with the USA during the early 1970s. In 1972 a US table tennis team and in 1975 an American track and field team visited China. The PRC's sports diplomacy also focused on the international sports federations; membership of at least five IFs was a prerequisite for Olympic acceptance. Although the PRC came as a supplicant it insisted that any IF that it joined must expel Taiwan. With some, including fencing and volleyball, it was a successful strategy, but with others it was, initially at least, a failure. Both FIFA and the IAAF rejected the People's Republic's insistence on Taiwanese expulsion and attempted to preserve a 'two Chinas' policy. The acceptability of the PRC's policy was the cause of considerable friction between the IOC and the Canadian government just prior to the Montreal Games in 1976. The Canadians insisted that, because of its policy of recognition towards the PRC, Taiwan athletes would not be admitted. The inability of the IOC either to persuade Canada to compromise or to devise a formula acceptable to the Taiwanese led to the latter's withdrawal from the Games (Espy 1979).

Up until the mid-1970s the IOC's 'two Chinas' policy was broadly supported by the two foremost IFs, namely FIFA and the IAAF (in contrast to the question of the GDR's recognition). However, during the latter part of the 1970s the IOC explored a number of formulations designed to keep both states within the Olympic movement. Eventually, in 1979, a broadly acceptable compromise was devised which allowed the PRC to adopt the name 'Chinese Olympic Committee' and to have the exclusive right to use the flag and anthem of the PRC while the Olympic committee of Taiwan was obliged to use the name 'Chinese Taipei Olympic Committee' and to adopt a new flag and anthem. Although Taiwan was unhappy with the solution it probably considered it preferable to the solution of the United Nations which had resulted in its expulsion from the UN and replacement by the PRC.

The solution was not ideal from the PRC's point of view either, as 'Taiwan' was still a member of the IOC though under the title Taipei. Thus the IOC was able to present the PRC with an expression of its willingness to grant recognition while also insisting that Nationalist China should not be expelled. By 1981 the IOC policy had proved successful, with the PRC and the Taiwanese accepting the Committee's solution and subsequently both competing in the 1984 Games.

In many respects the protracted dispute over China demonstrated the capacity of the IOC to act as an independent force in the international system. First, it devised, revised and defended its policy in the face of considerable pressure from powerful governments including those of Communist and Nationalist China, the USA and the Soviet Union. More specifically it influenced the PRC to modify its 'one China' policy and also persuaded Taiwan to accept a name change of its NOC to include reference to Taipei. In terms of practical diplomatic achievements it is possible to argue that the real demonstration of the IOC's capacity to pursue an independent policy on recognition lay not in its recognition of the PRC but in its refusal to abandon Taiwan. Second, the episode illustrates the capacity of the IOC to adopt a leading role within the international sports community. Chan refers to the 'enormous influence' of the IOC policy as reflected in the swift adoption of the 'IOC solution' by the other major IFs in preference to the UN solution based upon Taiwanese expulsion (Chan 1985: 487). Third, in contrast to the GDR issue the IOC developed and followed a policy path distinct from that of the UN. Finally, there is some evidence that the 'IOC solution' proved attractive to other international organisations (Chan 1985: 488).

This very positive analysis of the IOC must be balanced by the acknowledgement that the Committee proved unsuccessful in attempting to challenge Canada's insistence that only the PRC could refer to China in its title, thereby alienating Taiwan prior to the 1976 Games. In addition, Chan has suggested that the IOC solution was seen by the PRC as temporary and also that it was unlikely that the communist government would have compromised so readily if the stakes had been higher, as indeed they were over the question of UN membership where the PRC insisted on Taiwanese expulsion. Nevertheless, the 'two Chinas' issue must be seen as an indication of the power and resources of the IOC and its capacity as an actor in international politics.

In addition to the conflicts surrounding the two Germanies and two Chinas there have been a number of other, less prominent disputes over recognition. One of the most significant involved Israel. While Israel found it relatively easy to gain membership of the IOC and the major IFs and to participate in the Olympic Games and world championships, it had much greater difficulty participating in regional games such as the Mediterranean Games and the International Army Games. Israel's experience highlights the tensions in the relationship between the IOC, IFs and a number of individual states.

IOC recognition of regional games is important. For the organisers it ensures publicity and status in the eyes of the major IFs, and for the IOC the development of regional games enhances its influence and is a vehicle for its sport development role. The Mediterranean Games were suggested by Egypt in 1948 and were to be open to all countries that bordered the sea. The first games were scheduled for 1951, but by this date a new country, Israel, had been established in the eastern Mediterranean. The animosity between Israel and its Arab neighbours created a constant source of tension within the Olympic movement and, more generally, international sport.

Israel did not participate in the 1951 regional games due to the failure – deliberate according to Espy (1979: 29) – of the IOC to grant its NOC membership in time. Israel was invited to the second games to be held in Spain, only to have the invitation withdrawn due to intense pressure by the Arab states. The third and fourth games to be held in Lebanon and Italy respectively were also intended to take place without the Israelis. The response of Avery Brundage was at best equivocal, and at worst hostile to the Israeli requests that the IOC uphold its own rules regarding access to regional events (Guttmann 1984: 225–6). There is also no evidence that other members of the IOC were keen to act as advocates for Israel. It was not until 1963, and after a strong lead had been given by the IAAF, that Brundage and the IOC made a clear declaration of the movement's commitment to free access of athletes. The stimulus for this move was due less to the IOC's realisation of the immorality of its earlier equivocation, and more to its fear of losing leadership within the international sports community. Not only had the IAAF adopted a stronger line on free access but there were also clear indications that the attempts to isolate Israel were spreading to the Asian Games.

Although Israel had participated in the second and third Asian Games (Manila, 1954 and Tokyo, 1958) it was not allowed to participate in the 1962 Asian Games to be held in Jakarta. Despite sending an initial invitation to Israel the team was subsequently refused entry to Indonesia, a fate also shared by the Taiwanese. The IOC response was the immediate suspension of the Indonesian Olympic Committee and the strong declaration 'that free access to participation was an absolute precondition of IOC patronage for all regional games' (Guttmann 1984: 226). However, the Indonesians, with the support of the PRC, proceeded to organise a successful alternative competition (the Games of the New Emerging Forces, GANEFO). Unfortunately for Israel IOC resolve soon weakened in the wake of the success of GANEFO and the prospect of a major split in the Olympic movement. The IOC and the IFs were alarmed at the prospect of an international event being successfully organised by governments, thereby challenging the roles of both the IOC and the federations. In consequence Indonesia was reinstated in time for the 1964 Tokyo Olympics, and Israel's attempts to participate in subsequent Asian games continued to be frustrated.

For much of the 1950s and 1960s the IOC's indifference towards Israel was balanced by the general willingness of the IAAF to support Israeli claims to participation. Admittedly, in the 1960s the IOC did make firmer pronouncements critical of attempts to isolate Israel, but as we have seen took little firm action. The IAAF and FINA (the swimming IF) took a much stronger line with Indonesia and caused its withdrawal from the 1964 Olympics because they refused to lift the bans imposed on Indonesian athletes who had participated in the GANEFO events. But by the early 1970s Arab pressure to exclude Israel was mounting again. Arab oil money was becoming increasingly important in supporting the Asian Games and this growing influence was reflected in 1981 by the election of Sheikh Fahd of Kuwait to the IOC. Changes were also taking place within the IAAF where Israel's request to be allowed to join the European regional games was refused at about the same time that Palestine was granted IAAF membership (Simson and Jennings 1992: 123). While the IAAF was willing, albeit reluctantly, to accept Palestine on the basis that the Gaza Strip, although occupied by Israel, was part of the pre-1948 Palestine territory, it consistently prevaricated over the issue of allowing Israel to participate in the European regional competitions. When the Federation, and the European Athletic Association, eventually did agree to Israel's request it was made clear that they saw the solution as temporary and that the problem was one for the Asian federation to solve. Thus in fairness to the IAAF it can be argued that if it had allowed Israel to move promptly into the European group it would have been handing a victory to those who see boycotts as a legitimate tool in sport policy. The IAAF decision came when a number of other European federations, including those for swimming, gymnastics and boxing, had already accepted Israel's participation and it was therefore increasingly difficult for the IAAF to pursue a different policy.

The 1982 Asian Games, to be hosted by India, provided further evidence of the Arab states' attempts to exclude Israel from participation in regional events. While the IOC executive questioned the Indian decision not to invite Israel it accepted the tactical decision by the organisers to withdraw their request for official Olympic patronage of the event. Rather than challenge this manoeuvring the IOC gave every impression of colluding, as evidenced by the attendance of Samaranch (IOC President), a number of other IOC members and IAAF President Primo Nebiolo. Soon after the Asian Games had finished the Asian Games Federation was wound up and replaced by a new organisation, the Olympic Council for Asia, which did not invite Israel to join. The first President of the OCA was Sheikh Fahd who also, according to Simson and Jennings (1992: 125), provided a substantial amount for the organisation's running costs. Rather than withhold approval of the organisation until Israel had been allowed to join, the IOC accepted the OCA as a legitimate regional organising body.

In many ways the actions of the IOC and of President Samaranch can be seen as supine in the face of Arab pressure. The major IFs, such as FINA, FIFA and IAAF, generally took a stronger stand against the anti-Israeli lobby, and in particular were willing to allow Israel to join the relevant European competitions. Indeed at present Israel plays most of its sport in Europe rather than in Asia for it is now a member of eighteen European federations of Olympic sports. The most generous explanation for the behaviour of the IOC lies in its concern to preserve the unity of the Olympic movement, even if that meant ignoring the requirements of the Olympic Charter. But a more plausible explanation needs to acknowledge the awareness of the IOC of the consequences of alienating the Arab states and losing the significant financial contribution made to the development and support of Asian sport. To this must also be added the general and persistent indifference of the IOC towards Israel's position.

Conclusion

At the start of this chapter it was suggested that if the major sports INGOs were to be accepted as credible actors in the international political system they must at least have the capacity to lead on issues central to sport and be able to voice and defend their interests when sport issues are being discussed in other policy communities. Among the factors that underpin the capacity of an INGO to function effectively in the international system are a high degree of value consensus within the organisation; organisational capacity; and a core of other resources to deploy in bargaining. The major IFs and the IOC display a considerable degree of internal cohesion and consensus as reflected in the general absence of serious policy splits. On balance the same can also be said of the same organisations taken as a whole. While there clearly were differences between these core organisations, the differences were often over tactical matters rather than over strategic objectives. This is certainly the case with the anti-doping campaign. Even where divisions are more marked, as over the distribution of television and sponsorship income, there is general agreement over the fundamental values involved, which in this case are an acceptance of the commercialisation and professionalisation of international sport.

In terms of organisational capacity the major IFs and the IOC can boast wealth, expertise, moral authority, and an extensive pattern of contacts with other sports organisations and, more importantly, with individual governments and major international organisations. However, the possession of a range of resources may be a necessary criterion for success in international politics, but it is not always a sufficient criterion. On the issue of drug abuse the IAAF has, in conjunction with the IOC, done much to force the pace of policy development and implementation through its relations with domestic governing bodies, individual governments and other federations. Similarly, in relation to the growing professionalisation and commercialisation of sport, the IOC and the major federations, once the majority overcame their initial distaste for the trend, have managed to exert considerable influence on the direction of commercialisation (see Chapter 7). Both these issues required organisations not only to possess the necessary resources, but also to possess the organisational capacity and skill to deploy them to greatest effect.

Without wishing to detract too seriously from the general conclusion that sports INGOs are credible actors in the international system, it must be borne in mind that the anti-doping policy is in its early stages and also that the IAAF proved incapable of uncovering the state-sponsored doping of athletes in the GDR. On the issue of commercialisation it could be argued that the leadership given by the Olympic movement and the major IFs was more apparent than real and that their 'leadership' was due to the rapid acceptance of the requirements of the media, key sponsors and leading athletes.

The examples relating to recognition, while generally confirming the influence of the most significant sport INGOs, are not wholly unambiguous. As a sign of weakness one can point to the failure of the IOC to force Canada to allow Taiwanese athletes entry for the Montreal Games in 1976. In addition, one can also argue that the IOC's response to the 'two Germanies' problem was dictated more by its delicate relationship with the IFs than by its preferred policy of maximising participation in the Olympic movement. Yet both these points ignore the complexity of international political life. The success of the Canadian government in challenging IOC policy on entry of athletes has to be set against the number of occasions when the IOC has persuaded governments to modify their visa requirements for the period of the Games and has withstood the pressure of governments concerning the selection of venue. Similarly, the 'two Germanies' episode is better interpreted as a successful balancing by the IOC of its twin priorities of maximising participation in the Games and maintaining its own position at the heart of world sport. This view is supported by the Olympic Committee's handling of the 'two Chinas' problem where not only did it devise a solution that kept both countries in the Olympic movement but it also developed a solution that was distinct from that of the United Nations. The handling by the IOC of the German, Chinese and Israeli issues shows not only a degree of consistency in policy objectives comparable to other major INGOs, but also a capacity to implement a distinctive policy strategy.

If the IOC and the major federations are capable of controlling their own agenda the question still remains whether they are able to intervene to voice and protect sports interests when they are subject to debate in other policy communities. The links between the Olympic movement and the sports federations on the one hand and organisations such as UNESCO, the Council of Europe and the European Community are explored in the next chapter.

Notes

1 This threefold classification is adapted from Rosenau (1970).

4

Sport and international governmental organisations

Introduction

The sports organisations described in Chapter 3 form part of a hierarchy with domestic organisations, such as sport-specific governing bodies and interest-specific bodies for the disabled or student sport, forming the base upon which regional/continental organisations and then global bodies rest. Much of the policy activity of these organisations is clearly focused on sports issues which can be resolved within the network of sports bodies. Most aspects of the following would fall into this category of internal issues: rule changes, location of events and eligibility of athletes. However, there are a number of issues, and indeed some aspects of those just mentioned, which can be resolved only with the cooperation of governments. Among the issues in this category are drug abuse by athletes, the denial of athletes' human rights as in South Africa under apartheid, and the promotion of sport development in poor countries. Indeed, it is becoming clear that an increasing number of sports issues are incapable of being resolved by sports organisations alone or within a purely domestic context (Houlihan 1991).

It is these issues, which can only be managed adequately through contact with government, that make it important to explore the variety of international governmental organisations that can provide additional points of access to domestic government. Yet the flow of influence is not one-way. Governments and governmental organisations are developing, with greater frequency, policy with direct or indirect consequences for sport and these organisations will also be keen to utilise a range of contact points, at the domestic and international levels, with influential bodies in sport. Discussions on the content of the physical education curriculum or on the promotion of mass involvement in sport follow complex lines of dialogue between a large number of bodies forming an increasingly sharply defined policy community.[1]

Since the mid-1970s there has been a significant increase in the number of international governmental organisations (IGOs) concerned with sport, both at the global and at the regional levels, complementing the similar expansion on the international non-governmental side. Because Europe has the longest-established and largest number of IGOs involved in sport this chapter will focus on the European experience. Within the policy area of sport in Europe there are three international governmental organisations that are of especial significance: UNESCO, the Council of Europe, and the European Community (EC). While it is acknowledged that only the UN body is a truly global organisation the other two have a significance beyond the boundaries of Europe. The EC has a number of educational and cultural programmes that are directed at countries beyond the twelve existing members. More importantly the Council of Europe has developed policy in a number of areas of sport which has subsequently been influential in shaping policy in other continents. What makes these three organisations of interest is their capacity to shape sport policy at state level through the control of important resources such as information, finance and, in the case of the EC, legislation.

One of the key issues to arise from a consideration of the role and significance of IGOs is whether they are a force for the homogenisation of sport policy and sports practice or whether they have the capacity and sensitivity to protect and promote diversity of interests in sport. As the discussion of the 'Sport for All' campaign supported by the Council of Europe and UNESCO will show, there needs to be a closer analysis of what sport and whose sport is in fact being promoted by the campaign.

The United Nations Educational, Scientific and Cultural Organisation (UNESCO)

The United Nations was created in 1945 and two factors were particularly important in shaping the character of the new organisation. The first factor was the emerging bipolarity in world politics and was reflected, for example, in the establishment of the Security Council in which members, including the Soviet Union and the United States, had vetoes. The second factor that shaped the UN was the experience of the

League of Nations. While the League had serious deficiencies as a world organisation one of the few areas of success was in relation to health, economic and social matters. In 1939 the Bruce Committee, which was reviewing these aspects of the League's work, suggested that a specialised agency, the Central Committee for Economic and Social Questions, be created (Armstrong 1982). Although the collapse of the League prevented action on this recommendation the United Nations created a number of specialised agencies very much in line with the Bruce Committee recommendation that the 'primary object of international cooperation should rather be mutual help than reciprocal contract' (Armstrong 1982: 64).[2] Thus while the UN was primarily concerned with issues of global security it acknowledged that the maintenance of peace required, in part at least, a willingness to address a broad range of economic and social issues. As a result a number of new functional agencies were created in the 1940s, including UNESCO. The functionalist orientation within the UN is strong and reflects a widely held view that by developing collaborative efforts in relatively non-controversial areas there would be a beneficial 'spillover' effect such that 'the penchant for cooperation developed in one functional sector would lead to cooperation in other sectors' more directly related to the promotion of international peace such as human rights and arms control (Gregg 1972: 222; see also Taylor 1984; Sullivan 1976; Haas 1958).

UNESCO developed out of the League's International Institute for Intellectual Cooperation yet aspired to be more than a 'high level debating society', which was how it was characterised by Armstrong (1982: 69). Unfortunately its funds were limited and while it had ambitions to promote international collaboration in culture, education and science, it had little capacity for effective action. However, from the 1960s UNESCO began to be more interventionist and developed a more sharply defined set of issues to focus upon (Williams 1987). This was largely due to the rapid increase in UN membership with most new members being from among the poorer countries whose concerns included combating illiteracy, facilitating technology transfer, and controlling news communication. As might be expected the activities of the Organisation became controversial particularly when it began to debate issues of cultural imperialism and to support research into the cultural heritage and early history of African countries. Of particular significance was the launch of a campaign for a New International Information Order following the acceptance by UNESCO of the McBride Report (1980) on the problems of global communications. This campaign was the outcome of a series of discussions during the 1970s and involved the Organisation in intervening directly to establish alternative and locally controlled sources of information and news about Third World states. Such high-profile activity which challenged so directly the western and largely American monopoly on communication was bound to generate opposition from Europe and North America. It was therefore little surprise when the United States and Britain withdrew from UNESCO in the early 1980s, ostensibly on the grounds of concern at the poor quality of administration and financial management (Williams 1987: 27–32; 62–3).

It is within this context of growing political controversy between 1960 and the mid-1980s that UNESCO became increasingly involved in aspects of sport. Given the Organisation's concern with the curriculum it began to examine physical education teaching. Its early activity was largely confined to organising conferences and producing reports on levels of need. Due, in part, to the Organisation's small budget it was not able to intervene to attempt directly to influence the development of PE policy. Part of the explanation for inaction during the period up to the mid-1970s also lay in an inability to agree what the objectives of intervention might be. The prolonged period of discussion within UNESCO resulted eventually in a meeting of Ministers of Sport in 1976 when it was decided, *inter alia*, to establish a permanent intergovernmental committee on physical education and sport, to establish a fund to support its work, and to produce an international charter on PE and sport. The permanent committee was successfully created and met in 1977, but UNESCO had greater difficulty in raising finance and this limited its capacity to mount projects and influence government policy.

UNESCO's activity received much stimulus from the work of the Council of Europe which was at the same time refining its policy towards sport. From 1966 to 1975 the Council had been discussing the formulation of a policy for 'Sport for All'. The Council's document, discussed more fully below, was very influential in shaping UNESCO's thinking and in November 1978 the latter produced an International Charter of Physical Education and Sport. The Charter stressed the role of physical education and sport in the 'well balanced development of the human being' and in promoting 'the universal language of physical education and sport [which] contributes to the preservation of lasting peace, mutual respect and friendship and will thus create a propitious climate for solving international problems' (UNESCO 1978: 1, 3). The Charter claimed association with the 'Olympic ideal' that sport serve an educational purpose and 'must in no way be influenced by profit-seeking interests' (1978: 3). Even in 1978 this was a naïve objective. As regards implementation of the Charter UNESCO relied on the willingness of states to recognise the value of PE and sport and to accept its model of decentralised organisation.

Much of the activity that followed from the publication of the Charter was confined to desk research and occasional conferences. Of especial importance was the establishment of an International Committee for Sport and Physical Education in 1976 with a rolling membership of thirty states. The Committee developed links with a number of international sports organisations including the IOC and GAISF and focused on a range of sports issues concerning elite sport and mass participation. As will be shown, the Committee was able to claim little success regarding elite sport and only limited success on the latter issue. UNESCO had little money with which to support major field activity particularly after the withdrawal of the United States in the early 1980s and Britain in 1985. Some work was carried out in an attempt to encourage states to produce plans to interpret 'Sport for All' in ways suitable to each country but in general little was achieved (McIntosh 1980). However, it was those states which had a prior commitment to 'Sport for All', such as Britain, the Scandinavian countries, Canada and China, that made progress in refining their policies. Overall UNESCO made little contribution to the promotion of the values associated with PE and sport except by granting them a degree of legitimacy through association.

UNESCO's ineffectiveness in the area of international sport policy was not simply due to its discursive style of proceeding or to its lack of substantial resources. A far more important reason for its weakness was the rift that was opened between UNESCO and the major international sports organisations by the proposal that UNESCO should work towards a New International Sports Order and specifically seek to take over the running of the Olympic Games. In 1976, at a meeting of UNESCO in Nairobi, a resolution was proposed by France and supported by many Asian and African states that there should be an inquiry into the 'difficulties with the staging of international sports competitions'.[3] At the next meeting of UNESCO in Paris, where the Nairobi resolutions were to be considered, the Cuban representative proposed that UNESCO should take over responsibility for the Olympic Games from the IOC. Although this proposal was a surprise for most of the western representatives it needs to be seen in the context of the continuing conflict concerning the democratisation of the Olympic movement.

The Soviet attempts to alter the basis of IOC membership so as to reflect a greater degree of equality between member states was easily defeated in the mid-1950s. But far from this marking the end of the issue the arena and strategy simply shifted away from the IOC itself and to the national Olympic committees and the international federations. During the 1960s and 1970s pressure on the IOC was maintained by a strategy, largely inspired by Giulio Onesti, President of the Italian NOC (CONI), which sought to organise the NOCs into an effective lobby. At roughly the same time the international federations had begun to strengthen their capacity to lobby the IOC by forming, in 1967, the General Assembly of the International Sports Federations (GAISF). While the obvious point of conflict between the IOC and the GAISF was the distribution of television income the momentum within the NOCs was due to a feeling of neglect among the increasing number of Third World member states. Although the replacement of the adversarial Brundage with the more conciliatory Killanin in 1972 and the establishment of the sports development commission, Olympic Solidarity, calmed matters somewhat the issue of access by poorer states to Olympic decision-making had clearly not been resolved. Hence the proposal from the Cubans in Paris in 1976 which, although easily defeated, had the long-term effect of souring relations with the Olympic movement and also with a number of influential western states including Britain, the USA and West Germany. It is worth noting that one important reason for the ease with which the proposal was defeated was that by 1976 the 1980 Games had been awarded to the Soviet Union who realised the public relations opportunity this presented and were therefore not keen to offend the IOC and consequently failed to support the Cubans. A further reason for the prompt dismissal of the proposal was the rapid organisation of opposition by a number of states using the informal title of the Western Contacts Group. Prominent in this group were the USA, Britain, Australia, Japan and interestingly China which was suspicious of any proposal coming from what it considered to be a Soviet puppet state.

Espy notes that the IOC was deeply suspicious of UNESCO and its associated bodies such as ICSPE[4] and made it clear that it 'wanted nothing to do with ICSPE, considering it, like GANEFO, to be "a serious threat for the Olympic movement" ' (1979: 112). However, Coghlan (1990) paints a very different picture of the relationship between ICSPE and the IOC. For Coghlan the period from 1976 up to the present was one of increasingly close cooperation between the two organisations as evidenced by the granting to ICSPE of the status of a 'Recognised Organisation' by the IOC. During the 1980s ICSPE did cooperate with the IOC in designing a number of sports development projects but it is clear that the IOC was wary of the UNESCO body and as a result the sports policy initiatives of UNESCO were not able to benefit fully from cooperation with Olympic Solidarity or the IAAF Development Commission which both began to expand rapidly in the 1980s. Currently, UNESCO's involvement in sport is overseen by the Intergovernmental Committee for Physical Education and Sport (CIGEPS) with the Fund Internationale pour le Développement du Education Physique et Sport (FIDEPS) its main operational agency. But by 1989, according to Coghlan, UNESCO's development activity had largely atrophied due to 'lack of money and poor quality leadership' (1990: 235). However. at roughly the same time there were signs that UNESCO was beginning to rebuild its links with the Olympic movement, particularly following the departure of the controversial Director, M'Bow. In 1988, at UNESCO's second sports conference a memorandum of understanding was signed by the new Director-General Federico Mayor Zaragoza and IOC President Samaranch, and the Organisation is presently considering the development of a policy towards doping in sport.

During the period in the mid-1970s when the New International Sports Order was being promoted by Cuba the parallel issue of apartheid in South Africa was emerging as a major topic within the UN. The campaign within the UN to introduce stronger measures against South Africa resulted in a number of important decisions in the late 1970s and early 1980s. In 1977 the UN General Assembly adopted a resolution calling for a cultural boycott and in 1980 the UN Centre Against Apartheid began compiling and publishing every six months lists of athletes who had taken part in events in South Africa. The UN action, coming at the same time as similar declarations by the Commonwealth and by individual states, put considerable pressure on the South African government but also created strains within the international sports community.

For international sports organisations the point at issue was not opposition to apartheid, which was shared by most sports bodies, but the prospect of growing state interference in matters concerning team selection, the movement of athletes and the organisation of fixtures. Thus the concern expressed by the IFs was at the erosion of areas of traditional policy autonomy and the explicit support and legitimation that the UN decisions were giving to the interference by domestic governments in the decisions of their sport governing bodies. But it was not just the IOC and the IFs that were concerned; so too was the Council of Europe. The Council's members had all made statements opposing apartheid and most had in place clear policies along the lines of the UN resolution but, with the exception of Sweden and Cyprus, refused to sign the resolution as it contravened the spirit of the Council's Convention on Human Rights.

The recent history of UNESCO is interesting for a number of reasons. First, for demonstrating the capacity of western states to undermine an organisation of which they disapprove, for while the bid to take control of the Olympics was only a relatively minor irritation, of much greater significance was the discussion within UNESCO of ways of altering the existing distribution of power concerning the control of global information flows. The sustained criticism of UNESCO by the Americans and their subsequent withdrawal left the agency financially and politically weak. While much of the agency's work, especially in the field of physical education and promoting 'Sport for All', is non-controversial it has effectively been marginalised within the international policy community for sport and despite recent changes in personnel at the Paris headquarters there is little sign of its influence increasing. UNESCO's activity is also of interest because it highlights the delicacy of the relations between international governmental and non-governmental organisations in the sports policy area. The UN campaign against apartheid and the less significant challenge to control the Olympic Games soured relations between the governmental and non-governmental members of the international sports community and made progress on other important issues, such as Sport for All and drug abuse, less rapid.

The Council of Europe

The Council of Europe was created in 1949 as a grouping of non-communist European states. Its current central concerns include the promotion of democratic and parliamentary principles, the defence of human rights and the development of closer cooperation between member states. For much of its recent history it has lived in the shadow of the EC although with the collapse of communism at the end of the 1980s the Council has been reinvigorated and is playing a major role in supporting the fledgeling democracies in eastern and central Europe.

In mid-1993 the Council had 29 members with the most recent being Hungary (1990), Poland (1991), Czechoslovakia (1991, which in 1993 is expected to be accepted as the Czech and Slovak Republics), Bulgaria (1992), Estonia, Lithuania and Slovenia (1993). Albania and Russia are among the current applicants for membership.

The Council operates through a Parliamentary Assembly and a Committee of Ministers. The Assembly, whose members are drawn from the parliaments of member states, meets three times a year and makes recommendations to the Committee of Ministers. The Committee, which meets twice a year and comprises the Foreign Ministers of member states, decides the Council's programme of activities and approves its budget. In addition to the Committee of Ministers there are often meetings of specialist Ministers such as those for sport. Finally, the Council has extensive contacts with INGOs and has granted consultative status to over 350.

Without doubt the best-known and most impressive achievement of the Council was the formulation, in 1950, of the European Convention on Human Rights and the establishment of the European Court of Human Rights at Strasbourg. Over 19,000 cases have been brought under the terms of the Convention covering such issues as the use of corporal punishment, the prohibition of divorce, and prisoner's rights. Yet this is only one of over 140 conventions; others, for example, in the area of sport, cover doping and spectator violence.

The Committee for the Development of Sport (CDDS)

In 1960 the Council accepted responsibility for educational and cultural matters which, after a short period, was organised under the auspices of the Council for Cultural Cooperation (CCC). From 1962 until 1968 the sport and physical education functions were delegated to a subcommittee of the CCC. By 1968 there was growing recognition of the distinctiveness of the policy area, but establishing a more effective forum for debate and policy-making was difficult due to the wide variation in the allocation of responsibility for sport and PE between governmental and non-governmental bodies at member level (Coghlan 1990: 236).

Although 'Sport for All', the first major policy initiative of the Council of Europe relating to sport, was slowly being developed during the late 1960s and early 1970s it was not until the mid-1970s that an effective organisation for implementation was put in place. In 1975, at a conference of European Ministers for Sport, the decision was taken to establish a committee of experts on sport to replace the existing consultative body. The Committee for the Development of Sport met for the first time in 1977 with a broad brief covering research (into building design and legislative drafting, for example), promotion (of Sport for All, for example), and policy evaluation (of national sports plans). However, the central focus of the Committee's early activity was the promotion of Sport for All. In 1978 the Committee was given its present title (Comité Directeur pour le Développement du Sport) and was given equal status to the CCC and thus now reports directly to the Assembly.

The CDDS, with a mixture of governmental and non-governmental representatives, is involved in a complex web of relationships with other governmental and non-governmental international bodies. Of particular importance are its relationships with UNESCO, the Olympic movement, and the European Sports Conference, which are discussed in the section that follows. The relationship with the EC is of increasing importance and will be discussed later in this chapter when the role of the Community is explored.

The relationship with UNESCO

On the surface the relationship with UNESCO should be a close one. Not only do the patterns of responsibilities and interests of both organisations coincide, but they also have the advantage of geographical proximity as the UNESCO headquarters is also located in France. Unfortunately the relationship is poor and erratic. Although both organisations invite observers from the other, UNESCO attend CDDS events and meetings only occasionally. Part of the explanation for the weakness of the link is the greater concentration of expertise in the CDDS and the generally poor level of organisation in UNESCO. However, a further element in the explanation is the role that the Council played in organising opposition to the Cuban proposal to challenge the IOC's control of the Olympic Games. The basis of the Council's opposition lay in its perception of democracy as involving a balance between public and private/voluntary institutions such as the IFs and the IOC, and an implicit limit on the role of the state in cultural and sports policy. However, the interpretation of what constituted an acceptable balance and where the limit of state intervention lay varied among Council members. The Swedish government adopted a much more interventionist policy regarding sporting contact with South Africa (for example denying visas to South African athletes) and was in the forefront of the campaign within UNESCO to persuade the UN General Assembly to take a tougher line on apartheid. Sweden also mounted a similar campaign within the Council of Europe, most of whose members were not in favour of moving beyond a policy similar to that reflected in the Commonwealth 'Gleneagles Agreement' which aimed to discourage sporting contact.[5] The

Swedish campaign within the Council had a serious effect on the broader and less contentious aspects of CDDS activity and soured relations within the organisation. It was only in the late 1980s, when apartheid was beginning to crumble, that relations between Sweden and the majority of Council members began to improve.

The CDDS and the Olympic movement

There are two possible points of contact between the CDDS and the Olympic movement, the first being at the regional level with the Association of European National Olympic Committees (AENOC), and the second at the global level with the IOC. To date the closest relationship has been with the IOC due to the overlap of interest in anti-doping policy. However, the relationship has not been warm. The IOC has a standing invitation to attend most CDDS working groups but it rarely sends an observer. Almost certainly the main reason for the IOC reluctance to get too closely involved with the Council is its concern to maintain its distance from governmental organisations, even one which puts so much emphasis on the role of INGOs in decision-making. As regards AENOC there are signs that it is willing to work more closely with the Council, particularly concerning the provision of advice and support to the central and eastern European states. Nevertheless, it would be wrong to expect too much of this display of interest for it is important to remember that AENOC is merely a forum for NOCs, most of whom, in Europe especially, have a long tradition of autonomy. As a result it is rare for AENOC to give a policy lead and it certainly does not set a policy agenda; rather it responds to initiatives from individual NOCs.

The CDDS and the European Sports Conference

The European Sports Conference (ESC) was established in 1973, held its first conference in 1975 and has met every two years since then. As the title suggests it has no permanent location or secretariat although it does have an International Co-ordinating Committee, and since 1991 an Executive Committee, which operate between conferences and are primarily concerned with organising the next meeting.

At the time of its creation the ESC was the only body to bring together representatives of sports organisations from western and eastern Europe. In general, western participants tend to be NGO officers or academics while, until the last few years, the eastern states sent government officials. Sports aid, youth sport, drug abuse and most recently women in sport are among the topics covered by the ESC. The organisation's value within the European sports community has been its maintenance of contacts with eastern Europe during the latter part of the Cold War. This point of contact was especially useful in opening a dialogue on the question of doping at a time when there was growing suspicion of systematic and government-sanctioned drug abuse in many communist states and the ESC was consequently prominent in pressing the IOC to sanction out-of-competition testing. However, in general the ESC has access to few resources and the outcomes of its conferences have not been especially original or influential on the wider policy community. Indeed it is tempting to argue that its best days are behind it.

Since 1973 a number of other forums for discussing sports issues in Europe have emerged, including AENOC, the European Non-governmental Sports Organisations (ENGSO),[6] the EC, and the Council of Europe, which have covered similar topics often with overlapping membership. Since the collapse of European communism and the expansion of Council of Europe membership into eastern Europe the distinctiveness of the ESC's role has declined and led it to consider its future. One possibility is that it will link into the CDDS structure in some way, but a major stumbling-block to this arrangement is that the CDDS is essentially a governmental organisation whereas the ESC is not. The current position is that the Austrian state sports organisation has offered to provide and finance a permanent secretariat. Despite this development the long-term future of the Conference is at best uncertain.

Policy influence: doping and Sport for All

The CDDS is active across a wide range of sport policy areas, with doping and the promotion of Sport for All being two of the most important in recent years. As regards doping, it is easy to overlook the fact that significant challenges to drug abuse by athletes are very recent, dating from the mid-1980s, and that an effective policy to combat the problem has yet to be fully established. Progress in policy development has been slow and has been hampered by a number of factors: first, the scientific problems of developing reliable tests; second, the cost of mounting an adequate testing regime; and third, the large number of governmental and non-governmental interests whose cooperation is required in order to implement policy effectively (Houlihan 1991: 201ff.). It is the last of these factors concerning which that the Council of Europe and the CDDS have an important role to play.

As mentioned in Chapter 3 the implementing bodies face a number of issues: first, agreeing a list of proscribed substances and practices; second, agreeing a testing procedure; and third, agreeing sanctions. One factor which complicates implementation is the international nature of competition, coaching and training. Athletes will be registered with their home governing body, but may train in a number of other countries, and will participate in a global circuit. If testing is to be effective both at events and during out-of-competition periods then the cooperation of domestic governing bodies, international federations and a large number of governments is a prerequisite. Agreement is needed between states and IFs concerning entry by testing officers to countries, and state support for testing procedures and penalties.

Admittedly policy development is still at an early stage but there remains a considerable lack of uniformity between IFs and between states in their attitudes towards testing and levels of active support. The present cases involving Harry 'Butch' Reynolds and Katrin Krabbe, both of whom have challenged or are challenging decisions by the IAAF through the courts, are indicative of the problems that IFs face in building a policy consensus. These problems were compounded when a number of governments were clearly colluding with their domestic sports organisations in the systematic doping of athletes. Though many of the guilty states were in eastern Europe, there were several western states that were less than rigorous in implementing anti-doping policies.

It is in this area that the CDDS has played an important role. In 1984 the Council approved an Anti-Doping Charter which became a model for states and other organisations both within and outside Europe. Canada, for example, was keen to get the Charter adopted on a wider basis and a Charter group was established which included Canada, the US Olympic Committee, the Council of Europe, and the IOC with the aim of developing an international anti-doping charter. This was followed by a conference in Ottawa at which a slightly modified version of the Charter was adopted. At about the same time GAISF and AENOC gave their support to the Council's initiative followed by the IOC, which approved the Charter at its meeting in Seoul, and UNESCO which adopted it in November 1988.

Following the success of the Charter the Council and CDDS maintained their prominence in the policy area due to the proposal to strengthen the anti-doping campaign through the introduction of a Convention which, unlike the Charter, is binding on the governments that sign. The Convention was duly agreed in 1989 and has already been accepted by many states, with a number of east European states considering acceptance. Among the recent issues considered by the Convention

Monitoring Group is the need to press for greater uniformity between member states concerning the availability and control of anabolic steroids. While anabolic steroids are controlled substances in some states, in others, such as Belgium and Portugal, they can still be bought over the counter.

The Monitoring Group of the Convention is currently supporting a Working Party on Technical Questions related to policy implementation. Although its work is primarily concerned with issues such as training of testing officers and the accreditation of laboratories, some of the conclusions reached indicate the problems facing those who seek a more rigorous and consistent approach to the issue of doping. For example, the Working Party, in considering the need to achieve greater commonality on the list of banned substances, considered the possibility of trying to bring the IFs' lists more fully within the ambit of the Council of Europe's Anti-Doping Convention. The Group also stressed that it was inappropriate for IFs to be completely responsible for out-of-competition testing. Other suggestions to emanate from this Group include the establishment of an independent reference laboratory to help those accredited, or seeking accreditation, by sports governing bodies. What is at the heart of these suggestions is a concern that the self-policing of drug abuse by sports governing bodies was no guarantee of rigour; only governmental bodies or other disinterested organisations could guarantee effective implementation. It hardly needs saying that such suggestions are interpreted by IFs as a challenge to their control of sport and the IFs are quick to question the disinterestedness of governments.

One consequence of the mutual wariness between IFs and IGOs is the multiplication of overlapping working groups or committees on issues such as doping. In addition to the CDDS Convention Monitoring Group, the IOC has its own Medical Commission and there is also an International Working Group for the Permanent World Conference on Anti-Doping in Sport comprising mainly government representatives. Many of the members of one body are also members of the other two; for example, Prince Alexandre de Merode who chaired the CDDS group that produced its Anti-Doping Charter in 1984 is also chairman of the IOC Medical Commission which has responsibility for doping policy within the Olympic movement. On the one hand it is possible to argue that overlapping membership makes for consistency across the government–non-government divide and also consolidates effort. On the other hand a strong case can be made which suggests that the existing pattern is a fragmentation and dissipation of effort and has been consciously fostered by the IFs and the IOC as a way of diluting the perceived challenges to their authority. Nevertheless, this response by the IFs and the IOC is not aimed at undermining the anti-doping effort but is aimed at attempting to maintain their leadership within the policy community. Thus while the development of an effective policy is slowed by the divisions among IGOs and INGOs it has not altered the direction of policy change which is towards a greater degree of consistency across a broadening range of states.

The policy which has become known as 'Sport for All' first emerged in the early 1960s in Germany and the Nordic countries. It took root within the Council of Europe in 1968 when, at a meeting of the Council's Out of School Education Committee, the chairman, Armand Lams, suggested that the Committee should seek to define the concept and design a number of projects for its promotion. According to the Committee, 'Sport for All' concerned the provision of the 'conditions to enable the widest possible range of the population to practise regularly either sport proper or various physical activities calling for an effort adapted to individual capacities' (quoted in Marchand 1990: 3). The growing interest in the development of Sport for All led to the adoption of the European Sport for All Charter in 1975 which asserted that 'every individual had the right to participate in sport' and that it was a duty of government to support sport financially and organisationally (Council of Europe 1992a: 37).

The adoption of a commitment to Sport for All has proved to be the primary organising principle for the CDDS and the Council. Programmes have been developed to broaden the base of sports participation among women, the disabled, prisoners, migrants, the unemployed and the elderly. For prisoners the CDDS approved a policy which asserted the rights of prisoners to participation in sport, the contribution of sport in a pre-release process, and the importance of sport in providing an 'opportunity for learning self-control, a respect for rules and other attitudes which are useful in society' (Council of Europe 1992a: 105). As regards immigrants the CDDS developed a policy which, *inter alia*, was designed to 'promote the integration of immigrants into society'. The means of achieving this aim was through the development of such skills among immigrants as would enable them to develop and sustain their own organisations (and sports) which could act as a bridge into their adopted society.

The conception of Sport for All adopted by the CDDS is inclusive of elite sport and indeed the Committee is at pains to stress the need to take account of the elite level when developing policy. More importantly the commitment to Sport for All has allowed the Council to involve itself in a broad range of policy areas, including spectator behaviour where it was instrumental in facilitating cooperation between European states during the 1992 soccer European Championships in Sweden. More recently the CDDS has focused its attention on the problems of the new democracies of central and eastern Europe. The changes in Europe were considered to be so significant that a revised sports charter was needed. The European Sports Charter was duly approved at the 1992 meeting of the Conference of European Ministers Responsible for Sport.

Where the 1975 Charter was brief and epigrammatic, the 1992 Charter spelt out in more detail the values and priorities at the heart of the Council's conception of sport. Among its thirteen articles are statements concerning the complementary relationship between public and voluntary organisations, the need to cater for differing levels of ability, the importance of public financial support, and the need to develop organisations at domestic and international levels in order to achieve effective implementation. The new Charter was accompanied by a resolution on a code of ethics for sport which, according to the Secretary-General of the Council of Europe, developed values in sport, such as fairness, respect for others and compliance with rules, that are 'closely related to the values of democracy. Seen in this way, sport can be a veritable training ground for democracy' (quoted in Jenner 1992).

The significance of the Council of Europe

During the 1970s and early 1980s there was always a danger that the Council of Europe would be eclipsed by other international bodies such as the UN and UNESCO in particular, and regionally by the EC. However, not only has the Council survived but the collapse of communism in Europe has given it a renewed role in regional politics. From the point of view of sport policy and politics the Council is important because of its explicit role in the promotion of specific norms and values associated with democracy and its definition of sport as an important vehicle for the promotion of these norms and values.

In many respects the Council is well placed to use sport to foster its broader objectives. The CDDS has proved effective in bringing together representatives of governmental and non-governmental bodies responsible for sport and in gaining acceptance as an appropriate forum for the development of expert working groups to tackle particular issues. The CDDS has also proved successful in broadening its membership among the newly independent European states and involving them in its work. This general respect and legitimacy is based primarily on the leadership provided by the CDDS and the Council on issues such as doping, crowd behaviour and sports promotion. Indeed the CDDS is well placed to take a leading role on these ethical issues due to the strong association between the Council and the promotion and protection of human rights. The status of the Council has enabled it to exert a policy influence well beyond its regional boundaries. Anti-doping policy is a particularly good example where the Council's Charter was used by Canada and later the IOC as a model for their own statements on the issue.

Yet it is not just the ability to claim the moral high ground that provides the basis of CDDS effectiveness. The fact that the priorities of the Council differ from those of the EC is also an advantage. The Council is not weakened by the EC's economic concerns or legislative capacity, both of which are perceived as a potential threat by sports governing bodies and INGOs in particular, and also by some domestic governments. The Council has also not been bedevilled by the sectional politics that have marred the recent history of UNESCO, although this is probably because its membership is economically more homogeneous and, by definition, politically homogeneous.

Despite this positive assessment the work of the CDDS also indicates some of the problems that emerge at the interface between governmental and non-governmental organisations. While the Council clearly commands the respect of many in the world of international sport there is undoubtedly a significant degree of apprehension about the trend towards greater involvement in sports matters by IGOs. For example, the feeling among some governments and some within the Council that governing bodies of sport and their IFs are not the best organisations to administer and police anti-doping policy fuels the suspicion within IFs and the IOC that governments will continue to encroach upon their traditional areas of policy autonomy.

The clearest example of close cooperation between the Council and the IFs illustrates the dilemma. The work of the CDDS concerning the control of spectator violence and sporting events has generally been agreed to be a success as evidenced by the low level of violence at the recent European Championships for soccer in Sweden. The success of the policy depended upon close cooperation between member states, particularly their police forces, but also required a close working relationship with the European soccer governing body, UEFA. However, while UEFA's cooperation was fully given the organisation was well aware that the future of this competition and other club-level internationals rested with the decisions of governments rather than with its own organising committee. UEFA's support for the Council's initiative was given at least in part as a defensive measure and as an attempt to pre-empt more restrictive measures being adopted by individual governments.

In general, the relationship between the Council and the CDDS on the one hand, and the sports INGOs on the other, is amicable if not close. The cooperation between the two sets of organisations has produced tangible results and is likely to be particularly important as the eastern European states seek to establish independent sports organisations similar to those in much of the rest of Europe. The major significance of the Council is in its role of promoting a distinctive set of values and norms, for example associated with drug-free sport and ethical behaviour both on and off the field of play. It is also important in reinforcing a distinctive set of values associated with the organisation of sport and the role of government. In particular the work of the Council and the CDDS emphasises the importance of state financial support for sport, the importance of fostering voluntary organisations, and the general integrative effect of sport. The Council has therefore carved out a distinctive niche for itself in the international sport community, with the only immediate threat to its position being the growing interest of the EC in sports policy.

The European Community

There is little doubt that the EC is the most important regional intergovernmental organisation in the world. Established in the early 1950s to provide a basis for cooperative production and marketing of steel and coal the EC has developed into an organisation that touches most aspects of domestic political life of the twelve member states, and which is an increasingly important actor on the world stage. Although primarily an economic organisation the recent moves towards closer political integration following the establishment of the single European market in 1993 have given a stimulus to those within the EC who would like to see the development of a greater role in social and cultural policy. It is within this context that sport has emerged as a policy concern of the EC.

The decision-making heart of the EC is the Council of Ministers which comprises the Foreign Ministers of member states. Meetings of the Council are supplemented by periodic meetings of Prime Ministers or their equivalents and meetings of service-specific ministers. The work of the Council is supported by the Commission, the executive arm of the Community, which implements EC policy. The Commission is organised into twenty-two directorates-general (similar to British departments or ministries) organised along functional lines. Among the most important directorates-general are DG IV (competition) and DG XVI (regional policy), with DG X (audio-visual, information, communication and culture) having responsibility for sport. A third significant institution within the Community is the European Parliament which comprises 518 members directly elected from the member states in rough proportion to population size. In general the Parliament is peripheral to the decision-making processes of the Community although in recent years there have been attempts, by MEPs, to extend their role beyond advocacy and advice.

While the early history of the Community has been dominated by economic issues concerning agriculture, steel and coal it has always had a broader political purpose concerned with the integration of the states of Europe. In recent years, with the increasingly successful establishment of a common market for trade, the focus of EC concerns has shifted more towards other dimensions of integration including political, cultural and social. The phrase, an 'ever closer union', from the Treaty of Rome, has proved open to a variety of interpretations and has served to expose wide differences regarding the future direction for the Community. At the heart of the present debate is a dispute over the proper balance between national sovereignty and the supranational authority of the Community. If this issue represents a fundamental fault line through the twelve members then the recent attempts by the Community to expand its involvement in sport and general cultural matters is one way in which this fault line is manifest in policy terms.

There are two ways in which involvement of the EC in sport might be justified: first, simply on the basis that the single European market, due to the scope of the policy, is bound to impinge on aspects of the sports industry and general sports concerns and, second, that sport is an important tool for achieving greater social integration within the Community. As a recent Commission paper put it, 'The Community's approach to sport, then, has so far been by two parallel channels, treating it as an economic activity on the one hand, and as an activity with a high potential for public awareness-raising on the other' (Commission 1991: 2).

In many respects it was the latter concern with Community integration that first surfaced as an issue within the EC. Although there had been some discussion within the European Parliament in 1982 of the role of sport in the life of the Community it was not until 1985 that the issue was firmly placed on the agenda of the Community. In 1985 an *ad hoc* Committee was established to consider measures 'to strengthen and promote the EC's identity and its image for its citizens and for the rest of the world' (Commission 1985: 5). The report that followed (the Adonnino Report) explored a wide range of suggestions for developing a sense of belonging among citizens of the Community including tourism, the media and educational exchanges. The report also acknowledged the contribution that sport might make much in the same way that individual states have used and continue to use sport as a tool of nation-building. The report suggested the organisation of EC events 'such as cycle and running races through European countries', the creation of Community teams, encouragement to teams to wear, on occasion, the EC emblem, the development of a programme of athlete and coach exchanges, and the organising of EC sporting events for particular groups, such as the disabled (Commission 1985: 26). Since 1985 this view of the value of sport has gathered momentum within the Community, with a later report highlighting the potential for sport to act as a vehicle for achieving non-sport policy objectives such as those concerning health and the integration of migrants, and as a way of stimulating a greater awareness of the EC and its policies, especially among the young (Commission 1992). According to Jacques Delors, 'In the creation of one European Community, the Commission has given sport a priority position, as sports can be a vehicle to increase solidarity between the different member states within the EC' (Commission 1993: 2). In addition to exploiting sport for Community-building purposes the report also identified hooliganism as an issue of concern and suggested that the European Council should convene a meeting of sports ministers 'to step up concerted action as a matter of urgency' (Commission 1985: 27).

The recommendation in the Adonnino Report to take advantage of sport for purposes of Community integration gathered some, albeit limited, momentum during the late 1980s. One notable failure was the proposal to hold European Community Games every two years starting in 1989. The initiative for this proposal came from a consortium of commercial interests with only limited involvement of the EC itself. The Games were to include twenty-four sports and be organised across the Community on the basis of 'unity of time' rather than the conventional 'unity of space' (The British Archer 1988). The Games never took place partly because of problems with their commercial viability, partly due to the reluctance of European IFs to add another date to an already crowded calendar and partly due to a lukewarm response from athletes.

Despite the failure of the EC Games there have been other, limited, successes. Most notable is the EC Swimming Club Championships held annually since 1987. The championships are contested between the winners of domestic inter-club competitions and are not a competition between individuals, as this was felt by the IF to be too close in concept to the European Championship. Other sporting events supported by the EC and used for publicity purposes by the Community include: the 1992 Tour de France, which had a route that covered seven countries; the European School Games; the Youth Olympics, held in Brussels in 1991 and supported with a subsidy of ECU 300,000 with 1,200 competitors from 33 European states; and the Rugby Union World Cup, where the EC paid ECU 10,000 to display EC flags at the ground (Seary 1992). The EC has also supported major global sports events when held in Europe such as the 1991 World Student Games held in Sheffield, England and the 1992 Barcelona Olympic Games, where the EC used $15m to promote itself and even suggested that athletes from EC member states should march behind the EC flag rather than that of their own state.

Clearly the EC has recognised the public relations value of sport, just as national governments have done. Yet its ability to exploit the marketing opportunity presented by sport has been limited. There is no obvious coherence to its pattern of involvement beyond the purely opportunistic and, more fundamentally, the Community has had little success in building a sufficiently close relationship with the major European IFs who remain clearly suspicious of EC motives. Nevertheless the IFs are wary of dismissing EC overtures too bluntly for two reasons: first, the EC has significant financial resources available for sport (£1m in 1992), and second, because EC legislation is increasingly impinging on sports interests and therefore the European IFs are sensitive to the need to establish and maintain a good working relationship.

Although the Adonnino Report was primarily concerned to exploit sport for its propaganda value to the Community it also mentioned in passing the need for consideration of hooliganism by an appropriate meeting of the Council. Although the Adonnino Report did arouse some interest it was not responsible for the steady rise in Community involvement in sport. Indeed, this trend has not been the result of a specific strategy, but has developed in a haphazard way with the gradual accumulation of isolated decisions and policy developments. The overall effect of this accumulation is that the Community currently has the capacity to affect, in important ways, many of the activities of athletes.

At the heart of the EC's growing impact on sport is the emphasis given by the Community to sport as an industry rather than sport as a leisure activity. As an industry sport must therefore conform to the requirements of the single European market. There are two important aspects of the single market for sport: first, that sportsmen and sportswomen should have the same rights of movement as other workers and, second, that there is a conflict between the Community's progress towards a concept of 'European citizenship' and the eligibility rules most common in sport which are based on nationality, ancestry or length of residence.

One or two examples will serve to illustrate the actual and potential impact of the single market. A fundamental principle of the Community is the free movement of goods and workers. For sport this raises serious problems as international sport is defined by national differences between teams. The issue may be amply illustrated with regard to soccer professionals. Although in the 1950s and 1960s it was common for clubs to field teams with a high proportion of foreign players there has been a gradual tightening of eligibility rules. However, attempts to limit the number of foreign players conflict with EC principles. In 1991 a compromise agreement was reached with UEFA which allowed a minimum of three non-national players to participate in any single match. A similar conflict exists in basketball in France where a number of attempts have been made by the domestic governing body to prevent clubs filling their ranks with foreign players. So far the Community has compromised with the governing bodies and allowed them to retain nationality as the cornerstone of eligibility but this might not always remain the case. On the one hand there are pressures from within the Commission to bring sport, and especially professional sport, into line with Community law. Thus it is the view of a recent study that 'The intention is that [the Commission's periodic meetings with UEFA] will smooth the transition towards complete free movement of footballers' (Coopers Lybrand 1992: 7). On the other hand there are member states that would welcome a relaxation of eligibility rules in the interests of their own nationals. For example in the Irish Republic, which is unable to support a professional league, talented players are forced to work abroad if they are to make a career in soccer.

Transfer of professional soccer players is another area where EC law clashes with governing body practice. Although a transfer fee is understandable if a player is transferred during the period of his contract it is also routinely demanded when a player has completed his contract. In recent years a number of players have turned to the EC for support in challenging end-of-contract transfer fees. A case currently before the EC Commissioner for Competition concerns Hans Gilhaus who, having played for the Scottish team Aberdeen for two years, now wishes to return to Holland, but cannot join another club until a fee of £400,000 is paid to Aberdeen. The argument given by clubs and governing bodies in support of the system is that the end-of-contract fee is a way of recouping the initial outlay in recruiting the player and also that it helps to subsidise youth development. Neither of these arguments is likely to be found persuasive within the Commission.

It is not just in the major team sports that the EC has an effect on sport. Existing Community laws affect the freedom of movement of coaches and trainers, the movement of firearms (for shooting events), and the movement of horses (equestrian events). Community competition policy also affects sponsorship arrangements, the granting of exclusive broadcasting rights, the labelling of equipment as the 'official' racket or ball, etc., for a particular event or sport, and the granting of exclusive rights to sell tickets.

In addition to matters associated with trade and competition the Community has begun to involve itself in aspects of sport more remote from the economic. In 1990 the European Council passed a resolution concerned with doping which required the Commission to draw up a code of practice (published in 1992), develop publicity and undertake investigations of drug use and testing methods. The Community mounted an anti-doping campaign to coincide with the 1992 Olympic Games and as part of a growing interest in 'sport for all' the EC is currently developing policy initiatives in the areas of sport for the disabled and sport for young people.

The growing interest of the EC in European sport is viewed with a degree of trepidation among sports INGOs and domestic governing bodies. On the one hand the entry of the Community into the policy area of sport brings with it the prospect of EC resources – particularly funding, but also legitimacy and expertise. As we have seen, a number of sports have already benefited from EC finance. On the other hand the EC is also perceived as a distinct threat to the autonomy of sport. What is of particular concern is the narrowness of interest of the EC and especially its preoccupation with creating an infrastructure to accommodate market capitalism and its growing emphasis on 'European citizenship'.

We have already seen how delicate the relationship was between the Council of Europe and the sports INGOs, with the latter suspicious of governmental encroachment on their activities. Yet the Council of Europe is a decidedly less interventionist organisation by constitution and temperament than the EC. It is already clear that the EC sees sport as a convenient tool for achieving its own political objectives concerning European citizenship. This is not in itself a threat to the independence of sports organisations as it may simply be an additional source of sponsorship. But it is clear that the EC sees many of the rules regarding eligibility, and the relationships between clubs and their players, and governing bodies and sponsors as frequently in conflict with Community aims.

At present the EC is in the early stages of developing a set of policy objectives for sport. It is still taking stock of the implications of the single market for sport and the areas of current involvement. However, it has already shown an interest in a number of policy areas (doping, crowd management, sport for all, and youth and disabled sport) and has begun the process of establishing links with other interested organisations through the establishment of an EC Sports Forum. At present the Forum has a membership comprising governmental representatives, mainly civil servants, and NGOs, mainly drawn from the NOCs of member states. The Forum met for the first time in December 1991 when a series of general debates took place concerning its likely role. Although it is too soon to outline with any certainty the role of the Forum it is already apparent that there is considerable apprehension about any further expansion of EC interest.

From within the Council of Europe there is a concern felt by some that the EC will duplicate its role. Yet while this concern is borne out by the Community's interest in issues initially identified and promoted by the CDDS it is also possible to argue that the recent expansion of the Council's membership will help to sustain its distinctive role. The Council is also concerned that the delicate balance of IGO and INGO interests in the CDDS may be upset by EC intervention on issues such as doping and eligibility (Sevelius 1992). Of greatest concern both to the Council and to sports organisations is that the fundamental orientation of the EC is to treat sport as primarily an economic activity. This is borne out to a large extent by the initial report prepared by Coopers Lybrand which looks only in passing at non-economic aspects of sport. At present it seems as though the intervention of the EC will have the effect of reinforcing the commercialisation of sport, the exploitation of sport for political purposes and the trend towards greater state regulation.

This is not to deny that much of sport is highly commercial and that many of its more arcane practices need reform but the cost of regulating commercial sport and modernising its practices might be the downgrading of effort on the moral issues bedevilling sport such as drug abuse and at the expense of the highly valued but non-commercial endeavours such as Sport for All.

Conclusion

By the mid-1980s it was clear that a number of sports issues could no longer be resolved within domestic policy communities. Doping by athletes and spectator violence both required, as part of the process of policy development and implementation, the involvement of a number of international governmental and non-governmental actors. More recently issues such as eligibility, professionalism and sponsorship have moved out of the purely domestic sphere to be discussed within a number of international forums. In the last chapter it was shown how the role and significance of sports INGOs had increased and this chapter shows a parallel process among governmental organisations. Some organisations, like UNESCO, have made only a marginal impact on sport policy, but others such as the Council of Europe and the EC have exerted a considerable influence on the direction of policy.

At the heart of any analysis of the significance of IGOs is the need to assess the extent to which they act as an independent influence on policy or simply a point of access for domestic governments. UNESCO was the most radical policy source of those reviewed, yet seemed to be a conduit for sectional interests rather than an independent variable in the policy process. The ease with which it was marginalised within the policy process on broad cultural issues including sport is an important demonstration of the capacity of governments to rein in and undermine IGOs that forget the realities of the global balance of power.

The United Nations was undoubtedly more effective in policy development, but its policy on apartheid was also the product of sectional interests and it is difficult to discern a distinctive UN approach to this particular issue. By contrast the Council of Europe has developed a distinctive policy style and emphasis as reflected in its concern with the ethical dimension of policy and its acknowledgement of the autonomy of voluntary organisations. However, there is a danger of over-emphasising the capacity of the Council to act independently in the policy process.

The Council rarely takes actions which would alienate its members; consensus is the dominant mode of debate and decision-making, and the Council and its various committees are sharply sensitive of members' interests. By contrast the EC is a more assertive organisation and has demonstrated a capacity to pursue Commission policy in the face of considerable opposition from individual members. It is the EC that has the greatest potential to act with a high degree of independence on sports issues.

The extent to which IGOs are perceived as potential exploiters of sport is reflected in the uneasy relationship between sport INGOs and the governmental organisations discussed above. The INGOs are well aware of the resources that the EC, UNESCO, etc., have to offer but they are also aware that the price they may have to pay for a share of those resources may be the loss of independence in important areas of sport organisation, such as sponsorship arrangements, movement of players and control over ticket sales. Quite clearly there are many policy issues on which there is a general consensus between the two sets of organisations, such as drug abuse where considerable progress has been made, but even here the sports INGOs are conscious of losing their leadership role within the policy community. Thus while anti-doping policy is still focused on the lead given by the IOC and IAAF, UEFA lost control over football hooliganism to the European police forces and courts.

The growing involvement of IGOs in sports policy raises the question of whether the overall impact of their activity makes for an homogenisation of policy for and practice of sport or whether IGOs have the capacity to defend diversity. In other words, in relation to a policy such as Sport for All, whose sport is being promoted? All the evidence presented in this chapter suggests that IGO activity makes for a loss of heterogeneity. At one level apartheid in sport would be a form of diversity that few would defend and therefore the activity of the UN would gain the support of the vast majority of sports organisations. However, the activity of the EC in using sport for public relations purposes results in sponsorship being directed at the well-established global sports with little support for retaining the local sporting traditions found in many parts of Europe. Similarly the preoccupation of the Community with free market capitalism results in a dominant conception of sport as a commercial enterprise rather than an element in community welfare or personal development. The Council of Europe also contributes to the homogenisation process, though not in such a direct way as the EC. The Council is much more concerned with developing a consensus on the values which should underpin the participation of individuals in sport and the involvement of government. The Council's European Sports Charter legitimises government involvement in sport, emphasises the importance of organisational rationality in sport, and highlights the importance of values which are legitimated in terms of their contribution to the support of democratic government. If the EC is promoting sport as a support for the dominant economic system then the Council is promoting sport as a support for the dominant political system.

Notes

1 A policy community is one way of conceptualising the operation of the policy process. Among the attributes of the policy communities are a membership that includes government officials and interest groups; a degree of value consensus; and a degree of structure. For a fuller discussion see Friend *et al.* (1974), Hogwood (1987), Laffin (1986), Rhodes (1986) and Houlihan (1991).

2 Quoted in Walters (1952).

3 Quoted in Howell (1990: 288).

4 ICSPE (International Council for Sport and Physical Education) was established in 1958 under the aegis of UNESCO to conduct research and promote the study of sport and PE so as to inform policy. The first General Assembly of ICSPE took place in Rome at the time of the Olympic Games and received support from both UNESCO and the IOC. The organisation changed its title to the International Council for Sport Science and Physical Education (ICSSPE) in 1982.

5 The 'Gleneagles Agreement' is the popular title of the Commonwealth Statement on Apartheid in Sport, adopted in 1977.

6 ENGSO was formerly known as the NGO club and was established in the early 1970s to provide a forum for the leaders of national sports confederations. The UK is represented by the Central Council of Physical Recreation. ENGSO's aims are to share information and discuss current issues of concern. It recently established an EC working party to monitor developments in the Community of interest to sports organisations (Seary 1992: 81).

5

The Olympic movement

According to Avery Brundage, President of the IOC for twenty years and one of the most influential figures within the Olympic movement, 'The Olympic movement is a twentieth century religion, . . . a modern, exciting, dynamic religion, attractive to youth, and we of the International Olympic Committee are its disciples' (IOC Bulletin 1964: No. 88). There is always something disquieting about any organisation which describes itself as a 'religion' or 'movement' and adopts the language of mysticism as exemplified by the frequent references to 'the spirit of Olympism'. In contrast to other major international sporting events such as the soccer World Cup, the Wimbledon tennis championships and motor racing Grand Prix, the Olympic Games has been defined by the IOC as giving expression to a set of distinctive values encapsulated in the Olympic Charter. As with other organisations which express a commitment to a specific doctrine, analyses of the Olympic movement tend to provoke strong criticism or equally strong defence. At one extreme Simson and Jennings (1992) condemn the Olympic movement for its hypocrisy and pomposity and describe a movement perverted by greed and self-aggrandisement. While Simson and Jennings' analysis is weakened by its overblown rhetoric, Seppanen (1984) in a much more careful analysis is equally critical. For Seppanen the failure of the Olympic movement is that it has been unable to promote its ideals and has become 'an instrument in the hands of external and extraneous forces' (1984: 124). Hoberman goes even further, tracing the moral degeneration of the Olympic movement to a level he describes as amoral universalism 'which strives for global participation at all costs, even sacrificing rudimentary moral standards' (1986: 2). Yet the strength of this criticism is matched by a number of staunch defenders. Foremost among them is Lucas who, while not uncritical of the recent history of the Olympic movement, extols the 'unmatched leadership skill' of IOC President Juan Samaranch and sees the movement with the potential to play a 'real role in helping the world avoid brutal frontal assault or volatile international conflicts' (1992: 210, 215).

In Chapter 3 the IOC was located at the centre of the matrix of international sports organisations. Its leadership within the international sports community was supported by a capacity to articulate and defend many of its key interests and to exert influence on both governments and other international bodies. The international importance of the Olympic movement is clearly dependent on the continued success of the quadrennial Games. It is therefore not surprising that the Olympic movement and the modern Olympic Games have been the focus of intense pressure from both governmental and non-governmental interests. The purpose of this chapter is to analyse the Olympic movement in terms of its significance as an arena for nationalism and diplomatic manoeuvring over international issues and in terms of its capacity to develop and promote distinctive Olympic values.

The discussion that follows is structured around four questions. First, why are the Olympic movement and Games so attractive to governmental and non-governmental political interests; second, in what ways are the movement and Games used by these interests; third, to what extent is the Olympic movement vulnerable to political exploitation; and finally what values does the Olympic movement currently seek to uphold in international politics?

The attraction of the Olympics to political interests

Although all aspects of cultural life have been subject on occasion to exploitation for political purposes, the degree of involvement of political interests in international sport seems far greater, and within international sport the Olympic Games (along with the Commonwealth Games) seem to be disproportionately affected. One of the primary explanations arises from the conscious decision of the successive IOC Presidents to define the purpose of the Olympic movement in political terms (such as equality and fraternity) and to aspire to political influence. The Olympic Charter is peppered with statements that reflect the aspiration of the movement to have an influence far beyond competitive sport: 'Olympism is a philosophy of life' . . . 'the goal of the Olympic movement is to contribute to building a peaceful and better world' (IOC 1991: 7). Unlike other international governing bodies which seek to produce opportunities for the display of sporting excellence, and increasingly to generate profit, the Olympic movement has always been more ambitious. As Kanin observed, 'the Olympic Games were founded with expressly political goals in mind and have thrived on ties to global affairs' (1981: ix). Yet Kanin's observation, while accurate, does not do justice to the deep ambiguity at the heart of the movement. What is central to the Olympic movement is the capacity to promote an international political agenda while at the same time claiming that the movement and the Games are above politics. Ideally such a strategy allows the IOC to set standards of behaviour for host states, for example concerning the equal right of entry of all Olympic athletes for the period of the Games, while at the same time operating a policy of inequality with regard to IOC membership.

Such inherently contradictory policies are obviously difficult to sustain while not enabling other organisations to exploit their ambiguities. Thus governments can, on the one hand, justify non-intervention on an issue on the grounds that the Olympics are non-political, and on the other hand, intervene on the grounds that the Olympic Charter requires action. This ambiguity enabled a number of governments to avoid confronting the repression of domestic opposition by Germany prior to the 1936 Games and Mexico prior to the Games of 1968, yet withdraw from the Montreal Games because of the presence of a team from New Zealand, which had recent sporting ties with South Africa. The Olympics therefore provide a conveniently adaptable context for the furthering of interests.

A second explanation is that the structure of the Olympic Games and movement is almost ideal for expressions of national interest. As a number of writers have pointed out it is no accident that the modern Olympics were revived at a time that coincided with the high point of European nationalism (Mandle 1974; Caldwell 1982). From at least the 1904 Games the IOC consistently perceived issues of participation in the Games in terms of the eligibility of states rather than the eligibility of athletes (Espy 1979: 168–9). For example, the participation of Germany (unfortunately the host nation) in the 1936 Olympics and South Africa in the 1960 Olympics was more important than the exclusion of German Jewish or South African black athletes. Similarly, the exclusion of the Germans from the 1920 and 1924 Games and the refusal to admit immediately the Hungarians to the Olympic movement because they were on the losing side in the First World War are also evidence of the conceptual priority of state over individual. Consequently the dominance of the state as the organising unit of the movement, the reliance on national Olympic committees to select, finance and organise athletes and the dependence of most NOCs on the financial support of their government gave and still gives the latter a degree of leverage that is all too difficult to resist. The IOC, in allowing the perpetuation of the symbolic trappings of national identity as part of the Games and relying so heavily on state-based structures for their organisation, can hardly feel aggrieved when national interests seem to swamp Olympic idealism. In this context the attempt by the IOC to prevent the calculation of a medal league table in the early 1920s, surely an inevitable extension of nationalism, was absurd.

In practice, states have available a wide and finely graded repertoire of symbolic and substantive actions ranging from behaviour at opening ceremonies, and the use of flags/anthems, to the interference with the participation of particular athletes and boycotts. There are many examples of national interests using the Olympics as an opportunity to draw attention to a grievance or cause. In the 1908 London Games the American team marched in the opening ceremony with their flag at half-mast and did not lower the flag as they marched past the king and queen. According to Guttmann this show of disrespect was prompted by the large number of Irish-Americans in the team who wished to protest against the continued occupation of Ireland by Britain.[1] At the 1912 Games the Finns, protesting against Russian domination of their country, were allowed to march behind their own flag in the opening ceremony, much to the irritation of the Russians. Later in 1936 the Nazis excluded a number of world-class Jews from their team such as the high jumper, Gretel Bergmann although they did select the fencer, Helene Mayer and the ice hockey player, Rudi Ball, both of whom had some Jewish ancestry (Guttmann 1984 and 1992; Espy 1979; Hart-Davis 1986; Mandell 1976).

A third factor in explaining the attraction of the Olympics to political interests is the high level of media attention given to international sport in general and the Olympic Games in particular. From the very first modern Games when Prince Constantine and King George stood by the finishing line to meet the Greek victor of the marathon, political leaders have recognised the public relations opportunities of the Olympics. While the Greek monarch was able to make political capital out of the Greek marathon victory before 40,000 or so of his subjects the modern Olympic Games provide access to an audience of well over one billion.

Modern Olympic sport provides almost the ideal backdrop for the politically ambitious. Its association with health, youth, peace and enjoyment is a public relations manager's (or propagandist's) dream. In addition to the attraction to political interests of global access that the Games present there is the bonus that the cost of access is relatively low. Although the cost of hosting the Games has been considerable for some countries or cities, particularly Mexico and Montreal, it is far outweighed by the benefits of three weeks of global free publicity.

Although governments are best placed to exploit the publicity potential of the Games non-governmental interests have also made dramatic use of the high concentration of media attention. The tragic massacre of Israeli athletes at Munich contrasts with the quiet protest of John Carlos and Tommie Smith at the 1968 Games. Black American athletes Carlos and Smith, both medal winners in the 200 metres, raised a black-gloved clenched fist during the playing of the American national anthem in protest at the domestic policies of the US government. Their action helped to sharpen the debate in the USA about the civil rights of black Americans and remains one of the most vivid and poignant images of the modern Olympics.

Finally, a further reason why the Olympics is so attractive to political interests is the very fact that they are culturally so significant to such a large section of the world. The debate surrounding the globalisation of sport will be explored in Chapter 8 but it is worth emphasising here that the Olympic Games can justifiably claim to be, not merely a global event, but also an event about which many people feel passionately. Coubertin's claim that 'For me, sport is a religion with church, dogma, cult . . . but especially with religious feeling'[2] was undoubtedly influenced by the enthusiasm of the proselyte but nonetheless contained a considerable amount of truth. The attraction to political interests to tap into and manipulate that intensity of feeling is therefore understandably strong.

Given the relative ease of access of national governmental interests to the Olympics and the explicit ambition of the Olympic movement to be something more than an organiser of a major sporting event, it is not surprising that the modern Olympic Games have been the constant focus of international politics. In summary, political interests, especially governments, have structured points of access to the Olympic movement and Games; the Olympic movement aspires to international political involvement; and the intrinsic qualities of Olympic sport make the Games highly attractive as a political as well as sporting arena.

How political interests use the Olympics

With an organisation as large and as complex as the modern Olympics the options for political gestures and actions are extremely wide. For example, the (unsuccessful) Soviet insistence that Russian be accepted as a third official language of the IOC as a condition of its joining, was a gentle, if not very subtle, reminder that the USA was not the only global power. At the other end of the range there is the action of Hitler's National Socialists in using almost every aspect of the 1936 Games as an opportunity to propagandise on behalf of Nazism. Although the variety of political uses of the Olympics is wide there are two that are particularly important, namely the use of boycotts and the exploitation of the Games for propaganda purposes by the host state. It is these two actions, above all others, that illustrate the value of the Olympics to state political interests.

Boycotts of the Olympic Games seem to be going out of fashion. The Games held at Seoul and at Barcelona were both extremely well attended in marked contrast to the two previous Games at Los Angeles and Moscow. However, the likelihood of the boycott as a political resource disappearing from the Olympics for good is remote as its value has been too clearly demonstrated in the past. Yet boycotts are problematic resources as they are far from subtle, lacking the gradations of scale that diplomats prefer. With boycotts you either attend or you do not – it is not possible to attend a little, though some have tried! It is also a risky resource which frequently embarrasses the user, or the intermediary (often the IOC), more than the intended victim. In addition boycotts are a resource that cannot be used by all members of the Olympic movement. For many the benefits of attendance (international visibility and acceptance) must be carefully weighed against the costs of non-attendance. For example, at the 1960 Games in Rome the Taiwanese team who had been denied, by the IOC, the right to use the word 'China' in describing their team, preferred to attend rather than boycott. They did, however, produce a placard at the opening ceremony which read 'Under Protest' and in so doing made an effective and well-publicised point. Comparable dilemmas also faced the nascent German Democratic Republic in the 1960s. Despite these drawbacks the boycott, either threatened or actual, has been a feature of the Olympics for much of its history.

The first significant boycott attempt focused on the 1936 Berlin Games. Although the initial Nazi reaction to the inherited commitment to host the Games was highly critical Goebbels, the Propaganda Minister, soon realised the opportunity they presented both internally, as a means of galvanising support for the new government, and internationally, as a way of promoting the success of National Socialism. The anti-semitic policies of the Nazis prompted a prolonged and heated campaign, primarily in America, aimed at boycotting the Games. Brundage, then President of the American Olympic Association, fought hard to prevent a successful boycott campaign within the American Athletic Union. However, pressure of public opinion forced him to agree to make a fact-finding visit to Germany in 1934. His visit was brief, less than a week, and carefully stage-managed; not surprisingly the report he produced for the AAU was highly favourable (Hart-Davis 1986: 71). It is hard to avoid the conclusion that such a distorted report was partly the result of Brundage's admiration of the Nazis' anti-communism and his own underlying anti-semitism (Guttmann 1984: 72). Although the AAU vote was close (58.25 – 55.75) it was in favour of attending. Later in that Olympic year Brundage was rewarded with a seat on the IOC.

Twenty years later two major international crises resulted in renewed threats of boycotts. The first was prompted by the seizure by Egypt, of the Suez canal which was operated by a company owned predominantly by the French and British. After a brief period of negotiation the French and British arranged with the Israelis that the latter would invade Egypt thereby enabling an Anglo-French force to intervene on the pretext of separating the two sides and 'protecting' the canal. The level of international outrage at this action was such that both the USA and the Soviet Union called for the withdrawal of the invading forces. Without the support of the United States the French and British governments had little choice but to face the humiliation of withdrawal. Egypt, Lebanon and Iraq boycotted the Melbourne Games in protest primarily at the actions of the aggressors but also at the failure of the IOC to condemn or expel France and Britain from the Games. Such was the level of international condemnation of the invasion and such was the depth of British humiliation that the boycott seemed superfluous. It was also difficult to identify the purpose of the boycott as the invaders had already withdrawn. Finally, the small scale of the boycott had little effect on the success of the Games. Possibly the most significant factor in undermining the effectiveness of the boycott was that the Suez episode was soon overshadowed by the Soviet invasion of Hungary and the crushing of the attempt of Prime Minister Imre Nagy to assert Hungarian independence from the Soviet empire.

The Soviet invasion led to the boycott of the Games by Spain, Switzerland and the Netherlands, though Spain's action was possibly due more to shortage of money than to moral outrage (Espy 1979: 54). By far the most serious blow was the Swiss boycott due to the location of the IOC headquarters at Lausanne. The Swiss were eventually prevailed upon to reverse their decision but were unable to arrange transport. As with the boycott by the three Islamic states the boycott by the three European states had little effect on either the IOC, the success of the Games or the Soviet Union. The Hungarian team who had just left for the Games a few days before the invasion continued on to Melbourne where a number took the opportunity to defect.

Although boycotts featured in the dispute over the 'two Germanies' and the 'two Chinas', during the 1950s and 1960s the most extensive boycott campaign focused on the participation of South Africa (and Rhodesia) and the policy of apartheid. The context in which the attempt to isolate South Africa developed is important in explaining the actions of the black African states in particular. Of prime importance was the recent independence of many of the sub-Saharan states. Decolonialisation in the 1950s and 1960s created a large number of new states, most with borders set by the arbitrary outcome of imperial conquest rather than the result of the evolution of national identity. A key problem for government was the creation of a sense of national unity and sport provided a valuable resource. Not only was the generation of national sporting heroes a political asset but so too was the identification of a foreign policy issue which enabled the specification both of an 'enemy' and of an issue which would unite one state with its neighbours. In addition, apartheid provided an issue on which black African states could take an international lead while the Olympic movement provided access to a suitable international arena, and one which would lead to other more prestigious forums such as the United Nations and the Commonwealth. As Kanin notes, 'Upon achieving independence, African states found that they could compete more successfully in the Olympic Games than in the struggle for resources and power' (1981: 95). More cynically, one clear benefit of the boycott campaign was that it was a high-profile demonstration of political principle but did not preclude many black African states continuing to trade with South Africa for much of the period of the dispute.

The implications for sport of the emerging policy of apartheid were made clear in 1960 when, following the ban by the International Table Tennis Federation on an all-white South African team, the government used the law to ban interracial sport and outlined the implications of apartheid for sport. In 1962 the South African Non-Racial Olympic Committee (SAN-ROC) was formed and immediately approached the

IOC with the request that it be recognised as the NOC for South Africa on the grounds that the existing NOC was organised along racial lines that contravened the Olympic Charter. Just prior to the formation of SAN-ROC the IOC had presented South Africa with an ultimatum: either conform to IOC rules or risk exclusion. The failure of the South Africans to offer any concessions resulted in the IOC excluding them from the 1964 Games.

This decision applied only to the 1964 Games and thus the issue was reopened as preparations began for the 1968 Games which were scheduled for Mexico City. Partly in anticipation of the renewal of the dispute thirty-two African states established the Supreme Council for Sport in Africa (SCSA) in 1966 which had the express aim of using 'every means to obtain the expulsion of South African sports organisations from the Olympic movement and from International Federations should South Africa fail to comply fully with IOC rules' (quoted in Lapchick 1975: 80). The IOC persisted in attempting to find a formula which would enable South Africa to retain its membership. To ascribe this aim solely to the racism of the white-dominated IOC, as Lapchick (1977) does, is misleading. Racism undoubtedly played a part but so did the absence of a willingness to accept ex-colonial, black African states as equal members of the IOC and an overwhelming concern to prevent the loss of a member of the Olympic family. This latter concern blinkered the IOC so that it was unable to recognise the extent to which it was becoming detached from the new realities of international relations.

The IOC defended its decision to allow the South Africans to send a team to the 1968 Games on the grounds that the latter had made major concessions which would enable a multi-racial team to represent the country. Unfortunately when it became clear that the South African government was intent on overriding the commitments made by its NOC, the IOC persisted in rejecting calls for the expulsion of South Africa. The IOC seemed willing to brazen out the threat by the SCSA and its thirty-two members to boycott the Games. Yet if the IOC thought that the boycott would crumble then it made a serious misjudgement. Crucial to the campaign was the position of the Soviet Union who, in Lapchick's words, had to 'decide if Olympic gold was more important than third world prestige' (1977: 64). In March of 1968 the Soviets finally decided to back the boycott primarily because of its fear that China might exploit its participation and challenge its leadership of the communist bloc, thereby undermining its Third World influence. Once the Soviet decision became clear the IOC moved rapidly to save the Mexico Games and once again exclude South Africa. By now there was growing international momentum for expulsion, particularly following the United Nations resolution encouraging all countries to break off sporting relations with South Africa: expulsion finally came in 1970. The IOC decision to expel South Africa was taken very reluctantly and was determined less by sympathy with the critics of apartheid and more by a fear that the African states and the communist bloc might be persuaded to leave the Olympic movement and support some rival competition such as the GANEFO.

The success of the boycott campaign provides firm evidence of the vulnerability of the IOC to pressure from the emerging power blocs in the Olympic movement and the ability of the latter to exploit, *inter alia*, 'the ideological claims of modern sport' concerning 'notions of equal treatment and respect for one's co-competitor' (Kidd 1988: 648, 650). Yet it should be noted that the IOC took action later than the United Nations and only after it was faced with the prospect of the virtual collapse of the Mexico City Games. To conclude that the IOC was a soft target for boycott threats would therefore be wrong. This is a view confirmed by the events in 1976 when South Africa's internal politics again threatened the Olympic Games.

Spurred on by the success of the expulsion campaign SCSA continued to press for the complete isolation of South Africa from all forms of international sporting contact. New Zealand was one country that continued to retain its sporting contact with South Africa. A New Zealand rugby union tour was planned for 1976, just four months before the Olympics in Montreal. Tanzania was the first state to announce that it would boycott the Games and just two days before the opening ceremony a further fourteen states threatened not to attend if New Zealand was allowed to participate. The demand took the IOC by surprise for a number of reasons, one of which was the extent to which the Committee had been preoccupied with the dispute arising from the refusal by the Canadian government to permit the Taiwan team to enter the country. The surprise and irritation felt by the Committee was also due to the facts that 'New Zealand did not practise apartheid; rugby was not an Olympic sport; the New Zealand rugby Federation was not affiliated with the New Zealand Olympic Committee; and the IOC had expelled both Rhodesia and South Africa' (Espy 1979: 158). The IOC decided not to accede to the demands of the Africans and thirty states subsequently withdrew. The IOC's resistance on this occasion was due in part to the feeling that it was morally in a stronger position, but also due to the lack of support for the boycott from the communist bloc states.

The boycotts of 1980 and 1984 confirmed the importance of blocs within the Committee, but also illustrated the growing confidence of the IOC. The Moscow Games marked the first use by a superpower of a boycott as a weapon in the Cold War (Guttmann 1988). The 1980 boycott campaign, led by the US government, illustrated the danger that the boycott becomes the focus of debate rather than the policy that the boycott is intended to influence. As soon became clear, the issue of the Soviet invasion of Afghanistan was rapidly confused with the controversy over the relationship between sport and government/politics in western democracies, and the relationship between the USA and its NATO allies. In addition, the focus of the boycott campaign was blurred by the Soviet decision to sentence the prominent dissident Andrei Sakharov to internal exile near Gorky. The nature of the debate held in each country varied. In some, such as the USA and Britain, the issue of the invasion was overlaid with concerns about government interference in sport and the civil liberties of athletes (see below for a discussion of the impact on NOCs). The debates in Canada and West Germany were defined more in terms of whether they shared equal status with the USA in NATO or whether they were junior partners who were unable to determine their own foreign policy. In nearly all countries the issue was debated twice, once after the invasion and again after the sentence was passed on Sakharov.

The Games went ahead and were at best a modest success by comparison to previous Games. For the IOC the Games were a disappointment, but some comfort could have been taken from the fact that despite the US-led boycott the Games survived and were the major sporting event of 1980 with healthy television viewing figures throughout Europe. However, given that the next Games were to be hosted by Los Angeles the likelihood of full attendance was remote. One hundred and forty teams attended the twenty-third Olympiad but unsurprisingly the Soviet Union and sixteen of its allies did not participate. The 1984 boycott was primarily retaliatory, though the Soviets justified their action with claims of harassment by American officials and expressions of concern for the safety of their athletes. Yet as with the Moscow Games those in Los Angeles were claimed as a success by the organisers in terms of the quality of competition. In addition, Los Angeles could claim that despite the absence of the Soviet team the Games were also a considerable financial success.

For boycotts to be an effective diplomatic resource it is normally essential that the issue be, and remain, clear-cut; that there be some expectation that the boycott will have an eventual effect on policy; that the construction of the boycott take place without too much (visible) arm-twisting; and finally that the event be perceived to be diminished by the absence of the boycotting states. In 1980 and 1984 many of these requirements were either absent or present in only a muted form. The boycott, as a political resource, was at its most refined and effective over the issue of South Africa. In this case the issue of apartheid was clear-cut and the objective of the boycott was understood (the sporting isolation of South Africa). Also the boycott policy was already showing signs of success through the expulsion of South Africa from an increasing number of international sports federations. While 'arm-twisting' undoubtedly took place it was discreet and enabled the advocates of the boycott policy to claim the moral high ground. Finally, in 1968 at least, the IOC was convinced that a boycott would be of such a scale as to undermine the viability of the Games. The attractiveness and effectiveness of the boycott declined from 1968. By 1980 the boycott was seriously tarnished as a political resource and was further discredited in 1984.

While attention is often concentrated on the use of boycotts as a political resource the Olympics present an equally significant opportunity to those states selected to host the Games. The public relations potential of the Games is enormous. Not only is the host state the subject of intense, and largely uncritical, media attention for the three weeks of competition, but the host will also benefit from the publicity associated with the preparations in the years prior to the event.

Reflecting on the financial success of the Los Angeles, Seoul and Barcelona Games it is easy to forget that for most of its history finding a host for the Games has involved trying to find a government willing to act as sponsor and underwriter. Yet willing hosts were not too difficult to find as governments soon realised the propaganda potential of hosting a major international sports event. For some of the early hosts the propaganda benefits were largely internal. The Greek royal family were quick to recognise the opportunity that the 1896 Games presented to link them firmly to traditions of ancient Greece. This was important as the 'Greek' royal family was a branch of the Danish nobility imposed on Greece by the European powers after the War of Independence. The Games, and particularly the symbolism of the marathon, also gave the Greek king the opportunity to 'present Greece as a barrier against Turks and Slavs in modern times as it was against the Persians at Marathon' (Kanin 1981: 29). Eight years later the Games were hosted by

St Louis and Kanin remarked that the involvement of President Roosevelt indicated a clear appreciation of the opportunity presented by holding the Olympics in election year.

As media attention increased during the early part of the century the attraction of using the role of host to direct propaganda towards external targets also increased. Italy, the original host for the 1908 Games, saw an opportunity to establish its credentials as the new major power in Europe. Britain, who took over the role of host after the withdrawal of the Italians following the devastating eruption of Vesuvius, also recognised the propaganda value of the Games. Having just extricated itself from the long and internationally unpopular war in South Africa Britain was keen to use the Games as a way of rebuilding its links with its European neighbours (Kanin 1981: 32–3).

The exploitation of the 1936 Games by the Nazis has been well documented and needs no further comment here (see Hart-Davis 1986 and Mandell 1976). Although hosting the Games purely for the publicity value probably occurred only in 1936, states in recent years have been adept at using the Games for self-promotion. For Mexico the Games offered the opportunity to project the country as modernising, stable and north American and to shed its Third World debt-ridden image (J. Wilson 1988: 154). The bloodshed required to clean up Mexico City and prevent political demonstrations by students was the price paid (Hoberman 1986: 13–14). The attempt to showcase socialism at the Moscow Games was a limited success – especially when compared with the triumph of capitalism in Los Angeles! For the South Koreans hosting the 1988 games provided an immensely important opportunity to win international recognition at the expense of its northern rival. 'The 1988 Olympics will mark a turning point in that struggle with the South about to achieve international acclamation and the North virtually isolated even from its chief communist allies, the Soviet Union and China' (*The World & I* 1988: 22). Hosting the Games can therefore fulfil a number of political functions not only legitimising repression within host states, but also providing a sympathetic backdrop against which states can manipulate a largely compliant media.

The vulnerability of the Olympics to political manipulation

The primary source of weakness within the Olympic movement is the extent to which NOCs and individual IOC members are increasingly dependent on the support of their governments. It is not just the financially dependent NOCs from the poorer states that are politically dependent; even the richer NOCs, such as that of the United States, have faced problems resisting governmental pressure.

The vulnerability of NOCs to governmental pressure is amply illustrated by the response of the United States Olympic Committee (USOC) to government insistence on a boycott of the 1980 Moscow Olympics. At the end of 1979 the Soviet Union invaded Afghanistan and the US government of President Carter, frustrated at its inability to intervene effectively, ordered a boycott of the forthcoming Olympics. Hill (1992: 127–34; see also Guttmann 1992: 151–5) catalogues the range of pressures exerted on the USOC including the threats to reverse their tax benefits, to renegotiate the advantageous lease to their (government-owned) headquarters and training ground, and to take emergency powers, under the International Emergency Economic Powers Act, to stop athletes attending. These specific threats were backed by consistent and highly public pressure from the White House and Congress directed at the members of the USOC and members of the US Olympic team. Given the extent of intimidation that the USOC faced it is not surprising that they soon acquiesced and voted to accept the boycott. Although the USOC might have argued the case of the human rights of American athletes more forcefully, Guttmann is a little harsh in calling the USOC's actions 'abject capitulation' (1992: 151).[3]

The call by the United States for an international boycott was heeded by a number of other countries including Canada, West Germany, Japan and Israel, all of whom were heavily economically and/or militarily dependent on America. While the western democracies were used to decrying the boycotts instituted by predominantly communist and military dictatorships they proved in 1980 that their respect for the rights of athletes was just as poor. What was also demonstrated was that very few countries could claim confidently that their NOC was effectively independent of the state. Even among those countries that did attend only a small number of NOCs, the British Olympic Association being the most notable, defied the explicit policy of their home state.

It is not just the dependence of NOCs that undermines the autonomy of the Olympic movement, individual members of the IOC are also increasingly state nominees rather than the choice of the President and the Committee itself. As Brundage, then vice-President of the IOC, feared, the participation of the Soviet Union brought with it an insistence that the IOC should accept the nominee of the Soviet government, thus setting a precedent for other communist states. Both IOC Presidents Edstrom and Brundage were prepared to accept state nomination as the price of progress towards their goal of Olympic universalism (Guttmann 1984: 139–40). Consequently for much of the period between the mid-1950s and the present decision-making within the IOC (and in many international federations) has been seriously affected by the development of bloc voting determined by the political priorities of the home governments and/or the pattern of interdependence between states in the international system.

In addition to the consequences of the political dependence of many NOCs and IOC members the IOC is vulnerable to political manipulation due to its own internal workings and membership criteria. By comparison to most international federations (IFs), which operate on a basis of equality among members, reflected in a 'one member, one vote' system, the IOC remains a self-perpetuating oligarchy, albeit a fairly benign and paternalistic one. Alexandrakis and Krotee (1988) explain the composition of the IOC as a product of its period of formation, namely the specific stage of capitalist development, though they acknowledge that reconciling the spread of capitalist organisational rationality with the clearly feudal structure of the IOC is problematic. Without attempting to resolve this paradox the establishment of the modern Olympics undoubtedly took place within a highly distinctive context exemplified by, first the intensity of nationalist feeling, second the aristocratic domination of sport, and third the prominence of the aristocracy within diplomatic relations. The net effect was to lay the foundation of an elitist (and Eurocentric) culture which made an easy accommodation with decolonialisation and the development of communist and other power blocs unlikely.

The Eurocentrism of the Olympic movement is easily demonstrated by an analysis of the current membership of the IOC. Table 5.1 shows the breakdown of IOC membership by continent and illustrates the continuing dominance of Europe, even allowing for the recent increase in the number of states.

Table 5.1 Geographic distribution of IOC membership (1992)

	Europe	Asia	Africa	America	Oceania	Total
%	42 (21)	15 (23)	19 (28)	20 (23)	4 (5)	100 (100)

Note: Figures in brackets show the percentage of the world's nations included in each continent.

Source: Adapted from Alexandrakis and Krotee (1988).

The impression given by Table 5.1 is supported by the large number of European states (eleven out of a total of seventeen) that have two IOC members. In terms of social class the IOC is well represented by the aristocracy, business and the military justified, presumably, by the capacity to remain financially independent of government and other interests. Membership of the IOC is highly dependent upon the whim of the incumbent President, who may or may not seek advice (Hill 1992: 60), although it is clear that account is taken of the wealth and support for sport in individual states. In addition, there also seems to be an accepted period of apprenticeship for NOCs before they can expect an IOC member.

It has been argued, most notably by Brundage, that such a closed selection process and such a distorted pattern of geographical representation on the IOC allows the Olympic movement a degree of freedom from political interference. The IOC is seen as selecting only those who have a strong commitment to act as guardians of the Olympic spirit and who owe their position to the Committee and its President rather than to political sponsors in their home state. Following this logic it may be argued that the existing pattern of selection and membership ensures independence of action (for example over the selection of sites) and is consequently the best way of securing the future of the Olympic movement (see, for example, Killanin 1983; Lucas 1992). However, such an argument has obvious weaknesses as exemplified during the South African and Rhodesian crises. The small number of IOC members from Africa and other Third World states fuelled suspicion about the commitment of the IOC to opposing racism in general and apartheid in particular. In addition, the IOC was vulnerable to proposals from the Soviet Union that it should be reformed along the lines of the United Nations with each NOC and each Olympic IF President having a right to a seat on the Committee. While the Soviet Union can be accused of seeking to incorporate the current discontent among the IFs and NOCs about the distribution of Olympic income into its 'Cold War' strategy, the IOC found it extremely difficult to argue against plans to democratise the organisation without further alienating Third World members and thereby strengthening the Soviet voice (Espy 1979: 73–5).

For the IOC the problem is to maximise both freedom of action and authority in the world of international sport and politics. Having survived the turbulent Cold War years with the present arrangements intact it is possible to argue that there is now no reason to alter them. But buying off Third World states with sport development aid and co-opting powerful external critics from the federations is only a tactical response to pressure rather than a strategic view of the development of the Olympic movement, and is only as successful as the handling of the last crisis.

The final factor which contributes to the weakness of the Olympic movement is the seemingly unstoppable growth in the scale of the summer Olympic programme. As Hill points out, concern with 'gigantism' was voiced as early as the 1950s and the point is made that 'in practice only the richest of candidate cities, or those under the control of effective authoritarian governments, are plausible candidates' (1992: 241). Not only is the pool of plausible host cities becoming shallower as the logistics of mounting the Games increase in complexity, but also once the host city is selected the Olympic movement is locked into a delicate relationship with the city and its government. The need for substantial government co-operation in mounting the Games gives the state considerable leverage over the IOC, as illustrated by the difficulties the IOC faced in Montreal in 1976 and Los Angeles in 1984 over the guarantee of entry to all participants. In addition, as Hoberman argues, political stakes of hosting the Games are for most states so high that it encourages and indeed legitimises internal repressive measures as illustrated by the Tlatelolco massacre of students prior to the 1968 Mexico Olympics, the round-up of dissidents prior to the Moscow Games (1986: 12–15) and the arrests of many Catalan activists prior to the Barcelona Olympics (*Guardian* 17.2.1992). This combination of the narrowing of choice of venue for the Games and the behaviour of host governments makes it increasingly difficult for the IOC to avoid the accusation of 'amoral universalism' and to defend the spirit of the Olympic Charter and particularly its concern with fraternity and goodwill.

Contemporary Olympic values

As the foregoing discussion makes clear the Olympic movement has been closely involved in a number of major international issues both as a forum for others to operate within and as an actor in its own right. Although views differ as to the nobility of the IOC's values it displays many of the common traits of other actors in the international system. In the examples discussed above the President and Committee are on some occasions victims of more powerful interests while on others have been capable of sustaining an independent policy. On some issues the IOC has been able to articulate a reasonably clear set of policy aims while on other issues it has seemed directionless. Yet much the same might be said of the governmental actors involved in many of these issues.

Hoberman's condemnation of the Olympic movement for putting the maximisation of participation before the values encapsulated in the Olympic Charter and traditionally expressed by IOC Presidents carries considerable force. But we need to ask whether the mix of principle and pragmatism found in the IOC is any different from that found in similar international organisations. There is no reason why the organisations of the Olympic movement should contradict the accumulation of research from organisational sociology which suggests that organisations temper their commitment to public goals with a pragmatic concern for their own survival (see, for example, Benson 1982; Ranson *et al.* 1980). Yet the extent to which the Olympic movement moderates its principle with pragmatism is important for the study of its significance in international politics. It is important first because of the role that the movement plays in the transmission of cultural values across national boundaries. It is also important because it operates at the non-governmental level of transnational relations and greatly influences the conduct of a multiplicity of informal lines of transnational contact that are conducted through the medium of sport. The Olympic movement expresses its values in a number of ways and three of the most important are, first, the conduct of the Games, second the Olympic education programme, and third the activities of Olympic Solidarity.

In terms of the conduct of the Games much has already been said about the promotion of nationalism through the Games. The attitude of the IOC and the early Presidents of the Olympic movement towards nationalism was deeply ambivalent. A remark of Pierre de Coubertin, quoted by MacAloon (1981: 180), aptly sums up not only his disdain for democracy but also his contempt for nationalism. He describes the IOC as 'composed of three concentric circles; a small nucleus of active and convinced members; a nursery of members of good will who were capable of being educated; and finally, a facade of more or less useful men whose presence satisfied national pretensions while giving some prestige to the group'. What the 'nucleus' was 'convinced' of was the virtue of 'internationalism' over 'cosmopolitanism'. Whereas cosmopolitanism was the homogenisation of culture, internationalism was, by contrast, the acknowledgement and celebration of cultural difference. However well intentioned this formulation might have been, it proved increasingly difficult to sustain this view of nationalism as being defined and moderated within the context of Olympic internationalism.

Brundage, many years later, attempted to resist the nationalist tide. During the 1960s the Olympic movement was locked in a debate over amateurism part of which concerned the allegations that NOCs were colluding in selecting teams which contained 'state professionals'. One response by Brundage and many on the IOC was to attempt to reduce the opportunities for reinforcing nationalism presented at the Games as a way of diminishing the incentive to maximise national advantage. Having failed to get support for a suggestion in the early years of his presidency that the playing of national anthems and the flying of national flags at the medals ceremonies be abandoned, he tried once more in the early 1960s, but with a similar lack of success. Arguing that Olympic victors should be treated as 'sportsmen and not as representatives of a country' he proposed that the playing of anthems be replaced by a simple fanfare of trumpets.[4] For the motion to be successful the proposal required a two-thirds majority which it failed to achieve. Guttmann notes the irony that many of the opponents of Brundage's proposals were the 'internationalists' from the communist bloc (1984: 121). Since the 1960s there have been far fewer expressions of concern, from within the IOC, about the level of nationalism and there is no evidence that this issue is of concern to the present President.

During the last three decades the Olympic movement has consequently allowed national interests to become even more strongly associated with the whole fabric of the Games. At the heart of the debate about the relationship between the movement and nationalism is whether it is symbiotic or parasitic. The general view reflected in the statements of Olympic members and academics is that the relationship is best described as predominantly parasitic. The biographies and autobiographies of IOC Presidents (Guttmann 1984; Killanin 1983; Coubertin 1979) and the studies of many academics (for example Lucas 1992; Coakley 1986) all argue for a reduction in expressions of nationalism as a condition of the continuing health of the movement. There is plenty of evidence to support this view, for example in the exploitation of the IOC as a forum for pressing claims for diplomatic recognition (East Germany), pressing for the exclusion of rival governments (People's Republic of China), or more generally seeing the IOC as another forum for the playing out of Cold War politics.

Yet to describe nationalism as a parasite on the Olympic body is inadequate. The relationship is so intertwined at the ideological, structural and procedural levels that symbiosis is a much more accurate description. Particularly as the world moves away from the ideological confrontations of the last fifty years sport has become an increasingly important language for the conduct of international relations, even if mainly heard as part of the supporting chorus. In addition, the Olympic movement makes a prominent arena within which the dialogue can take place. Unfortunately, symbiosis requires a high degree of mutual dependence and while one could claim that nationalism and the Olympic movement are mutually reinforcing, nationalism would undoubtedly survive the demise of Olympism. By contrast it is hard to conceive of Olympism surviving without the adrenalin of nationalism.

The IOC, particularly under Samaranch, is wedded to functioning within a national structure and to the projection of nationalist values. The only serious potential challenge to that relationship is the rise of commercial interests and the increasing reliance of the Olympic movement on sponsorship and the fees from television companies. The Moscow boycott was a watershed in the Olympic movement which convinced many on the IOC, and the incoming President, that financial independence was an important element in going some way towards redressing the balance between the movement and the major world powers. The Olympic movement now has the task of weaving the interests of its commercial sponsors into the fabric of Olympism, itself a blend of mystical internationalism and pragmatic nationalism. The last twelve years have shown that, in general terms, the Games can be commercially successful, supportive of national interests and a major sporting event. This has been achieved primarily because, Moscow 1980 notwithstanding, commercial priorities and the interests of the major Olympic powers have been broadly in harmony. But, as Chapter 7 will suggest, the harmony may be short-lived.

The second way in which the Olympic movement expresses its values is through the Olympic education programme. Included in the Olympic Charter are a number of explicit references to the responsibility of the movement to foster the dissemination of the Olympic message through an education programme. The focus for Olympic education is, on the one hand, the International Olympic Academy (IOA) at Athens and, on the other a network of national Olympic academies or education programmes. For the enthusiasts in the Olympic movement the IOA was, according to Lucas, 'the philosophical center of the Olympic Movement, the metaphysical and spiritual repository for those invisible and precious ideas that transcend stadium activities' (1992: 172; see also Nissiotis 1982; Strong 1982). About sixty academies also exist in individual countries, including Germany, China, Hungary and Spain. The operation of the IOA and the national academies is centred upon the study and discussion of Olympic history, organisation and philosophy and has involved over 5,000 participants since their creation. The academies not only organise conferences and workshops on Olympic themes for athletes and particularly young people, they also act as a focus for lobbying activity within each country with an especial concern to influence the physical education curriculum (Parry 1988; Strong 1982). However, the range of activities of national academies varies widely and includes youth work, conservation of historic Olympic sites, such as the site of the Much Wenlock Games in Britain, and the organisation of 'Olympic Day' events (Parry 1992).

It is extremely difficult to assess the impact of the Olympic academies on the spread of modern Olympism. What can be noted is that the number of academies continues to increase, the number of athletes involved is also growing, and the range of activities continues to widen. Furthermore the workshops/conferences of the academies are frequently used as opportunities for courting political figures in the domestic government. While all these activities are of value in maintaining the profile of the Olympic movement, probably of greatest significance is the legitimacy that the academies and their educational programmes give to Olympism.

The third way in which the movement expresses its values is through its global sports development programme. In 1961 the IOC established the Commission for International Olympic Aid which had the aim of supporting sports development in the newly independent countries of Asia and Africa. Lack of money prevented the Commission making any significant contribution to sport development during the decade that followed. The Commission was revived and the name changed to Olympic Solidarity in 1972 when it was organised under the wing of the Italian NOC. Solidarity was given a further boost from 1974 by being allocated a share of the growing income from the sale of broadcasting rights. The activities of Solidarity are wide-ranging and include the awarding of scholarships for athletes and coaches to attend training centres in the USSR, the GDR and the United States, help with the purchase of equipment and the building of training facilities, and the organising of training events in the various regions of the world.

The motive for the establishment of Olympic Solidarity was in part altruistic and in part self-interested. There was a genuine awareness that a large number of the new members of the Olympic movement were ex-colonies, most of whom were desperately poor and seriously lacking in the necessary skills and infrastructure to enable them to participate effectively in the Games (Anthony 1988). But the IOC's concern for sports development was also prompted by the growing realisation during the period of decolonialisation that some means of locking the new states into the Olympic movement had to be found that avoided granting them all membership of the IOC itself. During the late 1950s and early 1960s the Soviet Union had sought to broaden the basis of IOC membership partly by giving a seat to each NOC president. Although this proposal failed it had, from Brundage's point of view, gained a worrying level of support from countries in eastern Europe, Asia and Africa. In addition, the GANEFO had taken place in 1963 and had been judged a success, thus creating a situation where 'If the IOC alienated Third World countries, they now had a viable rival, supported by a superpower (China), to turn to' (J. Wilson 1988: 164). Although the second GANEFO did not take place the IOC saw clearly that its monopoly was capable of being challenged. Consequently the establishment of Olympic Solidarity, and the steady increase in its budget and activities during the 1970s, was in part an attempt to lock Third World sports organisations into the movement.

In recent years the work of Solidarity has proved to be an important focus for the sports aid programmes of the major IFs, especially the IAAF. Indeed the IAAF's Development Commission (established in 1976) and Solidarity work in close cooperation in planning, funding and delivering courses for athletes, coaches and administrators (IAAF 1991). In 1988 the IOC spent over $11m on development and the transport of athletes to the Seoul Games. While some money is spent on individual athletes the primary concern is to reach and train administrators (judges and event organisers) and coaches who can pass on to others the practice of Olympic sports and the values of the Olympic movement.

At the beginning of this chapter it was pointed out that analyses of the Olympic Games and movement tend to generate committed advocates and equally committed critics. That the Olympics can produce such passion is surprising as is the depth of disagreement between supporters and detractors. To read Lucas followed by Hoberman it is hard to believe that they are talking about the same organisation. This chapter has been concerned to show how the ideals of Olympism and the pragmatism required to function as part of the international political system can lead to selective myopia on major world issues. In purely organisational terms the IOC has been remarkably successful not only in keeping the Olympic Games the world's greatest sporting event, but also in broadening and deepening the reach of the movement. In most parts of the world 'sport' is defined in terms of the Olympic programme, 'competition' is organised around Olympic qualification, and 'success' is confirmed by an Olympic medal. While it is easy to challenge the Olympic movement's willingness to operate by the values enshrined in the Charter, the success of the movement in becoming the global reference point for sporting organisation and culture is difficult to deny.

Notes

1 Kanin (1981: 34) provides an alternative explanation suggesting that the cause of the American action was a combination of a reaction to the 'oversight' of not displaying the US flag at the opening ceremony and the strong egalitarian and anti-aristocratic spirit of the American team.
2 Quoted in Kortzfleisch (1970: 232).
3 Guttmann (1992: 151) quotes from the 1977 Final Report of the President's Commission on Olympic Sports which deplored 'the actions of the governments which deny an athlete the right to take part in international competition' and observes that 'Carter indulged in a president's time-honoured right to ignore the resolutions of presidential commissions'.
4 Quoted in Guttmann (1984: 121).

6

The Commonwealth and sport

The changes in the title of the Commonwealth Games over the years reflect the transformation in the relationship between Britain and its Empire. The first British Empire Games were held in 1930 at a time when Britain's status as a world power was still intact. But by 1954 the title had been altered to the British Empire and Commonwealth Games to reflect, less the decline in status of Britain, but rather the rise in status of Canada and Australia. By 1970 the process of decolonialisation and Britain's relative economic decline had radically altered the relationship between members of the former Empire and this was reflected in the new title of the British Commonwealth Games. Finally, by 1978 pressure from member states to give greater public recognition of their independent status resulted in the word 'British' being dropped from the title of the four-yearly Games.

Apart from charting the evolution of Britain's relationship with members of its former Empire the changes in the title of the Games also reflect the capacity of the Commonwealth itself to adapt to the changes in the pattern of international relations in the twentieth century. The quadrennial Commonwealth Games are one of the most visible symbols of the most enduring international governmental organisation apart from the United Nations.

The Commonwealth

According to Groom and Taylor the Commonwealth 'is a voluntary association of those states which have experienced some form of British rule who wish to work together to further their individual and common interests' (1984: 7). In the early 1990s 51 states were members of the Commonwealth with Pakistan (rejoined in 1989) and Namibia (1990) being the most recent additions. The evolution of Empire into Commonwealth is due in large part to Prime Minister Nehru who, rather than take the newly independent India out of the Commonwealth, chose to remain within the organisation as an independent republic. Thus instead of the Commonwealth possibly contracting to become a largely white Anglo-Saxon club each phase of decolonialisation brought new independent members.

The present form of the Commonwealth dates from the early 1970s when an independent Secretariat was established. The Secretariat was created at a time of great strain within the organisation resulting partly from the conflict between Britain and the African and Asian members over South Africa, but also from Britain's recent membership of the European Community. More specifically, by the 1960s the idea of Commonwealth defence was long forgotten while the notion of Commonwealth economic preference was fast losing its significance. Of particular importance was the wish among the newly independent Commonwealth members to cast off any remnants of subordinate status. As Doxey observed, 'For the Commonwealth to remain relevant to them it had to satisfy national pride as well as national need; to reinforce sovereignty and be seen to do so' (1984: 18).

The effect of the establishment of the Secretariat was to weaken the formal Anglo-centricity of the organisation and to facilitate the emergence of non-British political figures within the Commonwealth. The Secretariat took over all the functions previously fulfilled by British civil servants, with the primary function being to service the meetings of Commonwealth Heads of Government (CHOG) which take place every two years, but also to co-ordinate the work of the wide range of international non-governmental organisations working within the Commonwealth (Jones 1991). Well over one hundred organisations, official and unofficial, are associated with the Commonwealth covering development cooperation, culture, education, information and media, youth, and sport. As this list suggests the focus of the Commonwealth is not on the major dimensions of international relations such as trade and defence, but rather on culture, education and information. While at the formal CHOG level Anglo-centricity is low, it is much more apparent at the INGO level. This may be illustrated with reference to the Commonwealth Foundation, formed in 1965 to facilitate interchanges between professional bodies within the Commonwealth, where the majority of the constituent organisations have a London base with the rest located largely in countries of the 'white' Commonwealth (Chadwick 1982).

The contemporary Commonwealth is founded upon a mix of value consensus and pragmatic diplomacy, supported by a common language, a broadly similar set of administrative and, frequently, legal processes, and a sense of common identity. The last factor is described by Groom as a 'distant cousin syndrome' which results in a predisposition for cooperation (Groom 1988: 185). In 1971 at the Singapore CHOG meeting the Declaration of Commonwealth Principles was adopted. The Declaration expressed support for the United Nations, a belief 'in the liberty of the individual, in equal rights for all citizens regardless of race, colour, creed or political belief, and in their inalienable right to participate by means of free and democratic political processes in framing the society in which they live', a policy of non-discussion of members' internal affairs without their agreement, and a method of operation based on consultation and cooperation (Commonwealth Secretariat 1987: 156–7). Decision-making is therefore generally limited to the making of recommendations and the avoidance of attempts at coercion.

This mix of basic values and operational guidelines is reinforced by many members who recognise the diplomatic opportunities that membership of the Commonwealth provides. The Commonwealth has survived some turbulent periods, most notably in 1971 over the British decision to sell arms to South Africa and in the 1980s over Britain's reluctance to pursue a stronger sanctions policy towards South Africa. Despite the tensions that were clearly evident in the Commonwealth it has survived and even at the most difficult times the transnational activity of the NGOs has remained largely undisturbed. Part of the explanation of the durability of the organisation lies in its value to many of its members. One feature of the Commonwealth is the number of very small states that are members. Of the 55 'states' in the world with a population of less than one million 20 have a connection with the Commonwealth, indeed 30 members of the Commonwealth have a population of less than three million (World Bank 1990; Julien 1992). It provides access to a world stage for those states that would otherwise have little chance of making their views known in other forums such as the United Nations. It also provides small states with a supportive environment in which to try out ideas and policy proposals. Julien notes that those states that have attempted to operate within other transnational organisations such as the Organisation of American States and the Group of 77 have found the experience uncomfortable (1992: 48). Even the larger states, such as many in Africa, despite comprising almost one-third of the UN membership find influence on global decision-making difficult to achieve. This is particularly the case following the decline of apartheid as a major issue at the UN. The UN Special Committee on Apartheid gave African states a prominent voice within the General Assembly but one which is weakening rapidly. In addition to the marginalisation of the Third World in the UN resulting from the easing of tension over apartheid there is also the decline in Third World influence resulting from the ending of the Cold War, which has reduced the capacity of Third World states to use their strategic location to play one superpower against another (Aluko 1991). As a result of this decline in leverage it is likely that the Commonwealth will become a more significant point of access to the major forums of world politics.

Yet the Commonwealth is also of value to medium powers such as Australia and Canada. Although Canada in particular sees the UN, OECD and NATO as the major forums through which to pursue its policy objectives the Commonwealth provides a useful addition. As Delvoie notes the 'Commonwealth is not at the centre of Canadian foreign policy concerns [nor is it] an instrument of the first importance in pursuit of its major and enduring foreign policy objectives' (1989: 140). However, the Commonwealth is of use in defining Canada's international personality and differentiating it from the USA. It is also of value in the pursuit of specific policy objectives such as the isolation of South Africa. Finally, the Commonwealth provides Canada with a basis for implementing its development policy towards the Third World (Delvoie 1989: 140–2). Indeed one of the major strengths of the Commonwealth is its acceptability as a link between North and South (Groom 1988: 186).

Attempting to assess the significance of the Commonwealth as an element in the international system, either as an independent actor or as a conduit for its members, is not easy. Its impact on major global issues such as security, trade and the environment is modest, though on the latter issue the Secretariat is hopeful that the Commonwealth can play a more prominent role (Bourne 1992). Yet it extends the reach of the international system into corners of the globe that the major international organisations often miss and it can claim to have influenced the outcome on some important problems. According to Groom the Commonwealth 'has been successful in easing some of the problems in NIEO (New International Economic Order), in the ACP–EC relationship and in individual cases such as the negotiations between Papua New Guinea and Rio

Tinto Zinc' (1988:187). Akinrinade adds to this list the significant part played by the Commonwealth in promoting democracy among its members, for example through the monitoring of elections and in the devising of constitutions for newly independent states. The Commonwealth has also been active in facilitating decolonialisation, both for members and for non-members. The Commonwealth Secretariat played an important part in the negotiations between Portugal and Frelimo over the independence of Mozambique (Akinrinade 1992). Perhaps the most significant contribution of the Commonwealth was in pushing the British government to adopt and retain a policy of firm opposition to the rebel regime in Rhodesia and in moderating Britain's willingness to support South Africa.[1]

In summary, the Commonwealth is not a first-order international organisation, it is clearly overshadowed by the UN, NATO and OECD. It is not just that the Commonwealth lacks the same prestigious superpower membership, it also lacks the degree of functional specialism as the Singapore Declaration of Commonwealth Principles is a long way from being a policy agenda. Yet the Commonwealth clearly has found a valuable niche in the international system. The niche can be defined both in terms of membership and also in terms of issues or, at least, approach to issues. The general stability of membership and its shared history, the high proportion of small states, and the geographical spread provide it with a distinctive character. The mode of debate within the Commonwealth, the non-interventionist assumptions and the organisational emphasis on issues relating to culture, information and human rights also add to its distinctive qualities.

However, in order for an international organisation such as the Commonwealth to survive it must convince its members of its value and also demonstrate its vitality to the outside world. The key to meeting both these requirements is the achievement of policy objectives, but the maintenance of a high level of international visibility is also important. As will be shown the Commonwealth Games have an important contribution to make to both the achievement of policy objectives and the promotion of the institution's image.

The Commonwealth Games

The idea for a four-yearly sports festival for the countries of the Empire was first suggested in 1891. Initially there was some debate about whether

America should participate on the basis of its Anglo-Saxon heritage but the idea was soon dropped in favour of limiting eligibility to the (implicitly white and 'well-born') subjects of the Queen and Empress (Moore 1986). A limited 'Inter-Empire Championships' was held in 1911, but it was not until 1930 that the first British Empire Games were held in Hamilton, Canada. Some 400 competitors took part from eleven countries. The purpose of the Games is summed up in the following, often quoted, passage.

> It will be designed on the Olympic model, both in general construction and the stern definition of amateur. But the Games will be very different, free from both the excessive stimulus and babel of the international stadium. They should be merrier and less stern, and will substitute the stimulus of a novel adventure for the pressure of international rivalry. (quoted in Commonwealth Games Federation 1987)

Although this statement seems anachronistic now in the light of the compromises on professionalism and commercialism it reflects the mix of idealism, social snobbery and Anglo-centricity that characterised the early Games.

In 1932 the British Empire Games Federation was formed to oversee the organisation of future events and to promote sport throughout the Empire. Its successor, the Commonwealth Games Federation (CGF), until recently had no assets and, apart from a part-time secretary, no permanent staff. It relied on voluntary effort and goodwill to survive. The role of the Federation is to promote and organise the four-yearly Games, to establish rules and regulations for the conduct of the Games, and to encourage amateur sport throughout the Commonwealth. The Games have generally followed the model of the Olympic Games, particularly in terms of the commitment to amateurism and the explicit stand against all forms of discrimination. But the Games differ from the Olympics in a number of important ways, most obviously in their explicit political foundation, but also in the way in which the event is organised, for example in the exclusion of team sports. In addition, the Commonwealth Games were, until recently, limited to only ten sports, of which two must be athletics and swimming, with the other eight selected by the country hosting the Games from a list of approved sports established by the CGF. Thus over the years fencing and rowing have both ceased to be regularly included in the programme and have been replaced by sports such as shooting, weightlifting and gymnastics. For a new sport to be added to the list of approved sports it must be played in a wide range of countries, have only one international federation (IF), not be solely a team game, not be unduly costly, and not rely on mechanical means. Tennis, table tennis and judo are the most recent sports to be accepted on to the approved list and, as an exception to the ban on team games and because of its popularity within the Commonwealth, netball has been approved for inclusion for 1998.

Achieving the status of an approved sport is often the result of considerable lobbying by international sports federations seeking participation in the Games, even if some see Commonwealth acceptance as primarily a stepping-stone to Olympic eligibility. Karate, handball and triathlon have all attempted to emulate netball's recent success and gain acceptance. There is also increasing pressure on the CGF to admit popular team games such as cricket, volleyball and basketball, and also to allow competitions, particularly single-event championships and regional competitions, outside the Games themselves but under the aegis of the CGF.

The decision-making forum of the CGF is the annual General Assembly at which each member country has one vote (in contrast to the weighted voting system of the IOC). The main responsibility of the General Assembly is to select the venue for the next Games. Most other matters are delegated to an Executive Committee comprising vice-presidents of the Regions (continental groupings) and the officers of the Federation. The main source of income for the CGF is from the country hosting the next Games and, for the 1994 Games, amounts to four annual payments of £100,000, although this figure is set to increase to £250,000 for the 1998 Games. To run a major international multi-sport competition with such a fragile financial base is a tribute to the considerable amount of voluntary effort provided. Unfortunately, the financial weakness of the CGF, by contrast to the IOC which has built up a reserve fund of over $72m, is causing some serious problems. For example, on the question of drug testing, the CGF can only ensure limited consistency of procedure from one Games to the next because it is dependent on the host country to finance and provide testing facilities.

An assessment of the significance of the Commonwealth Games in the pattern of international relations can be approached in a number of ways: first in terms of its importance to the Commonwealth, second in terms of its value as a vehicle for the diplomatic ambitions of individual Commonwealth members, and third in terms of the relationship between Commonwealth sports bodies and other international NGOs in sport such as the IOC and the major IFs. Two issues provide an opportunity to explore the political role of the Games: the first is the policy towards South Africa and the second concerns the current debate about the future of the Games.

South Africa

The policy of apartheid in South Africa dominated the Commonwealth Games (and the Commonwealth), as it did the Olympic Games, for much of the 1970s and 1980s.[2] Although apartheid was a clear source of tension within the Commonwealth it was also the issue which helped to define the principles upon which the organisation was based. Given the nature and style of the biennial CHOG meetings where votes were normally avoided, direct criticism of domestic policy of members was rare, and a preference for the maintenance of consensus existed, the opportunities for resolving an issue where there was such a conflict of views were limited. Although this broad consensus broke down partially during the mid-1980s, when Britain's isolation was made clear, the conflict over South Africa was largely displaced to the Commonwealth Games where more aggressive actions, such as boycotts, could be taken without jeopardising participation in the main forum, the CHOG meetings.

The internal politics of South Africa has been a prominent, and often a dominant, issue in the Commonwealth for thirty years from 1961 when South Africa withdrew from the organisation. During that period the black African states sought to isolate South Africa through the application of a comprehensive range of sanctions. Sport was a particularly important focus for the campaign partly because of its high public visibility and low cost to relatively poor states, and partly because of the important cultural significance of sport in the republic and also because the major sports (cricket and rugby union) and sporting partners of South Africa were limited in number and the latter were members of the Commonwealth. It should be noted that neither cricket nor rugby were Olympic sports and therefore the Commonwealth could not rely on immediate support from the IOC for its actions. In addition, both sports were among the more commercially successful and therefore were less dependent on government subsidy. Although the issue of apartheid was present as a background to much Commonwealth activity during this period there were a number of occasions when the issue surfaced and dominated the organisation's agenda.

Three such occasions amply illustrate the interplay between sport and politics in the Commonwealth, namely the formulation of the 1977 Gleneagles Agreement, the threatened boycott of the 1978 Edmonton Games, and the boycott of the 1986 Edinburgh Games. As mentioned in Chapter 5 the 1976 Olympic Games were disrupted by a boycott by thirty states because of the refusal of the IOC to withdraw its invitation to New Zealand. The cause of the boycott was the decision by the New Zealand rugby union authorities to send a side to tour South Africa and the clear expression of support given to the proposal by Prime Minister Muldoon. While the black Commonwealth states were incensed at the decision, Canada was also concerned. Canada, although not particularly active on Third World issues in the 1970s, was motivated by a general antipathy to racism, and also by a concern to maintain both the role of the Commonwealth in protecting western interests during the Cold War and Canada's reputation as an international peacebroker (Macintosh and Black 1994). The fact that Canada was scheduled to host the Commonwealth Games in 1978 was an additional factor of considerable importance. However, matters were likely to come to a head sooner as the next CHOG meeting was arranged for 1977 in London. As Payne makes clear, defusing this conflict owed much to the diplomatic skills of the Secretary-General of the Commonwealth, Shridath (Sonny) Ramphal and the style of CHOG meetings. Ramphal encouraged the African members to moderate their criticism of Muldoon while also persuading Australia, New Zealand's closest political ally, to make clearer its support for the African position (Payne 1991). In this way he made Muldoon's isolation clear. In addition, Ramphal was supported in his endeavours by Trudeau who embarked upon a vigorous round of diplomacy among the African states.

The technique for getting Muldoon off the hook and building a stronger Commonwealth anti-apartheid consensus was the production of the Commonwealth Statement on Apartheid in Sport (commonly referred to as the Gleneagles Agreement). The idea for the Agreement came from the British minister Howell with the support of Australia and Canada, but was largely written by Ramphal. Trudeau, who was seen as instrumental along with Ramphal in getting the Agreement accepted, was also important in obtaining the support of the Organisation of African Unity which he lobbied through Canada's Francophone links (Macintosh and Black 1994). The Agreement drew a veil over previous conflicts while establishing a set of expectations regarding members' responses to apartheid which was probably as precise as could be expected from a meeting of over forty heads of state. The document not only saved the Edmonton Games, but also opened the way for the CGF to exclude members who failed to live up to the spirit of the Agreement.[3] Yet the issue rumbled on prompted in part by the decision of the New Zealand rugby union authority to invite the South African Springboks to tour in 1981. Many members of the Commonwealth saw this proposal as a test of commitment to stand by the Gleneagles Agreement. The fact that the tour took place may be seen as a set-back; however, it also provided an opportunity to clarify and strengthen the Agreement.

In 1982 a Code of Conduct applicable to each national association was drafted which set out what would constitute a breach of the Agreement. The Code gave the Federation new powers to exclude a country which seriously breached the terms of the Agreement (Payne 1991: 425). The Code obtained wide support among African states because it was seen partly as a clarification and strengthening of the Gleneagles Agreement and partly as an important step in redefining the anti-apartheid strategy. Up until the early 1980s the African states and athletes had borne the brunt of the policy of isolating South Africa. Consequently there was a growing view that the boycotts were harming the boycotting states, and especially their athletes, as much as South Africa and that the strategy also limited the opportunity to use sporting contact as a political tool for other purposes.[4]

During the mid-1980s a series of rebel tours took place indicating the difficulty South Africa faced in arranging official tours. With the election of David Lange and a Labour government replacing Muldoon's National Party, New Zealand ceased to be the focus of Commonwealth criticism. However, New Zealand's place was quickly taken by Britain which was sharply criticised for its unwillingness to impose economic sanctions on South Africa. The net effect of the confrontation between Britain and its Commonwealth partners was that 32 states boycotted the 1986 Edinburgh Games. Despite growing scepticism about the wisdom of boycotts the tactic presented the black African states with a 'relatively cost-free way of demonstrating their displeasure with Britain' (Payne 1991: 427), or in other words the costs were borne by their athletes and not their merchants. Despite the attendance of three African states the remaining participants gave the Edinburgh Games the look of an 'old' Commonwealth club meeting. From 1986 the issue of apartheid began to decline, initially because of the lack of any government-supported challenge to Gleneagles, and later due to the programme of reform ushered in by De Klerk towards the end of the decade.

The future of the Commonwealth Games

By the end of the 1980s South Africa as a political issue for Commonwealth sport was moving down the international agenda. For the Commonwealth as a whole this was both a welcome relief and also a cause of concern. It was a relief insofar as it removed the issue that had divided the Commonwealth most sharply and at times had seemed to threatened its long-term survival. But it was a cause of concern because the thirty-year debate over apartheid was the catalyst that had sharpened the Commonwealth's identity and sense of political purpose. The declining significance of apartheid also posed problems for the Commonwealth Games. Not only had the Games been one of the most important arenas for the public display of anti-apartheid policy, but they had also diverted attention from other issues related to the role and organisation of the Games. Among the most important issues were the viability of the Games in an increasingly commercial sports world, the underlying disquiet concerning the traditional location of the Games outside the Third World, the role of the Games in the Commonwealth, and the content of the Games.

Many of these issues surfaced in the late 1980s when the Commonwealth undertook a review of the Games on the initiative of the Canadian External Affairs Secretary, Joe Clarke. The immediate context of the Canadian proposal for a review of the Games lay in the recent decision to award the 1994 Games to the city of Victoria in Canada. Since the first Games were held in Hamilton, Canada in 1930 they have only once moved out of the 'white' core of the Commonwealth when they were held in Kingston, Jamaica in 1966. Even New Zealand with its small population has hosted the Games on three occasions, most recently in 1990. In 1986, when Auckland was chosen as the host for the 1990 Games, there was a widespread assumption that the next hosts would come from a Third World country. New Delhi, India was seen as the most likely contender. Yet when the CGFs General Assembly met in Seoul it chose Victoria in preference to New Delhi and Cardiff, Wales. Although Victoria's success was based on the votes of many Third World delegates it was also due to the adoption of a style of campaigning for votes that was associated more with the Olympics than the Commonwealth Games. There were strong allegations that Victoria had, on the one hand, bought the Games with promises of financial assistance for teams from poorer countries and promotional visits by delegates to Canada, and on the other scared delegates away from casting their vote for New Delhi with rumours of poor sanitation and health risks. New Delhi's case was strong.

It already had most of the necessary facilities in place and had recently hosted the far larger and more complex Asian Games. However, New Delhi lost decisively on the first ballot, not because of the votes of the 'old' Commonwealth but because the smaller Caribbean and Pacific members voted for the Canadian city.

The Federation's decision to select Victoria represented the immediate political context but it is also important not to lose sight of the wider commercial context. The need for the Games to confront the growing commercialism of sport was recognised in the mid-1980s. The success of the Los Angeles Olympic Games in 1984 in attracting commercial sponsorship and making a profit was an important catalyst, but of greater importance was the trend towards professionalism among athletes. The route taken by tennis and golf in abandoning amateurism for their elite sportsmen and women was now being followed by track and field. While the track and field elite have not gone as far as golf and tennis in exerting 'player power' it was clear by the mid-1980s that the assumption that athletes would meekly follow the instructions of their governing bodies was under threat. Part of the source of change lay in the rapid growth in the sponsored grand prix circuit in athletics and the trend for IFs to organise their own world championships. The Commonwealth Games were therefore under pressure through the growing concern among athletes for prize money and the increasingly crowded calendar of competitions.

It was against this background that Canada launched its proposal to review the Games. The Clarke proposals stressed the symbolic importance of the Games for the Commonwealth and also the need to involve as many members as possible in hosting and taking part in the Games (Secretary of State for External Affairs 1989). The document addressed a set of interrelated issues: the administrative capacity of the CGF, the sports development needs of poorer members, and the provision of financial support to Third World hosts. As regards the CGF the document included proposals to provide financial assistance via a Commonwealth Sport Trust and also through the adoption of modern marketing techniques by the Federation along the lines of the Olympic movement. The document also suggested that the CGF might be relocated away from London, possibly to Jamaica. In proposing aid to developing countries Clarke gave a high priority to the provision of travel support for teams, through a Travel Stabilisation Fund. However, this would only be one part of a much wider programme of sports development assistance. As regards hosting future Games the document stressed the economic and sporting opportunities that hosting the Games presented to a country.

Clarke also emphasised the importance of the 1998 Games being awarded to a developing country, but recognised the need to provide financial and administrative support to many prospective hosts.

The Clarke document was discussed at the CHOG meeting in Kuala Lumpur in 1989 when the Heads of Government noted the significance of the Games as 'a highly visible and important symbol of Commonwealth unity', and agreed to the formation of a working party, under the chairmanship of Roy McMurtry, to consider its suggestions (Commonwealth Secretariat 1989: 43). The preliminary report of the working party provided an analysis of the problems facing the Commonwealth. Acknowledging the role of sport in nation-building the report stressed its similar role in the Commonwealth. It saw sport and the Games reflecting the 'core values [of the Commonwealth] of non-racialism, equality and fair play', and identified sport as ranking with other primary Commonwealth links such as language and law. It also highlighted the fact that sport is particularly attractive to the young and that almost two-thirds of the Commonwealth's population of 1.6 billion is under 16 years of age. Finally the report recognised that sport might provide a counterweight to factors weakening the Commonwealth.

> With some Commonwealth countries experiencing significant levels of immigration from non-Commonwealth countries, the traditional Commonwealth bonds are, to an extent, being weakened. These changes in patterns of immigration are matched by diminishing economic ties and the emergence of regional economic blocs. In our view, sport is a powerful antidote for these erosive influences on the Commonwealth association. (McMurtry 1990: 5)

The proposals aired in the report focused on the need to strengthen the Federation, particularly the need to provide a secure source of finance. The report, while noting the difficulty in making the Games self-funding along the lines of the Olympics, clearly saw this as a priority. Thus the marketing of a Commonwealth logo was suggested along with the minting of commemorative coins and the development of sponsorship deals. The report also highlighted the question of the range of eligible sports.

The final report followed closely the issues identified in the preliminary report and made sixteen recommendations covering a broad range of topics including suggestions for putting the financing and organisation of the CGF on a firmer footing, the establishment of a sports development programme, and alterations to the content of the Games. The basis of the final report's recommendations was an acknowledgement of the importance of the Games as a reinforcement and visible expression of the core values of the Commonwealth.

> Sport imparts values and principles which help form a foundation for broader Commonwealth understanding – principles such as: the equality and dignity of the individual; non-discrimination on the basis of race, sex, colour, creed, economic status or political belief; fair play. (Commonwealth Secretariat 1991a: 2)

In terms of the content of the Games the final report noted the dominance within the programme of western European sports and argued that it was important that the Games reflected the sports most widely played in the Commonwealth. Yet the most popular sports according to the report are team sports such as soccer, netball, basketball, volleyball, cricket, hockey and rugby, most of which have their origins in western Europe or North America. The report received a warm reception from the 1991 CHOG meeting in Harare, Zimbabwe. The communiqué welcomed the report and the sports development initiatives and referred to the Games as the cornerstone of the Commonwealth. The meeting decided to establish an *ad hoc* committee, chaired by McMurtry, to meet biennially and continue the working party's activities over the coming four years.

The successful implementation of the recommendations included in the final report is by no means a foregone conclusion. To date progress has been mixed. There have been changes in the funding of the CGF which will put it on a much more secure footing, but there has been little progress in the crucial area of sports development beyond the preparation of a distance learning pack for athletes and administrators. Much depends on the willingness of governments, in a time of deep recession, to allocate finance to support the expanded role of the CGF. Many of the suggestions regarding the streamlining of the organisation of the Games and the sports content depend crucially on the success of the 1998 Games to be hosted by Kuala Lumpur. If the choice of Kuala Lumpur proves, like Kingston in 1966, to be an exception rather than a break with tradition, the prospects for implementation of the rest of the McMurtry recommendations will substantially diminish.

Conclusion

Assessing the significance of sport, and particularly the Games, to the politics of the Commonwealth is understandably difficult. In such a complex pattern of international relations as surround issues such as apartheid it is not possible to make definite statements about cause and effect. However, while acknowledging the importance of this caveat, a number of observations can be offered. As regards the importance of the Games to the institution of the Commonwealth it is clear that the Games provided an arena where individual members felt that they were able to employ a broader range of policy positions. The restraining protocols of the CHOG meetings were absent from involvement in the Games and members could adopt more radical stances without undermining their participation in CHOG meetings. Thus the Games provide a useful political resource both as an additional medium for policy communication, but more importantly as a safety valve for political positions that the CHOG meetings might not be able to accommodate.

Yet this level of analysis deals only with the rather superficial pattern of behaviour of members, not the fabric of values, attitudes and expectations that underpin diplomatic activity. For J. Wilson the Commonwealth Games, like the Olympic Games, 'began to serve as a public reinforcement of the myths of Western civilisation's superiority over colonial peoples' (1988: 156). In a similar vein Stoddart argues that 'As the formal, political ties with the imperial power have declined, the informal cultural ones have been strengthened to maintain a strong power relationship and a particular vision of social order' (1986: 125). There is much force and substance in both these evaluations and they need to be explored before the richness of the political significance of sport in the Commonwealth can be fully appreciated.

Wilson is correct in his analysis of the racial politics of the Games, but the impact of the Commonwealth Games is not to highlight the cultural gap between western and colonial peoples; rather it serves to exemplify and, to an extent, set the terms of admission to the modern, developed world. Those terms are not just the commitment to liberal democracy and market economics but also the acceptance of rational bureaucratic organisation as a basis of social and sporting order. A similar amplification may be made of Stoddart's analysis. He identifies the dominant relationship within the Commonwealth as being between Britain and her former colonies, with the 'old' Commonwealth states forming a set of close allies. Even in 1986 this underestimated the degree of change in the power relations within the Commonwealth. Not only had British power and centrality seriously declined but other potential focal states had grown in stature, for example Canada, Australia and India. More importantly the content of the cultural message of the Games had changed from one of replicating imperial power to one concerned with wider economic and political values dominant in Britain and North America during the Thatcher and Reagan years in the 1980s. The Commonwealth is culturally significant, but less as a means of retaining imperial domination and more as a means of economic and political assimilation.

In this sense the Games provide highly visible evidence of the presence of the Commonwealth and, according to the McMurtry Report, provide a graphic illustration of the core values of the organisation. Here the Commonwealth faces a dilemma. The liberal democratic values of equality, fair play and non-discrimination quoted above are being augmented by the liberal market values of sponsorship, marketing and commercialisation. Yet this development is consistent with trends in the broader Commonwealth. In the Harare Declaration the promotion of sustainable development and the alleviation of poverty are to be achieved through a combination of economic stability and a recognition of the central role of the market economy (Commonwealth Secretariat 1991b: 6). The attraction of a market economy approach to the Games is also reflected in the discussions over the choice of sports for inclusion. The proposal to include a limited number of team games is justified partly on the basis of their popularity within the Commonwealth but also because sports such as limited-over cricket would 'attract a huge world-wide television audience' (Commonwealth Secretariat 1991a: 7).

However, commercial opportunities are not the only motive for reconsidering the range of eligible sports. The McMurtry Report makes clear its concern to include popularity throughout the Commonwealth as an important criterion for eligibility. But at the very least there is a tension here between commercial attraction and Commonwealth popularity. It will be interesting to see how the Federation balances the highly televisual and marketable cricket, rugby and basketball against hockey and volleyball, which are arguably popular with a greater number of Commonwealth countries. It has been suggested that New Delhi's inclusion of three racket sports in its bid for the 1994 Games lost it votes in the Caribbean where sport is more strongly influenced by western culture (Ingham 1988). Breaking the tradition of Commonwealth Games based predominantly on European sports is difficult enough, but will be especially so if commercial considerations become more important.

The Games also fulfil a function in terms of their value as a vehicle for the political ambitions of individual, or groups of, members. Collectively, the African members were able to pursue a policy objective towards South Africa within a forum where their impact was likely to be greater and where the sports politics agenda was not crowded with other issues. It is interesting to contrast the controversy within the Olympic movement prior to the 1976 Montreal Games with that surrounding the 1978 Edmonton Commonwealth Games. In 1976 the issue of apartheid was marginalised due to the controversy over the 'two Chinas' issue and Canada's refusal to accept the Taiwanese team as representatives of the Republic of China. Even though thirty states, many of them Commonwealth members, boycotted the Games the impact on the international debate on apartheid was weak. The Commonwealth Games, by contrast, have not been an arena for east–west tension, nor a focus for battles over diplomatic recognition, and consequently provided a clearer agenda for organising opposition to apartheid.

It is not just the African, and to a lesser extent the Caribbean, states that have used the Games to further political ambitions. Canada has clearly seen apartheid and the Games as political opportunities. According to Macintosh and Black (1994) the Gleneagles Agreement was a crucial foundation for Canada's ambitions to adopt a leadership role in the Commonwealth as well as enhancing its influence in the United Nations on the issue of apartheid. From 1984 Mulroney, building upon Trudeau's efforts, adopted a much more interventionist foreign policy than his predecessor. The motivation of the Mulroney government for involvement in this issue lay in the perception of a broad strategic interest in achieving a peaceful transition in South Africa, and a culture within the new government that gave a high priority to human rights issues (Wood 1990: 284–6). Saul (1988, quoted in Macintosh and Black 1994) argues that part of the motivation for Mulroney's opposition to apartheid was the view that apartheid's abolition was necessary if South Africa was to be saved for capitalism. Canada also saw apartheid and the Commonwealth as an issue and forum where it could adopt a leading role and move out from the shadow of both the USA and Britain. Canada's choice of sport and apartheid as issues on which to build their diplomatic influence was shrewd as, unlike Britain, New Zealand and Australia, neither cricket nor rugby were major domestic sports. Thus an aggressive sports foreign policy could be pursued without arousing internal opposition and without running the risk of being embarrassed by Canadian sportsmen and sportswomen breaking ranks.

The third area where the significance of the Games can be assessed is in terms of the relationship between the Commonwealth Games organisations and those of the Olympics and the major IFs. In general, the relationship between the CGF and other major sports organisations is weak primarily due to suspicion of organisations that are closely linked to political organisations. This suspicion was given substance by the production of the Gleneagles Agreement which, as Coghlan observed, 'presented [sports bodies] with a fait accompli [which] has been resented ever since' (1990: 142). While the issue of apartheid might be fading, an emerging tension relates to the problems of fitting the Commonwealth Games into an increasingly crowded and commercially based sports calendar. This is potentially a serious problem for track and field sports in particular.

Among the few areas where there has been cooperation, doping is the most significant. However, this has been limited on the part of the CGF to the adoption of the IOC list of banned substances and practices. As noted earlier the effectiveness of drug testing at each Games depends primarily on the resources of the host state. The one area where cooperation is most promising concerns sport development. The Commonwealth is clearly keen to support the development of elite and grass-roots sports in poorer states, and while few Commonwealth initiatives exist to date it is clear that Olympic Solidarity and the IAAF would welcome any addition to the resources devoted to sports development activity. The advantage that the CGF possesses over the Olympic movement is its contacts with states, for example the smaller islands in the Caribbean and Oceania, that are members of the CGF but are not members of the IOC.

While the membership of the CGF helps to extend the global reach of organised sport it also provides a voice for smaller nations to raise issues with major sports INGOs, particularly over issues of sports development and travel costs for major competitions. However, it is not only the small states that see the CGF as a useful point of access to the international sports community. Britain, which has gradually lost its leading role in world sports administration, values the CGF as one of the few remaining international sport bodies which retains a strong British influence. As a result the British International Sports Committee, which has a broad concern to enhance the influence of Britain in international sport, sees the CGF as an important focus for its activities. The payment of a grant by the Sports Council to the CGF from 1990 and the provision of accommodation from 1992 are seen as prudent investments.

Finally, it is important to form some assessment of the impact of Commonwealth membership on the behaviour of the member states. It is clear that the Commonwealth was able to exert some collective influence over New Zealand's policy of support for sporting contact with South Africa. New Zealand has few diplomatic contacts with Third World states and this self-imposed diplomatic isolation is compounded by its geographical isolation and narrow range of trade relations. The Commonwealth was one of the few forums where Muldoon was exposed to a broader range of world opinion. While bringing New Zealand into line with Commonwealth policy was a considerable achievement the Commonwealth also affected the strategy adopted by the African states. Given that the organisation has little practical involvement in matters of defence or trade the dispute over apartheid was able to be funnelled into the relatively harmless policy area of sport. Commonwealth debates on apartheid were in effect a diplomatic cul-de-sac rather than a springboard for firmer, more aggressive action. The character of the Gleneagles Agreement is ample proof of this. The Agreement undermined any intention that the African states had of pursuing, more rigorously, their challenge to New Zealand's policy. In Payne's words the Commonwealth was effective in urging them 'not to demand too much of New Zealand' (1991: 419).

The current significance of the Commonwealth Games, either to the future of the Commonwealth as an institution or to the majority of participants, is not in doubt. It is perhaps fitting that the CGF is currently discussing with sports officials of the former Soviet Union the possibility of a sports event in May 1995 which will involve both the Commonwealth and the states of the former USSR. If the event takes place it will bring together the two sets of states which have used sport as an explicit vehicle for promoting their respective political ideologies. However, the Soviet Spartakiade sports festivals and the ideology that went with them have disappeared while the Commonwealth has adapted to change with a considerable degree of success and the CGF is looking forward to the next century.

Notes

1 There is an interesting argument that the controversy over South Africa and the friction between Britain and the majority in the Commonwealth was important in sharpening the focus of the organisation and providing it with a clearer sense of purpose. Thus rather than being a threat to its future apartheid was an important catalyst in defining the modern Commonwealth (Austin 1988; Akinrinade 1992; Chan 1988).

2 Although the issue of apartheid in sport came to a head in the 1970s it had had an impact on the Commonwealth much earlier when the 1934 Games, scheduled for

South Africa, were moved to London because of concern with the former's racial policies.

3 Due to some perceived 'backsliding' by Muldoon Nigeria did not send a team to Edmonton, but it was the only state to withdraw.

4 Guttmann (1992: 141) gives an interesting illustration of the personal consequences associated with the persistent use of the boycott. Youssef Assad, an Egyptian shot-putter, did not participate in the 1972 Olympic Games due to his country's desire to show solidarity with the Palestinian cause; he missed the 1976 Games because of the boycott in protest against New Zealand; and he missed the 1980 Games because his government chose to boycott as a protest against the Soviet invasion of Afghanistan.

7

Business and sport

As with the relationship between sport and politics that between sport and business is surrounded by more rhetoric and assertion than analysis. Yet while there has always been a connection between sport and business it is in the last forty years that it has helped to transform sport from a largely parochial and temporally distant event or events to a global and immediate spectacle. The source of this transformation has been television. Sport is now not only a business, and a major source of profit, in its own right, but also an important element in the business strategies of multi-national corporations whose products and services have little or no relation to sport. While there is a long history of athletes making a living from their sport and others making a living from organising sports events it is only comparatively recently that businesses not directly associated with sport have begun to see sport as an ingredient in profitability.

The attempt by the British, in the late nineteenth and twentieth centuries, to define sport as an amateur activity resulted in a long period of conflict in sport, leaving many rifts that have hardened into lasting divisions. Yet there were always challenges to amateurism, and particularly the social elitism that gave it its logic. During the 1880s rugby and soccer were emerging as substantial spectator sports and were soon professionalised – rugby through an acrimonious split which resulted in the development of two distinct games, rugby union and rugby league, and soccer without any significant split though only with the adoption of almost feudal controls over the freedom of players. Other sports slowly followed this lead, with tennis accepting professional players from the late 1960s and track and field from the early 1980s. Today, in Britain as in the rest of the world, there is a general acceptance that it is legitimate to aspire to make a living from one's sport and also the desire to make a profit out of organising sport is recognised, if not yet readily approved.

By the 1920s, on both sides of the Atlantic, sport was fast becoming a major spectator attraction. The soccer Cup Final of 1923 was watched by 200,000 while in the USA boxing was attracting audiences of over 100,000 (Cashmore 1990). The widespread ownership of radios, by the 1930s, made the business sponsorship of sports broadcasts increasingly attractive for product marketing. Ford and Gillette in the United States and brewers, such as Whitbread, in Britain, though slightly later, were among the first to recognise the potential of sponsoring sports events. The advent of mass television ownership in the 1950s further tightened the link between sport and business. Today sport and business are closely interlocked and their relationship raises a number of important questions related to sport's significance in world politics. Of particular importance is the effect that the increasing commercialisation is having on the role of sport in international relations. If commercial patronage is challenging political patronage, is there evidence that the malleability of sport as a foreign policy tool is lessening? A related question concerns the values or characteristics of sport that are especially attractive to commerce. Third, as sport has expanded internationally and become more commercial, how have the character and role of the international federations and international organising bodies, such as the International Olympic Committee (IOC) and Commonwealth Games Federation (CGF), altered? In particular, are they altering their character so as to share more of the traits of multi-national corporations? Following a brief examination of the major elements of the current debate on the role and significance of multinational corporations the rest of this chapter will seek answers to these questions through an examination of the role of the media and business in cultivating a global audience for sport and their capacity to influence the development of major sports.

Sport and multi-national corporations

Multi-national corporations (MNCs) are typified by a corporate headquarters located in a First World state, ownership concentrated in First World states, manufacturing or service production dispersed among a number of states, often in the Third World, and finally, a global market. There are many businesses that have a heavy involvement in international sport and possess many or all of these characteristics. Businesses such as Visa, Kodak, Coca-Cola and McDonald's are major sponsors of sport while media corporations such as News International, ABC and NBC are prominent as both sponsors and broadcasters of sport.

The traditional debates concerning the role of MNCs have tended to focus on manufacturing businesses, though in recent years closer attention has been paid to the significance of media corporations. Understandably research into the impact of MNCs has focused on whether the overall effect on Third World countries is beneficial or harmful to their individual economic growth. Since the early 1970s when the potential significance of MNCs was first examined there has been an increasing concern first, to explore the political side-effects of their presence in Third World countries and second, and more recently, to explore their impact on national or ethnic cultures. In other words the focus of interest has shifted from concern to delineate the forms of exploitation of raw materials and labour as a contribution to the reduction in the costs of production, to a focus on the ways in which social and political support for the exploitative relationship is maintained and the way in which an exploited country can nonetheless be an eager market for the products and services of First World businesses. Part of the explanation for this shift in focus lies in a growing awareness of the links between economic relations and political power at the global level, and partly in an acknowledgement that conceptualising the relationship in terms of exploiter and exploited is a gross oversimplification of a complex multi-layered relationship between countries in the global economy. What Leonard (1980: 456) refers to as the political side-effects that tend to accompany the presence of multi-nationals needs to be expanded to include an appreciation of the cultural side-effects.

As the global economy has expanded so the relationship between MNCs and individual states has become less a pattern of bilateral arrangements and more the incorporation of individual states into a system of international trade and marketing. While the former might be managed by states the latter is less susceptible to the influence of individual states. A state might nationalise a particular industry but will still be dependent upon an international market over which it is likely to have little control. Sport is an integral part of the means of fostering and promoting that system of international trade and marketing.

The debates about the content, process of transmission and impact of global culture are explored in the next chapter. The purpose of this chapter is to examine the degree of interpenetration of sport and international business so as to indicate whether sport has the potential to play a significant part in the process of globalisation.

Sport and the Media

Over the last thirty years sport has emerged as one of the most important ingredients in a television company's scheduling. In Australia in 1966 some 250 hours of sport were broadcast on three channels while by 1986 this figure had increased to just under 1,400 hours over five channels (McKay and Miller 1991: 88). A similar trend is found in Britain where the BBC showed over 1,600 hours of sport on two channels in 1992, almost 20% of its entire output. In any one year the typical proportion of broadcast sport in North America will be 15% (Kennard and Hofstetter 1983). Real (1986) estimated that around two-thirds of adults in developed countries regularly watched the 1984 Olympic Games. The estimated world-wide audience for the 1984 Olympic Games was 2.5bn.

The global interest in major international sporting events is clear but for most countries outside the developed world the view they receive of the Olympics and other major international sporting occasions such as the soccer World Cup and the athletics World Championships is one that has been produced and edited by foreign television companies. Most of Africa, for example, sees a version of the Olympics and the World Cup in which the European Broadcasting Union defines what is worth seeing and knowing (Geraghty *et al.* 1986). Bearing in mind the recent success of African athletes at the Seoul Games and at the World Cup few newspapers have the resources to send correspondents and photographers to cover events. As a result not only is there little coverage of Third World athletes relative to their recent success, but also images of African achievement in sport are chosen by Europeans (Kidane 1987). There is a similar relationship between the US broadcasters and South America where images of South American athletes are processed by their northern neighbour.

Meadow, in one of the few detailed studies of television coverage of the Games, analysed all 166 hours of the ABC broadcast. His conclusions indicate an overwhelming, if not unsurprising, preoccupation with American athletes and preferred American sports. When Americans were not on screen the preferred alternatives were, in Meadow's words, 'favoured allies including Britain, Germany and Japan' (1987: 6–12). Of especial interest is the extent to which Third World athletes are ignored. While the US, Canadian, British, Japanese and West German athletes received 66% of television coverage (of which US received 44.7%), African athletes received just 2.8% and South Americans 2%. As Meadow observed the message that comes across from the ABC coverage is that 'the Olympics are not about international competition, but about competition between America and the world' (1987: 6–12).

In 1960 the European Broadcasting Union which negotiates on behalf of most European television companies agreed to pay $0.67m for the rights to the Rome Games, in 1972 the sum was $1.7m, in 1984 $19m, and in 1992 the total had reached $90m. Although this rate of price inflation is impressive it is dwarfed by the escalation in price paid by US companies where the figure rose from a mere $0.4m in 1960 to $7.5m in 1972, $225m in 1984 and $401m in 1992. In 1992 the estimated total income to the Olympic movement from the sale of television rights was $0.6bn. The expectation of the Atlanta Organising Committee is that TV rights will cost over $500m in the USA alone. While this might be an overestimate it is likely that non-US rights will increase dramatically in value, taking the total value of rights sales beyond that from Barcelona. Of greater significance than the growth of fees for television rights is the effect it has had on the pattern of Olympic income. In 1976 government provided 81% of the revenue to finance the Montreal Games with TV providing just 6% and sponsorship 2% of overall income. However, by 1984 the government's contribution to the summer Games had fallen to 5% and TV rights risen to 42%, with sponsorship accounting for 18% of income (Official Reports 1976 and 1984).

It is only in the last twenty years or so that the Olympic Games have become the subject of serious attention by the world's television companies. The redefinition of the Games from a quirky side-show in a company's main sports broadcasting schedule to its centrepiece took place during the 1960s and early 1970s. Among the factors which were significant was the development of satellite transmission which enabled events to be shown live around the world. Geostationary satellite transmission was available for the Tokyo Games, but the difference in time zones meant that viewing figures in the crucial US east coast advertising market were low.

The second factor was the rise in public interest in both the summer and winter Olympics. In many countries, and particularly the USA, there was a consensus among television companies that there was not a market for multi-sport events and particularly ones that had so many little-known sports, such as modern pentathlon, shooting and luge. Two developments were important in changing this consensus. First, the superimposition of east–west rivalry on the Games and the gradual adoption of Cold War metaphors by the media to crystallise the distinctiveness of the Games. This was aided by the emergence of the East Germans as a major athletic force in their own right in 1972 and the steady improvement in the success of the Soviets during the 1960s. This process was aided by the emergence in the Munich Games of two major media stars, Mark Spitz and Olga Korbut. The American swimmer Spitz, who set four world records, and Korbut, the young Soviet gymnast, were both subject to intense media coverage. From the broadcaster's point of view the stimulation of public interest in personalities from two minority sports helped greatly to generate interest in the whole Olympic programme and was also part of a process of transforming sport into the conventional model of television entertainment 'television brings to sport the values that it seeks in other forms of entertainment – an emphasis on spectacle, star individuals, and swift emotional reactions' (Geraghty *et al.* 1986: 27). The second development which helped to make the Olympic Games a focus of world attention was the terrorist attack by the Palestinian group Black September. As Klatell and Marcus note, 'The 1972 Munich kidnapping and massacre of Israeli athletes turned an otherwise sleepy American awareness of the Games into riveted, near obsessive viewing' (1988: 165).

A third factor which helped to contribute to the increasing importance of the Games to the television media was the more varied viewing profile of the Games. The Olympics seemed to attract a higher proportion of younger, better-educated and female viewers than other sports broadcasts, thus making the Games attractive to a broader range of advertisers (Klatell and Marcus 1988; Geraghty *et al.* 1986).

Having the 1976 Games in Montreal helped to confirm the value of the Olympics as an advertising opportunity. Companies that had bought advertising time during 1972 had benefited greatly from the upsurge in viewing figures. The television companies also began to see the Games as an opportunity, not only to sell advertising slots at high prices, but also to market their own programmes, thereby hoping to increase viewing figures, and charges to advertisers, for the period after the Games. What was also becoming apparent was the malleability of the Olympic imagery. Just as the Nazis, the Soviets and the United States had been able to exploit Olympic symbolism and imagery as props to their ideologies, so advertisers were realising that there were few products that could not be marketed against an Olympic backdrop.

By the early 1980s the Olympics and television were tightly integrated. For the US television companies, covering the Olympics was seen as a key element in their sports broadcasting policy, while the IOC and local Olympic organising committees were beginning to realise the potential gold-mine that television fees represented. The 1980s were therefore a period in which the television companies sought to influence the organisation of the Games so as to protect their financial return and the IOC sought to maximise its TV income. In the relationship between television and the Olympic movement the US companies are the major actors on the media side. Even though their contribution to Olympic TV income has reduced during the 1980s it still accounted for 65% of the total in 1992 (as opposed to 79% in 1984).

The influence of the media has affected the scheduling of events and their timing as well as the length of the Games. The Calgary Games, for which ABC paid just over $300m, are a good example. The Calgary organising committee agreed to extend the Games from twelve to sixteen days thus encompassing three weekends for prime viewing; 50% of events were scheduled for weekends or other prime-time periods; and the quantity of events was increased to include a number of especially televisual demonstration events, such as freestyle skiing and short circuit speed skating. In addition, the ice hockey play-offs were structured so that Canada and USA would play at peak viewing times, and also arranged in such a way that the USA would avoid the more powerful teams in the early rounds. In Seoul many events were scheduled for early morning so as to fit prime-time viewing in the USA (Klatell and Marcus 1988: 173).[1]

To assume that the IOC and the local organising committee are being pushed around by heavyweight business organisations would be wrong. Despite some early disquiet about the demands of the media the Olympic movement (and even the Moscow organising committee) rapidly became willing partners in the commercialisation of the Games. A recent illustration of the IOC's willingness to cooperate was the decision to hold the winter Games, not in the same year as the summer Olympics as in the past, but two years after the summer Games from 1992. The logic behind this change was that it would allow the television companies to spread the cost of the Games more evenly and also increase the fees obtained for the winter Games (Sabljak 1987). As Don Miller, Executive Director of the US Olympic Committee, said, 'I have repeatedly heard the word commercialism as something bad. But commercialism is as much part of the Olympic Games as doves and the Olympic flame' (*Sport International* 20.12.1984).

It is not only the Olympics that have forged an accommodation with television. In the past the main motives for altering the rules of a game were, *inter alia*, to preserve or enhance its boundary with similar sports or to maintain the original rationale or distinctive qualities for the sport

(Kew 1988). However, in recent years there have been many examples of governing bodies altering their rules to make their sport more attractive to TV companies and advertisers. Professional boxing reduced the number of rounds from fifteen to twelve because this pattern fitted more neatly into a one-hour time slot and also allowed time for advertisements. Other sports also adapted: golf moved from medal play to stroke play; tennis introduced the tie-break; and squash altered its scoring system and the 'tin' height (see Whannel 1992: 79–84 and also Greendorfer 1981 for further discussion). As well as changes in rules changes can also take place in the fundamental structure of sports. For example, the increase in the number of 'one-day' cricket matches in Britain and in Australia was largely as a response to pressure from sponsors and the formation of a break-away circuit by Australian television company owner, Kerry Packer (Stewart 1986). From the point of view of the sponsors and the television companies their preference was for a cricket series for television 'but one that could be televised start to finish and that would attract a new cricketing audience by offering a beginning, a middle and an end, but above all a definite result' (Whannel 1992: 80). In addition, one-day cricket could be marketed 'to emphasise aggression, speed and danger, rather than grace, patience and subtlety; a twentieth century gladiatorial sport rather than a leisurely nineteenth century pastime' (Goldlust 1987: 163).

Sponsorship and the Olympics

Sports sponsorship has grown rapidly over recent years. In Britain it has risen from £2.5m in 1971 to £240m in 1991, and in the USA from $900m in 1980 to $2.1bn in 1992. Sponsorship may be of specific events (the brewers Tuborg have paid £0.5m to sponsor the 1993 World Cycling Championships), leagues (the brewers Whitbread paid £2.14m to sponsor the Welsh Rugby League from 1992/3 to 1995/6 and Bass have recently paid £12m to the Football Association for the right to sponsor the soccer Premier League for the next four seasons), teams (the car producer Opel paid £2.2m to advertise on the shirts of soccer club Bayern Munich), or individual athletes (Nick Faldo received £0.33m to wear Pringle sweaters).

Although there are some examples of companies sponsoring sports events that are not televised they are in general rare as the primary attraction for the sponsor is the access that it provides to the television audience. In Britain, as in many countries, tobacco companies figure prominently among the major sponsors of sport, with one of the most significant being Gallaher, the manufacturer of Benson and Hedges cigarettes. According to N. Wilson the guiding principles behind Gallaher's strategy are as follows:

1 Only major activities in sport.
2 Guaranteed national television.
3 Guaranteed national radio and national press.
4 Total name identification.
5 Simplicity of title.
6 Prestige event.
7 No multi-sponsorship.
8 No fragmentation.
9 Events should be cost effective.
10 Right target market. (1988: 161)

Using these guidelines Benson and Hedges have acted as major sponsors for cricket, snooker and golf and have taken a major share of the estimated 400 hours of television exposure that tobacco products receive through sponsorship. As the guidelines also suggest businesses will select the sports they choose to sponsor very carefully. Sports that are not compatible with the company's marketing strategy are either ignored or else abandoned. Wilson recounts how squash was sponsored by Benson and Hedges but later dropped. The explanation is given by the sales promotion manager of B & H: 'It [squash] was a purely physical activity and we were slightly incongruous in it. I always felt I was in the wrong place. You could have a cigarette when playing golf or cricket and even the hockey crowd were a cosmopolitan bunch who enjoyed the odd drink and a cigarette. Squash was more obsessive.' (quoted in N. Wilson 1988: 163). Hockey, which B & H sponsored for six years, was dropped despite its 'cosmopolitan' image because it failed to become a mass appeal (highly televised) sport.

It is not only events that receive sponsorship as many companies will see greater advantage in developing a link with an individual sportsman or sportswoman. However, the same basic ground rules as adopted by Gallaher apply. But as Aris points out, 'To the corporate mind, sporting success is only one ingredient in the marketing mix. Far more important is the star's image and personality' (1990: 41). For Puma, the long-time rival to Adidas, the West German tennis player Boris Becker was the ideal vehicle for their products. Although Puma were reputed to have paid Becker $24m in 1985 to promote their products, their investment was handsomely repaid, doubtless boosted by Becker's Wimbledon victory later that year. In two years Puma's racket sales rose from 15,000 to 300,000, making them one of the best-selling brands in Europe. Deutsche Bank and Coca-Cola have also found the Becker personality a useful marketing tool.

The golfer Nick Faldo is also a highly marketable sportsman; handsome, polite and co-operative. As a result, in 1988, Faldo made an estimated £1.5m in addition to his competition winnings of £0.3m through the promotion of products such as Pringle sweaters, Wilson clubs and Stylo shoes. However, while there are a number of sportsmen and sportswomen whose earnings from sponsorship are spectacular there are many others who are ignored either because they fail to fit the preferred marketing image or because they lose their value. Aris relates the explanation given by an Adidas executive of the difficulty of using Fatima Whitbread to market sports clothes, noting that while she has made a major contribution to women's sport she is not likely to sell sports clothes to women. Britain's other javelin star, Tessa Sanderson, lost a £50,000 sponsorship deal with a US computer company because she was injured at the time of the Seoul Olympics.

The speed at which sports sponsorship has grown even during recessions is remarkable. In Britain, for track and field alone, sponsorship has grown from £300,000 in 1985 to £4m in 1992. In the United States sponsorship has grown at over 10% a year for the last eight years. One area where the growth has been most striking is in relation to the Olympic Games, and it is the Olympic experience which is fast becoming the model for other IFs and for the Commonwealth Games.

Given the unrivalled global attraction of the Olympic Games it is understandable that it has established an extremely successful programme of sponsorship. ISL Marketing is one of the most successful marketing companies in the world and it has been instrumental in developing the sponsorship potential of the major sports events including the soccer World Cup, the IAAF track and field World Championships, and most importantly of all the Olympic Games. In a short period of less than ten years ISL has provided the Olympic movement with a third major source of income to add to the huge fees from television companies and the subsidy from host governments.

The 1980 boycott of the Moscow Games coincided with the election of Samaranch as President. Samaranch was much more willing to explore ways in which the income of the movement could be augmented by sponsorship than his predecessor. The Moscow boycott confirmed his concern at the vulnerability of the Games to government policy changes and, although the sale of TV rights was producing a substantial income, Samaranch was keen to develop sponsorship as a further source of income. However, there were serious difficulties in marketing the Olympics globally. Foremost among them was the fact that the rights to the Olympic five-ring symbol, its most valuable asset, were owned not by the IOC but by each national Olympic committee. Given the tension between the NOCs and the IOC during the 1970s it was a surprise that so many were willing to transfer their rights.

ISL, established by Horst Dassler – the owner of Adidas, one of the largest sports goods manufacturers in the world, was given the contract to market the Olympics in 1985. Despite the problems of buying out the rights to the Olympic logo from over 150 separate NOCs, ISL was very successful largely due to its ability to persuade the NOCs that a considerable amount of additional income could be generated by a concerted, global sale of rights. The marketing vehicle was The Olympic Programme (TOP)[2] which companies could buy into and thereby acquire the right to use the Olympic logo throughout the world up to and including the 1988 Games. The only exceptions were the small number of countries, for example Iraq and Cuba, where the NOC decided to retain their rights. Coca-Cola, Visa, Federal Express and Philips were among the companies to buy into TOP, contributing to the $90m total raised. The second round of TOP which coincided with the Seoul Games is set to raise over $170m from twelve corporate sponsors, with Coca-Cola rumoured to have paid $33m alone. ISL is estimated to take 25% commission with half the remainder being divided between the organising committees of the forthcoming summer and winter Games and the remaining funds going to the IOC and the 167 participating NOCs. In terms of the return on the $10–20m investment by companies they achieve association with an event that projects an image that is deemed complimentary to their product. Elements of that image include youth, high performance, glamour, success, excitement and spectacle. They also know that they are able to use one of the most frequently recognised logos in the world as part of their own global marketing strategy.

The implications for sport are significant for, in return for the income from business, governing bodies and teams need to ensure that they consistently provide the positive advertising backdrop that business requires. Aggression and drama are required but not too much violence; spectacle, excitement and success are required but not if (too overtly) the product of drugs; a gloss of national rivalry is helpful but only so long as it does not interfere with a global marketing strategy.

Sports businesses

The development of the sports goods industry dates from the last quarter of the nineteenth century, paralleling the growth of organised sport. Almost from the outset manufacturers developed close relationships with clubs and leagues as part of their sales strategies. In the United States, for example, early baseball manufacturers competed to have their product adopted as the 'official' ball of a league (Hardy 1990). Moreover, they sponsored leagues at home and promotional tours overseas. AG Spalding, one of the major manufacturers of baseball equipment, sponsored a 'world tour' in the late 1880s by a series of 'all-star' teams which played exhibition games in a wide range of countries including Italy, England, Australia, Ceylon and Egypt (Levine 1985). As Hardy observes sporting goods entrepreneurs were 'hardly content to leave promotional efforts in the hands of liberal theologians and urban reformers' (1990: 86). The involvement of sports businesses in the global promotion of sport has been a constant feature of modern sport. More recently Maguire (1990) has shown how the corporate arm of the US National Football League was closely involved in developing interest in American football in Britain in the 1980s.

The activities of governing bodies, sports manufacturers and colonists not only helped to spread awareness of new western sports, but also served to develop sports that required standardised equipment. Thus the moves by governing bodies to standardise rules were complemented by the manufacturers' desire to standardise equipment. The power of governing bodies to give official approval to equipment gave the manufacturers the protected market they wanted while the governing bodies could be seen to be acting as guardians of the sport.

This mutually beneficial relationship between sport and the sports goods business has persisted from these early days up to the present. A modern illustration was the relationship between the Hummel sports clothing company and the Tottenham Hotspurs soccer team. One of the central reasons for Hummel's sponsorship of Tottenham was the access this afforded to international markets. At the time of the sponsorship the Football League was providing recorded matches for 41 countries with live broadcasts to Scandinavia (N. Wilson 1988). Tottenham was a key element in Hummel's, ultimately unsuccessful, bid to break the hold of Adidas on the market for soccer clothing.

The sports goods business has grown from small nationally based cottage industries of the 1880s to a series of vast global corporations foremost among which is Adidas. Adidas had sales of $2bn in 1991 and although sales declined to $1.7bn in 1992 it still remains a major sports goods manufacturer with world-wide sales. By way of comparison Nike, the world's largest sports goods company, had sales of $3.8bn in the 1992/3 financial year, and Reebok had sales of $3.02bn for the 1992 calendar year. Although Adidas has lost its dominant position in terms of global sales it used its close relationship with the Olympic movement to achieve the market leadership it enjoyed in the 1980s and has used its Olympic links to protect its current position. In the late 1980s it was estimated that Adidas products were worn by about 80% of all athletes competing in the Los Angeles Games. Yet the company's influence was not confined to the Olympics for at the soccer World Cup in Italy fifteen of the twenty-four participating countries were wearing Adidas kit.

Adidas was, until 1987, controlled by Horst Dassler, one of the most influential figures in international sport. According to some reports Dassler systematically developed links with the poorer African and central European states and thus gained access to the decision-making of a number of IFs. The basis of this strategy was, first, the realisation that television was becoming more interested in sport and, second, an assumption that the federations 'would be the ones to decide what the athletes would wear and that if he could control them, everybody out there would be wearing his product' (Simson and Jennings 1992: 31). The provision of cheap or free equipment was the key element in the Adidas strategy. Gaining influence within IFs and the IOC was then used to influence the choice of venue for events, the election of officers, and the development of sports. For example, it is suggested that Dassler used his influence to get Seoul selected as the venue for the 1988 Games in preference to Nagoya in Japan because the former was thought to be more amenable to foreign corporate involvement (Lawrence 1986a: 208).

In addition to sports goods businesses exerting influence over governing bodies there are also examples of non-sports companies seeking to supplant the governing body, as Kerry Packer attempted successfully, or examples of the players supplanting the governing body, as has happened to a great extent in tennis and golf. In 1977 Kerry Packer, the owner of the Channel 9 television company in Australia, announced that he had recruited enough first-class cricket players to enable him to organise an international cricket event as a rival to the Test Match series organised by the International Cricket Conference (ICC), the sport's IF. Packer's proposed World Series Cricket would, not surprisingly, be broadcast on his own Channel 9. During subsequent negotiations with the ICC Packer made it clear that a fundamental requirement for a solution was the granting of exclusive coverage of Australian cricket to Channel 9. The response of the ICC was first to ignore the threat, ban players who had signed up with Packer, and finally to challenge his proposal in the courts. None of these strategies worked; virtually an entire West Indies squad signed for World Series Cricket and the British legal challenge failed in the High Court. World Series Cricket went ahead and as Jack Bailey, at the time secretary to the ICC, comments, '[Packer] had introduced day/night cricket which did capture the Australian public and he had certainly hit the Australian Cricket Board where it hurt, chiefly in the pocket but also in the way he had overcome seemingly unsurmountable obstacles' (1989: 110).

The ICC realised that a compromise was inevitable and agreed to the Australian Board negotiating a solution with Packer. The agreement that eventually emerged was more a capitulation than a compromise. Packer got everything he wanted: exclusive broadcasting rights for ten years, an increase in one-day matches, day/evening matches, coloured clothing, and a say in which teams toured Australia. Packer demonstrated that the love of money linked players and promoters more tightly than the love of the sport linked players to administrators. Packer's concern was to be in a position to influence the development of cricket so that it was a more attractive television spectacle. As Whannel noted, 'Packer . . . had no interest in running cricket, but merely wanted to clinch the television rights. He did.' (1992: 76)

The recent history of professional tennis also demonstrates the vulnerability of governing bodies to commercial interests. By contrast to cricket the challenge to the tennis IF came less from an external business interest, though the BBC was influential in persuading Wimbledon to accept open tennis, and more from the players.[3] The acceptance of open tennis in the late 1960s led to a number of professional tennis circuits being established by a variety of entrepreneurs, leading eventually in 1970 to the establishment of a grand prix circuit under the aegis of the International Tennis Federation. However, at roughly the same time both men and women tennis players were forming their own organisations to represent their interests in negotiations with the IFs. The Association of Tennis Professionals (the men's body, formed in 1972) soon sought to gain greater control over the organisation of competitions and the distribution of prize money by threatening to boycott the Wimbledon Championships. The eventual compromise gave professional players a voice equal to those of the governing body and the tournament directors on a newly formed Men's Tennis Council. But this proved to be only a temporary arrangement, for in the early 1980s the ATP broke away from the Council and formed the ATP Tour in conjunction with the tournament directors. The Tour administers 77 grand prix events leaving the ITF to administer the four Grand Slam events. In effect the players, determined to maximise their income, and the competition organisers have successfully excluded the ITF from shaping the development of tennis.

Tennis is by no means alone in seeing the development of player-power undermining the authority of governing bodies. The influence of players on the game of golf through the Professional Golfers Association is well established. More recently chess and athletics have shown similar symptoms of revolt against the role of the IF, and for similar income-maximising reasons. The finalists in the 1993 International Chess Federation's (FIDE) World Championship, Nigel Short and Garry Kasparov, decided to organise the final independently of the Federation and under the aegis of the newly formed Professional Chess Association, and so reduce the Federation levy on the prize money from 30% to 10%.

There is a similar motivation behind the proposals of the International Association of Athletes' Representatives (IAAR). Major changes have taken place in the organisation of international athletics. Of particular relevance is the growth of a strong grand prix circuit, the introduction of IAAF World Championships every two (rather than four) years, and the attraction of large sums in sponsorship and in television rights. The IAAF recently sold the television rights for the next two World Championships for $91m to the European Broadcasting Union. The response of the grand prix organisers was to form their own consortium to market their events. The reaction of the athletes to the rapid rise in income to the Federation and the commercial organisers was to develop the IAAR to negotiate on their behalf, much as the ATP did for tennis players. At present the IAAR, which claims to represent 90% of the top 50 athletes in each event, is proposing prize money for the World Championships and a relaxing of rules on advertising on clothing. If the IAAF fails to agree the IAAR has made a thinly veiled threat to organise its own events or reach an agreement with the grand prix organisers. In its submission to the IAAF the IAAR report concluded: 'Approval of these proposals will allow the IAAF to continue to control and run athletics throughout the world in a benevolent manner. A denial of these proposals by the IAAF could lead to the formation of a new organisation which will adopt these proposals.'[4]

One important consequence of sport's closer involvement with business is that the former is beginning to adopt the organisational characteristics and values of the latter. More IFs and even individual clubs have marketing and public relations departments, legal staff and secretive decision-making procedures which help to transform sports into products and athletes into commodities (admittedly expensive commodities for the elite). There are a number of factors motivating the IFs and organisations such as the IOC and the CGF to adopt a more commercial approach to running their sports. First, many IFs see commercialisation as a means of promoting and developing their sport; second, it is seen as a safeguard against an over-reliance on government finance; and third, it is undoubtedly a defensive measure aimed at retaining control over the sport in the face of pressure from players and event organisers for greater income or profit.

Conclusion

The media have been essential for the global spread of western sport and the western concept of competition. Yet from the earliest days of international sport this process has been contested. The suspicion and resistance, particularly by the French and Germans, to Coubertin's Olympics on the grounds that there were too many English sports may have been overcome, but there are still areas of the globe where there is unease or outright resentment at the cultural invasion that western and Olympic sport represent (Weber 1970; Glassford 1976, 1981; Paraschak 1991). However, for most of the world western sports and the western definition of sport reign supreme. Though countries might view sports events selectively there is little variation in the extent to which countries throughout the world accept, and increasingly promote, sports that are organised in a rational, specialised and bureaucratic fashion and marginalise those that fail to conform (Guttmann 1978; Paraschak 1991). There is also a growing acceptance of commercialised professional sport which relies heavily on corporate support. Yet as sport has become a source of profit in its own right, through the sports goods business or through the marketing of TV rights, corporate interests have become more aware of the need to protect that source of profit. Thus just as corporate interests will lobby and advise IFs about how to make their sports more commercially attractive and lobby governments for sympathetic treatment, so they will also attempt to influence major organisers such as the IOC over the location of Games and the selection of sports.

In summary, the corporate influence on sport, and on sport's relationship with international politics, is evident in a number of areas. First, business attempts to affect the extent to which sport is used for governmental and other political purposes. Second, business exerts a leverage over sport which increasingly rivals that of government. Thirdly, business has an important effect on the values projected by sport, pushing to the fore values associated with capitalism and the international free market. Finally, corporate involvement in sport has an impact on the language and conduct of international relations.

The attitude of television companies to politics in sport, and especially the Olympics, is ambivalent. On the one hand the east–west rivalry of the Cold War period was a valuable selling point for viewers. From 1952 when the Soviet team first entered the Games at Helsinki the attraction of beating the communists has been a useful marketing angle in stimulating a degree of nationalism and increasing viewing figures. However, while an ideological undercurrent gives competition an added attraction the intrusion of too many overt political issues into the Olympic arena is a threat to the attractiveness and profitability of the event. TV companies therefore will try to ensure that their investment is protected and will add their support to the tendency for host governments to adopt exceptional repressive measures for the duration of the Games.

The current relationship between sport and business is such that business now has considerable leverage over sports organisations. As yet there are few signs that the love affair between international sport and international business has cooled, but it is instructive to remember how important business income from TV rights and sponsorship is to modern sport at both domestic and international levels. In Australia only 30% of the total net income from the England cricket tour came from gate receipts, the rest coming from business. The pattern is the same for tennis in Australia where gate receipts as a proportion of total net income dropped from 62% in 1973/4 to 29% in 1983/4 (Stewart 1986: 81). At the Wimbledon tennis championships TV fees increased as a proportion of total income from under 20% in the early 1970s to nearly 70% in 1992. For the Olympic Games the picture is broadly similar (business income rising from 8% in 1976 to 60% in 1984), but with the increase in business income replacing government subsidy rather than income from ticket sales (Official Reports 1976 and 1984).

Among sports administrators it is fashionable to talk of the increasingly symbiotic relationship between sport and business. Sport benefits from wider coverage and financial support while business benefits from the use of sport as a vehicle for the 'globalisation of consumerism' (McKay and Miller 1991: 93). It may be that the relationship continues happily for many years but there are distinct areas of concern, particularly regarding the effect of commercialisation on the nature of particular sports and the relationship between participation and spectating. In the late nineteenth century sports goods manufacturers were credited with responsibility for making sports such as ice hockey and American football more violent by making more effective protective clothing, and in the 1970s the same happened in cricket. In the television age the same accusation is made due to the tendency for the media to emphasise aggression, drama, conflict in sport thereby creating a dangerous role model for the next generation of players (Coakley 1986; Lawrence 1986b). In addition, television has an interest in promoting sporting 'heroes', but while this is good for advertising campaigns it also has the effect of making the gap between the ordinary player and the elite seem unbridgeable. The result may be a growing division between participation and passive spectating, and between elite performance and the ideal of 'sport for all'. Sports goods manufacturers already know that passive involvement in sport is no threat to their sales. Indeed most sports clothing is sold as leisure wear rather than specialist sports wear. Ultimately, business will continue to invest in sport only as long as it sees sport as a valuable commodity from which to extract a profit or as a vehicle for marketing non-sporting goods.

The involvement of television companies in the Games affects not only the superficial politics that results in governments and the Olympic movement making the Games safe for the media; it also affects the 'deep structure' of the Games, the taken-for-granted web of attitudes and values upon which the Games rest. Kidd, in expressing a similar concern with the 'domination and manipulation of Olympic meanings – values, received history, and significance of events', suggests that the 'result has been coverage which heavily favours male team sports . . . and which is highly patriarchal, at times gladiatorial, nationalistic, and confirming of existing hierarchies and inequalities' (1987: 1–6; see also Whannel 1984; Hoch 1972). The individualisation of achievement and the presentation of the athlete as 'hero'; the emphasis on risks and danger; and the celebration of the work ethic and pushing the individual to breaking point are all part of a solemnisation of the competitive individualism at the core of capitalism. Thus on the one hand the media's involvement with sport helps to promote and legitimise core values of capitalism, while on the other reinforcing a nationalistic view of the world which underpins international sports organisation. Yet there is a tension here for there would seem to be many examples where business and business values seem to be undermining nationalism. For example, in golf, tennis and to a lesser extent motor racing a TV market has been created that is largely unaffected by the presence or absence of national stars. Britain is still waiting for a realistic challenger for the Wimbledon title, but the competition nonetheless continues to remain popular in the country. In both golf and motor racing sportsmen are promoted as global citizens and personalities rather than parochial national champions. In a similar fashion it is also possible to argue that commercial pressures have led some team sports at club level to build more cosmopolitan sides thus weakening the link between club and country. Soccer in many parts of Europe is a good example with Italian, French and British elite clubs recruiting their teams globally, restrained only by UEFA rules. This policy receives strong support in Europe with the EC exerting pressure on UEFA to create a free market in players, within the EC at least.

Despite these signs of commercialism undermining nationalism in sport the latter is still the dominant value which largely forces commercialism to adapt. Thus a Formula 1 motor racing team may be managed by a Briton and use a car built in Britain with a Japanese engine, but if the driver is Brazilian or French it is still perceived as essentially a Brazilian or French victory. Similarly the Dutchmen, Van Bastan or Gullit, may score the goals for AC Milan but the victory remains Italian. Nationalism is still therefore the dominant value in international sport and international competition, and the Olympic movement in particular provides a very supportive context for nationalist ideology. This is particularly important at present with so many communities aspiring to national self-determination in the wake of the collapse of communism. Yet national aspirations are not just supported by the opportunity that international sport and the attendant media coverage provide to play the national anthem and see the flag flying over the stadium. Of equal significance is the aura of upward mobility that international sport promotes (Lawrence 1986b: 174). The emphasis in international sport on elitism and meritocracy filters through to international politics. The message that the media transmit is that just as individual sportsmen and sportswomen can use sport as a route to wealth, status and security so too can countries. The

Olympic success of East Germany, the success of Brazil and Argentina in soccer's World Cup, and the West Indies in cricket all 'demonstrate' the opportunities available in return for dedication, hard work and conformity to the dominant values and norms of the international political system.

One might add that, in terms of values significant to international politics, the media's coverage of international sport in general, and the Olympics in particular, emphasises participation in western international sport as a criterion of modernity and, increasingly, as an indicator of eligibility to join the capitalist world.[5] In his study of the significance of the Seoul Games to South Korea's domestic and foreign policy aspirations Hoberman highlights the importance of the Olympic 'halo effect' in legitimising such policy. The Olympic movement, as one of a family of right-wing INGOs, is particularly valuable in conferring legitimacy on anti-communist governments (Hoberman 1987b: 11–38).

The way sport is presented by corporate sponsors and the media produces a 'halo effect' in another way as well. Sport and major competitions are rule-based events. Operating within a framework of rules, or 'laws' as some sports term them, is an integral aspect of international sport. Over the years rulebooks have got fatter and more aspects of a sport are rule-governed, with debates on amendments to rules and disputes over their interpretation being an increasing part of broadcasting. While it would be rash to over-emphasise the significance of this change it is important to acknowledge the extent to which creativity and spontaneity in sport are controlled and limited, and the extent to which sport becomes a more apt metaphor for society and the practice of politics even at the international level. As Galliher and Hessler suggest, 'Sports, particularly international competition such as the US–USSR track meet, the America's Cup yacht races, and the Olympics, are excellent structures for promoting high levels of controlled and reasonably predictable international competition' (1979: 17). Thus the international language of rules, whether the 'rules of engagement' of UN soldiers or the rules of trade set by GATT, is constantly reinforced by the developments in sport and the media coverage of international sport. The conduct of international sport and its refinement and promotion through a global media is part of the construction and reinforcement of a global political culture of international relations. The dominance of Eurocentric standards of international behaviour discussed by Bull (1984) and Robertson (1992) among others have been consistently reinforced by international sport and its treatment by television.

Notes

1 Geraghty *et al.* (1986) note similar scheduling priorities during the 1970 and 1978 soccer World Cup competitions. They quoted Evans (1982) who gives the example of England playing their match against Brazil, in Mexico, at noon so as to coincide with European peak viewing times.
2 See Hill (1992) for a thorough examination of the details of TOP and the various categories of sponsorship offered by ISL.
3 See Kramer (1979) for an account of the role of the BBC in the pressure on the Wimbledon authorities to accept open tennis in order to stop the steady flow of talented players to the professional circuits.
4 Quoted in *The Guardian*, 14.10.1992.
5 James (1990: 140–1), for example, reports how the victory of 'Australia II' in the 1983 America's Cup yacht race was reflected in the domestic media as 'signifying the onset of a new age of post-industrial, hi-tech capitalism'.

8

Sport, culture and globalisation

Introduction

In Chapter 1 it was suggested that there were, superficially at least, a number of developments in sport that indicated that a global sporting culture was emerging. In the chapters that followed it was established that the organisational infrastructure for globalisation of sport existed. The international federations of sport are now well established in the major sports as the arbiter of the rules of individual sports. In addition, most have a clear policy towards sports development and are content, or more accurately eager, to work closely with the media. Governments have also developed an international framework for discussing sports issues, most fully developed in Europe through the European Community and the Council of Europe. Further there are now a number of firmly established global sports events, either single-sports world championships and professional circuits, or major multi-sport events such as the Olympic Games and the Commonwealth Games. Finally, the infrastructure of globalisation is completed by the enthusiastic embracing of sport by the media and by television in particular. Sponsors can feel confident that when the soccer World Cup final or one of the blue riband Olympic events is being broadcast something approaching a quarter of the world's adult population is watching.

Yet having an infrastructure supportive of globalisation of culture in place is not sufficient to claim that a process of globalisation of culture is taking place. It is first necessary to explore more precisely the nature of the concept of globalisation, how the process might be defined and recognised and finally how the impact might be assessed. Addressing these issues provides the focus for this chapter.

Culture and globalisation

As with any relatively new concept the early stages of the evolution of the concept of globalisation have been marked by a period of definitional imprecision. Although there has been much discussion of the nature of globalisation, progress towards a consensus is slow. In order to pick a way through the definitional undergrowth, and to assess the utility of the concept for the study of sport and international relations, it is helpful to identify the key elements in the debate.

There are four elements of the debate on globalisation that are particularly relevant to sport: first, identifying the key attributes of global culture; second, determining whether the direction of globalisation is top-down (from rich to poor; from west to east and south) or more diffuse; third, identifying whether the prime mover in the process is a particular state, a set of states, capitalism or indeed some other source; and fourth, whether the role of the people in the receiving states is that of passive recipients or participants and if they are participants whether they can reject, as well as modify and accept, the external culture. Additional elements relate to how the impact of globalisation might be measured; determining what is fundamental change and what is superficial; deciding whether the primary impact is the erosion of local culture and the adoption of global culture or the integration of global with local culture.

The key attributes of global culture

Culture is generally conceptualised in one of two ways: first, in broadly anthropological terms as those values, beliefs and ways of doing things that distinguish one group from another; and second, in humanistic terms as the concern for 'higher' arts within any particular community. In many ways such a distinction is artificial and it is best to see those elements of 'high' culture as an integral part of the overall set of values, beliefs and ways of doing things that provide the context for human interaction and give meaning to actions.

Yet clearly some basis for the disaggregation of the notion of culture is required. Hannerz (1990b) suggests a particularly useful basis in terms of 'cultural flows'. He identifies four distinct cultural flows and suggests that only one is an element in the globalisation process. The first flow concerns cultural commodities which move within a market framework and would include the media's presentation of sport, as well as sports goods and clothing. It is this flow that carries the potential for cultural homogenisation that is a preoccupation of many of those concerned with globalisation. Bagdikian refers to the aim of 'the lords of the global village' as being to create a predisposition to consume (1989: 818), while Tomlinson and Whannel (1984), referring specifically to sport, paint a similar picture of the manipulation of the Olympic Games by the interlocking interests of the media, the advertising agencies and the consumer goods manufacturers (For similar analyses see also Sklair 1991; Esteinou Madrid 1986; Hamelink 1984).

The second cultural flow concerns the actions of the state as an organisational form and as a manager of meaning. This activity is often directed towards goals of nation-building and thus while it involves a degree of cultural engineering aimed at developing a strong sense of national identity and consequently homogenisation, there is also the countervailing pressure to manipulate cultural engineering in such a way as to distinguish one nation from another. A key element in the development of a sense of national identity is the capacity to define oneself in terms of the world. Therefore the state is interested in balancing internal homogenisation and external distinctiveness. Clearly sport is an important element in this process as many ex-colonies, such as Canada and Australia, and new states in post-war Europe used sport quite explicitly as a tool for nation-building.

The third cultural flow is the 'form of life' which Hannerz uses to describe the 'habitual perspectives and dispositions' (1990b: 114) developed as part of the routine of daily life. Largely untouched by other flows there is scope here for a degree of cultural autonomy. The important question in relation to this flow is the extent to which it conditions the reception of market- or state-inspired flows. The final flow is a series of 'movements' or causes that periodically capture the popular imagination such as the women's movement, environmentalism and the peace movement.

The value of Hannerz's typology of flows is that it suggests where the weight of global culture falls and which elements of local culture are least likely to be affected. This enables us to explore the interaction between global and local culture not just in terms of globalisation but also in terms of a process of de-localisation of culture, with the implication being that the latter process is one that is more under the control of the 'recipient' community.

While Hannerz's typology is wide-ranging it is possible to identify a further 'flow', namely that associated with the cultural elements of the discourse between states. Given that most of today's states joined an international system that was already established it is appropriate to ask what values system were they participating in and, usually, accepting? As Featherstone notes, 'international relations theory focuses on international relations and neglects the international state system in the form of culture (independent diplomatic languages – Latin then French – and systems of representation linked to the Church and dynastic families in the Middle Ages) which arose alongside state action and made it possible' (1990: 5). Giddens makes a similar point when he establishes an analytical distinction between the global state system and the 'global information system' which describes the context of discourse between states (1987: 276; see also Der Derian and Shapiro 1989 for a collection of essays which explore the relationship between the language of international relations and its practice; and Korzenny and Ting-Toomey 1990 for explorations of diplomacy and negotiation across cultures). Thus while Hannerz is correct to identify the market-based commodity flow as a major carrier of global culture it is important to look beyond the boundaries of the state and acknowledge the significance of the diplomatic cultural flow. In this context it is possible to argue that the symbolism, practice and organisation of international sport may be particularly suited to the existing diplomatic culture exemplified by the withdrawal of representatives, the boycotting of international meetings, and the fostering of bilateral relationships.

It is the interweaving of these five cultural flows which gives each group (community or nation) its distinctive 'cultural recipe' and where the process of globalisation affects only some ingredients. The implication of the above categorisation is that the impact of globalisation is relatively discrete. This, however, is unlikely as a change in one cultural ingredient will affect others and will consequently affect the overall culture of the group. Yet, with the qualification that elements of a culture cannot be treated in isolation, Hannerz provides an important starting point for investigation.

The process of globalisation

King underlines the ambiguities in the notion of globalisation by asking 'Does it, for example, merely imply a state of inter-connectedness? Or does the inter-connectedness take a special form (as in an international division of labour)? Does it imply cultural homogenization, cultural synchronization or cultural proliferation? What does it say about the direction of cultural flows?' (1990: 12). For most writers the direction is clearly top-down, from the rich, capitalist states to the poorer eastern and southern states. Hannerz sums up this position as a loss of the pre-twentieth-century world which was essentially a cultural mosaic 'of separate pieces with hard edges' and its replacement by 'a global ecumene of persistent interaction and exchange'. Yet the exchange is unequal and the resulting relationship is 'structured as an asymmetry of centre and periphery . . . the periphery out there in a distant territory, is more the taker than the giver of meaning and meaningful form' (1990b: 107).

This is a view shared by King who sees this development as closely associated with the present period of 'post-colonialism', a conceptualisation which has clear echoes of the notion of imperialism outlined by Galtung (see Chapter 2) where culture may be one medium through which the imperialist relationship is maintained. Yet Galtung, and in a modified form Robertson, also suggested that the development of global culture was highly contested as it involved conflict over what was worth knowing and that the motor of globalisation was a combination of the development of a world-wide media system, the spread of capitalism and western imperialism (Galtung 1971; Robertson 1990b).

For Schiller the prime mover in the process of globalisation is capitalism in general and multi-national corporations in particular. Preferring the description 'cultural imperialism' Schiller sees the mass media, 'saturating the cultural space of the nation', as the capitalist's Trojan horse (1985: 18). The purpose of this process is the 'cultural take over of the penetrated society' (1976: 8; see also Mattelart 1983) and the net effect of the process is the systematic undermining of distinctive national cultures to the extent that Hamelink can claim that the 'survival of autonomous cultural systems in many areas of the Third World is very much in question' (1983: xiii). Hall (1990: 27) would certainly accept that the prime mover is western capitalism but would go even further and argue that globalisation is essentially an American product, though arguing that the end product is not uniformity of culture but a manipulated diversity.

The views of the process of globalisation expressed above do not, however, represent a consensus but rather one side of a fundamental fault line in the discussion of globalisation. On one side of this line there is the conceptualisation of globalisation as a process either of catching up (by the Third World with the First) or of the imposition by the First World on the Third (cultural imperialism). Both these variants see the relationship as one between the centre and periphery where the source and motor of cultural transmission is located firmly at the centre. This analysis has not been without challenge. Hannerz (1990b) and Boyd-Barrett (1982) among others have suggested that there has been a generally uncritical acceptance that the prime mover in the development of globalisation is western capitalism with the conclusion of the globalisation process a replication of a western consumer culture. In essence they both argue that the concept of globalisation is too complex to be reduced to a uni-directional process. This is certainly true for there are at least three aspects of globalisation where the inadequacy of the cultural imperialism thesis is at best under-researched and at worst a naive over-simplification: namely, first, the role of the state in the process; second, the nature of the cultural products which are transmitted; and third, the impact of global culture. Wallerstein (1990), like Hannerz, in considering the role of the state agrees that the capitalist world economy working through states is the prime mover in the process of globalisation. However, he also argues that the state is schizophrenic in that it is an integral part of the infrastructure of world capitalism and hence the globalisation process, yet is also a powerful force for establishing and defending the cultural distinctiveness of a state. The work by Hannerz referred to above notes the need to disaggregate culture and to avoid the temptation to see all aspects of the culture of a group as equally vulnerable to external pressures. Finally, the impact of globalisation is highly contested and is discussed in detail below.

If cultural imperialism represents one side of the fault line then the other is represented by the view of globalisation that notes its degree of dissociation from First World states and cultures and stresses instead elements of the global culture that require a reorientation by First *and* Third World states. Using a variety of terminology writers have identified a process within the contemporary world such that a global 'third' culture (Featherstone 1990: 9) is emerging which is essentially trans-national or even a-national (King 1990: 4). Robertson states the position succinctly when he refers to the rise of national society as an aspect of globalisation. For him globalisation is a process associated with, rather than dependent upon, the nation-state (Robertson 1989, 1990b). Wagner argues that 'What we are seeing around the world, and this is perhaps most evident in Asia and Africa, is a blending of many sports traditions' (1990: 400). For Wagner the end result of this process is greater homogenisation but this is not imperialistic; it is explained as reflecting the 'will of the people' (402). While these views represent a serious challenge to the notion of cultural imperialism they are far less clearly articulated and represent the degree of dissatisfaction with existing conceptualisations rather than a coherent alternative.

The impact of globalisation: decoding the global culture

One of the most striking conclusions from a review of the literature on cultural imperialism and globalisation is that far more attention has been paid to identifying the quantity and range of cultural products transferred from the rich western states, than to the impact of that transfer (Fejes 1981; Schlesinger 1987). As a result a degree of caution is required when making assumptions about the likely impact of sport globalisation, as existing work is drawn from a range of studies in the broad area of cultural studies.

Existing studies suggest a number of distinctive relationships which vary according to the 'reach' of the culture-exporter and the 'response' of the culture-importer. In general these relationships fall into one of four categories as shown in Figure 8.1. The two dimensions of the figure reflect the divisions in the literature which tend to focus on the extent to which the exported culture permeates all aspects of the recipient group. One reason for partial 'reach' might result from the deliberate strategy of the exporting group or it might reflect the resistance of the target group. Hence the second dimension of debate concerns the degree to which the response of the recipient/target group is passive acceptance, or cooperative/contested participation.

With the dimensions of the current debate in mind a valuable starting point is the work of Hannerz. Following Hannerz's four-fold classification of cultural flows it is possible to argue that the elements of a domestic culture that are affected by globalisation are the more superficial or peripheral ones. For example, the popularity of basketball in Israel or baseball in Japan does not signal a homogenisation or an Americanisation of these respective cultures because either sport in general or these sports in particular are accepted within the cultures as being part of the ephemera of cultural life and far removed from core cultural values and practices. While this view might have a logic to it, it is not persuasive as the later review of baseball in Japan will show. The assumption that elements of culture can be so neatly compartmentalised in either community or personal terms is hard to accept.

In contrast to this view Hall (1990) argues much more strongly that globalisation does result in homogenisation – a homogenisation in terms defined by western capitalism. Brohm, also arguing from a Marxist

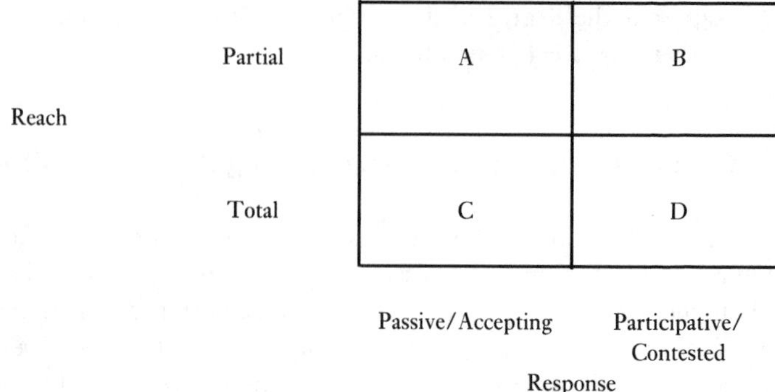

Figure 8.1 Patterns of globalisation.

perspective, articulates the global significance of modern sport in the following terms: 'it ideologically reproduces bourgeois social relations such as selection and hierarchy, subservience, obedience etc.; secondly, it spreads an organisational ideology specific to the institution of sport; and thirdly, it transmits on a huge scale the general themes of ruling bourgeois ideology like the myth of the superman, individualism, social advancement, success, efficiency etc' (1978: 77). The implications of Brohm's analysis are clearly that the scope for cultural resistance within modern sport is slight and, more importantly, that awareness of the manipulative force of sport is also slight. In terms of the categorisation suggested in Figure 8.1 globalisation is both total and largely uncontested.

Although superficially similar to Brohm's position Hall's is much more subtle and persuasive. He suggests that global mass culture is 'a particular form of homogenisation . . . [which] is not absolutely complete, and it does not work for completeness. . . . It is wanting to recognise and absorb those (cultural) differences within a larger overarching framework of what is essentially an American conception of the world' (1990: 28). Thus for Hall globalisation does not equate with the destruction and replacement of local cultures; rather, it is manipulation of local culture (see Sussman and Lent 1991 for a series of examples of the overpowering effect of multi-national media interests). In other words the 'reach' is selective/partial though still largely uncontested. However, this view is persuasive only in that it recognises the failure of global culture to manifest itself in the form of a homogeneous cultural form. What Hall is suggesting has the ring of tautology in that because local cultures persist in the face of the onslaught of American-led 'westoxification' (Featherstone 1990: 11) the only grounds upon which they can be accommodated within a Marxian framework is by dismissing them as corrupted forms (community false consciousness) which in the last instance will operate in the interests of the external cultural power. There is a further weakness in Hall's reference to a specific territorial source for the dominant culture. As Sklair points out, while the 'American dream' is a central element of capitalist consumerism the latter 'is mystified by reference to Americanization' (1991: 134). Such a mystification falsely implies that if American influence can be excluded from a state so too can the capitalist culture.

Despite these weaknesses in Hall's argument his analysis has considerable merit for it draws our attention to the need to explain the apparent resistance of local cultures to the global invader, or the apparent capacity of local cultures to absorb major elements of the global culture, adapt them to the local context, and redefine them in a way that is supportive of local values. Zayed (1987) provides a good example of the acceptance of and then resistance to the cultural invader and he suggests that religious fundamentalism is one form of resistance.

Much of the recent research into the impact of media discourses provides support for the adaptive capacity of local cultures. Morley (1986), for example, has shown how the 'decoding' of television programmes varies according to the social position of the receiver. Similarly Katz and Liebes (1985) demonstrated the variation among different ethnic groups in terms of their response to the American television programme, 'Dallas', and concluded that the meaning of a programme is a negotiation between the story or message on the screen and the culture of the viewer.[1] In the context of sport an interesting example explored below is the attempt by the Gaelic Athletic Association to prevent the spread of rugby union in Ireland because it was defined as an attempt by Britain (specifically England) to undermine the local culture whereas (white) South Africans, who also fought against British imperial power, redefined the same cultural product so that it symbolised the Afrikaans character and Afrikaner resistance (Van der Merwe 1985).

Robertson reaches similar conclusions when considering the question of the impact of global culture on recipient communities for, while acknowledging the constraints that arise from the unequal distribution of power in the international system, he stresses the importance of 'choice' in cultural change. For him global culture is a contested terrain where 'what is taken to be a worthy direction of societal aspiration – is something which is constructed in the global arena in relation to the constraints upon [most] societies to maintain their own identities and senses of community' (Robertson 1987: 38).

Similarly, Hannerz, in response to the view of non-western cultures as passive, unresisting recipients of external cultural forms, makes a particularly telling point when he reminds us that the engagement between the First and Third Worlds has been a very long one and is not just a product of the post-war years. 'There is often an idea that peripheral cultures come defenceless, unprepared to the encounter with metropolitan culture, . . . and are taken by surprise . . . this notion would frequently entail a measure of ignorance of the continuous historical development of centre–periphery contacts. It may well be that the First World has been present in the consciousness of many Third World people a great deal longer than the Third World has been on the minds of most First World people' (1990b: 110).

Developing this line of thought Hannerz suggests that the concept of 'creolisation' is a more appropriate description of the complexities of the interaction between the local and the global. Creolisation is a process where 'people actively engage in making their own syntheses . . . [such that] . . . When the peripheral culture absorbs the influx of meanings and symbolic forms from the centre [it] transforms them to make them in some considerable degree their own' (1990b: 127). Friedman provides an interesting illustration of this phenomenon in his study of the Ainu of Japan. He shows how they were stimulated by their absorption into the global tourism industry to re-create their culture. Being the subject of tourist interest led to a revival of traditional crafts, ceremonies and language. What was of central importance was the degree of control that the group was able to exert over the production of their 'culture-for-others' for, as Friedman notes, 'It is in defining themselves for the Japanese, their significant Other, that they establish their specificity' (1990: 321).

The assumption that meaning is negotiated rather than determined is undoubtedly an attractive source of hypotheses, yet is far from convincing as a full explanation of the interaction between global and local culture. To conclude that culture is negotiated begs a series of questions such as who sets the limits of negotiation, and who is negotiating from the position of greater strength. In other words what is the nature of the power relations that provide the context and limits to the negotiating process? Feld exemplifies this problem in his study of the relationship between African and American popular music and shows clearly that there has been considerable cultural interplay between the two continents and their respective musical styles; a mutual process of import, adaptation and export which suggests the capacity of peripheral cultures to act as full participants in the cultural market-place. However, Feld also points out that 'This voice is harmonised by a counter-melody of power, even control and domination' which produces a situation where this interweaving of musical styles takes place within a framework of values and exchange determined and controlled by the American record companies (Feld 1988: 31; see also Roncagliolo 1986 for a similar analysis of the international media).

In practice it is likely that for some local cultures the awareness and acknowledgement of a global culture is an important element in defining their own identity and distinctiveness, in the same way that sailors in the past used the same reference points (stars) to identify their particular and distinctive location on the seas. Thus watching the same sporting event or playing the same sport may fulfil the function of highlighting the essential (and distinctive) qualities of local cultures. But while the superficial cultural products of globalisation may be malleable by local communities, the context of interaction between the local and global cultures is set by deeper ideological forces more attuned to the prevailing pattern of economic power distribution. Thus while a gold medal at the Olympics for Cuba may superficially enhance the status of Cuban socialism, at a deeper level it confirms the achievement principle, specialisation, professionalisation and a series of other values more in tune with the consumerism of the west and Japan than the ideals of international socialism.

Wallerstein makes a parallel point when he highlights the apparent paradox of the state as the prime mover in the development of national culture and national differentiation and the similarity in the modes of expression of these differences. Thus the cultural particularity of the nation-state is expressed in profoundly uniform ways, whether they are forms of political decision-making, such as a legislature, a constitution and a national currency, or whether they are artistic forms such as a national anthem and a flag. As Wallerstein comments, 'It is almost as though the more intense the nationalist fervour in the world, the more identical seem the expressions of this nationalism' (1990: 93). Robertson makes essentially the same point when he refers to the establishment of standards of civilisation as a set of 'regulative principles concerning inter-state relations' (Robertson 1992: 218) to which states wishing to participate in the European-centred international system of the nineteenth and early twentieth centuries had to conform. Bull's basic contention is that 'the demand of Asian and African peoples for equality of rights in international law was one that the latter did not put forward until they had first absorbed ideas of equal rights of states to sovereignty, of peoples to self-determination, and of persons of different races to individual rights, which before their contact with Europe played no part in their experience' (1984: ix). Even though Bull admits that the period characterised by the dominance of Eurocentric standards of international behaviour has now passed he argues that the attempt to delineate the present norms and values of 'international society' remains an important theme in international relations literature (Gong 1984; Bull and Watson 1985) and is based on the assumption that global norms and values can be sustained.

What is implicit in Wallerstein's observation, and those of the international society school of international relations theory, is the layered nature of globalisation whereby the prime effect of globalisation is the establishment of an homogeneous frame of reference within which local particularity is constructed. This development has a clear parallel in sport. When globalisation of sport is discussed what is most often referred to is the spread and adoption of certain events or particular sports, such as the Olympic track and field events and soccer, rather than the ideology of organisational rationality as reflected in a concern with rules of competition, timing, record-keeping and, more nebulously, standards of play. What is important here is the analytical separation of the globalised cultural products from the underlying ideology which smooths their flow. Only by acknowledging the existence of distinctive layers of global culture can we reconcile the paradox between claims to globalisation and the apparent ability of states to use sport to demonstrate cultural diversity. In terms of international relations sport can best be seen as a valuable global Esperanto which states use to say very different things about themselves, about others and to each other, yet seemingly unaware that the common language they are using has its own inherent structure which sharply affects what may be said and how it may be said.

In a number of the examples that will be explored below states and sub-state cultural groups use sport as a tool of cultural, and often explicitly political, resistance. Yet many do so in terms which merely reinforce the dominant global culture. For example, the investment in sport in the German Democratic Republic, Cuba and the Soviet Union was partly justified in terms of demonstrating the superiority of the socialist way of life. This was achieved by being more competitive than western teams or athletes, more determined to win medals, and more concerned with record times. Thus far from replacing the capitalist values embodied in international sport the communist states integrated themselves into the very system of values they were opposing. The same is true of the Gaelic sports movement in Ireland where the cost of undermining local interest in 'English' sports was the necessity to imitate the organisational features of English sport such as leagues and competitions. To paraphrase Wallerstein, what was intended to be a difference of substance was little more than a difference of form (1990: 101).

The notion of an overarching culture of organisational rationality as a framework for international sport follows Weber's argument that the bureaucratisation of society was both unavoidable and universal (1947). For Weber the onward march of bureaucratic rationalism would replace a creative humanity with the bureaucratisation of all spheres of life. This picture was clearly unduly pessimistic as much empirical research draws attention to the irrationality of some organisations and the general limitations of bureaucratic organisation (see, for example, Fine 1984; Strauss 1978; Mayhew 1983; Haferkamp 1987). Although Weber misjudged the depth of bureaucratisation there is much evidence to support his view concerning its spread beyond the major organisations such as the churches, the military and the state and into other areas of social life such as sport.

For many years there has been a debate among academics and among politicians about the nature of sport. On the one hand are those who see sport as a rare opportunity for the expression of individuality (Scruton 1980; Risse 1921 quoted by Guttmann 1981) and on the other those who argue that sport is subject to the same pressures for rational organisation as any other aspect of life (Brohm 1978; Rigauer 1981). That sport is an opportunity for free expression is an argument that is increasingly difficult to sustain in the face of an accumulation of evidence that suggests that it is highly routinised and regimented. Rigauer, arguing from a neo-Marxist perspective, suggests that sport is subject to the same concern to strive for some form of recognised excellence as are other professions. In order for excellence to be adequately recognised, rationalised standards for participation are required. Such standards are found in the measurement of achievement in centimetres, points, seconds and pounds (it is no longer sufficient simply to record the winner, we need to be able to quantify the victory). Rational standards are also found in training and also in the general increase in specialisation within sport. Most importantly, the satisfactory functioning of the achievement principle requires a bureaucratic form of organisation. As Rigauer points out, 'Rationalization assumes logically necessary forms when it goes on to become bureaucratization and administration of top level sport' (1981: 44). This process of the commodification of the sport results in the 'constant narrow[ing of] the individual's room for choice' (1981: 47). Ironically it is within the communist bloc that the rationalisation and bureaucratisation of sport reached its most fully developed form. Brohm, who shares many of Rigauer's views, in his analysis of sport in the GDR observed that: 'As a prioritised branch of the bureaucratic state apparatus, sport itself has become *bureaucratic, State-sport: cybernetic sport*' (1978: 79).

A similar picture is painted by Hinings and Slack, though writing from a Weberian standpoint. In tracing the development of amateur sports organisations in Canada they highlight the change 'from structures characterised by undifferentiated task arrangements, low formalisation of procedures and participative decision-making to structures that now exhibit higher degrees of specialisation and formalisation and where decisions are made by centralised bodies' (1987: 3). According to Cunningham *et al.* (1987; see also Slack 1985; Hinings and Slack 1987) the impetus for the trend towards greater professionalisation and bureaucratisation was provided by the federal government and its concern to produce elite athletes.

The emergence of rationality as the dominant form of organisation in sport is undoubtedly an important element in the argument concerning globalisation. While Weber saw bureaucracy as largely neutral in ideological and interest terms Marcuse (1955), by contrast, saw bureaucratic rationality as an organisational imperative that is ideologically hegemonic. The emergence of bureaucracy in sport has been the product of the same forces that promoted it in work and other areas of society, namely the growth in size of administrative units, the development of a money economy, the increase in occupational specialism, the dominance of the profit principle (Blau 1956; Ingham 1975). The process has been referred to by Elias as the 'sportisation of pastimes': the transformation of pastimes where the 'game and the players were still largely identical' into sports where the establishment of regulating bodies endows 'the game with a measure of autonomy in relation to the players' (1986: 39). The impetus for this process was the ruling class and their desire to control and centralise.

Picking a way through these layers of debate and ambiguity is difficult, but two fairly coherent positions on the issue of globalisation can be identified. In the first globalisation is a conceptual extension of the longer-established notion of cultural imperialism. In this conception the cultural relationship mirrors the economic power relationships in a capitalist world; the driving force of globalisation is exploitation and ideological manipulation of communities and people as markets, consumers and workers. Similar views to this have been referred to as 'Americanisation' and 'commercialisation'. This view is much more closely associated with the matrix of interests that ties capitalism to particular states, most obviously the USA. Given the prominent role of the state in this position the suggestion that globalisation is essentially a variant of imperialism suggests that it may be accommodated fairly comfortably within the broad dependency/globalist perspective and even within the realist model insofar as there is a basic correlation between economic resources and military (and cultural) power.

The second position defines globalisation as an outcome which requires a reorientation by both the First and the Third Worlds. Here the global culture is less confidently associated with an identifiable source such as the USA or capitalism. In the words of Hannerz, 'The world culture is created through the increasing interconnection of varied local cultures, as well as through the development of cultures without a clear anchorage in any one territory' (1990a: 237). This view sits less comfortably within the realist or dependency perspectives as it casts doubt on the centrality to the process of globalisation of the state and/or specific MNCs. The implicit consideration given to a role for organisations such as international sports federations and the IOC, etc., reflects the support this position gives to the pluralist conceptualisation of international relations.

In seeking to test the significance of sport for the relationships between nations in terms of cultural imperialism or some form of participative globalisation, a series of different types of relationships will be explored in the remainder of this chapter. It is possible to identify four groups of states where the relationship between the external culture and importer is distinctive. The first group includes those states which are generally poor with a low level of industrialisation and few strong local sporting traditions, and which were once colonies of a European power and remain economically dependent on either European or North American states. This group would contain most of the Caribbean states (though Cuba might claim different status), most of South America and Africa. It is within this group that evidence in support of the cultural imperialism hypothesis should be most easily found.

The second group contains those states and communities which were, or still are, in a colonial position but which differ from the first group in that they possess a recognisable local sporting tradition. Included in this group would be the Irish Republic, Scotland, the Basque regions of France and Spain and the Inuit areas of North America. Within this group one would expect to find evidence for the cultural imperialism hypothesis, yet also a higher level of conflict at the interface between the external and local cultures. The third group consists of the richer ex-colonies which have large numbers of settlers from the ex-imperial power. States such as Australia, Canada, South Africa and New Zealand would be included in this group. It is in this group that one would expect to find support for the participative model of globalisation. The final group is a variation on the previous category for it refers to states which are generally industrial but non-western and without strong local sporting traditions. Included in this group are Israel and Japan and one would expect these states to be in a participative relationship with globalisation.

Of course there are other possible groupings that can be identified and the four outlined above can be subdivided, added to and refined, but they have the merit of reflecting recognised categories. In addition, many of the states within each group have been the subject of research into the nature and organisation of domestic sport and thus provide a body of empirical data for analysis.

Poorer dependent states

The role of sport in nation-building, already noted in Chapter 1, continues to be a feature of many of the colonies that gained their independence in the 1950s and 1960s. Writers examining the relationship between Britain and its former Caribbean colonies have argued that the relationship as mediated by sport, particularly cricket, is an imperial one in which the former colonies' sporting assets are stripped, with the majority of top Caribbean cricketers playing most of their first-class cricket outside their home states; and also a relationship which achieves not only the cultural subordination of the Caribbean states but also the denigration of the black population. As Tiffin argues the progress of Caribbean blacks towards greater participation in cricket was very much on the white man's terms for 'he was really only being offered the opportunity to be as good as his master; he had little chance of redefining the moral assumptions behind the game' (1981: 187). Patterson goes even further by suggesting that the dominance of British culture, of which sport is a key element, has stymied the development of a coherent Afro-Jamaican culture. He observes: 'Hence it [cricket] becomes on the symbolic level the English culture we have been forced to love, for it is the only real one we have, but the culture we must despise for what it has done to us, for what it has made of the hopeless cultural shambles, the incoherent social patchwork, that we have called Afro-Jamaican culture' (1969: 24). For

Stoddart (1987) the cultural legacy of cricket for Barbadian society is the inculcation of a high degree of conservatism that has helped avoid conflict between the social elite and the mass. The symbolism of the sporting relationship mirrors and reinforces other facets of the relationship between the 'British' Caribbean and the developed world such that any progress towards economic, diplomatic and cultural independence takes place only within the framework established by western states and Britain in particular.

The analysis of the relationship between the USA and the Dominican Republic by Klein (1991b) also provides much support for the cultural imperialism hypothesis. In many ways the Dominican Republic is the archetypical case of dependency: twice invaded by the USA this century; led by politicians frequently imposed by the USA; and heavily dependent on the US market for the only major crop, sugar. Baseball was largely introduced and fostered by American servicemen in the early part of the century and by the 1930s the game was firmly established as the national sport. As Klein remarks the sport grew in popularity 'as North American political, military, and economic domination increased' (1991b: 151). By the 1950s American baseball clubs became aware of the actual and potential talent within the Dominican Republic league. There began a flow of talented players across to the USA which can be seen as of some mutual benefit to the sport in both countries as players received first-class training and could play in the USA in the summer and return home for the winter league in the Republic. Unfortunately what started as mutual benefit was soon transformed into the systematic expropriation of the sporting talent of the Dominican Republic and the undermining of the domestic league. American clubs began to establish locally based baseball 'academies' which systematically sifted potential talent, exporting the most promising to the States. As Klein points out, 'the academies established by the North Americans undercut the traditional role of Dominican amateur baseball as a developer of talent, and the advent of free agency in the United States had the unforeseen effect of discouraging Dominican stars from taking part in winter play' (1991b: 152). Klein concludes that 'the political and economic domination of the game had an ideological consequence: the passing on of the belief that culture in general and baseball in particular was better in the United States than in the Dominican Republic' (1991b: 152).

The evidence presented seems to be strongly supportive of the cultural imperialism hypothesis, yet Klein in his analysis of baseball and many of those who have analysed Caribbean cricket find evidence which also supports the view that sport may also be the basis for the development of a national culture and consequently a capacity to resist hegemonic pressures. Klein suggests that Dominicans infuse the game with distinctive characteristics and qualities and that sport in Latin America has a capacity for radical political expression. He concludes that the 'Dominicans are a beleaguered people who may someday rebel; to predict when the flashpoint will occur, look first to the firefights being waged in a game that has inspired their confidence' (1991b: 156). However, this conclusion runs counter to much of the evidence that Klein accumulated and owes more to the tendency to romanticise the oppressed rather than acknowledge the effectiveness of their oppression.[2]

Klein's conclusion concerning the tension between hegemony and resistance in Dominican baseball is also found within analyses of Caribbean cricket, most notably in the work of Patterson. However, there are others who argue that cricket in the Caribbean has been transformed and redefined. Burton, for example, suggests that 'West Indian cricket . . . has retained its English form while being injected with a new and specifically West Indian content and meaning . . . [it] has been comprehensively creolised' (1991: 8). Similarly to Klein, Burton suggests that cricket is imbued with 'street qualities' such as style, panache and flamboyance which are at odds with the dominant norms which emphasise respectability, seriousness and moderation. While this is plausible it is not very convincing for, while the style of involvement may be different, the substance is essentially the same and defined externally to the Caribbean: the substance being the basic structure and values of the game and, more importantly, the bureaucratic pattern of rules and administration within which the game is organised. Thus while the accent and intonation may be different the language is the same and has been produced elsewhere.

The main conclusion to be drawn from this section is that where the sporting traditions are imported by a dominant economic power it is immensely difficult for the dependent state to redefine the sporting experience in a way that seriously challenges the cultural hegemony of the former. Indeed the recipient state, at worst, merely reshapes the sport at the margins in order for it to sit more comfortably within the peripheral culture or, at best, devises an acceptable accommodation with the dominant culture. To refer to either of these outcomes as creolisation is accurate only in the sense that the recipient culture has been involved in shaping the surface manifestation of the underlying power relationship.

Culturally strong (ex-)colonies

In Ireland, the intertwining of cultural/sporting, military and political opposition to English rule has been intense for over a hundred years. Sport has not only been of symbolic significance in the relationship between the two countries, it has also been a locus for the organisation of political opposition and, at least in the early part of the century, a source of paramilitary recruits. The focus for Irish opposition to the English sporting tradition was the Gaelic Athletic Association (GAA), established in 1884 with the express aim of promoting traditional Gaelic sport such as hurling and Gaelic football, and actively resisting English sports such as rugby, soccer and cricket.[3] An aggressive campaign, closely linked with the militantly nationalist Irish Republican Brotherhood, resulted in a revival of the moribund sport of hurling (displacing its more genteel version, hurley) and was instrumental in defining Gaelic football and distinguishing it from English rugby. As an example of cultural resistance the success of the GAA is impressive and resulted from its strong emotional appeal to nationalism and strict enforcement of the rules that prohibited members from playing English sports as well as Gaelic and which prohibited contact with clubs subscribing to English sports. Consequently during the first half of this century sport, through the GAA, was both a potent symbol of resistance to English rule as well as being a key element in the political and military campaigns to oust the English from Ireland. Even today the significance of sport in the politics of Northern Ireland is great and the GAA remains a central structure in the definition and promotion of Irish nationalism (see Sugden and Bairner 1986; Knox 1986).

To be consistent with the analysis of Caribbean cricket and Dominican baseball we need to ask whether the achievements of the GAA were similarly superficial. At first glance the answer would be no, for the Irish Catholic majority, through the GAA, were able to define and then reject 'alien' English sports and replace them with traditional sports which subsequently put down deep roots. In addition, and at a more profound level, one could also argue that the GAA was able to challenge effectively the organisational assumptions of English sport, particularly regarding notions of professionalism and middle-class exclusivity. However, Mandle makes clear that a similar process of challenge was taking place at roughly the same time (late nineteenth century) in England with soccer and rugby dividing over the issue of payment of athletes. More importantly, Mandle argues that despite the aggressive anti-English foundation of the GAA and the success of the rejection of English sports the GAA was operating within a definition of sport that was essentially English. He sums up the position in the following terms: 'While adopting hostility to all England, and particularly English sport, stood for, the Association was forced, unconsciously as it may be, to imitate the features of Victorian sport – its emphasis on morality, on health, on organisation, codification and competition. Much of what the GAA regarded as distinctive about the meaning of its games was merely the result of the substitution of the word "Ireland" for "Britain" or "England"' (1987: 14). But as Mandle noted it is not surprising that Ireland and the GAA followed the rest of the industrialised world in adopting English sports and the attendant underlying values. While each country may play each sport in its own style 'the purposes behind the games revolution – the philosophic heightening of their meaning, the moralising . . . were everywhere the same order. . . . Even the use of sport to proclaim national distinctiveness was a British invention' (Mandle 1987: 14).

Irish sport then may be seen in a similar fashion to that in the Caribbean characterised by superficial resistance within an imperial hegemony. Yet to draw such a conclusion would be seriously to underplay the importance of sport in the Irish anti-colonial struggle. While it must be accepted that the underlying values and much of the organisational form of Irish sport are identical to that found in Britain and throughout the industrialised world the major role of sport both as a symbol of resistance and as an actual focus for the independence movement must also be acknowledged. It is therefore possible to develop a local culture within the cultural hegemony of an imperial power and work towards objectives alien to the interests of that power.

Paraschak provides a second example which considers the maintenance of community identity in the face of imperial pressure in her exploration of the attempts by native northern Canadians to preserve their sporting traditions in the face of pressure from the Eurocanadian 'power-bloc' (1991). In the two examples she outlines there are clear pressures to make the sporting contests conform to western conceptions of organisation and structure, in much the same way that lacrosse, originally a native game, was codified and renamed to suit a European heritage (Salter 1972). The Arctic Winter Games established in 1970 are sponsored by the government and comprise a diet of sports selected predominantly from a European heritage. The Northern Games were organised in reaction to the Arctic Winter Games and include traditional sports. Paraschak shows clearly that both these Games have been the focus of tension between Eurocanadian sports and organisational expectations and local sports and games and forms of organisation. Over the twenty or so years that these Games have been held there has been a degree of compromise, with more native sports being included in the Arctic Winter Games while the Northern Games have moved closer to a 'Eurocanadian, meritocratic model of sport' (1991: ch. 4, p. 16). In her conclusion Paraschak notes that the greatest degree of change has been to the Northern Games yet nonetheless suggests that the changes in both Games reflect the 'ongoing ability of native people to shape their own future' (1991: ibid.). However, this may be an unduly optimistic conclusion for what is also clear is that the motive of the Canadian government is cultural incorporation and that to a considerable extent they have been successful. The nature of that 'incorporation' is not necessarily into a culture exemplified by the participation in Eurocanadian sports, but rather the incorporation into the deeper values reflected in a bureaucratic form of social organisation.

An interesting comparison to the work of Paraschak is provided by Jarvie who analysed the phases of development of the Highland Gatherings in Scotland. His conclusions broadly support Paraschak in that he charts the destruction of the Highland Gatherings as an expression of popular Highland culture in the eighteenth and early nineteenth centuries and then their reinvention, by the Scottish aristocracy, in the mid- to late nineteenth century in a sanitised and politically neutered form. Jarvie notes that by the twentieth century the 'Gatherings became increasingly bureaucratised, standardised, and dependent upon a romantic cultural identity divorced from the social context in which such traditions were originally experienced' (1986: 354).

While the Irish had accepted the values underpinning organised sport the native Canadians are still committed to sports and pastimes that reflected social values and priorities that are not only markedly different from the dominant Eurocanadian culture, but which also reflect the self-contained and independent nature of native Canadian culture. It is much harder to reach a cultural accommodation in the Canadian case than in the Irish as with the former there is far less common ground. In the Scottish example the traditional Highland culture was transformed into a more acceptable form, while the majority of urban and Lowland Scots came to see soccer, and to a lesser extent rugby union, as more appropriate sports through which to assert their identity.

Richer ex-colonies

The third group of states to be considered is that which is characterised by ex-colonial status, and a large settlement of migrants from the imperial state or some other developed industrial state. In general these states are relatively wealthy and the 'imperial migrants' are numerically and/or economically dominant. In the states that were once British colonies, particularly Australia, New Zealand and Canada, the early phase of their colonial history was typified by a desire to maintain a strong political and cultural identity with the home country and with the maintenance of the British Empire. Thus all three countries displayed, in the eighteenth and nineteenth centuries, an experience of sport similar to that found in England. Sport was used to establish cultural identification with the homeland and to demonstrate cultural superiority to the local population.

While the sporting history of these three countries has much in common the degree of commonality declined sharply in the present century. In Canada, as in England, the public schools were central to the development of sport. Even after confederation in 1867 the Canadian elite retained a strong cultural link with Britain. According to Brown (1984) the Canadian elite saw nationalism and imperialism as interlocked and symbolised by their attachment to British sport, especially cricket. However, during the late nineteenth and early twentieth centuries Canadians developed their own sports derived in part from their contact with local cultures (lacrosse) and in part from an adaptation to local climatic conditions (ice hockey and Canadian football). Yet despite this high degree of innovation and adaptation in the types of games played, which certainly reflected the search for a sense of Canadian identity, 'the moral theory of games was unquestionably British in its association. . . . Orthodox values were easily grafted on to Canadian activities' (Brown 1984: 132). Yet Canada could not remain immune from the influence of its southern neighbour and the decline in cricket and rise in popularity of baseball, basketball and football are symptomatic of the decline in British cultural influence and the rise of American. This shift is reflected not only in the change in the popularity of particular sports but also in the rapid adoption of commercial organisation and values.

Canada seems therefore to be both part of the globalisation of the Anglo-Saxon sports philosophy in its relationship to native sports, but also a recipient of an American sporting culture. Yet to see Canada as the passive recipient of a global culture would not be entirely fair. Canada has exerted considerable influence over the development of international sport, particularly the Olympics. In addition Canada, in its commitment to sport in the Commonwealth and its plans to support the Commonwealth Games, may be seen as imposing its own definition of sport on the international stage even if it does seem to be perpetuating a Victorian conception of imperial sport. Canada's early history is one of a perception of the values of sport shared with Britain; its more recent history shows it coming increasingly (and to an extent unwillingly) under the influence of American sport yet also having the capacity to determine a national and an international sports policy of its own. However, neither its domestic policy nor its contribution to international sports policy have differed greatly from the dominant pattern found in most western/industrial states.

For New Zealand and Australia sport was also a confirmation of links with the homeland but also, later, a barometer by which its growing independence could be measured. Both these countries saw visits by touring English cricket or rugby teams, and eventual victories over them, as important milestones in their 'coming of age'. In this sense they had much in common with the Caribbean colonies, but with far less ambiguity towards success at English sports. For Australian and New Zealand settlers cricket and rugby were part of the cultural baggage of the migrant. As Mitchell observes, 'Australian cricketing nationalism was like the rivalry of a loving child, a sign of a continuing loyalty to Britain' (1992: 290). This is not to say that success at English sports did not pose problems for nascent national identity, but it is clear that in both countries a common sporting heritage was seen as an important reference point for establishing separate identity (Crawford 1984; Harriss 1986). Also both countries had little hesitation in deviating from English views, on amateurism in particular and the relationship between commerce and sport in general.

In common with Canada, Australia and New Zealand have both had a significant impact on the organisation of the sports they play. Australia has had a major impact on cricket in particular. The introduction of the one-day game and the commercialisation that followed the creation, by Kerry Packer, of World Series Cricket have left lasting marks on the rules, format and values of the game. By contrast the West Indies, the dominant cricket team for much of the 1970s and 1980s, has affected merely the style of play, most notably the selection of four fast bowlers in a team.

Clearly the countries in this category are not simply recipients of a global culture. Their present culture is one that developed from the culture they brought with them and one that the majority in the country feel comfortable with. While all three countries do feel a degree of tension in their relationship with culturally hegemonic powers – initially Britain and more recently the United States – they have been able to develop a sporting culture that they are able to define as their own. In addition, at least Canada and Australia have either helped to redefine a particular sport at a fundamental level or else have proved to be major forces in shaping global sport in their own right. These countries therefore must be seen as possessing the resources (wealth, relatively independent media and sporting success) to enable them to participate in the development and dissemination of a global sporting culture which requires the reorientation by both the traditionally hegemonic power and the recipient countries.

Israel and Japan

At first sight Israel and Japan have much in common: they have both been relatively isolated in their respective regions for much of the post-war period; neither has a strong tradition of competitive sport; and both have a current pattern of sport that is largely imported. As regards Israel, Oren (1975) points out that sport is not part of Jewish culture and even though there have been attempts to trace a Jewish athletic tradition back to the Old Testament it is clear that sport is a twentieth-century addition to Jewish life (Laemmer 1974; Soreq 1984). Indeed, as Laemmer points out, there was a general disdain for sport as opposed to intellectual activities and it was only very slowly that it became an accepted element of culture among Jews and within the new Israeli state. Two factors were particularly important in forming a background against which sport developed within modern Jewish culture: first, the recognition of the strong association in many countries between nationalism and sport at the early part of this century; and second, the need to rebut the seeming confirmation of anti-semitic prejudices that the absence of physical culture implied (Reshef and Paltiel 1989).

In the twentieth century such Jewish involvement in sport that there was followed the strong gymnastic tradition in central Europe. Participation was boosted by Max Nordau's call for a 'Muskeljudentum' (muscular Jewry) linked firmly to the fostering of a sense of Jewish nationalism, which led eventually in 1921 to the formation of the Maccabi World Union (Hanak 1974). In part the involvement in gymnastics was simply a reflection of the dominant sports tradition in central Europe at the turn of the century; it was also in part a conscious reaction to the exclusion of Jews from the two major gymnastic movements in Europe, the Deutsche Turnerschaft and the slavic Sokol organisation. From the 1920s and particularly since the establishment of the state of Israel sport has moved away from a narrow base in gymnastics and embraced a much wider range of, largely Olympic, sports with the focus for participation being on the one hand the quadrennial Maccabiah Games first held in 1932 and the Olympic Games.

Given that sport was only weakly linked to Jewish culture it is hardly surprising that Israel's present range of sports is eclectic. Also any assessment of the extent to which Israeli sports reflect the outcome of globalisation must bear in mind that Jewish sport in this century has always been deliberately international, as one of the primary motives is to develop and foster international links between Jews throughout the world. Although figures such as Nordau extolled the virtues of sport as a focus for Jewish nationalism it was not because particular sports were seen as encapsulating core Jewish values. Sport was seen in much more instrumental terms as being an organisational focus for Jewish youth. Indeed, in the early years of the Israeli state political parties, who were the main organisers of sports clubs, selected sports, such as soccer, on the basis of their capacity to attract a large following.

In conclusion, while modern Jewish sport has much in common with that found in Europe and North America it is still a more ephemeral element in Israeli culture. Consequently, the relationship between Jewish sport and the process of globalisation is primarily one of participation rather than the outcome of a process of cultural imperialism.

In the mid-nineteenth century Japan, like much of Asia, was vulnerable to imperialist advance. Although a number of countries had contact with Japan it was the United States that saw Japan as part of its sphere of influence. Yet from the 1850s to the turn of the century Japan gradually strengthened its economic and military position and ceased to be merely an exotic curiosity and became 'Japan the competitor' (Iriye 1975). By this time baseball was a major sport in Japan and remains so today. The central question is: how did baseball, the quintessentially American sport, survive in Japan during a period of intense nationalism and anti-Americanism?

Like Israel, Japan had no strong team sport tradition. Among the elite, intellectual skills were more highly prized and until the late nineteenth century contact between Japanese and foreigners was extremely limited.

The context within which baseball was initially accepted suggests how the Japanese can reconcile the apparent contradiction of satisfying nationalist fervour with an imported sport. Rosenstone (1980) rightly cautions against the easy acceptance of the cultural stereotype that the Japanese are basically an imitative people and joins Roden (1980) in arguing that the answer lies in the capacity of the Japanese to assimilate effectively elements of external culture. Against a background of growing nationalism Japanese students sought a national game and because judo and kendo were seen as too solitary, attention turned to western team sports and baseball in particular. Baseball was seen as reflecting key Japanese values of order, harmony, perseverance and self-restraint. 'Despite foreign provenance, baseball reputedly nourished traditional virtues of loyalty, honour, and courage and therefore symbolised the "new bushido" spirit of the age . . . [W]hile Americans in Yokohama played baseball to be more American, Japanese students . . . turned to baseball in an effort to reify traditional values and to establish a new basis for national pride' (Roden 1980: 520). But it was not just Japanese national pride that was enhanced by success at baseball, it also helped to redefine Japan's international image in a more positive light, at least according to the Japanese.

The growth in popularity of baseball in Japan coincided with an awareness in America among politicians and sports administrators of the role of baseball in the spread of American influence and values (Crepeau 1982). To many influential Americans 'Baseball promised the maturation of the Japanese national identity and the dissolution of cultural barriers between the Orient and the Occident' (Sinclair 1985: 46). Unfortunately, during the 1920s and 1930s US–Japan relations steadily worsened and despite the continuation of large crowds for American tours of Japan there was clearly an undercurrent among Japanese nationalists that associated baseball with the 'emerging enemy'. Initially there was an attempt to make more explicit the 'Japanisation' of the sport with English phrases being replaced with Japanese terminology. Eventually, as war moved closer baseball was banned in Japan. What is surprising is the rapidity with which baseball re-emerged in post-war Japan and assumed its earlier popularity, illustrated by the formation of national organising bodies for students in 1946 and for adults in 1948 (Kusaka 1987).

Part of the explanation lies in the capacity (and confidence) of the Japanese to absorb and adapt external cultural products. In sport there are many examples of this cultural eclecticism. Sasajima shows how sports imported from China in the ninth and tenth centuries had their rules subtly altered, and later when baseball and tennis were imported they were played in a 'Japanized' style (1972: 110; see also Reader 1989 and Culyer 1985). This view of the relationship between sport and Japanese culture is supported from similar analyses of religion and Japanese culture. Robertson, for example, in attempting to explain Japan's capacity to assimilate such a broad range of external religious influences and beliefs and yet retain a resilient national-societal identity points to the strong cultural strand in Japan concerning rituals of purification which mark the boundaries between internal and external, and inside and outside, and he argues that through the use of such rituals Japan is able to reject some external ideas and purify those that it wishes to adopt. In other words Japan has a societally satisfactory way of 'systematically import[ing] ideas and worldviews with relatively little "contamination"' (1987: 41).[4]

While both Israel and Japan must be seen as exhibiting a participative relationship to globalisation the explanations are very different. In Israel, where sports roots are shallow within Jewish culture, there has been a clear instrumental approach to sport, namely as a vehicle for nation-building, a basis for building and maintaining party political support in the domestic political arena, and in highlighting Israel's international problems with its immediate neighbours and, more importantly, with anti-Israeli states beyond the Middle East region. It must also be noted that Jewish culture, while not overtly positive towards sport, was not antipathic towards it and the way it was organised, apart from a mild aversion to boxing and a concern that organised sport should respect religious conventions, for example regarding sport on the sabbath. In Japan there was also little aversion to many of the aspects of modern sport such as its commercialisation and form of organisation and as far as specific sports were concerned their cultural significance could be successfully redefined.

The above brief examinations of the relationships found between global culture and local culture demonstrate the difficulty of making generalisations concerning the nature and process of globalisation, especially in the area of sport. Rather than attempting to categorise the cases as examples of either cultural imperialism or participative globalisation the evidence would seem to suggest that the two-dimensional framework described in Figure 8.1 is a better starting point for analysis. However, even this does not capture the complexity of the possible permutations in the relationship between the more static local culture and the more mobile global culture.

Of particular significance is the need to reassess the relative importance of the division between the spread of specific sports and the spread of attitudes and values associated with the rational organisation of sport. What the cases show clearly is that powerful political statements can be made at what was originally suggested to be the more superficial level of cultural uniformity. The example of Ireland is of particular interest, where a relatively weak country was (and to a degree still is) able to use sport to organise political resistance to the imperial power. Similarly, Israel's highly instrumental attitude towards sport makes it an effective political tool in international relations. What Israel and Ireland illustrate is the capacity of local cultures to make effective choices concerning which sports they adopt and, more importantly, the meaning and significance that these sports hold.

It would not be appropriate to describe the experience of Ireland and Israel as examples of creolisation for this would underplay the degree of choice that was exercised. However, creolisation would be a fair description of many of the patterns of sport identified in the cases, particularly those where the relationship is between states that each possess substantial resources. Thus creolisation (the absorption and redefinition, and possible re-export, of sports) is only possible where resources are available to support the process. There is consequently a danger of describing cosmetic changes as creolisation, a description which ignores and helps to obscure the realities of power relationships. Thus the case of baseball in Japan would be aptly described as creolisation whereas the case of cricket in the Caribbean would not.

Turning to consider the global spread of organisational rationality as the basis upon which international sport takes place, it is fair to conclude that this is indeed a development of great significance for the practice of international relations as it provides a common set of structures and procedures which different states can work within and apply when they wish to use sport politically. Just as the protocols of modern diplomacy need to be carefully internalised by states so that the subtleties and nuances of diplomatic actions can be properly understood, so too must the 'protocols' of the world of international sport. As was mentioned earlier in this chapter the symbolism, practice and organisation of international sport are ideally suited to the existing pattern of diplomatic procedures and actions such as the symbolic gestures of the withdrawal of representatives and the boycotting of international meetings.

Globalisation, as related to sport, is therefore most evident and significant in providing governments with a further medium through which to conduct international politics. However, at the deeper level of facilitating the internalisation of capitalist and consumerist values within local communities globalisation is also successful, though it is extremely difficult to identify the extent to which sport has been a primary vehicle for propagation of these values.

In terms of the major perspectives on international relations the focus on globalisation does not present an alternative perspective or approach. Its significance is that it encourages students to take account of a broader range of influences, strategies and processes in the relations between states. Just as it is better to see the pluralist perspective as an exhortation to the realist school not to ignore the significance of non-state organisations, so globalisation of sport similarly exhorts those working within the realist perspective to take greater account of the significance of global cultural flows in order to capture the richness of international politics. Referring back to Tables 2.1 and 2.2 in Chapter 2 the globalisation of sport helps to integrate international interaction at the less formal and personal levels into broader theoretical patterns.

Notes

1 Schiller (1989) is rightly sceptical of the increasingly common assumption that the audience is an active participant in the communication process, that 'meaning' is bestowed upon a product not by the producer but by the consumer. For Schiller this assumption involves ignoring the structures of power that underpin the relationship.

2 For a discussion of the potential for sport to provide a site for political resistance see Hargreaves (1982); Taylor (1982); and Donnelly (1988).

3 This section draws on research carried out by W.F. Mandle (1977; 1980; 1983; 1987).

4 There is some interesting research which explores the importation and redefinition of Japanese sports in the west. See, for example, Goodger and Goodger (1980) and Forster (1986).

9

□

Sport and international politics

For much of the post-war period the pattern of international sport politics has been dominated, as has international relations in general, by the twin fault lines of the Cold War and South African apartheid. Particularly over the twenty years between the late 1960s and the late 1980s the sports diplomacy associated with these two issues had almost become a sport in its own right, with informal rules, game strategies and tactics of play. The world of sport had become aware of, and adept at handling, the processes of compromise and bargaining around well-known issues where national and organisational positions were fairly clearly established. Not only were there elements of ritual apparent in the practice of sport, but they were also present in the practice of sport politics. The abrupt collapse of communism and the more predictable, but nonetheless surprisingly swift, retreat from apartheid has undermined the certainties of modern diplomatic life.

From one standpoint these developments can be seen as freeing international sport from a set of tensions and restrictions that have hampered the global aspirations for sports development of the international federations and the major organising bodies. Thus a repetition of the damaging boycotts of the 1970s and 1980s and the various attempts to undermine the Olympic movement through breakaway competitions, such as GANEFO, or challenges to the authority of the International Olympic Committee, by UNESCO, should be less likely. However, to view the recent history of sports politics in purely negative terms would be a mistake. It is equally plausible to argue that despite the traumas of boycotts and challenges to IOC authority, domestic and international sport have benefited greatly from being involved in the world's major issues.

The decision by the German Democratic Republic to use international sport as a stepping-stone to diplomatic recognition, and the acknowledgement by the Soviet Union and its allies of the value of sport as one way of promoting socialism, not only gave a powerful stimulus to the development of sport in central and eastern Europe but also had a similar effect in the United States and among its allies. Cold War rivalry was an important impetus for government support for sport in countries such as the USA and Britain where free market economics and jealously guarded governing body independence made for an unpromising context for government intervention. In addition to providing support for domestic sport Cold War rivalry also stimulated an interest in sport as a focus for aid and non-financial forms of sport development activity. Both the USA and the Soviet Union and their respective allies saw sport as providing an opportunity to court Third World states. For many Third World states this came in the form of competition against visiting teams – often deliberately weakened to flatter the hosts. But there was also a considerable flow of real resources in the form of expertise (coaches, scholarships and subsidised conferences and training sessions) and facilities (tracks and sports halls). While for most Third World states trade concessions, medical aid and arms were higher priorities there is little doubt that sport in poorer parts of the world benefited from Cold War tension and mistrust. A similar argument may be made with regard to apartheid. While the practice of apartheid prevented the development of black sporting talent in South Africa the organisation of the anti-apartheid campaign did much for the development of sport and national identity in many African countries. For if black African states were to be in a position to use sport as a political weapon they needed to produce a squad of athletes that would be missed from an international event if a boycott were called.

If one acknowledges the boost to sport that international tension provided then one would also have to accept that these benefits were far from cost-free. For example, while drug abuse by athletes pre-dates the emergence of east–west rivalry it was clearly legitimised in many states by the Cold War. This applies not just in the communist states but also to many western states where most anti-doping campaigns are characterised by, at best, a lethargic approach to the issue and, at worst, collusion or the turning of a deliberate blind eye to its practice. One might also argue that the dominance of the Cold War and apartheid has enabled sports organisations to avoid addressing other major sports issues. One might have expected the concentration on the practice of racial discrimination in South Africa to have resulted in a sharper sensitivity towards other forms of discrimination in sport, but this does not seem to have been the case. The preoccupation with apartheid enabled sports organisations to ignore similar forms of discrimination against women and against those who participate in minority, and non-western, sports. The lack of sports opportunities for women to participate at the highest level remains a damning indictment of most IFs and particularly of the IOC, given its rhetoric of universalism. In addition, in most IFs the representation of women in positions of authority is abysmally low (Bowles and Chappell 1986; White and Brackenridge 1985). As regards the discrimination in favour of western European sports neither the IOC nor the Commonwealth Games Federation have sought to define sports development as anything other than the reinforcement of the western sporting tradition. The claims of regional sports, such as the various martial arts, to exposure on the Olympic stage have been ignored and progressively marginalised. The eligibility rules of the IOC in particular, which require among other criteria that the sport be practised in at least fifty countries across three continents, make it extremely difficult for popular regional sports to get the opportunity to be displayed before a global audience. Thus while tennis and golf find the path to Olympic status relatively smooth non-European sports face considerable barriers.

Although an audit of the last thirty years of international sport would produce differing calculations of costs and benefits, attempts to assess the likely direction of sport in the post-Cold War and post-apartheid world are much more difficult. Without the stimulus for government interest and intervention that the Cold War provided and at a time of global economic recession there are signs that governments will seek to reap a peace dividend from sport as well as from their defence budgets. The elaborate sports infrastructure in the former GDR and Soviet Union have been largely dismantled and this has already been reflected in a decline in performance, by the constituent states, at the 1992 Olympic Games. In Britain the spending on sport by local authorities has declined by between 30% and 40% since 1990 while the budget of the Sports Council has been frozen at its 1992 level.

While the decline in government support for sport in developed states might be compensated for by an increase in commercial sponsorship the same is not likely to be the case for Third World states. Part of the motivation for the establishment of Olympic Solidarity and the development strategies of major IFs such as FIFA and the IAAF was indeed to promote and strengthen sport in poorer countries but an important motivation was also the garnering of votes and the maintenance of the balance of power within federations and the IOC. With the fragmentation of the communist bloc the political motive for supporting sports development programmes has weakened, if not quite disappeared. It may continue but the dependent position of most Third World states on the developed world is likely to increase and make challenges to First World dominance of global sport far less likely.

The role and significance of sport for international relations

It is within the context of rapid global political change that the role and significance of international sport need to be assessed. In Chapter 1 five themes for analysis were outlined, namely the relationship between sport and diplomacy, ideology, nation-building, access and money. As regards providing opportunities for diplomacy sport has proved extremely valuable both as a resource and as an arena. As a resource sport enables states to make approaches to hostile states through a medium which benefits from its non-political image. As a current example South Korea is edging closer to North Korea by proposing a joint team for the 1994 Asian Games. This follows the disappointment of the failure to secure agreement on a joint team for the Barcelona Olympics, but the success of joint teams in the FIFA World Youth tournament in 1991 and in the table tennis world championships in Japan also held in 1991.

Sport can be used to strengthen relations between allies, for example within the Commonwealth and also through the medium of aid for sport development. Governments have not simply relied on their ability to gain the cooperation of domestic governing bodies to help further diplomatic interests, they have also fostered the emergence of sports issues on the agendas of international governmental organisations. For example, the current activities of the Council of Europe fit in very closely with the diplomatic aims of western European states of encouraging the development of free market economics and liberal democracy in former communist states. This strategy allowed early approaches from states that were previously considered enemies to be directed to a relatively non-controversial area of social life. In retrospect such caution was unnecessary as the former communist states were only too eager to jettison central planning in favour of the free market but in 1989 the sporting links via the Council provided western governments with a more broadly based strategy. As a final illustration of the value of sport as a resource the decisions about location of major events still remain an important diplomatic opportunity. The decision to locate the 1994 Commonwealth Games in Victoria, Canada rather than New Delhi was recognised by all concerned as a serious diplomatic error, perpetuating the image of the Games as a white Commonwealth preserve. Notwithstanding the fact that many Third World Commonwealth members must have voted for Victoria it was strongly urged by senior Commonwealth figures, including John Major, that the Games must go outside the 'old' Commonwealth in 1998. The choice of Kuala Lumpur, while not one of the poorest of states, was seen as an important diplomatic decision for the stability of internal Commonwealth relations.

Just as sport remains a valuable diplomatic resource it also remains an important arena in which states can publicise positions regarding the policies of others and project domestic policy. The last two Olympic Games have been largely free of boycotts and consequently the main diplomatic advantage has been to the host countries, with both South Korea and Spain maximising the political benefits of the role of host.

The utility of sport as a diplomatic resource or as a forum for international contact may, however, be diminishing. The end of the 1980s saw the emergence of an international sports movement radically different from that of only ten years previously. Not only are international sports bodies much wealthier, but they have also developed a close and, so far, advantageous relationship with the media. The growing commercialism of sport and the emergence of the Olympic Games as a multi-million dollar enterprise have changed considerably the relationship between sport and government, especially in richer states. On the one hand these developments have given international sports organisations resources with which to withstand, in theory at least, a degree of government pressure. The IAAF World Championships, the soccer World Cup and the Olympics are no longer in the position of looking for subsidy from the host government but are now courted by governments who are all too eager to demonstrate their commitment to sport. In addition, elite sportsmen and women in many sports possess a degree of financial security that allows them to act independently of their governments and increasingly their governing body.

Yet the picture painted above of economic wealth leading to greater autonomy applies only to a small group of sports and participants. The vast majority of competitors and sports are still heavily dependent on state subsidy in most countries. Even those that have gained a degree of financial independence have simply moved from state patronage to a frequently more demanding and intrusive commercial patronage. More importantly the contrasts that might emerge between government and business priorities for the conduct of international sport are likely to be superficial, especially in western countries, for at a fundamental level both government and business share a common liberal democratic, free market ideology. In addition, as international sport has become more attractive to commercial interests it has also become much more complex to organise and administer. The problems that now face many governing bodies require the active cooperation of governments. The accrual of greater wealth, rather than granting autonomy, frequently leads to more involved organisational and financial structures that in turn increase the membership and complexity of policy communities. For example, soccer in Britain and in many other European countries has greatly increased its income from sponsorship but has nonetheless found that the issues of football spectator violence and (in the European Community) free movement of players involved governing bodies in intense negotiations with government and IGOs. The problems associated with drug abuse, in part the direct result of commercialisation, have similarly involved governing bodies and IFs in complex patterns of relationships with governments (and their court systems) and IGOs. Thus the commercialisation of sport has altered the relationship between governments and sports organisations but not to any profound extent; indeed it has simply created the impression within sports organisations of being in control of the direction of the sport's development.

The growth of commercialisation of sport highlights the debates about the relationship between sport and ideology. In Chapter 8 the question of globalisation was explored and one of the key conclusions was that to refer to globalisation as a process of homogenisation was not supported by the evidence. At a superficial level it may be possible to argue that, pockets of regional idiosyncrasy notwithstanding, an increasing proportion of the world's population is playing and watching a similar western-defined and governed range of sports. Yet a contrary conclusion can also be argued which suggests that significant variation still exists in terms of the sports people participate in and watch, and a number of examples of resistance and rejection of 'alien' sports were provided in support. However, this argument is only plausible if analysis is confined to the surface level of phenomena. Brazil may affect the style of play of soccer and the West Indies that of cricket but the substance of power and the ability to determine the direction of sports development remains lodged firmly in the First World. What was clear from the examination of the infrastructure of international sport was the extent to which it had developed a capacity to facilitate the process of globalisation.

The emergence of a global sports infrastructure in the last thirty years is of major importance. The chapters that examined the role of business and that of international governmental and non-governmental organisations showed clearly that domestic sport is firmly embedded in a network of international organisational relations. The capacity of domestic sports organisations, particularly those of poorer countries, to insulate their practices and traditions from external pressures, and their capacity to engage with the international sports community on their own terms, is slight. While the global media facilitate globalisation by fostering the desire to participate in international sport, other organisations such as Olympic Solidarity and the Commonwealth Games have the capacity to provide poorer countries with the means by which they can fulfil their aspirations. Olympic Solidarity and the development programmes of the major IFs enable athletes from poorer countries to participate on the international sports circuits thus providing local role models and 'heroes'. The IFs and the Commonwealth also enable countries to participate in and absorb the values and norms associated with the organisation of international sport.

The substance of globalisation lies at a more profound level than the practice of particular sports. It lies in the legitimation that the presentation and practice of international sport give to a particular set of western values. The rationalised and bureaucratised form of international sport provides a supportive backcloth to the practice of other forms of international contact, for example through diplomacy or business. As was suggested at the end of Chapter 8 the globalisation of the sport has provided a set of common reference points and a common language for dialogue to be used by states, but the reference points and the form and structure of the language have been determined on the basis of western power.

Perhaps the most enduring value of sport to governments is as a basis for nation-building, and as a basis for recognition of claims to national distinctiveness. For the Baltic states the reactivation of their Olympic membership was one of their first actions following the loosening of ties with the Soviet Union. Other states emerging from the collapse of the Soviet Union have also seen membership of the Olympic movement and the major IFs as a first independent step on the international stage. Uzbekistan even bid to host the 2000 Olympic Games at Tashkent, demonstrating an acute awareness of the benefits of being the Olympic host, if rather misjudging the costs. At sub-national level sport still retains its attraction as a medium for asserting claims to national identity and self-determination. The 1992 Barcelona Olympic Games provided an important opportunity for the Catalan nationalists to draw attention to their cause. In Australia Aborigine groups are campaigning against the current bid by Sydney to host the 2000 Games on the grounds of denial of their human rights.

The variation on this standard theme linking international sport and nation-building is the use of sport to develop a sense of identity at the supra-national level. Most notable is the attempt by the EC to develop and enhance a sense of Community citizenship through the association of the EC with sports events. Equally significant is the Commonwealth's increasing reliance on sport to demonstrate the vitality of the organisation and to symbolise its values. The continued attraction of sport to states, international organisations and aspiring nation-states is a testament to the richness and adaptability of the sports metaphor and the malleability of sports administrators.

In conclusion, sport has always been a resource within the international system available primarily to governments, but also to other non-governmental political interests, and while it has, on occasion, been the primary tool of diplomacy and policy implementation, it has more often been an element of a broader and more comprehensive political strategy. Sport provides governments in particular with an elaborate but low-key network for contact and dialogue where strategies can be tested and tentative approaches made within a context where the stakes are generally low and where media attention is high but generally malleable, naive and uncritical in its analysis of sports politics. But it is not just that sport, through actions such as boycotts or the opportunity to host major events, provides an extension to the diplomatic repertoire possessed by states, sport is also significant in terms of its contribution to the establishment of a set of norms and values supportive of capitalist interests and of western diplomatic activity.

Over the last thirty years a sophisticated and truly global and elaborate infrastructure has been constructed around sport comprising not just sport IGOs and a set of INGOs which see sport as a significant element in their range of interests, but also a global media that sees sport as an essential element in its capacity to maintain market share and profitability. The network of IGOs and INGOs reaches states and communities of the world that are not part of the other major world institutions such as the UN. As a result governmental and non-governmental sports organisations provide an important point of access for the world's microstates (as well as for some middle-rank powers), and also provide a means by which the global sporting culture maximises its penetration.

If the primary conclusion of this study is to highlight the extensive opportunities that the development of an international sport infrastructure provides for the pursuit of national and organisational interests, then an important secondary conclusion relates to the significance of the less formal forms of transnational contact between states. The flow of athletes, supporters and administrators between countries is a major phenomenon and an important element in the process of globalisation and cannot be confidently seen as an extension of global media penetration. International sport operates extensively at this less formal level of contact and plays an important role in spreading values and norms associated with a particularly western view of sport.

The elaborate international infrastructure of sport and the interpenetration of sport and politics outlined and analysed in this book add weight to the pluralist approach to understanding international politics. However, the analysis does not require a rejection of the emphasis given to the realist assumptions concerning the core interests of the state, especially security. Rather the discussion provides much evidence which confirms the centrality of these realist concerns. What the analysis demonstrates is the existence of a set of international actors with a capacity to establish and pursue their own interests, while acknowledging that these interests are often the product of negotiation with states and are rarely capable of being sustained in the face of determined state opposition. Yet sports organisations cannot be ignored by states and are indeed treated with a high degree of respect in recognition of their status as significant actors in the international system.

References

Agnell, R.C. (1969), *Peace on the March: Transnational Participation*, New York: Van Nostrand Reinhold.

Akinrinade, O. (1992), 'The 1971 Declaration of Commonwealth Principles after 20 years', *The Round Table*, 321, pp. 23–35.

Alexandrakis, A. and Krotee, M.L. (1988), 'The dialectics of the International Olympic Committee', *International Review for Sociology of Sport*, vol. 23, 4, pp. 325–43.

Alker, H.R. (1981), 'Dialectical foundations of global disparities', in Hollist, W.L. and Rosenau, J.N., (eds.), *World System Structure: Continuity and change*, Beverly Hills, Calif.: Sage, pp. 80–109.

Allison, G. (1969), 'Conceptual models and the Cuban Missile Crisis', *American Political Science Review*, 63, Sept., pp. 689–718.

Allison, G. (1971), *Essence of Decision*, Boston, Mass.: Little, Brown & Co.

Allison, G. and Halperin, M.H. (1972), 'Bureaucratic politics: a paradigm and some policy implications,' in Tanter, R., and Ullman, R.H. (eds.), *Theory and Policy in International Relations*, Princeton, NJ: Princeton University Press, pp. 40–79.

Allison, L. (ed.) (1986), *The Politics of Sport*, Manchester: Manchester University Press.

Aluko, O. (1991), 'The foreign policies of African states in the 1990s', *The Round Table*, 317, pp. 33–44.

Anthony, D. (1988), 'Olympic Solidarity', *Coaching Focus*, 8, 3–5.

Aris, S. (1990), *Sportsbiz: Inside the sports business*, London: Hutchinson.

Armstrong, D. (1982), *The Rise of the International Organisation: A short history*, London: Macmillan.

Austin, D. (1988), *The Commonwealth and Britain*, London: Routledge and Kegan Paul.

Bagdikian, B. (1989), 'The lords of the global village', *The Nation*, 12 June, pp. 805–20.

Bailey, J. (1989), *Conflicts in Cricket*, London: Kingswood Press.

Bailey, P. (1979), *Leisure and Class in Victorian England*, London: Routledge and Kegan Paul.

Bennett, A.L. (1991), *International Organisations: Principles & issues*, Englewood Cliffs, New Jersey: Prentice-Hall.

Benson, J.K. (1979), *Interorganisational Networks and Policy Sectors: Notes towards comparative analysis*, mimeo, University of Missouri.

Benson, J.K. (1982), 'A framework for policy analysis', in Whetton, D.H. and Rogers, D.L. (eds.), *Interorganisational Coordination*, Iowa: Iowa University Press, pp. 137–76.

Binder, L. (1986), 'The natural history of development theory', *Comparative Studies in Society and History*, 28, pp. 3–33.

Blau, P.M. (1956), *Bureaucracy in Modern Society*, New York: Random House.

Bourne, R. (1992), 'Commonwealth at UNCED', *The Round Table*, 324, pp. 457–63.

Bowles, S. and Chappell, R. (1986), 'Women and athletics', *Athletics Coach*, vol. 20, 2, June, pp. 8–11.

Boyd-Barrett, J.O. (1982), 'Cultural dependency and the mass media', in Gurevitch, M., Bennett, T., Curran, J. and Woollacot, J. (eds.), *Culture, Society and the Media*, London: Methuen.

The British Archer (1988), 'New concept for European Community Games in 1989', *The British Archer*, vol. 39, 4, pp. 166–8.

Brohm, J.-M., (1978), *Sport: A prison of measured time*, London: Pluto Press.

Brown, D.W. (1984), 'Imperialism and games on the playing fields of Canada's private schools', in Muller, N. and Kuhl, J.K. (eds.), *Olympic Scientific Congress, Official Report, Sports History*, Niederhausen, Germany: Schors, pp. 129–38.

Bueno de Mesquita, B. (1981), *The War Trap*, New Haven, Conn.: Yale University Press.

Bull, H. (1977), *The Anarchical Society: A study of order in world politics*, London: Macmillan.

Bull, H. (1984), 'Forward', in Gong, G. *The Standard of Civilisation in International Society*, Oxford: The Clarendon Press, pp. v–xi.

Bull, H. and Watson, A. (1985), 'Introduction', in Bull, H. and Watson, A. (eds.), *The Expansion of International Society*, Oxford: The Clarendon Press, pp. 1–9.

Burton, R.D.E. (1991), 'Cricket, carnival and street culture in the Caribbean', in Jarvie, G. (ed.), *Sport, Racism and Ethnicity*, London: Falmer Press, pp. 7–29.

Caldwell, G. (1982), 'International sport and national identity', *International Social Science Journal*, 92, pp. 172–83.

Cameron, I.O. (1989), 'Canada, the Commonwealth and South Africa: National foreign policy-making in a multilateral environment', *Millennium*, vol. 18, 2, pp. 205–25.

Cantelon, H. and Gruneau, R., (1982), *Sport, Culture and the Modern State*, Toronto: University of Toronto Press.

Cardoso, F.H. and Faletto, E. (1979), *Dependency and Development in Latin America*, Berkeley, Calif.: University of California Press.

Carr, G.A. (1976), 'The birth of the German Democratic Republic and the organisation of East German sport', *Canadian Journal of History of Sport and Physical Education*, vol. VII, 1, pp. 1–21.

Cashmore, E. (1990), *Making Sense of Sport*, London: Routledge.

Chadwick, J. (1982), *The Unofficial Commonwealth: The story of the Commonwealth Foundation 1965–1980*, London: George Allen & Unwin.

Chan, G. (1985), 'The "two-Chinas" problem and the Olympic formula', *Pacific Affairs*, vol. 58, 3, pp. 473–90.

Chan, S. (1988), *The Commonwealth in World Politics: A study of international action 1965–1985*, London: Lester Crook Academic Publishing.

Coakley, J.J. (1986), *Sport in Society: Issues and controversies*, St Louis: Times Mirror/Mosby College Publishing.

Coghlan, J., (1990), *Sport and British Politics Since 1960*, Basingstoke: Falmer Press.

Cohen, E. (1977), 'Towards a sociology of international tourism', *Social Research*, vol. 39, 1, pp. 164–82.

Commission of the European Communities [Adonnino Report] (1985), *A People's Europe*, (Bulletin of the European Communities: Supplement 7/85), Brussels: Commission of the European Communities.

Commission of the European Communities (1991), *The European Community and Sport*, (SEC [91] 1438 final), Brussels: Commission of the European Communities.

Commission of the European Communities (1992), *European File: The European Community and Sport* 2/1992, Brussels: Commission of the European Communities.

Commission of the European Communities (1993), *Commission of the European Communities and Sports for Disabled People*, Brussels: Commission of the European Communities.

Commonwealth Games Federation (1987), *The Commonwealth Games Federation and the Commonwealth Games*, London: Commonwealth Games Federation.

Commonwealth Secretariat (1987), *The Commonwealth at the Summit: Communiqués of the Commonwealth Heads of Government meetings 1944–1986*, London: Commonwealth Secretariat.

Commonwealth Secretariat (1989), *Commonwealth Heads of Government: The Kuala Lumpur communiqué, October 1989*, London: Commonwealth Secretariat.

Commonwealth Secretariat (1991a), *Working Party on Strengthening Commonwealth Sport: Final report*, London: Commonwealth Secretariat.

Commonwealth Secretariat (1991b), *Commonwealth Heads of Government Meeting: The Harare communiqué*, London: Commonwealth Secretariat.

Constantino, R., (1978), *Neocolonial Identity and Counter-Consciousness: Essays on cultural decolonialization*, London: Merlin Press.

Coombs, P.H. (1964), *The Fourth Dimension of Foreign Policy: Educational and cultural affairs*, New York: Harper & Row.

Coopers Lybrand (1992), *The Impact of European Community Activities on Sport: Preliminary report*, Brussels: Coopers Lybrand.

Coubertin, P. de (1979), *Olympic Memoirs*, Lausanne, Switzerland: International Olympic Committee.

Council of Europe (1992a), *The Council of Europe's Work on Sport: 1967–91*, vol. 1, Strasbourg: Council of Europe.

Council of Europe (1992b), *The Council of Europe's Work on Sport: 1967–91*, vol. 2, Strasbourg: Council of Europe.

Cox, R.W. (1981), 'Social forces, states and world order: Beyond international relations theory', *Journal of International Studies: Millennium*, vol. 10, 2, pp. 126–55.

Crawford, S. (1984), ' "We have rough labour, but we can afford a day for recreation too": A thematic analysis of recreation and sport in colonial New Zealand', *Stadion*, X, pp. 95–134.

Crepeau, R.C. (1980), *Baseball: America's Diamond Mind, 1919–1941*, Orlando, Fla.: University of Central Florida Press.

Crepeau, R.C. (1982), 'Pearl Harbour: A failure of baseball?', *Journal of Popular Culture*, 19, pp. 67–74.

Crick, B. (1964), *In Defence of Politics*, Harmondsworth: Penguin.

Culyer, P. (1985), *From Rite to Sport*, New York: Weatherhill.

Cunningham, D., Slack, T. and Hinings, B. (1987), 'Changing design archetypes in amateur sport organisations', in Slack, T. and Hinings, C.R. (eds.), *The Organisation and Administration of Sport*, London, Ontario: Sport Dynamics, pp. 59–81.

Cutler, L.N. (1978), *Global Interdependence and the Multi-national Firm*, Headline Series No. 239 (April), New York: Foreign Policy Association.

Dahl, R. (1961), 'The behaviourial approach to political science', *American Political Science Review*, vol. 55, 4, December, pp. 37–51.

Dahl, R. (1963), *A Preface to Democratic Theory*, Chicago: University of Chicago Press.

Daoudi, M.S. and Dajani, M.S. (1983), *Economic Sanctions: Ideals and experience*, London: Routledge and Kegan Paul.

Delvoie, L.A. (1989), 'The Commonwealth in Canadian foreign policy', *The Round Table*, 310, pp. 137–43.

Der Derian, J. and Shapiro, M.J. (1989), *International/Intertextual Relations: Postmodern readings of world politics*, Lexington, Mass.: Lexington Books.

De Witt, B.D. and Kirton, J.J. (1983), *Canada as a Principal Power*, Toronto: John Wiley.

Donnelly, P. (1988), 'Sport as a site for popular resistance', in Gruneau, R. (ed.), *Popular Cultures and Political Practices*, Toronto: Garamond Press, pp. 69–82.

Donohoe, T. and Johnson, N. (1986), *Foul Play: Drug abuse in sports*, Oxford: Basil Blackwell.

Doxey, M. (1984), 'The Commonwealth Secretariat', in Groom, A.J.R and Taylor, P. (eds.), *The Commonwealth in the 1980s: Challenges and opportunities*, London: Macmillan, pp. 42–63.

Dunning, E.G., Murphy, P. and Williams, J. (1988), *Roots of Football Hooliganism*, London: Routledge and Kegan Paul.

Dye, T. (1975), *Understanding Public Policy*, 2nd edn., Englewood Cliffs, New Jersey: Prentice-Hall.

East, M. (1980), 'The organisational impact of interdependence on foreign policy-making: The case of Norway', in Kegley, C. and McGowan, P. (eds.) *The Political Economy of Foreign Policy Behaviour*, Beverly Hills, Calif.: Sage, pp. 137–61.

Edwards, H., (1973), *Sociology of Sport*, Homewood, Ill.: The Dorsey Press.

Eichberg, H. (1984), 'Olympic sport: Neocolonialism and its alternatives', *International Review for the Sociology of Sport*, 19, pp. 97–105.

Elias, N. (1986), 'Introduction', in Elias, N. and Dunning, E., *Quest for Excitement: Sport and leisure in the civilizing process*, Oxford: Basil Blackwell, pp. 7–41.

Erisman, H.M. (1983), 'Tourism and cultural dependency in the West Indies', *Annals of Tourism Research*, vol. 10, pp. 337–61.

Espy, R. (1979), *The Politics of the Olympic Games*, Berkeley, Calif.: California University Press.

Esteinou Madrid, J. (1986), 'Means of communication and construction of hegemony', in Atwood, R. and McAnany, E., *Communication and Latin American Society: Trends in critical research, 1960–1985*, Madison: University of Wisconsin Press, pp. 104–26.

Evans, P. (1982), *World Cup 1982*, London: Knight.

Featherstone, M. (1987), 'Consumer culture, symbolic power and universalism', in Stauth, G. and Zubaida, S. (eds.), *Mass Culture, Popular Culture and Social Life in the Middle East*, Boulder: Westport Press, p. 107–26.

Featherstone, M., (1990), 'Global culture: An introduction', in Featherstone, M. (ed.), *Global Culture: Nationalism, globalisation and modernity*, London: Sage, pp. 1–14.

Fejes, F. (1981), 'Media imperialism: An assessment', *Media, Culture and Society*, vol. 3, 3, pp. 281–9.

Feld, S. (1988), 'Notes on world beat', in *Public Culture Bulletin*, vol. 1, 1, pp. 31–7.

Fine, G.A. (1984), 'Negotiated orders and organisational cultures', *Annual Review of Sociology*, 10, pp. 239–62.

Forster, A. (1986), 'The nature of martial arts and their change in the West', in Kleinman, S. (ed.) *Mind and Body: East meets West*, Champaign, Ill.: Human Kinetics Publishers Inc., pp. 83–7.

Friedman, J. (1990), 'Being in the world: Globalisation and localisation', in Featherstone, M. (ed.), *Global Culture: Nationalism, globalisation and modernity*, London: Sage, pp. 311–28.

Friend, J., Power, J.M. and Yewlett, C.J.L. (1974), *Public Planning: The inter-corporate dimension*, London: Tavistock.

Fukuyama, F. (1992), *The End of History and the Last Man*, London: Penguin.

Galliher, J.F. and Hessler, R.M. (1979), 'Sports competition and international capitalism', *The Journal of Sport and Social Issues*, Spring, pp. 10–21.

Galtung, J. (1971), 'A structural theory of imperialism', *Journal of Peace Research*, vol. 13, 2, pp. 81–94.

Geraghty, C., Simpson, P. and Whannel, G. (1986), 'Tunnel vision: Television's World Cup', in Tomlinson, A. and Whannel, G. (eds.), *Off The Ball: The football World Cup*, London: Pluto Press, pp. 20–35.

Giddens, A. (1987), *The Nation State and Violence*, Berkeley, Calif.: University of California Press.

Gilpin, R. (1981), *War and Change in World Politics*, New York: Cambridge University Press.

Glassford, G. (1976), *Application of a Theory of Games to the Transitional Eskimo Culture*, New York: Arno.

Glassford, G.R. (1981), 'Life and games of the traditional Canadian Eskimo', in Luschen, G.R.F. and Sage, G.H., *Handbook of Social Sciences of Sport*, Champaign, Ill.: Stipes, pp. 78–92.

Goldlust, J. (1988), *Playing for Keeps: Sport, the media and society*, Melbourne: Longman Cheshire.

Gong, G. (1984), *The Standard of 'Civilization' in International Society*, Oxford: Clarendon Press.

Goodger, B.C. and Goodger, J.M. (1980), 'Organisational and cultural change in post-war British judo, *International Review of Sport Sociology*, vol. 15, pp. 21–48.

Greendorfer, S.H. (1981), 'Sport and the mass media', in Luschen, G.R.F. and Sage, G.H., *Handbook of Social Sciences of Sport*, Champaign, Ill.: Stipes, pp. 160–80.

Gregg, R.W. (1972), 'UN economic, social and technical activities', in Barros, J. (ed.), *The United Nations: Past, present and future*, New York: Free Press, p. 212–30.

Groom, A.J.R. (1988), 'The advent of international organisation', in Taylor, P. and Groom, A.J.R., (eds.), *International Institutions at Work*, London: Pinter, pp. 3–20.

Groom, A.J.R. and Taylor, P. (1984), 'The continuing Commonwealth: Its origins and characteristics', in Groom, A.J.R. and Taylor, P. (eds.), *The Commonwealth in the 1980s: Challenges and opportunities*, London: Macmillan, pp. 2–3.

Groom, A.J.R. and Taylor, P. (eds.) (1988), *International Institutions at Work*, London: Pinter.

Guttmann, A. (1978), *From Ritual to Record*, New York: Columbia University Press.

Guttmann, A. (1981), 'Translator's introduction', in Rigauer, B., *Sport and Work*, New York: Columbia University Press, pp. 1–17.

Guttmann, A. (1984), *The Games Must Go On: Avery Brundage and the Olympic movement*, New York: Columbia University Press.

Guttmann, A. (1988), 'The Cold War and the Olympics', *International Journal*, XLIII, Autumn, pp. 554–67.

Guttmann, A. (1992), *The Olympics: A history of the modern Games*, Urbana, Ill.: University of Illinois Press.

Haas, E. (1958), *The Uniting of Europe: Political, social and economic forces 1950–1957*, Stanford: Stanford University Press.

Haferkamp, H. (1987), 'Beyond the iron cage of modernity? Achievement, negotiation and changes in the power structure', *Theory, Culture and Society*, vol. 4, pp. 31–54.

Hall, S. (1990), 'The local and the global: Globalisation and ethnicity', in King, A.D. (ed.), *Culture, Globalisation and the World System*, Basingstoke: Macmillan, pp. 19–40.

Hamelink, C.J. (1983), *Cultural Autonomy in Global Communications: Planning national information policy*, London: Longman.

Hamelink, C. (1984), *Transnational Data Flows in the Information Age*, Lund, Sweden: Studentliteratur.

Hanak, A. (1974), 'The historical background of the creation of the "Maccabi World Union"', in *Physical Education and Sports in the Jewish History and Culture: Proceedings of an international seminar at Wingate Institute, July 1973*, Natanya, Israel: Wingate Institute, pp. 147–60.

Hannerz, U. (1990a), 'Cosmopolitans and locals in world culture', in Featherstone, M., *Global Culture: Nationalism, globalisation and modernity*, London: Sage, pp. 237–52.

Hannerz, U. (1990b), 'Scenarios for peripheral cultures', in King, A.D. (ed.), *Culture, Globalisation and the World System*, Basingstoke: Macmillan, pp. 107–28.

Hardman, K. (1987), 'Politics, ideology and physical education in the German Democratic Republic', *British Journal of Physical Education*, vol. 18, 1, pp. 20–2.

Hardy, S. (1990), ' "Adopted by all the leading clubs": Sporting goods and the shaping of leisure, 1800–1900', in Butsch, R. (ed.), *For Fun and Profit: The transformation of leisure into consumption*, Philadelphia: Temple University Press, pp. 71–103.

Hargreaves, J. (1975), 'Mass sport and ideological hegemony', in Parker, S. *et al.* (eds.), *Sport and Leisure in Contemporary Society*, London: Polytechnic of Central London, pp. 53–64.

Hargreaves, J. (1982), 'Sport, culture and ideology', in Hargreaves, J. (ed.), *Sport, Culture and Ideology*, London: Routledge, pp. 30–61.

Hargreaves, J. (1986), *Sport, Power and Culture*, Cambridge: Polity Press.

Harrison, D. (1988), *The Sociology of Modernisation and Development*, Basingstoke: Macmillan.

Harriss, I. (1986), 'Cricket and bourgeois ideology', in Lawrence, G. and Rowe, D., *Power Play: Essays in the sociology of Australian sport*, Sydney, Australia: Hale & Iremonger, pp. 179–95.

Hart-Davis, D. (1986), *Hitler's Games: The 1936 Olympics*, New York: Harper & Row.

Heinila, K. (1985), 'Sport and international understanding – a contradiction in terms?', *Sociology of Sport Journal*, 2, pp. 240–8.

Hill, C.R. (1992), *Olympic Politics*, Manchester: Manchester University Press.

Hinings, B. and Slack, T. (1987), 'The dynamics of quadrennial plan implementation in national sport organisations', in Slack, T. and Hinings, C.R. (eds.), *The Organisation and Administration of Sport*, London, Ontario: Sport Dynamics, pp. 127–51.

Hoberman, J.M. (1986), *The Olympic Crisis: Sport, politics and the moral order*, New Rochelle, NY: Aristide, D. Caratzas.

Hoberman, J.M. (1987a), 'Sport and social change: The transformation of Maoist sport', *Sociology of Sport Journal*, 4, 156–70.

Hoberman, J.M. (1987b), 'Olympic internationalism and the Korea Herald', in Jackson, R. and McPhail, T., *The Olympic Movement and the Mass Media: Past, present and future issues, Conference Proceedings*, University of Calgary: Canada, pp. 11.35–11.42.

Hobson, J.A. (1965), *Imperialism: A study*, Ann Arbor: University of Michigan Press.

Hoch, P. (1972), *Rip Off the Big Game: The exploitation of sport by the power elite*, New York: Doubleday.

Hoffman, S. (1977), 'An American social science: International relations', *Daedalus*, vol. 106, 3, pp. 40–63.

Hogwood, B. (1987), *From Crisis to Complacency*, Oxford: Oxford University Press.

Hollis, M. and Smith, S. (1991), *Explaining and Understanding International Theory*, Oxford: Clarendon Press.

Holt, R. (1989), *Sport and the British: A modern history*, Oxford: Oxford University Press.

Houlihan, B. (1991), *The Government and Politics of Sport*, London: Routledge.

Howell, D. (1990), *Made in Birmingham: The memoirs of Denis Howell*, London: Queen Anne Press.

Hufbauer, G.C. and Schott, J.J. (1985), *Economic Sanctions Reconsidered: History and current policy*, Washington DC: Institute for International Economics.

Humphrey, J. (1986), 'No holding Brazil: Football, nationalism and politics', in Tomlinson, A. and Whannel, G. (eds.), *Off The Ball: The football World Cup*, London: Pluto Press, pp. 127–39.

Igbinovia, P.E. (1985), 'Soccer hooliganism in black Africa', *International Journal of Offender Therapy and Comparative Criminology*, vol. 29, 2, pp. 135–46.

Illmarinen, M. (ed) (1982), *Sport and International Understanding: Proceedings of the Congress, Helsinki July 7–10*, Berlin: Springer-Verlag.

Ingham, A.G. (1975), 'Occupational sub-cultures in the work world of sport', in Ball, D.W. and Loy, J.W., *Sport and Social Order: Contributions to the sociology of sport*, Reading, Mass.: Addison-Wesley, pp. 333–90.

Ingham, D. (1988), *Olympic-Style Bidding Threatens the Commonwealth Games*, London: Gemini News Service.

International Amateur Athletic Federation (1991), *Development Cooperation: A situation analysis and a strategy for the world-wide development of athletics*, London: IAAF.

International Olympic Committee (1964), *Olympic Bulletin*, no. 88, Lausanne, Switzerland: IOC.

International Olympic Committee (1991), *The Olympic Charter*, Lausanne, Switzerland: IOC.

Iriye, A. (1975), 'Japan as a competitor, 1895–1917', in Iriye, A. (ed.), *Mutual Images: Essays in American–Japanese relations*, Cambridge, Mass.: DC Heath, pp. 56–73.

James, C.L.R. (1963), *Beyond a Boundary*, London: Stanley Paul.

James, C.L.R. (1977), *The Future in the Past*, New York: Lawrence Hill.

Janis, I.L. (1972), *Victims of Groupthink*, Boston, Mass.: Houghton Mifflin.

James, P. (1990), 'The ideology of winning: cultural politics and the America's Cup', in Lawrence, G. and Rowe, D. (eds.), *Power Play: Essays in the sociology of Australian sport*, Sydney: Hale and Iremonger.

Jarvie, G. (1986), 'Highland Gatherings, sport and social class', *Sociology of Sport Journal*, vol. 3, pp. 344–55.

Jenner, B. (1992), *The Council of Europe and Sport: A reappraisal of 'Sport for All in Europe' by Jacques Marchand*, Strasbourg: Council of Europe.

Jervis, R. (1976), *Perception and Misperception in International Politics*, Princeton, Mass.: Princeton University Press.

Jones, A. (1991), 'The first Commonwealth forum for non-governmental organisations: A voice for the NGOs of the Commonwealth', *The Round Table*, 320, pp. 401–11.

Julien, K.S. (1992), 'The problems of small states', *The Round Table*, 321, pp. 45–50.

Kanin, D.B. (1978), 'Ideology and diplomacy: The international dimensions of Chinese political sport', in Lowe, B., Kanin, D.B. and Strenk, A., *Sport and International Relations*, Champaign, Ill.: Stipes, pp. 263–78.

Kanin, D.B. (1980), 'The Olympic boycott in diplomatic context', *Journal of Sport and Social Issues*, vol. 4, 1, pp. 1–24.

Kanin, D.B. (1981), *A Political History of the Olympic Games*, Boulder, Colo.: Westview Press.

Katz, E. and Liebes, T. (1985), 'Mutual aid in decoding "Dallas": Preliminary notes from a cross cultural study', in Drummond, P. and Paterson, R. (eds.), *Television in Transition*, London: British Film Institute, pp. 187–98.

Kegley, C.W. and Wittkopf, E.R. (1989), *World Politics*, 3rd edn., Basingstoke: Macmillan.

Kennard, J.A. and Hofstetter, E.O. (1983), 'Sport and television: A bibliography', *Arena Review*, vol. 7, 2, pp. 28–38.

Kennedy, P. (1988), *The Rise and Fall of Great Powers*, London: Unwin Hyman.

Keohane, R.O. (1980), 'The theory of hegemonic stability and changes in international economic regimes, 1967–77', in Holsti, O. *et al.*, *Change in the International System*, Boulder, Colo.: Westview Press, p. 131–62.

Keohane, R.O. (1984), *After Hegemony: Cooperation and discord in the world political economy*, Princeton, New Jersey: Princeton University Press.

Keohane, R.O. (1989), *International Institutions and State Power: Essays in international relations theory*, Boulder, Colo.: Westview Press.

Keohane, R.O. and Nye, J.S. (1974), 'Transgovernmental relations and international organisations', *World Politics*, vol. XXVII, 1, pp. 39–62, pp. 186–99.

Keohane, R.O. and Nye, J.S. (1975), 'International interdependence and integration', in Greestein, F.I. and Polsby, N.W. (eds.), *International Politics: Handbook of social science*, vol. 18, Reading, Mass.: Addison-Wesley.

Keohane, R.O. and Nye, J.S. (1989), *Power and Interdependence: World politics in transition*, 2nd edn., Boston, Mass.: Little, Brown & Co.

Kesselman, M. (1973), 'Order or movement? The literature of political development as ideology', *World Politics*, vol. 26, 2, pp. 163–97.

Kew, F. (1988), *How Games Change: The structuring and re-structuring of games (with particular reference to Gaelic/Australian football)*, Paper presented to the International Leisure Studies Association Conference, Brighton, England.

Kidane, F. (1987), 'The Olympic movement and the mass media in Third World countries', in Jackson, R. and McPhail, T., *The Olympic Movement and the Mass Media: Past, present and future issues, Conference Proceedings*, University of Calgary: Canada, pp. 4.19–4.28.

Kidd, B. (1987), 'The Olympic movement and the sports–media complex', in Jackson, R. and McPhail, T., *The Olympic Movement and the Mass Media: Past, present and future issues, Conference Proceedings*, University of Calgary: Canada, pp. 1.3–2.0.

Kidd, B. (1988), 'The campaign against sport in South Africa', *International Journal*, XLIII, Autumn, pp. 643–63.

Killanin, Lord (1983), *My Olympic Years*, London: Secker & Warburg.

King, A.D. (1990), 'Introduction: Spaces of culture, spaces of knowledge', in King, A.D. (ed.), *Culture, Globalisation and the World System*, Basingstoke: Macmillan, pp. 1–18.

Klatell, D.A. and Marcus, N. (1988), *Sports For Sale: Television, money and the fans*, New York: Oxford University Press.

Klein, A. (1989), 'Baseball as underdevelopment: The political economy of sport in the Dominican Republic', *Sociology of Sport Journal*, 6, pp. 95–112.

Klein, A. (1991a), 'Sport and culture as contested terrain: Americanisation in the Caribbean', *Sociology of Sport*, 8, pp. 79–85.

Klein, A., (1991b), *Sugarball: The American game, the Dominican dream*, New Haven, Conn.: Yale University Press.

Knorr, K. (1970), *Military Power and Potential*, Cambridge, Mass.: DC Heath.

Knox, C. (1986), 'Political symbolism and leisure provision in Northern Ireland local government', *Local Government Studies*, Sept.–Oct., 12, 5, pp. 37–5.

Kolatch, J. (1972), *Sport, Politics and Ideology in China*, New York: Jonathan David Publishers.

Kortzfleisch, S. von (1970), 'Religious Olympism', *Social Research*, vol. 37, pp. 231–6.

Korzenny, F. and Ting-Toomey, S. (1990), 'Communicating for peace: Diplomacy and negotiation', *International and Intercultural Communication Annual*, vol. XIV, pp. 136–56.

Kramer, J. (1979), *The Game: My forty years in tennis*, London: Andre Deutsch.

Krasner, S.D. (ed.) (1983), *International Regimes*, Ithaca, NY: Cornell University Press.

Kropke, R. (1974), 'International sports and the social sciences', *Quest*, 22, June, pp. 25–32.

Kurdle, R.T. (1987), 'The several faces of the multi-national corporation: Political reactions and policy response', in Frieden, J.A. and Lake, D.A. (eds.) *International Political Economy*, New York: St Martin's Press, pp. 107–30.

Kusaka, Y. (1987), 'The development of baseball organisations in Japan', *International Review of the Sociology of Sport*, vol. 22, pp. 263–77.

Laemmer, M. (1974), 'Ideological tendencies in the historiography of sport in the Jewish culture (with particular consideration of the Biblical and Hellenic-Talmudic eras)', in *Physical Education and Sports in the Jewish History and Culture: Proceedings of an international seminar at Wingate Institute, July 1973*, Natanya, Israel: Wingate Institute, pp. 54–77.

Laffin, M. (1986), 'Professional communities and policy communities in central–local relations', in Goldsmith, M. (ed.), *New Research in Central–Local Relations*, Aldershot: Gower, pp. 108–21.

Lapchick, R.E. (1975), *The Politics of Race and International Sport: The case of South Africa*, Westport, Conn.: Greenwood Press.

Lapchick, R.E. (1977), 'Apartheid sport: South Africa's use of sport in its foreign policy', *Journal of Sport and Social Issues*, vol. 1, 1, pp. 52–79.

Lawrence, G. (1986a), 'In the race for profit', in Lawrence, G. and Rowe, D., *Power Play: Essays in the sociology of Australian Sport*, Sydney: Hale & Iremonger, pp. 204–14.

Lawrence, G. (1986b), 'It's just not cricket!', in Lawrence, G. and Rowe, D., *Power Play: Essays in the sociology of Australian Sport*, Sydney: Hale & Iremonger, pp. 151–65.

Lawrence, G. and Rowe, D. (1986), *Power Play: Essays in the sociology of Australian sport*, Sydney: Hale & Iremonger.

Leftwich, A. (1984), *What is Politics?*, Oxford: Blackwell.

Lenin, V.I. (1966), *Imperialism, The Highest Stage of Capitalism*, 13th edn., Moscow: Progress Publishers.

Leonard, H.J. (1980), 'Multinational corporations and politics in developing countries', *World Politics*, XXXIII, 4, pp. 454–83.

Lerner, D. (1958), *The Passing of Traditional Society*, Glencoe: Free Press.

Levine, P. (1985), *AG Spalding and the Rise of Baseball: The promise of American sport*, New York: Oxford University Press.

Lindblom, C.E. (1977), *Politics and Markets: The world's political economic systems*, New York: Basic Books.

Locksley, G. (1986), 'Information technology and capitalist development', *Capital and Class*, 27, pp. 81–105.

Lowe, B., Kanin, D.B. and Strenk, A. (eds.) (1978), *Sport and International Relations*, Champaign, Ill.: Stipes.

Lucas, J.A. (1992), *Future of the Olympic Games*, Champaign, Ill.: Human Kinetics Books.

Luschen, G. (1982), 'Sport, conflict and conflict resolution', *International Social Science Journal*, XXXIV, 2, pp. 185–96.

MacAloon, J. (1981), *This Great Symbol: Pierre Coubertin and the origins of the modern Olympic Games*, Chicago: University of Chicago Press.

McBride, S. (1980), *Many Voices, One World: Communication and society, today and tomorrow*, New York: United Nations.

Macintosh, D. and Black, D. (1994), *Sport and Canadian Diplomacy*, Toronto: McGill-Queen's University Press.

Macintosh, D., Bedecki, T. and Franks, N. (1987), *Sport and Politics in Canada: Federal government involvement since 1961*, Montreal: McGill-Queen's University Press.

McIntosh, P. (1963), *Sport in Society*, London: C A Watts & Co.

McIntosh, P. (1980), *'Sport for All' Programmes Throughout the World*, Report submitted to UNESCO, Paris: UNESCO.

McIntosh, P. (1987), *Sport in Society*, revised edn., London: West London Press.

McKay, J. and Miller, T. (1991), 'From old boys to men and women of the corporation: The Americanisation and commodification of Australian sport', *Sociology of Sport Journal*, vol. 8, pp. 86–94.

McLellan, D. (1986), *Ideology*, Milton Keynes: Open University Press.

McMurtry, R. (1990), *Commonwealth Heads of Government Working Party on Strengthening Commonwealth Sport: Preliminary report (Chairman Sir R. McMurtry)*, London: Commonwealth Secretariat.

Maguire, J. (1990), 'More than a sporting touchdown: The making of American football in England 1982–1990', *Sociology of Sport Journal*, vol. 7, pp. 213–37.

Mandell, R. (1971), *The Nazi Olympics*, New York: Macmillan.

Mandell, R. (1976), *The Nazi Olympics*, Urbana, Ill.: University of Illinois Press.

Mandle, B. (1973), 'Cricket and Australian nationalism in the nineteenth century', *Journal of the Royal Australian Society*, 59, December, pp. 18–25.

Mandle, B. (1974), *Winners Can Laugh: Sport and society*, Harmondsworth: Penguin.

Mandle, J.R. and Mandle, J.D. (1990), 'Open cultural space: Grassroots basketball in the English-speaking Caribbean', *Arena Review*, vol. 14, 1, pp. 68–74.

Mandle, W.F. (1977), 'The Irish Republican Brotherhood and the beginnings of the Gaelic Athletic Association', *Irish Historical Studies*, XX, 80, pp. 418–38.

Mandle, W.F. (1980), 'Sport as politics: The Gaelic Athletic Association 1884–1916', in Cashman, R. and McKernan, M. (eds.), *Sport in History*, Brisbane: University of Queensland Press, pp. 99–123.

Mandle, W.F. (1983), 'The Gaelic Athletic Association and popular culture 1884–1924', in MacDonagh O., Mandle, W.F. and Travers, P. (eds.), *Culture and Nationalism in Ireland 1750–1950*, Canberra: Macmillan, pp.

Mandle, W.F. (1987), *The Gaelic Athletic Association and Irish Nationalist Politics 1884–1924*, London: Christopher Helm.

Marchand, J. (1990), *Sport for All in Europe*, London: HMSO.

Marcuse, H. (1955), *Eros and Civilization*, Boston, Mass.: Little, Brown & Co.

Mattelart, A. (1983), *Transnationals and the Third World: The struggle for culture*, South Hadley, Mass.: Bergin and Garvey Publishers Inc.

Matthews, H.G. (1978), *International Tourism: A political and social analysis*, Cambridge, Mass.: Schenken Publishing Company.

Mayhew, B. (1983), 'Hierarchical differentiation in imperatively coordinated associations', in Bacharach, S.B. (ed.), *Research in the Sociology of Organisations 2*, Greenwich: JAI Press, pp. 87–101.

Mazrui, A. (1976), *A World Federation of Cultures: An African perspective*, New York: The Free Press.

Meadow, R.G. (1987), 'The architecture of Olympic broadcasting', in Jackson, R. and McPhail, T., *The Olympic Movement and the Mass Media: Past, present and future issues, Conference Proceedings*, University of Calgary: Canada, pp. 6.7–6.20.

Migdal, J. (1983), 'Studying the politics of development and change: The state of the art', in Finifter, A. (ed.), *Political Science: The state of the discipline*, Washington DC: American Political Science Association, pp. 26–52.

Millar, J.D.B. (1962), *The Nature of Politics*, London: Duckworth.

Mitchell, B. (1992), 'A national game goes international: Baseball in Australia', *The International Journal of the History of Sport*, vol. 9, 2, pp. 288–301.

Modelski, G. (1978), 'The long cycle of global politics and the nation state', *Comparative Studies in Society and History*, vol. 20, 2, pp. 214–35.

Monnington, T. (1986), *The Politics of Black African Sport*, in Allison, L. (ed.), *The Politics of Sport*, Manchester: Manchester University Press, pp. 149–73.

Moore, K.E. (1986), 'Strange bedfellows and cooperative partners: The influence of the Olympic Games on the establishment of the British Empire Games', in Redmond, G., *Sport and Politics*, Toronto: Human Kinetics Publishers Inc., pp. 117–21.

Morley, D. (1986), *Family Television: Cultural power and domestic leisure*, London: Comedia.

Morrow, D. (1992), 'The institutionalisation of sport: A case study of Canadian lacrosse, 1844–1914', *The International Journal of the History of Sport*, vol. 9, 2, pp. 236–51.

Morton, H.W. (1982), 'Soviet sport reassessed', in Cantelon, H. and Gruneau R., *Sport, Culture and the Modern State*, Toronto: University of Toronto Press, pp. 209–19.

Nafziger, J.A.R. (1978), 'The regulation of transnational sports competition: Down from Mount Olympus', in Lowe *et al.* (eds.), *Sport and International Relations*, Champaign, Ill.: Stipes, pp. 160–90.

Nash, D. (1978), 'Tourism as a form of imperialism', in Smith, V.L. (ed.), *Hosts and Guests: The anthropology of tourism*, Oxford: Basil Blackwell, pp. 33–47.

Nissiotis, N. (1982), 'The educational work of the International Olympic Academies', *Arena Review*, vol. 6, 2, pp. 27–38.

Nossal, K.P. (1989), 'International sanctions as international punishment', *International Organisation*, vol. 43, 2, Spring, pp. 301–22.

O'Connor, J. (1970), 'The meaning of economic imperialism', in Rhodes, R.I., *Imperialism and Underdevelopment*, New York: Monthly Review Press, pp. 101–54.

Official Report (1976), *Official Report of the XXI Olympiad*, Montreal, Lausanne: IOC.

Official Report (1984), *Official Report of the XXIII Olympiad*, Los Angeles, Lausanne: IOC.

Oren, Y. (1975), 'Present problems of Israel's sport and physical education', in *1974 Proceedings of the Society on the History of Physical Education and Sport in Asia and Pacific Area*, Natanya, Israel: Wingate Institute for Physical Education and Sport, pp. 7–14.

Organski, A.F.K. (1968), *World Politics*, New York: Knopf.

Paraschak, V. (1991), 'Sports festivals and race relations in the Northwest Territories of Canada', in Jarvie, G. (ed.), *Sport, Racialism and Ethnicity*, London: Falmer Press.

Parry, J. (1988), 'Olympic education and higher education', *British Journal of Physical Education*, vol. 19, 1, pp. 6–27.

Parry, J. (1992), 'Olympic philosophy and Olympic education', *British Journal of Physical Education*, vol. 23, 2, pp. 23–5.

Parsons, T. (1964), 'Evolutionary universals in society', *American Sociological Review*, 29, pp. 339–57.

Patterson, O. (1969), 'The ritual of cricket', *Jamaica Journal*, vol. 3, 1, pp. 23–5.

Payne, A. (1991), 'The international politics of the Gleneagles Agreement', *The Round Table*, 320, pp. 417–30.

Pearson, K. (1979), *Surfing Sub-cultures of Australia and New Zealand*, St Lucia: University of Queensland Press.

Pendleton, B. (1983), *The 'Two Chinas' Imbroglio in International Sport: Proceedings of 26th ICHPER World Congress*, Natanya, Israel: Wingate Institute, pp. 13–20.

Pendleton, B.B. (1986), 'Deuce or double fault? The defection of Hu Na: A study of China–United States sport diplomacy', in Redmond, G., *Sport and Politics*, Champaign, Ill.: Human Kinetics Publishing Inc.

Pentland, C. (1976), 'International organisations and their roles', in Thompson, K.W. and Boyd, G. (eds.), *World Politics*, New York: Free Press, pp. 638–58.

Piccone, P. (1978), 'The crisis of one-dimensionality', *Telos*, 35, Spring, pp. 27–43.

Plamenatz, J. (1970), *Ideology*, London: Macmillan.

Polsby, N. (1963), *Community Power and Political Theory*, New Haven, Conn.: Yale University Press.

Ranson, S., Hinings, B. and Greenwood, R. (1980), 'The structuring of organisational structures', *Administrative Science Quarterly*, March, pp. 72–95.

Reader, I. (1989), 'Sumo: The recent history of an ethical model for Japanese society', *The International Journal of the History of Sport*, vol. 6, 3, pp. 285-9.

Real, M. (1986), *Global Ritual: Olympic media coverage and international understanding*, Unpublished paper, University of Calgary: Canada.

Redmond, G. (1986), *Sport and Politics*, Toronto: Human Kinetics Publishers Inc.

Reshef, N. and Paltiel, J. (1989), 'Partisanship and sport: the unique case of politics and sport in Israel, *Sociology of Sport Journal*, vol. 6, pp. 305–18.

Rhodes, R.A.W. (1986), *The National World of Local Government*, London: Macmillan.

Rigauer, B. (1981), *Sport and Work*, New York: Columbia University Press.

Riordan, J. (1978) (ed.), *Sport Under Communism*, London: Hurst.

Risse, H. (1921), *Soziologie des Sports*, Berlin: Verlag von August Reher.

Robertson, R. (1987), 'Globalisation and societal modernisation: A note on Japan and Japanese religion', *Sociological Analysis*, 47, Summer, pp. 35–43.

Robertson, R. (1989), 'Globalisation, politics and religion', in Beckford, J.A. and Luckman, T. (eds.), *The Changing Face of Religion*, London: Sage, pp. 10–23.

Robertson, R. (1990a), 'Globality, global culture and images of world order', in Haferkamp, H. and Smelser, N. (eds.), *Social Change and Modernity*, Berkeley, Calif.: University of California Press, pp. 47–63.

Robertson, R. (1990b), 'Mapping the global condition: Globalisation as a central concept', in Featherstone, M. (ed.), *Global Culture: Nationalism, globalisation and modernity*, London: Sage, pp. 15–30.

Robertson, R. (1992), ' "Civilization" and the civilizing process: Elias, globalisation and analytic synthesis', *Theory, Culture and Society*, vol. 9, pp. 211–27.

Roden, D. (1980), 'Baseball and the quest for national dignity in Meiji Japan', *American Historical Review*, vol. 85, 3, pp. 511–34.

Roncagliolo, R. (1986), 'Transnational communications and culture', in Atwood, R. and McAnany (eds.), *Communications and Latin American Society: Trends in critical research, 1960–85*, Madison, Wisconsin: University of Wisconsin Press, Ch. 4.

Rosenau, J. (1970), *The Adaptation of National Societies: A theory of political systems behaviour and transformation*, New York: McCabeb Seiler.

Rosenstone, R.A. (1980), 'Learning from those "Imitative" Japanese: Another side of the American experience in the Mikado's empire', *American Historical Review*, vol. 85, 3, pp. 572–95.

Rostow, W.W. (1962), *The Process of Economic Growth*, New York: W.W. Norton.

Rothstein, R.L. (1972), 'On the costs of realism', *Political Science Quarterly*, vol. 87, 3, pp. 347–62.

Sabljak, M. (1987), 'How the media cover economics in the Olympic movement', in Jackson, R. and McPhail, T., *The Olympic Movement and the Mass Media: Past, present and future issues, Conference Proceedings*, University of Calgary: Canada, pp. 3.3–3.10.

St Pierre, M. (1990), 'West Indian cricket: A cultural contradiction?', *Arena Review*, vol. 14, 1, pp. 13–24.

Salter, M. (1972), 'The effect of acculturation on the game of lacrosse and on its role as an agent of Indian survival', *Canadian Journal of History of Sport and Physical Education*, III, 2, pp. 28–43.

Sasajima, K. (1972), 'Foreign sports brought into Japan and their Japanization', in Simri, U. (ed.), *Proceedings of the Pre-Olympic Seminar on the History of Physical Education and Sport in Asia*, Natanya, Israel: Wingate Institute for Physical Education and Sport, pp. 97–112.

Saul, J. (1988), 'Militant Mulroney? The Tories and South Africa', paper presented to the annual meeting of the Canadian Association of African Studies, Kingston, Canada.

Schiller, H.I. (1976), *Communication and Cultural Domination*, New York: International Arts and Sciences Press.

Schiller, H.I. (1985), 'Electronic information flows: New basis for global domination?', in Drummond, P. and Paterson, R. (eds.), *Television in Transition*, London: BFI Books, pp. 11–20.

Schiller, H.I. (1989), *Culture Inc.: The corporate takeover of public expression*, Oxford: Oxford University Press.

Schlesinger, P. (1987), 'On national identity: Some conceptions and misconceptions criticized', *Social Science Information*, vol. 26, 2, pp. 219–64.

Scruton, R. (1980), *The Meaning of Conservatism*, Basingstoke: Macmillan.

Seary, B. (1992), *Brussels in Focus: EC access for sport*, London: Sports Council.

Secretary of State for External Affairs (1989), *A Proposal to Strengthen the Commonwealth Games: A firmer foundation – a brighter future*, Ottawa: External Affairs and International Trade Canada.

Seppanen, P. (1984), 'The Olympics: A sociological perspective', *International Review for the Sociology of Sport*, vol. 19, 2, pp. 113–27.

Sevelius, B. (1992), Speech given to the first meeting of European Sports Forum, Strasbourg: Council of Europe.

Sharp, P. (1987), 'Small state foreign policy and international regimes: The case of Ireland and the European Monetary System and the Common Fisheries Policy', *Millennium*, vol. 16, 1, pp. 55–71.

Shinnick, P.K. (1978), 'Sport and cultural hegemony', in Lowe, B. *et al.* (eds.) *Sport and International Relations*, Champaign, Ill.: Stipes, pp. 95–107.

Sie, S. (1978), 'Sport and politics: The case of the Asian Games and the GANEFO', in Lowe, B. *et al.* (eds.), *Sports and International Relations*, Champaign, Ill.: Stipes, pp. 279–95.

Simri, U. (1983), *Israel and the Asian Games: Proceedings of an international seminar, 26th ICHPER World Congress 1983*, Natanya, Israel: Wingate Institute.

Simson, V. and Jennings, A. (1992), *The Lords of the Rings: Power, money and drugs in the modern Olympics*, London: Simon & Schuster.

Sinclair, R.J. (1985), 'Baseball's rising sun: American interwar baseball diplomacy and Japan', *Canadian Journal of History of Sport*, XVI, 2, pp. 44–53.

Singer, J.D., Bremer, S. and Stuckey, J. (1972), 'Capability distribution, uncertainty, and major power war, 1820–1965', in Russett, B. (ed.), *Peace, War and Numbers*, Beverley Hills, Calif.: Sage, pp. 19–48.

Sklair, L. (1988), 'Transcending the impasse: Metatheory, theory and empirical research in the sociology of development and underdevelopment', *World Development*, 16, June, pp. 697–709.

Sklair, L. (1991), *Sociology of the Global System*, London: Harvester Wheatsheaf.

Slack, T. (1985), 'The bureaucratization of a voluntary sport organisation', *International Review for the Sociology of Sport*, vol. 20, pp. 145–65.

Smith, B. (1979), *Policy-making in British Government*, London: Martin Robertson.

Snyder, R., Bruck, H.W. and Sapin, B. (eds.) (1962), *Foreign Policy Decision Making*, New York: Free Press.

Soreq, Y. (1984), 'Diasporal Jewish participation in gymnastic life', in Muller, N. and Kuhl, J.K. (eds.), *Olympic Scientific Congress, Official Report, Sports History*, Niederhausen, Germany: Schors, pp. 432–41.

Spanier, J. (1987), *Games Nations Play*, Washington: CQ Press.

Spero, J.E. (1985), *The Politics of International Economic Relations*, 3rd edn., New York: St Martin's Press.

Stewart, B. (1986), 'Sport as big business', in Lawrence, G. and Rowe, D., *Power Play: Essays in the sociology of Australian sport*, Sydney: Hale & Iremonger, pp. 64–84.

Stoddart, B. (1986), 'Sport, culture, and postcolonial relations: A preliminary analysis of the Commonwealth Games', in Redmond, G., *Sport and Politics*, Toronto: Human Kinetics Publishing Inc., pp. 123–31.

Stoddart, B. (1987), 'Cricket, social formation and cultural continuity in Barbados: A preliminary ethnography', *Journal of Sport History*, vol. 14, 3, pp. 317–40.

Stoessinger, J. (1973), *The Might of Nations*, New York: Random House.

Strauss, A. (1978), *Negotiation: Varieties, process and social order*, San Francisco: Jossey-Bass.

Strenk, A. (1978), 'Diplomats in tracksuits: Linkages between sports and foreign policy in the German Democratic Republic', in Lowe *et al. Sport and International Relations*, Champaign, Ill.: Stipes, pp. 34–45

Strenk, A. (1980), 'Diplomats in tracksuits: The role of sports in the German Democratic Republic', in *The Journal of Sport and Social Issues*, vol. 4, 1, pp. 34–45.

Strong, C.H. (1982), 'Education as a social force in promoting Olympism', *Arena Review*, vol. 6, 2, pp. 10–21.

Sugden, J. and Bairner, A. (1986), 'Northern Ireland: The politics of leisure in a divided society', *Leisure Studies*, 5, pp. 341–52.

Sugden J., Tomlinson, A. and McCarten, E. (1990), 'The making of white lightning in Cuba: Politics, sport and physical education 30 years after the revolution', *Arena Review*, vol. 14, 1, pp. 101–9.

Sullivan, M.P. (1976), *International Relations Theories and Evidence*, Englewood Cliffs, New Jersey: Prentice-Hall.

Sunkel, O. (1972), 'Big business and dependencia: A Latin American view', *Foreign Affairs*, 50, 3, pp. 517–31.

Sussman, G. and Lent, J.A. (1991), *Transnational Communication: Wiring the Third World*, Newbury Park: Sage.

Tatz, C. (1986), 'The corruption of sport', in Lawrence, G. and Rowe, D., *Power Play: Essays in the sociology of Australian sport*, Sydney: Hale & Iremonger, pp. 46–63.

Taylor, I. (1982), 'Class, violence and sport: The case of soccer hooliganism in Britain', in Cantelon, H. and Gruneau, R. (eds.), *Sport, Culture and the Modern State*, Toronto: Toronto University Press, pp. 39–96.

Taylor, P. (1984), *Nonstate Actors in International Politics: From transregional to substate organisations*, Boulder, Colo.: Westview Press.

Taylor, T. (1988), 'Sport and world politics: Functionalism and the state system', *International Journal*, XLIII, Autumn, pp. 531–53.

Theonig, J.C. (1978), 'State bureaucrats and local government in France', in Hanf, K. and Scharpf, F.W., *Interorganisational Policy Making*, Beverly Hills, Calif.: Sage, pp. 66–82.

Tiffin, H. (1981), 'Cricket, literature and the politics of de-colonisation: The case of CLR James', in Cashman, R. and McKernan, M. (eds.) *Sport, Money Morality and the Media*, Kensington, NSW: New South Wales University Press, p. 177–93.

Tomlinson, A. and Whannel, G. (1984), *Five Ring Circus: Money, power and politics at the Olympic Games*, London: Pluto Press.

Toohey, D.P. (1986), 'The politics of the 1984 Los Angeles Olympics', in Redmond' G., *Sport and Politics*, Toronto: Human Kinetics Publishers Inc., pp. 161–9.

UNESCO (1978), *International Charter of Physical Education and Sport*, Paris: UNESCO.

Uwechue, R.C. (1978), 'Nation building and sport in Africa', in Lowe *et al.* (eds.), *Sport and International Relations*, Champaign, Ill.: Stipes, pp. 538–50.

Van der Merwe, F.J.G. (1985), 'Afrikaner nationalism in sport', *Canadian Journal of History of Sport and Physical Education*, XVI, 2, pp. 34–46.

Vinokur, M. (1988), *More Than a Game: Sports and politics*, New York: Greenwood Press.

Viotti, P.R. and Kauppi, M.V. (1987), *International Relations Theory: Realism, pluralism and globalism*, New York, Macmillan.

Wagner, E.A. (1990), 'Sport in Asia and Africa: Americanisation or mundialisation?', *Sociology of Sport Journal*, 7, pp. 399–402.

Wallerstein, I. (1974), 'The rise and future demise of the world capitalist system: Concepts for comparative analysis', *Comparative Studies in Society and History*, 16, 4, pp. 387–415.

Wallerstein, I. (1979), *The Capitalist World-Economy*, Cambridge: Cambridge University Press.

Wallerstein, I. (1990), 'The national and the universal: Can there be such a thing as a world culture?', in King, A.D. (ed.), *Culture, Globalisation and the World System*, Basingstoke: Macmillan, pp. 91–106.

Walters, F.P. (1952), *A History of the League of Nations*, London: Oxford University Press.

Waltz, K.N. (1979), *Theory of International Politics*, Reading, Mass.: Addison-Wesley.

Weber, E. (1970), 'Pierre de Coubertin and the introduction of organised sport in France, *Journal of Contemporary History*, 5, pp. 3–26.

Weber, M. (1947), *The Theory of Social and Economic Organisation*, New York: Oxford University Press.

Weber, M. (1958), *The Protestant Ethic and the Spirit of Capitalism*, New York: Charles Scribner's & Sons.

Weiner, M. and Huntington, S. (eds.) (1987), *Understanding Political Development*, Boston, Mass.: Little, Brown & Co.

Wernick, A. (1991), 'Promo culture: The cultural triumph of exchange', *Theory, Culture and Society*, vol. 7, 4, pp. 89–110.

Whannel, G. (1984), 'The television spectacular', in Tomlinson, A. and Whannel, G. (eds), *Five Ring Circus*, London: Pluto Press, pp. 31–43.

Whannel, G. (1992), *Fields in Vision: Television sport and cultural transformation*, London: Routledge.

White, S. and Brackenridge, J. (1985), 'Who rules sport? Gender divisions in the power structure of British sports organisations from 1960', *International Review of the Sociology of Sport*, 20, pp. 95–107.

Williams, D. (1987), *The Specialised Agencies and the United Nations: The system in crisis*, London: C Hurst & Co.

Williams, J., Dunning, E.G. and Murphy, P.J. (1984), *Hooligans Abroad*, London: Routledge & Kegan Paul.

Wilson, J. (1988), *Politics and Leisure*, London: Unwin-Hyman.

Wilson, N. (1988), *The Sports Business: The men and the money*, London: Judy Piatkus.

Wood, B. (1990), 'Canada and Southern Africa: A return to middle power activism', *The Round Table*, 315, pp. 280–90.

The World and I (1988), Editorial, Special Issue on the Seoul Olympics, October, pp. 22–3.

World Bank (1990), *The World Development Report 1990*, Washington, DC: World Bank.

Wren-Lewis, J. and Clarke, A. (1983), 'The World Cup – a political football', *Theory, Culture and Society*, vol. 1, 3, pp. 123–32.

Young, O. (1980), 'International regimes: Problems of concept formation', *World Politics*, vol. XXXII, April, pp. 331–56.

Zayed, A. (1987), 'Popular culture and consumerism in underdeveloped urban areas: A study of the Cairene Quarter of Al-Sharrabiyya', in Stauth, G. and Zubaida, S. (eds.), *Mass Culture, Popular Culture, and Social Life in the Middle East*, Boulder, Colo.: Westview Press, pp. 287–312.

Index

Books by Paul Theroux

FICTION

Waldo
Fong and the Indians
Girls at Play
Murder in Mount Holly
Jungle Lovers
Sinning with Annie
Saint Jack
The Black House
The Family Arsenal
The Consul's File
A Christmas Card
Picture Palace
London Snow
World's End
The Mosquito Coast
The London Embassy
Half Moon Street
Doctor Slaughter
O-Zone
The White Man's Burden
My Secret History
Chicago Loop
Millroy the Magician
The Greenest Island
My Other Life
Kowloon Tong
Hotel Honolulu
The Stranger at the Palazzo d'Oro
Blinding Light
The Elephanta Suite
A Dead Hand

CRITICISM

V. S. Naipaul

NON-FICTION

The Great Railway Bazaar
The Old Patagonian Express
The Kingdom by the Sea
Sailing Through China
Sunrise with Seamonsters
The Imperial Way
Riding the Iron Rooster
To the Ends of the Earth
The Happy Isles of Oceania
The Pillars of Hercules
Sir Vidia's Shadow
Fresh-Air Fiend
Nurse Wolf and Dr Sacks
Dark Star Safari
Ghost Train to the Eastern Star
The Tao of Travel

Saint Jack

PAUL THEROUX

PENGUIN BOOKS

PENGUIN BOOKS

Published by the Penguin Group
Penguin Books Ltd, 80 Strand, London WC2R 0RL, England
Penguin Group (USA) Inc., 375 Hudson Street, New York, New York 10014, USA
Penguin Group (Canada), 90 Eglinton Avenue East, Suite 700, Toronto, Ontario, Canada M4P 2Y3
(a division of Pearson Penguin Canada Inc.)
Penguin Ireland, 25 St Stephen's Green, Dublin 2, Ireland (a division of Penguin Books Ltd)
Penguin Group (Australia), 250 Camberwell Road,
Camberwell, Victoria 3124, Australia (a division of Pearson Australia Group Pty Ltd)
Penguin Books India Pvt Ltd, 11 Community Centre, Panchsheel Park,
New Delhi – 110 017, India
Penguin Group (NZ), 67 Apollo Drive, Rosedale, Auckland 0632, New Zealand
(a division of Pearson New Zealand Ltd)
Penguin Books (South Africa) (Pty) Ltd, 24 Sturdee Avenue, Rosebank, Johannesburg 2196, South Africa

Penguin Books Ltd, Registered Offices: 80 Strand, London WC2R 0RL, England

www.penguin.com

First published by Hamish Hamilton 1976
Published in Penguin Books 1977
Reissued in this edition 2011
1

Set in 11/13pt Dante MT Std
Typeset by Palimpsest Book Production Limited, Falkirk, Stirlingshire
Printed in Great Britain by Clays Ltd, St Ives plc

ISBN: 978-0-241-95514-7

www.greenpenguin.co.uk

For Anne, as always, with love

And for good friends in twenty tropical places

Action will furnish belief – but will that belief be the true one?

A. H. Clough, *Amours de Voyage*

PART ONE

I

In any memoir it is usual for the first sentence to reveal as much as possible of your subject's nature by illustrating it in a vivid and memorable motto, and with my own first sentence now drawing to a finish I see I have failed to do this! But writing is made with the fingers, and all writing, even the clumsy kind, exposes in its loops and slants a yearning deeper than an intention, the soul of the writer flapping on the clothes-peg of his exclamation mark. Including the sentence scribbled above: being slow to disclose my nature is characteristic of me. So I am not off to such a bad start after all. My mutters make me remember. Later, I will talk about my girls.

I was going to get under way with an exchange which took place one morning last year between Gopi and me. Gopi was our *peon* – pronounced 'pyoon', messenger, to distinguish him from 'pee-on', the slave. He was a Tamil and had a bad leg. He sidled into my cubicle. He showed me two large damp palms and two discoloured eyes and said, 'Mister Hing vaunting Mister Jack in a hurry-*lah*.'

That summons was the beginning. At the time I did not know enough to find it dramatic. In fact, it annoyed me. Though it seems an innocent request, when it is repeated practically every day for fourteen years it tends to swaddle one with oppression. That 'hurry-*lah*' stung me more than the summons. Mr Hing, my *towkay*, my boss, was an impatient feller. I was a sitting duck for summonings.

'No one tells Jack Flowers to hurry,' I said, turning back to my blue desk diary. I was resolute. I entered a girl's name beside a circled day. He can whistle and wait, I thought, the bugger. 'Gopi, tell him I'm busy.'

Carrying that message made the *peon* liable to share the blame. I suspected that was why I said it – not a cheering thought. But I couldn't go straight up to Mister Hing. Gopi left slowly, dragging his bad leg after him. When he was gone I slammed my diary and then, as if stricken with grief, and sighing on each rung, I mounted the narrow step-ladder to Mr Hing's office.

Mr Hing, a clean tubby Cantonese, got brutal haircuts, one a week, the sort given to inmates of asylums, leaving him a bristly pelt of brush on top and the rest shaven white. He had high Chinese eyebrows and his smile, not really a smile, showed a carved treasure of gold teeth. His smile was anger. He was angry half the time, with the Chinese agony, an impulsive belly-aching *Ying* swimming against a cowardly *Yang*: the personality in deadlock. So the Chinese may gaze with waxen placidity into your face, or refuse to reply, or snort and fart when you want a word of encouragement. The secrecy is only half the story. In the other half they yell and fling themselves from rooftops, guzzle weed-killer and caustic soda and die horribly to inconvenience their relatives, or gibber in the street with knives. What kept Mr Hing from suicide was perhaps the thought that he couldn't kill himself by jumping from the crenelated roof of his low two-storey shop-house. The two opposing parts of his nature made him a frugal but obsessive gambler, a tyrannical philanthropist, a tortured villain, almost my friend. He had a dog. He choked it with good food and kicked it for no reason – he may have kicked it because he fed it, the kindness making him cruel. When it ran away, which was often, Mr Hing placed an expensive ad in the *Straits Times* to get the poor beast back. Mr Hing was short, about fifty-three, and every morning he did exercises called 'burpees' in his locked office. He had few pleasures. Until six in the evening, when he changed into striped pyjamas and dandled his grandson on his knee, he wore an ordinary white shirt, an expensive watch, plain trousers and cheap rubber sandals which he kicked off when he sat cross-legged on his chair. He was seated that way the morning I entered his office.

He was slightly more agitated than usual, and the appearance of agitation was heightened by a black fan on a shelf moving its humming face from side to side very rapidly and disturbing the clutter of papers on his desk. Papers trembled and rose, and Mr Hing clapped them flat as the fan turned away; then it happened again, another squall, another slap.

Mr Hing's brother perched beside him in a crouch, his knees drawn up, his arms folded into the trough of his lap. He was wearing a T-shirt, the collar stretched, showing his hairless chest, and large khaki shorts. I thought of him as Little Hing; he was skinnier and younger and his youthful hungry face made him seem to me most untrustworthy. Together, their faces eight inches apart, staring at me from behind the desk, they resembled the pair of fraternal faces you see fixed in two lozenge-shaped frames on a square-shouldered bottle of Chinese patent medicine, Tiger Tonic, Three Wheels Brain Fluid or (Mr Hing's favourite) Rhino Water. Big Hing was especially agitated and saying everything twice. 'Sit down, sit down', then, 'We got a problem, got a problem.'

True Chinese speech is impossible to reproduce without distraction, and in this narrative I intend to avoid the conventional howlers. The 'flied lice' and 'No tickee, no shirtee' variety is really no closer to the real thing than the plain speech I have just put in Big Hing's mouth. Chinese do more than transpose *r* and *l*, and *v* and *b*, and *s* and *sh*. They swallow most of their consonants and they seldom give a word an ending: a glottal stop amputates every final syllable. So what Big Hing really said was, 'Shi' duh'' and, 'We go' a pro'luh''; there is no point in being faithful to this yammering. Little Hing's English was much better than Big's, though Little spoke very fast; but when they were in the same room Little didn't open his trap, except to mutter in Cantonese. That morning he sat in silence, his teeth locked together, the lowers jutting out, fencing the uppers with yellow pickets.

The conversation, I knew, would be brief, and the only reason Big Hing asked me to sit down was that I towered over the desk like a sweaty bear, panting with annoyance, my tattoos showing. My size bothered them especially. I was a foot taller than Big Hing and a foot and a half taller than Little – when they were standing. I sat and sank into a chair of plastic mesh, and as I was sinking Big Hing started to explain.

A month before, he was told that a man was coming from Hong-Kong to audit our books. There was another Hing in Hong-Kong, a *towkay* bigger than Big Hing, and the auditing was an annual affair. It was also an annual humiliation because Big Hing didn't like his accounts questioned. Still, it happened every year; at one time it was a sallow little man who always arrived ravaged from travelling deck class on a freighter; then, for a few years, a skeletal soul with a kindly smile and popping eyes, who hugged a briefcase – turned to suede by wear – to his starched smock with frog buttons. The auditors stayed for a week, snapping the abacus and thumbing the ledger; Big Hing sat close by, pouring tea, saying nothing. Last year it was a man called Lee, and he was the problem, though Big Hing didn't say so. All he said was, 'Meet this man at the airport.'

It was why Hing was agitated. He assumed Lee was Cantonese or at least Chinese. But he discovered, I never learned how, that Lee was an *ang moh*, a red-head. The *ang mohs* were my department. It was the reason I was employed by Hing – *Chop Hing Kheng Fatt: Ship Chandlers & Provisioners*, as the shop-sign read. Hing was peeved that he was mistaken about the name, and furious that his books were going to be scrutinized by an *ang moh*. He beamed with anger and banged his fist down upon the fluttering papers, repeating Lee's name and my orders to meet him at the airport. I drew my own conclusions, and I was correct in every detail except the spelling, which was Leigh.

'My car's at the garage,' I said. I was not being difficult. It was a noisy ten-year-old Renault with 93,000 miles on the clock. One wheel, the front right, had come unstuck from the chassis and made the front end shimmy at any speed, a motion that rubbed the tread from the tyres. 'I'll have to take a taxi.'

'Can, can,' said Big Hing.

Little Hing whispered something, staring at me, keeping his teeth locked, a coward's ventriloquism. For Little Hing I was the ultimate barbarian: my hair was once reddish, I am hairy, my arms are profusely tattooed – a savage, 'just out of the trees,' as Yardley used to say.

'Bus to airport, taxi to town,' said Big Hing. That was Little's whispered suggestion.

It was a two-dollar taxi fare; the bus was forty cents. There was no direct bus. I hated sitting at an out-of-town bus shelter, in the heat, with twenty schoolchildren. But I said okay because I could see Big Hing's anger make him determined that I should save one-sixty and know who was boss. I didn't start arguments I knew in advance I was going to lose. Big Hing was my *towkay*: I couldn't win. But my dealings with him were small.

He counted out $2.40 from petty cash and looked at his watch.

'What time is his plane due in?' I asked.

Big Hing thought three-thirty; Little murmured in Cantonese, and I expected an amendment, but Big stuck to three-thirty and gave me the flight number. I went down to consult my *Bus Guide*.

So far it had been an unpleasant day, ruined first by the *peon* telling me to hurry and second by the command to take the bus all the way out to the airport. After looking at the *Bus Guide* I saw that several things were in my favour. I was right about there being no direct bus, but the 18-A Singapore Traction Company bus passed by Moulmein Green. I could have lunch at home for a change, and if I hurried a quick nap. The change would have to be made on Paya Lebar Road – a stroke of luck: I could see if Gladys was available before continuing on the 93 to the airport. None of this would cost a penny extra; out of two humiliations I had rescued a measure of self-respect. And if Gladys was free and Leigh was interested I stood to make nine dollars. In any event, I was anxious to meet him. It was nice to see a new face, and an *ang moh*'s was more welcome than most. We were lonelier than we admitted to; after many years of residence in Singapore, we all went for the mail twice a day, even Yardley and Smale, who never got any.

This is the beginning of my story, and already I can see that it represents my fortunes more faithfully, in the haphazard recollection of a single morning's interruption, than if I had planned it as carefully as I once intended and began with the rumbling factual sentence I used to repeat to myself in the days when I believed my early life mattered, before I went away – about being born in the year 1918, in the North End of the city of Boston, the second child of two transplanted Italians; and then the part about my earliest memory (the warm room, my wet thumb and velvet cushion, my father singing with the opera on the radio). There is no space for that here.

2

Fourteen years ago, lowering myself on a rope from the rusty stern of the *Allegro*, anchored then in the Straits of Malacca ('the financial straits,' Yardley said), I did not think I was an old man – though if anyone had insisted I was old I would have believed him. Most people are willing to make fools of themselves with a little persuasion, and the question of age is answered by the most foolishness. Now I know that old and young make little difference: the old man talks easily to a child.

They say every age is more barbarous than the last. It is possible. If there is an error in the statement it doesn't matter, because the people who say this are either very young or very old, just starting out and with no experience, or musing in life's sundowner with false flickers of half-forgotten memories. The age, as they call it, is too big to see, but they have time on their hands: it is too early for one and too late for the other to worry about being wrong. What they don't know is that, however awful the age is, it is placid and hopeful compared to a certain age in man.

Fifty: it is a dangerous age – for all men, and especially for one like me who has a tendency to board sinking ships. Middle age has all the scares one man feels halfway across a busy street, caught in traffic and losing his way, or another one blundering in a black upstairs room, full of furniture, afraid to turn on the lights because he'll see the cockroaches he smells. The man of fifty has the most to say, but no one will listen. His fears sound incredible because they are so new – he might be making them up. His body alarms him; it starts playing tricks on him, his teeth warn him, his stomach scolds, he's balding at last; a pimple might be cancer, indigestion a heart attack. He's feeling an unapparent fatigue; he wants to be young but he knows he ought to be old.

He's neither one and terrified. His friends all resemble him, so there can be no hope of rescue. To be this age and very far from where you started out, unconsoled by any possibility of a miracle – that is bad; to look forward and start counting the empty years left is enough to tempt you into some aptly named crime, or else to pray. Success is nasty and spoils you, the successful say, and only failures listen, who know nastiness without the winch of money. Then it is clear: the ship is swamped to its gunwales, and the man of fifty swims to shore, to be marooned on a little island from which there is no rescue, but only different kinds of defeat.

That was how I recognized Mr Leigh, the man they sent from Hong-Kong to audit our books. I knew his name and his flight number – nothing else. I waited at Gate Three and watched the passengers file through Health and Immigration. First the early birds, the ones who rush off the plane with briefcases, journalists and junior executives with Chinese girlfriends, niftily dressed, wearing big sun-glasses; then the two Chinese sisters in matching outfits; a lady with a little boy and further back her husband holding the baby and juggling his passport; a pop group with blank faces and wigs of frizzy hair, looking like a delegation from New Guinea, anxious to be met; the missionary priest with a goatee and a cheroot, addressing porters in their own language; a few overdressed ones, their Zurich topcoats over their arms. Lagging behind, a lady in a wheel chair about whom people say, 'I don't know how she does it', a man with a big box, a returning student with new eyeglasses, and Mr Leigh. I knew him as soon as I set eyes on him: he was the only one who looked remotely like me.

He was red-faced and breathless, and, unaccustomed to the heat, he was mopping his face with a hanky. He was a bit heavier than he should have been – his balance was wrong, his clothes too small. I waved to him through the glass doors. He nodded and turned away to claim his suitcase. I went into the men's room, just to look in the mirror. I was reassured by my hair, not white like Leigh's and still quite thick. But I wished I had more hair. My face was lined: my nap had made me look older. I was dishevelled from the bus-ride and looked more rumpled than usual because I had rolled my sleeves down and buttoned the cuffs. It was my tattoos. I hid them from strangers. Strangers' eyes fix on tattoos as they fix on scars in unlikely places. A person spots a tattoo and he has you pegged: you're a sailor, or you do some sort of poorly paid manual labour; one day you got drunk with your friends and they got tattooed, and to be one of the gang so did you. It did not happen this way with me, but that is the only version strangers know of a tattooing.

Mr Leigh was just pushing through the glass doors as I came back from the toilet smoothing my sleeves. I said hello and tried to take his suitcase. He wouldn't let go; he seemed offended that I should try to help. I knew the feeling. He was abrupt and wheezing and his movements tried to be quick. It is usually this way with people who have just left a plane: they are over-excited in a foreign place, their rhythm is different – they are attempting a new rhythm – and they are not sure what is going to happen next. The sentence they have been practising on the plane, a greeting, a quip, they know to be inappropriate as soon as they say it. Leigh said, 'So they didn't send the mayor', then, 'You don't look Chinese to me.'

I suggested a beer in the lounge.

'What time are they expecting me?' he asked. He had just arrived and already he was worried about Hing. I knew this man: he didn't want to lose his job or his dignity; but it is impossible to keep both.

'They weren't too sure what time your plane was coming in,' I said. We both knew who 'they' were. He put down his suitcase.

One reason I remember the first conversation I had with Mr Leigh (or William, as he insisted I call him, though I found this more formal than Mister; he didn't reply to 'Bill') is that I had the same conversation with every *ang moh* I met in Singapore. We were in the lounge having a beer, sharing a large Anchor; every few minutes the loudspeakers became noisy with adenoidal announcements of arrivals and departures in three languages.

Leigh was still keyed-up and he sat forward in his chair, taking quick gulps of beer and then staring into his glass.

I asked about the flight and the weather in – William being English, I attempted some slang – 'Honkers'. This made him look up from his glass and squint straight at me, so I gave up. And was it a direct flight? No, he said, it landed for fuelling at Bangkok.

'Now *that's* a well-named place!' I said and grinned. I can't remember whether it got a rise out of him. I asked if he had a meal on the plane.

'Yes,' he said, 'perfectly hideous.'

'Well, that food is always so damned hideous,' I said, trying to sound more disgusted than he. The word stuck to my tongue. I wasn't telling the truth. I thought airplane food was very good, always the correct colour and each course in its own little covered trough on the tray, the knives and forks wrapped up and all the rest of the utensils in clean envelopes and in fitted slots and compartments. I had to agree the food was hideous. He was a guest, and I had plans for him.

The next thing I said to him was what I said to everyone who came through. I said it slowly, with suggestive emphasis on the right syllables. 'If there's anything you want in Singapore – anything at all' – I smiled here – 'just let me know and I'll see what I can fix up.'

He replied, as most strangers did, but he was not smiling, 'I'm sure you don't mean *any*thing.'

'Anything.' I took a drink of my beer to show I wasn't going to qualify the promise.

He mopped his face. 'I was wondering –'

And I knew what he was wondering. The choice wasn't large, but people didn't realize that. A tout could follow a tourist on the sidewalk and in the space of a minute offer everything that tourist could conceivably want. The touts who didn't know English handed over a crudely printed three-by-five card to the man with a curious idle face. The card had half a dozen choices on it: blue movies; girls; boys; exhibition; massage; *ganja* – a menu which covered the whole appetite of longing. No new longings were likely, and the tout who breathed, 'You want something special?' had in mind a combination based on the six choices.

Leigh was perspiring heavily. Vice, I was thinking: it sounded like what it was, it squeezed, expressing the grape of fantasy. Gladys was free. It was possible to stop off at her place on the way back from the airport – Leigh would appreciate the convenience – and I was going to say so. But it is a mistake to make explicit suggestions: I discovered that very early. If I suggested a girl and the feller wanted a boy he would be ashamed to admit it and the deal would be off. It was always wrong to offer an exhibition – like saying, 'You can't cut the mustard, but how about watching?' – and if a person was thinking of having a go he would refuse if I suggested it. Most people thought their longings were original, but they weren't: they could only be one of six, or else a combination. Various as fantasy, but fantasy didn't allow for the irregular performance of man's engine. I knew the folly of expectation, and how to caution a feller against despairing of his poor engine and perhaps hitting his pecker with a hammer.

I sized up Leigh as he was blotting his cheeks and pulling at his collar, counting the whirring fans in the lounge. I took him to be an exhibition man, with a massage to follow – not an ordinary massage, something special, Lillian jumping naked on his spine. Intimacy, as the girls called it – or *boochakong*, to use the common Chinese term I preferred to the English verb – would still be a strong possibility, I was thinking. There was no such thing as impotence: it was successful as soon as money changed hands. It wasn't the money, but the ritual.

'What do you say?' I asked, as brightly as I could. Usually it wasn't so hard; when it was, it meant the feller was worried about asking for something I couldn't provide.

'Oh, I don't know,' he said, and drew a deep breath. So I was wrong about the exhibition, and just as well, I thought; I hated those monkeyshines. I guessed Leigh was slightly bent; his particular crimp was a weakness for transvestites, of which, as is well known, there is a whole sorority in Singapore. Very few fellers admitted to this yen; they were the hardest ones to handle, but over the years I had seen how they reacted to the Chinese boys who in skirts were more winsome than girls. Middle age may be an emergence of this comfort, too, a fling at play-acting with a pretty boy, a reasonable occasion for gaiety, the surprise of costuming and merry vestments. If I detected the wish I took the fellers down to Bugis Street and steered them over to the reliable ones, Tiny or Gina. Lucy had the operation which sometimes disappointed the fellers. Your bashful fruit pretended he was talking to a girl, but just so we knew where we stood I said, 'Take Gina – he's a very nice feller.' The client looked surprised and said, 'You mean –?' And then, 'I might as well take him home – I'm too drunk to notice the difference,' and going out would slip me ten dollars.

'What did you have in mind?' asked Leigh.

A very uncommon question. I was going to say nothing, just keep smiling in a willing fashion. But he looked as though he meant it and wouldn't tumble to my willingness.

I said, 'I thought . . . if you were interested in anything illegal, hyah-yah, I might be able to –'

'Illegal?' said Leigh and put his hanky down. He leaned over and, puzzled and interested, asked, 'You mean a prostitute?'

I tried to laugh again, but the expression on his face turning from puzzlement to disgust rattled me. It had been a mistake to say anything.

'No,' I said, 'of course not.' But it came too late; my tardy denial only confirmed the truth, and Leigh was so indignant – he had straightened up and stopped drinking – that shame, unfamiliar as regret, tugged at my neck hairs. Through the glass-topped table in front of me I could see I was curling my toes and clawing at my sandals.

'Let's go,' I said. 'I'll call a taxi.' I started to get up. I was hot; I wanted to roll up my sleeves, now damply stuck to my tattoos, revealing them.

'Flowers,' he said, and narrowed his eyes at me, 'are you a ponce?'

'Me? Hyah-mn! What a thing to say!' It was a loud hollow protest with a false echo. Prostitute, he had said, pimp, whore, queer, ponce – what words people use to name the things they hate (liking them, they leave them nameless, the human voice duplicating the suspicion that passion is unspeakable). 'I'm a sort of pornocrat,' I was going to say, to mock him. I decided not to. His incredulity was a prompting for me to lie.

The waitress passed by.

Leigh said, '*Wan arn*!' greeting her in vilely accented Mandarin.

''Scuse me?' she said. She took a pad from the pocket of her dress, a pencil from her hair. 'Anudda Anchor?'

'*Nee hao ma*,' said Leigh. He had turned away from me and was looking at the girl. But the girl was looking at me. '*Nee hway bu hway* –'

'Mister,' said the girl to me, 'what ship your flend flom?'

Leigh cleared his throat and said we'd better be going. In the taxi he said hopelessly, 'I was wondering if I might get a chance to play a little squash.'

'Sure thing,' I said, pouncing. 'I can fix that up for you in a jiffy.' *Squash*? He was wheezing still, and red as a beet. Carrying his suitcase to the taxi-rank he kept changing hands and groaning, and then he put his face out of the taxi window and let the breeze blow into his mouth, taking gulps of it the way dogs do in a car. He had swallowed two little white pills with his beer. He looked closely at his palms from time to time. And he wanted to play squash!

'What's your club, Flowers?'

We had agreed that I was to call him William if he called me Jack. I liked my nursery-rhyme name. Now I felt he was cheating.

'Name it,' I said, and to remind him of our agreement I added, 'William.'

I had an application pending at the Cricket Club once, or at least 'the Eggs', two elderly bald clients of mine who were members, said I did. I had been trying to join a club in Singapore for a long time. Then it was too late. I couldn't apply for membership without giving myself away, for I often drank in the clubs and most of the members – they knew me well – thought I had joined years before. There wasn't a club on the island I couldn't visit one way or another. I had clients at all of them.

'Cricket Club's got some squash courts, but the Tanglin's just put up new ones – you may want to have a look at those. There's none at the Swimming Club so far, though we've got a marvellous sauna room.' I thumped his knee. 'We'll find something, William.'

'Sounds very agreeable,' he said, pulling his head back into the taxi. He was calm now. 'How do you manage three clubs? I'm told the entrance fees are killing.'

'They *are* pretty killing,' I said, using his dialect again, 'but I reckon it's worth it.'

'You're not a squash-player yourself?'

'No,' I said, 'I'm just an old beachcomber – drinking's my sport, nyah!'

That made him chuckle; I was laughing too, and as I shifted on the seat I felt a lump in my back pocket press into my butt: two thick envelopes of pornographic pictures I had brought along just in case he asked. Their reminding pressure stopped me laughing.

The taxi-driver tilted his head back and said, 'Bloomies? Eshbishin wid two gull. You want boy? Mushudge? What you want I get. What you like?'

'Just a game of squash, driver, thank you very much,' I said in a pompous fruity voice to this poor feller for the benefit of the horse's ass next to me. Then I smiled at William and tried to tip him a wink, but his head was out of the window and he was blinking and gulping at the breeze and probably wondering what he was doing on that tedious little island.

3

I walked into a bar where they did not know me well and I could hear the Chinese whispers: 'Who does that jackass think he is?' and then they ceased: my face made silence. It was not the face you expected in Ho's or Toby's or the Honey Bar, in the Golden Treasure or Loon's Tip-top. Years ago I had not minded, but later my heart sank on the evenings all my regulars were tied up and I had to go into these joints recruiting. I got stares from round-shouldered youths sitting with plump hostesses; and the secret society members watched me – in Ho's the Three Dots, in the Honey Bar the Flying Dragons. There was no goblin as frightening as a member of a secret society staring me down: he first appeared to have no eyes, then the slits became apparent and I guessed he was peering at me from somewhere behind the slits. I never saw the eyes. The slits didn't speak; and it was impossible to read the face, too smooth for a message. I turned away and slipped the manager a few dollars to release the girl, and when I was hurrying out I heard growls and grunts I didn't understand, then titters. On the sidewalk I heard the whole bar crackle and explode into yelling laughter. Now they had eyes; but I was outside.

One night a thug spoke to me. He was sitting up front at the bar eating a cold pork pie with his fingers. He was wearing the secret-society uniform, a short-sleeved shirt with the top four buttons undone, sun-glasses – though it was dark – and his hair rather long, with wispy wing-tufts hanging past his ears. I didn't think he saw me talking to the manager, and after I passed the money over and turned to go the thug put his hand on my shoulder and, rubbing pork flakes into it, said gruffly, 'Where you does wuck?'

I didn't answer. I hurried down the gloomy single aisle of the bar, past eerily lit Chinese faces. The thug called out, '*Where you wucking?*' That was in the Tai-Hwa on Cecil Street, and I never went near it again.

'Who is he?' they murmured in the Belvedere, the Hilton, the Goodwood, when I was in the lobby flicking through a magazine, waiting for one of my girls to finish upstairs. I could have passed for a golf pro when I was wearing my monogrammed red knitted jersey – the one with long sleeves – and my mustard-coloured slacks and white ventilated shoes. No one knew I had a good tan because I worked for Hing who refused to pay for taxis in town and who sent me everywhere, but always to redheads, with parcels. In my short-sleeved flowered batik shirt, with my tattoos displayed, they took me for a beachcomber with a private income or a profitable sideline, perhaps 'an interesting character'. Once, in the Pebble Bar of the Hotel Singapura, an American lady who was three sheets to the wind said I looked like a movie actor she knew, but she couldn't think of his name.

'What's your name?' she asked.

I smiled, to give her the impression that I might be that actor, said, 'Take a guess, sweetheart' and then I left; leaving, I heard some hoots from the gang of oil-riggers who always drank there.

My appearance, the look of a millionaire down on his luck, which is also the look of a bum attempting to be princely, was never quite right for most of the places I had to go. I was the wrong colour in the Tai-Hwa and all the other Chinese joints – that was clear: at the Starlight, strictly Cantonese, they seated me with elderly hostesses and overcharged me. I was too dressy for the settler hang-outs and never had enough money for more than one drink at the Hilton or Raffles, though I looked as if I might have belonged in those hotels. I certainly looked like a member of the Tanglin Club, the Swiss Club, the Cricket Club and all the others where my chits were signed for me by fellers who liked my discretion. I was always welcome in the clubs, but that was a business matter. And they did not laugh at the Bandung: they knew me there.

In the taxi I mentioned the Bandung to Leigh; he didn't say no, but he thought we should stop at Hing's first – 'Let's have a look at the *towkay*' was what he said. We got stuck in rush-hour traffic, a solid unmoving line of cars. There was an accident up front and the cars were passing the wrecked sedan at a crawl to note down the licence number so they could play it on the lottery. There was a bus in front of us displaying the bewildering sign *I Don't Know Why, But I Prefer Sanyo*. The local phrase for beeping was 'horning', and they were horning to beat the band. We sat and sweated, gagging on the exhaust fumes; it was after five by the time we got to Hing's.

Little Hing was sitting on the shop entrance reading the racing form. He sat like a roosting fowl, his feet on the seat, his knees drawn up under his chin. Seeing us, he turned his bony face and bawled upstairs, then he locked his teeth and snuffled and paddled the air with his free hand, which meant we were to wait.

'Your oriental politeness,' I said. 'He'll spit in a minute, probably hock a louie on your shoes, so watch out.'

We had made Big Hing wait; now, to save face, he was making us wait. Hing spent the best part of a day saving face, and Yardley said, 'When you see his face you wonder why he bothers.'

Gopi, the *peon*, brought a wooden stool for Leigh, but Leigh just winced at it and studied Hing's sign: *Chop Hing Kheng Fatt: Ship Chandlers & Provisioners*, and below that in smaller assured script: *Catering & Victualling, Marine Hardware, Importers, Wholesale Drygoods & Foodstuffs, Licensed Agents, Frozen Meat*, and the motto: *'All Kinds of Deck & Engine Stores & Bonded Stores & Sundries'*. 'Sundries' was my department. The signs on the shops to the left and right of Hing, and on all the other shops – biscuit-coloured, peeling, cracked and trying to collapse, a dusty terrace of shop-houses sinking shoulder to shoulder on Beach Road – were identical but for the owner's name; even the stains and cracks were reduplicated down the road as far as you could see. But there was something final in the decline, an air of ramshackle permanency common in Eastern ports, as if, having fallen so far, they would fall no further.

'What's your club in Hong-Kong?' I asked.

'Just one, I'm afraid,' he said. He paused and smiled. 'The Royal Hong-Kong.'

'Jockey or Yacht?'

'Yacht,' he said quickly, losing his smile.

Little Hing spat and went back to his racing form without bothering to see where the gob landed.

'Missed again,' I said, winking at Leigh. 'I've heard the Yacht Club's a smashing place,' I said, and he looked at me the way he had when I said 'Honkers'. 'You're in luck, actually. You have a reciprocal membership with the Tanglin here and probably a couple of others as well.'

'No,' he said, 'I inquired about that before I came down. Bit of a nuisance, really. But there it is.'

He was lying. I knew the Royal Hong-Kong Yacht Club and the Tanglin Club had reciprocal memberships and privileges; a member of one could sign bar chits at the other and use all the club's facilities. So he was not a member, and there we were standing on the Beach Road sidewalk, on the lip of its smelly monsoon drain, at the beck and call of a surly little *towkay* who had chosen to sulk upstairs, lying about clubs we didn't belong to. It made me sad, like the pictures hidden in my back pocket I would never admit to having: two grown men practising lies, and why?

Big Hing came out in his pyjamas and gave Leigh that secret society stare. Hing was not a member; he was a paid-up victim of the Red Eleven who controlled Beach Road and collected 'coffee-money' for protection. The payment gave Hing a certain standing, for, having victimized him, the Red Eleven would stick by him and fight anyone who tried to squeeze him. Leigh handed over a letter, and we waited while Hing gnawed the sealing wax from the flap. He put on his old wire glasses and read the column of characters, then he smiled his angry eyeless smile and nodded at Leigh.

'I trust everything is in order,' said Leigh to Hing.

It was a wasted remark; Hing was muttering to Little Hing, and Little replied by muttering into the racing form he held against his face.

'Where's our friend going to put up?' I asked.

'Booked at the Strand,' said Big Hing. 'Can come tomorrow.' He picked up his grandson and bounced the trouserless little feller to show the interview was over.

The Strand Hotel was on Scotts Road, diagonally across the road from the Tanglin Club. As we were pulling into the Strand's driveway, under the arch with the sign reading: *European Cuisine – Weddings – Parties – Reasonable Prices*, Leigh saw the Tanglin signboard and said, 'Why don't we pop over for a drink?'

I let my watch horrify me. 'God,' I said, 'it's nearly half-past six. That place is a mad-house this time of day. Fellers having a drink after work. Look, William, I know a quiet little –'

'I'd love to have a look at those new squash courts of yours,' he said. He hit me hard on the arm and said heartily, 'Come on, Flowers, I'll buy you a drink.' He gave his suitcase to the room-boy at the Strand, signed the register and then clapped his stomach with two hands. 'Ready?'

I'll buy you a drink, he had said, but that was impossible because money was not allowed and only a member could sign chits. The brass plaque on the club entrance – *Members Only* – mocked us both. I looked for someone I knew, but all I could see were tanned long-legged mothers, fine women in towelling smocks, holding beach-bags and children's hands, waiting for their *syce*-driven cars after a day at the club pool. They were eagerly whispering to each other and laughing; the sight of that joy lifted my heart – I couldn't help but think they were plotting some trivial infidelity.

'The new squash courts are over there,' I said, stepping nimbly past the doorman and bounding up the stairs.

'Drink first,' said Leigh. 'I'm absolutely parched.' He was enjoying himself and he seemed right at home. He led the way into the Churchill Room, and 'Very agreeable,' he said, twice, as he looked for an opening at the bar.

The Churchill Room had just been renovated: thick wall-to-wall carpets, a new photograph of Winston, a raised bar and a very efficient air-conditioning system. In spite of the cool air I was perspiring, a damp panel of shirt clung to my back; I was searching for a familiar face, someone I knew who might sign a drink chit. The bar was packed with men in white shirts and ties, some wearing stiff planter's shorts, standing close to the counter in groups of three or four, braying to their companions or sort of climbing over each other and waving chit-pads at the barmen. Leigh was pushing ahead of me and I had just reached out to tap him on the shoulder and tell him I had remembered something important – my nerve had failed me so completely I could not think what, and prayed for necessity's inspiration – when I saw old Gunstone over in the corner at one of the small tables, drinking alone.

Gunstone was one of my first clients; he was in his seventies and had come to Singapore when it was a rubber estate and a few rows of shop-houses and go-downs. During the war he was captured by the Japanese and put to work on the Siamese Death Railway. He told me how he had buried his friend on the Burmese border, a statement like a motto of hopeless devotion, an obscure form of rescue: *I buried my friend*. He was the only client who took me to lunch when he wanted a girl, but he was also the cagiest because I had to make all the arrangements for him and even put my own name on the hotel register. What he did with the girls I never knew – I never asked: I did not monkey with a feller's confidence – but it was my abiding fear that one day Gunstone's engine was going to stop in a hotel room I had reserved and I was going to have to explain my name in the register. I never saw Gunstone's wife; he only took her to the club at night and most of my club work was in the day-time.

'Jack,' he said, welcoming me, showing me an empty chair. Good old Gunstone.

'Evening, Mr Gunstone,' I said. It was a servile greeting, I knew, but I could not see Leigh and I was worried.

Gunstone seemed glad to see me; that was a relief. I feared questions like, 'Who are you and what are you doing here?'

'What'll you have?' asked Gunstone.

'Small Anchor,' I said, and as Gunstone turned to find a waiter Leigh appeared with a drink in his hand.

'Chappie here wants your signature, Flowers,' said Leigh.

I took the chit-pad from the waiter and put it on Gunstone's table, saying, 'All in good time', then introduced Leigh. Gunstone said, 'Ever run into old So-and-so in Hong-Kong?' and Leigh said charmingly, 'I've never had the pleasure.' Gunstone began describing the feller, saying, 'He's got the vilest habits and he's incredibly mean and nasty and' – Gunstone smiled – 'perfectly fascinating. He might be in U.K. now, on leave.'

'Do you ever go back to U.K.?' Leigh asked.

'Used to,' said Gunstone. 'But the last time I was there they passed a bill making homosexuality legal. I said to my wife, "Let's get out of here before they make the blasted thing compulsory!"'

Leigh laughed. 'I meant to ask you, Flowers,' he said. 'Are you married?'

'Nope,' I said. Leigh went on talking to Gunstone. Once, and it was at the Tanglin Club, I used to fix up a certain feller with girls. The feller was married and I eventually got friendly with the wife and 'She's ever so nice,' I said to the feller. On the afternoons when he had one of my girls I visited his wife at their house in Bukit Timah and had no fear that he would show up. But there were children; she hollered at them and sent them out with the *amah*. She was very sweet to me the moment after she had cuffed the children. One afternoon I was in the Bandung. I had agreed we should meet, but I realized I was late, delaying over a large gin. She was waiting; I was waiting; I did not want to go. It was like marriage. I went on drinking, and lost her.

'I must be going,' said Gunstone. He pulled the chit-pads over and signed them. He said, 'I scratch your back, you scratch mine.'

'Tomorrow,' I said, and winked.

'Lunch,' said Gunstone. 'The usual time, what?'

'Sounds frightfully hush-hush,' said Leigh.

To Gunstone I said, 'We were just leaving, too,' which made it impossible for Leigh to object. It was unfair to do this, but I was sore: Leigh's two gin-slings were going to cost me a whole afternoon of waiting in the lobby of a hotel, cooling my heels and worrying about Gunstone's engine.

Yardley was telling his joke about the Irishman and the love-starved gorilla as we entered the Bandung. We walked over to the bar and, perversely I thought, Yardley delivered the punch-line to Leigh: '"One thing more, sair," says O'Flanagan to the zoo-keeper. "If there's any issue – any issue at all – it's got to be raised a Roman Catholic."'

They started to laugh – Yates, Smale, Frogget, and, loudest of all and closing his eyes with mirth, Yardley himself. I smiled, though I had heard it before. Leigh wasn't amused; he said, 'Yes, well'. That was his first mistake in the Bandung, not laughing at Yardley's joke. Yardley, an old-timer, had been drinking in the Bandung for years, and one day when Yardley was out of the room Frogget said, 'Yardley *is* the Bandung.' Every bar had a senior member; Yardley was ours. Frogget, a large shy feller, balding but not old, was Yardley's ape. Frogget – Desmond Frogget – ate like a horse, but he was sensitive about his weight; it was considered impolite to remark on the amount of food Frogget ate, the platters of noodles he hoovered up. Frogget could not have been much more than thirty-five, but the ridiculous man had that English knack of assuming elderly biases and a confounding grumpiness that made him seem twice his age. He regretted the absence of clipper ships, he remembered things that happened before he was born and, like other equally annoying youths who drank at the Bandung, started sentences with 'I always' and 'I never'.

'Don't believe we've met,' said Yardley, putting his hand out to Leigh.

Leigh hinted at reluctance by frowning as he offered his hand, but the worst offence was that after he said his name he spelled it.

'Been in Singapore long?' asked Smale. Smale was a short ruddy-faced man whose squarish shape gave the impression of having been carpentered. He carried a can of mentholated cigarettes with him wherever he went. He was working the cutter on the lid as he asked Leigh the question.

'No,' I said, 'he just –'

'To be precise,' said Leigh in a prissy voice, and checking his watch, 'four hours and forty-five minutes.'

'We like to be precise around here,' said Yardley, nudging Frogget. 'Don't we, Froggy? I mean, seeing as how we're all on the slag-heap of life, it's a bloody good thing to know the time of day, what, Froggy?'

'I always wear my watch to bed,' said Frogget.

'You come down from K.L.?' Yates asked, seeing Yardley getting hot under the collar.

'Hong-Kong,' said Leigh, stressing the *Hong* the way residents do. He looked around the room, as if trying to locate an exit.

The Bandung was a huge place – in its prime a private house with an elegant garden, birdbath and sundial and intersecting cobblestone paths. But the garden had fallen to ruin and the trellises had broken under the weight of vines which had become thick, leaning on and pinching the frail trellis ladders. I liked the garden in this wild state, the elastic fig-trees strangling the palms, the roots of the white-blossomed frangipanis cracking the stone benches and showing knuckles between the cobblestones. And the vines, now more powerful than the trellises that had once supported them, needed no propping; they made a cool leafy cavern from the walled front entrance to the verandah, where there were pots of orchids hanging from wires, with gawking blossoms and damp dangling roots.

The bar itself stood in what had once been a vast parlour,

coloured glazed tiles on the floor and a ceiling so high there were often some confused swallows flying in circles near the top. The windows were also large, and Yardley said a swarm of bees flew in one day, passed over the heads of those drinking at the bar and flew out the other side without disturbing a soul. The adjoining room we called 'the lounge', where there was a jumble of rattan furniture, a sofa, the piano Ogham used to play and little tables and potted palms. No one sat there except the barman, Wallace Thumboo, when he was totting up the day's chits at midnight, sorting them into piles according to the signatures. I was seeing the Bandung now with Leigh's eyes, and I could understand his discomfort though I didn't share it.

'Could use a coat of paint,' Leigh said. 'Do I smell cats?' He wrinkled his nose.

'I was in Hong-Kong a few years back,' said Yardley. 'My *towkay* sent me up to get some estimates on iron sheeting. I was supposed to stay for a month, until the auction, but after two days I came back. Couldn't stick the place. They treated me like dirt. Told the *towkay* the deal was up the spout. Ever been to Hong-Kong, Froggy?'

Frogget said yes, it was awful.

'What's the beer like?' Smale asked Leigh.

'My dear fellow,' said Leigh, 'I haven't the remotest idea.'

That annoyed everyone, and Yardley said, 'Got a right one 'ere.' At that point I wasn't sure who I disliked more – Yardley for being rude to Leigh, or Leigh for spelling his name and saying, 'I haven't the remotest idea' to what was meant as a friendly question. The next thing Leigh said put me on Yardley's side.

'Flowers,' said Leigh sharply, ignoring the others, 'I thought you said we could get a drink here.'

This magisterial 'Flowers', in front of my friends! Frogget grinned, Smale winked and raised his glass to me, Yates frowned, and Yardley smirked as if to say, 'You poor suffering bastard' – all of this behind Leigh's stiffened back.

I knocked for Wally and ordered two gins. Leigh wrapped his

hanky around his glass and drank disgustedly. It may have been anger or the heat, but Leigh was reddening and beads of sweat began percolating out of his face. Ordinarily, Yardley would have behaved the same as Gunstone and said, 'Ever run into old So-and-so in Kowloon?' which might have brought Leigh around. Or he would have told his story about the day the swarm of bees flew through the window, and if he was in a good mood he would have embellished it by imitating the bees, running from one side of the room to the other, flapping his arms and buzzing until he was breathless.

'Bit stuffy in here,' Smale said.

Yardley was looking at Leigh. Leigh seemed unaware that he had nettled Yardley. Yates said he had to go home and Yardley said, 'I don't blame you.'

'Say good night to Flowers,' said Frogget.

'*Mister* Flowers to you, Froggy,' I said.

Yates left, saying good night to everyone by name, but omitting Leigh. Leigh said, 'Tiffin-time – isn't that what they call it here?'

Yardley had not taken his eyes off Leigh. I thought Yardley might sock him, but his tactic was different. He told his McCoy joke, the one he always told when there was a woman in the bar he wanted to drive out. It concerned four recruits being interviewed for the army. The sergeant asks them what they do for a living and the first one, saying his name's McCoy, mutters that he's a cork-sacker ('puts the cork into sacks, you see'); the next one, also a McCoy, is a cork-soaker ('soaks it in water, you understand'); the third McCoy is a coke-sacker ('sacks coke for a dealer in fuel') and the last one, a mincing feller in satin tights, says that he's the real McCoy. Yardley told it in several accents, lengthening it with slurs and pauses ('What's that you say?') and obnoxiously set it in Hong-Kong.

Leigh made no comment. He ordered a gin for himself, but none for me.

'You giving up the booze, Jack?' said Smale, who noticed.

'A double, Wally,' I said.

Yardley giggled. 'I must have my tiffin,' he said.

'Tiffin-time, breh-heh,' said Frogget.

'Take care of yourself, Jack,' said Yardley, and left with Frogget shambling after him.

'I think I'll go whore-hopping,' said Smale in a thoughtful voice. He pressed down the lid of his cigarette-tin and said, 'Say, Jack, what was the name of that skinny one you fixed me up with? Gladys? Gloria?'

I pretended not to hear.

'Give me her number. God, she was a lively bit of crumpet.' He stared at Leigh and said, 'She does marvellous things to your arse.'

'Ask Wally,' I said.

'It was like being dead,' said Smale, still addressing Leigh. He grinned. 'You know. Paradise.'

Wally was polishing glasses at the far end of the bar, smiling at the glasses as he smiled at the counter when he wiped it and at the gin bottle when he poured. Wally said, 'What you want, Mister Smale? You want mushudge?' He nodded. 'Can.'

'Aw hell,' said Smale. 'Maybe I should forget it. I could have another double whisky, toss myself off in the loo and go down to the amusement park and play the pin-ball machines. What do you think?' He leered at me, then snorted and sloped off.

Leigh did not say anything right away. He climbed on to a bar stool and dabbed at the perspiration on his upper lip with his finger. He looked at his finger and, feelingly, said, 'How do you stand it?'

It made me cringe. It happened, this moment of worry, when, hearing a question that had never occurred to me, I discovered that I had an answer, as once in the Tai-Hwa on Cecil Street, a stranger wearing dark glasses had asked, 'Where you does wuck'? and I remembered and was afraid.

4

In my cubicle, irritably dialling a third hotel, I heard Gopi coming. Then, in Singapore, disability determined the job; Gopi, a cripple, was a *peon* from birth. He could be heard approaching by the sigh-shuffle-thump of his curious bike-riding gait. One leg was shorter than the other, and the knee in that rickety limb bent inward, collapsing into the good leg and making Gopi lean at a dangerous angle as he put his weight on it. A long step with his good leg checked his fall, and that was how he went, heaving along, dancing forward, swaying from side to side, like the standing dance of a man pumping a bike up a steep hill.

Some years ago a horse named Gopi's Dream ran an eight-furlong race at the Singapore Turf Club. I was not a member of that club, but two dollars got me into the grandstand with the howling mob; and it was there that I spent at least one afternoon of every race meeting. I had just arrived and was getting my bearings when I saw that the horse I had picked for the first race had been scratched. There were poor odds on all the others except Gopi's Dream, and the logic of choosing this horse was plain to me. I put ten dollars on him to win, though my usual bet was a deuce on a long shot for a place, bolstered by a prayer which I screamed into my hands as the ponies leaped down the home stretch. I told myself that half the bet was Gopi's Deepavali present. Gopi's Dream won, as all horses do when the logic is irrefutable, and it paid two hundred dollars; half I put away for Gopi, the rest I lost in the course of the afternoon.

The next day I took Gopi to a shop over on Armenian Street and had him fitted for a brace and a boot with a five-inch sole. He was a bit rocky on it at first, but soon he got the hang of it and instead of his cyclist's swaying he learned a jerking limp, dragging the enormous boot and clumping it ahead of him and then chasing it with the other leg. The brace clinked and the boot gave out long twisting squeaks. The odd thing was that although he walked fairly straight he walked much more slowly, perspiring and pulling and swinging the boot along.

He stopped wearing the apparatus. He told me in Malay that it was 'biting' his leg and that it was at the cobbler's being put right. After a week I asked him about it; he started wearing it – two days of clinks and squeaks, then he stopped. I asked why. It was biting. The brace was a greater affliction than the limp, a cure more painful than the ailment; the incident cured me of certain regrets.

'All full up,' the voice was saying to me over the phone. Gopi pedalled over and I slammed the receiver into its cradle.

'Hupstairs,' said Gopi, pointing his slender finger to indicate that Leigh was in Hing's office. He clamped his tongue at the side of his mouth and scribbled in an invisible ledger to show he had seen Leigh writing. Then he asked me about Leigh. Who was he? Where was he from? Did he have children? Was he a Eurasian?'

I told Gopi what I knew and asked what time Leigh had arrived.

'Seven-something.'

That was news. As an eager new employee at Hing's, with the hunch that if I did a good job I had a chance for promotion, I used to come in at seven-something, too. By the time Hing rolled in I was already in a sweat, saying, 'Right you are, Mr Hing', and 'Just leave it to me'. There was no promotion. I asked for Christmas off; Hing said, 'I am Buddhist, but wucking on Besak Day, birthday of Buddha, isn't it?' I started to come in at eight-something and never said, 'Leave it to me', and after I made a go of my enterprise it was ten before I showed my face. I would not be promoted, but neither would I be sacked: he could never have gotten another *ang moh* for what he paid me. In the acceptance of this continuing meekness, the denial of any ambition, was an unvarying condition of security and the annual promise of a renewed work permit. It was an angle, but it cost me my pride. When someone at a club bar or hotel lounge said, 'Go on, Jack, have another one', I was happy: I had the satisfaction of having earned my reward. The reminder that the drink would never have been offered if I hadn't had a girl in tow was something that didn't worry me unless a feller like Leigh woke up my scruples with 'How do you stand it?' A feller who lived in Singapore and knew me would never have asked that. The real question was not how but why: my answer would have unstrung him, or anyone.

Leigh was eager to please Hing – that was plain. He had not found out it was no use. And who was he, this accountant from Hong-Kong? A clerkly fugitive, lying low after an incautious embezzlement in London? Sacked by a British bank for interfering with a woman in Fixed Deposits or for incompetence, and, like many *ang mohs* in the East, seeking cover in a Chinese shop, consoling himself with clubby fantasies and the fact that he was too far away to be of concern, an alien at a great distance, the bird of passage who mentioned from time to time when things got rough that there was always Australia? He had lied about his clubs – the first time anyone had tried that on me – but so had I, three times over. It could not be held against him.

The feeling I had for him was an inward clutching at self-pity. There was so much I could have told him if only he had been friendly and stopped calling me Flowers. 'Go away and save yourself', I wanted to say; I could have watched him do that and watching him given myself hope. I had my girls; I knew the limits of employment; I had faith in extraordinary kinds of rescue, miraculous recoveries; I knew a thing or two about love. What was his alternative? I decided to watch him closely, this version of myself; his nervy question still rankled, and pity prevented me from asking him the same. He was not aware of how much I knew.

Seeing me engrossed, Gopi left, shoulders heaving. His arms did not swing or give him motion. They dangled uselessly as he pedalled. He was a small man, and sometimes I believed that without him I would have floundered.

I dialled another hotel for Gunstone and got another refusal.

That was the last of his Victoria Street favourites. It was nearly lunchtime, so I called the Belvedere. I was at the airport, I told the receptionist, and did they have an air-conditioned double room for one night?

'All our rooms – we got eight-hundred plus – they are all air-conditioned,' she said.

'That's very nice,' I said, and made the reservation. 'If Hing asks,' I told Gopi, leaving him holding the can as usual – but who except the meekest man would hold it? – 'tell him I'm down with the 'flu.'

Since it was going to be lunch at the Tanglin, then off to the Belvedere, I thought I'd better change my duds.

'Why the black suit?' Gunstone asked.

'My others are at the cleaner's,' I said, still rolling 'I've just come from a funeral' around on my tongue. He would have asked who died, or perhaps have been spooked by the announcement. I had the fluent liar's sense of proportion and foresight. Gunstone was calmed.

Lunch was the Friday special, my favourite, seafood buffet. I followed Gunstone, taking the same things he did, in the same amounts, and I soon realized that I was heaping my plate with oysters and prawns which I liked less than the crab and lobster Gunstone took in two small helpings. I put some oysters back and got a frown from the Malay chef.

At the table I said, 'I hope I haven't boobed, Mr Gunstone, but I've fixed you up at the Belvedere this afternoon.'

He stabbed a prawn and peeled off the shell and dunked the naked finger of pink meat into a saucer of chilli paste. 'Don't believe we've ever been to the Belvedere before, have we, Jack?'

'The other places were full,' I said.

'Quite all right,' he said. 'But I ate at the Belvedere last week. It wasn't much good, you know.'

'Oh, I know what you mean, Mr Gunstone,' I said. 'That food is perfectly hideous.'

'Exactly,' said Gunstone. 'How's your salmon?'

I had not started to eat. I took a forkful, smeared it in mayonnaise and ate it. 'Delicious,' I said.

'Mine's awful,' he said, and he pushed his salmon to the side of his plate.

'Now that you mention it,' I said, 'it *does* taste rather –'

'Desiccated,' said Gunstone.

'Exactly,' I said. I pushed my salmon over to the side and covered it with a lettuce leaf. I was sorry; I liked salmon the way it tasted out of a can.

'Lobster's pretty dreadful, too,' said Gunstone a moment later.

I was just emptying a large claw. It was excellent, and I ate the whole claw before saying, 'Right again, Mr Gunstone. Tastes like they fished it out of the Muar River.'

'We'll shunt that over, shall we?' said Gunstone. He moved a lobster tail next to the discarded salmon.

I did the same, then as quickly as I could ate all my crab-salad before he could say it was bad. I gnawed a hard roll and started on the oysters.

'The prawns are a success,' he said.

'The oysters are –' I didn't want to finish the sentence, but Gunstone was no help '– sort of limp.'

'They're cockles, actually,' said Gunstone. 'And they're a damned insult. Steward!' A Malay waiter came over. 'Take this away.'

Demanding that food be sent back to the kitchen is a special skill. It is done with *panache* by people who use that word. I admired people who did it, but could not imitate them.

'Yours, *tuan*?' asked the waiter.

'Yes, take it away,' I said sadly.

'Do you want more, *tuan*?' the waiter asked Gunstone.

'If I wanted more, would I be asking you to remove that plate?' Gunstone said.

The waiter slid my lunch away. I buttered a hard roll and ate it, making crumbs shower down the front of my suit.

'That steward,' said Gunstone, shaking his head. 'The most intelligent thing I ever heard him say was, "If you move your lump of ice-cream a bit to the right, *tuan*, you will find a strawberry." God help us.'

I laughed and brushed my jacket. 'Still,' I said, 'I wouldn't mind joining this club.'

'You don't want to join this club,' said Gunstone.

'I do,' I said, and saw myself lying in the sun, by the pool, and one of those tanned long-legged women whispering urgently, 'Jack, where have you been? I've been looking everywhere for you. *It's all set.*'

'Why, whatever for?'

'A place to go, I suppose,' I said. The Bandung's only publicity was the matchboxes Wallace Thumboo had printed with the slogan, *There's Always Someone You Know At The Bandung!*

Gunstone chuckled. 'If they can pronounce your name you can join.'

'Flowers is pretty easy.'

'I should say so!'

But Fiori isn't, I thought. And Fiori was my name, Flowers an approximation and a mask.

'Now,' said Gunstone, looking at his watch, 'how about dessert?'

Gunstone's joke: it was time to fetch Djamila.

The old-timers, I found, tended to prefer Malays, while the newcomers went for the Chinese, and the Malays preferred each other. The Chinese clients, of whom I had several, liked the big-boned Australian girls; Germans were fond of Tamils, and the English fellers liked anything young, but preferred their girls boyish and their women mannish. British sailors from H.M.S. *Terror* enjoyed fighting each other in the presence of transvestites. Americans liked clean sporty ones, to whom they would give nicknames, like 'Skeezix' and 'Pussycat' (the English made an effort to learn the girl's real name), and would spend a whole afternoon trying to teach one of my girls how to swim in a hotel pool, although it was costing them fifteen dollars an hour to do it. Americans also went in for a lot of hugging in the taxi, smooching and kidding around, and sort of stumbling down the sidewalk, gripping the girl hard and saying, 'Aw, honey, whoddle ah do?' Later they wrote them letters, and the girls pestered me to help them reply.

Djamila – 'Jampot' an American feller used to call her, and it suited her – was very reliable and easy to contact. She was waiting by the Hong-Kong and Shanghai Bank with my trusty suitcase as we pulled up in the taxi. I hopped out and opened the door for her, then got into the front seat and put the suitcase between my knees. Djamila climbed in with Gunstone and sat smiling, rocking her handbag in her lap.

Smiling is something girls with buck teeth seldom do with any pleasure; Djamila showed hers happily, charming things, very white in her broad mouth. She had small ears, a narrow moonlit face, large darting eyes and heavy eyebrows. A slight girl, even skinny, but having said that one would have to add that her breasts were large and full, her bum high and handsome as a pumpkin. Her breasts were her virtue, the virtue of most of my Malay girls; unlike the Chinese bulbs that disappeared in a frock fold, these were a pair of substantial jugs, something extra that moved and made a rolling wobble of her walk. That was the measure of acceptable size, that bobbing, one a second later than the other, each responding to the step of Djamila's small feet. Her bottom moved on the same prompting, but in a different rhythm, a wonderful agitation in the willowy body, a glorious heaving to and fro, the breasts nodding above the black lace of the tight-waisted blouse, the packed-in bum lifting, one buttock pumping against the other, creeping around her sarong as she shuffled, showing her big teeth.

'Jack, you look very smart,' said Djamila. 'New suit and whatnot.'

'I put it on for you, sweetheart,' I said. 'This here's Mr Gunstone, an old pal of mine.'

Djamila shook his hand and said, 'Jack got nice friends.'

'Where's that little car of yours, Jack?' Gunstone asked.

'It packed up,' I said. 'Being fixed.'

'What's the trouble this time?'

'Suspension, I think. Front end sort of shimmies, like Djamila but not as pretty.'

'It's always the way with those little French cars. Problems. It's the workmanship.'

The taxi pulled up in front of the Belvedere. The doorman in a top hat and tails snatched the door open and let Gunstone out. I handed over the suitcase; it was a good solid Antler, a sober pebbly grey, filled with copies of the *Straits Times* and an RAF first-aid kit, a useful item – once we had to use the tourniquet on a Russian seaman, and the little plasters were always handy for scratches.

'You should get yourself a Morris,' said Gunstone at the reception desk.

I could not answer right away because I was signing my name on the register and the clerk was welcoming me with a copy of *What's On in Singapore*. I was not worried about being asked about Gunstone and Djamila; anything is possible in a big expensive hotel, and the manager will always smile and say he remembers you. In the elevator I said, 'Yes, your Morris is a good buy.'

'I like Chevy,' said Djamila.

The elevator boy and the bell-hop stared at her. My girls looked fine, very pretty in bars and on the street, but in well-lighted hotels they looked different, not out of place, but prominent and identifiable.

'I hate these American cars,' said Gunstone.

'So do I,' I said. 'Waste of money.'

'Nice and big,' said Djamila. She gave a low throaty laugh. Most of my girls had bad throats: it was the line of work, all those germs.

'Here you are, sah. Seven-oh-five,' said the bell-hop. He followed us in and swung the suitcase over to a low table; I could hear the newspapers shift inside. He started his spiel about the lights and if there's anything you want, but I interrupted him and pressed fifty dollars into his hand and he took off.

'Your lights,' I said, discovering the switch and turning them all on. I went around the room naming appliances and opening doors, as the bell-hop would have done if I had given him a chance. 'Your TV, your washroom, window-blinds, radio' – switching that on, I got a melody from *Doctor Zhivago*. 'I think everything is in order.'

'You couldn't do better than a Morris,' said Gunstone. He came over to me and said, 'What's she like?' in a whisper.

'Very rewarding,' I said. 'Very rewarding indeed.'

Djamila was sitting on the edge of the large double bed, removing her silver bracelets; she did it with dainty grace, admiring her arm and showing herself her fingernails as she pulled each bracelet past them.

Gunstone, on a stuffed chair, sighed and twisted off one of his shoes. He had pulled off a sock and was intently poking the limp thing into the empty shoe with his trembling finger, when I said, 'I'll leave you two to get on with it. Bye for now.'

The elevator boy, seeing the feller he had just deposited on that floor, looked away from me at the button he was punching, and I could tell from the movement of his ears and a peculiar tightening of a section of scalp on the back of his head that he had summed up the situation and was grinning foolishly. I felt like socking him.

'What's your name?'

'Tony-*lah*,' he said. A person sobers up when he has to tell a stranger his name.

'Here you are, Tony.' I handed him a dollar. 'Don't blab,' I said. 'Nobody likes a blabber.'

That dollar would have come in handy, and I could have saved it if I had gone down the fire stairs, which was what I usually did. But seven flights of dusty-smelling unpainted cement was more than a man my age should tolerate. A little arithmetic satisfied me that I could afford one drink; in the Belvedere lounge-bar the *hors d'oeuvres* were free.

Avoiding the lobby, I nipped into the lounge, found a cool leather armchair and sat very happily for a few minutes reading *What's On* and looking up every so often to admire the decor. Yardley and the rest did not think much of the new Singapore hotels – too shiny and tacky, they said: no character at all. Character was weevils in your food, metal folding chairs and a grouchy barman who insulted you as he overcharged you; it was a monsoon drain that hadn't been cleared for months and a toilet – like the one in the Bandung – located in the middle of the kitchen. Some day, I thought, I'm going to reserve a room at the Belvedere and burrow in the blankets of a wide bed – the air-conditioner on full – and sleep for a week. The ground floor of the Belvedere was Italian marble and there was a chandelier hanging in the lobby that must have taken years to make. I was enjoying myself in the solid comfort, sipping my gin, looking at a sea-shell mural on the lounge wall, periwinkles spilling out of conches, gilded sea-urchins and fingers of coral; but I became anxious.

It was not my habitual worry about Gunstone's engine. It was the annoying suspicion that the seven or eight tourists in the lounge were staring in my direction. They had seen me come in with Gunstone and Djamila and like Tony they had guessed what I was up to. The ones that weren't laughing at me, despised me. If I had been younger they would have said, 'Ah what a sharp lad, a real operator – you've got to hand it to him.' But a middle-aged man doing the same thing was a dull dirty procurer. I tried to look unruffled, crossing my legs and flicking through the little pamphlet. Recrossing my legs, I felt an uncommon breeze against my ankles: I wasn't wearing any socks.

How could I be so stupid? There I was in the lounge of an expensive hotel, wearing my black Ah Chum worsted, a dark tie and white shirt and shoes my *amah* had buffed to a high gloss – and sockless! That was how they knew my trade, by my nude ankles. I wanted to leave, but I couldn't without calling attention to myself. So I sat in the chair in a way which made it possible for me to push at the knees of my pants and lower my cuffs over my ankles. I tried to convince myself that these staring tourists didn't matter – they'd all be on the morning flight to Bangkok.

I lifted my drink and caught a lady's eye. She looked away. Returning to my reading, I sensed her eyes drift over to me again. You never knew with these American ladies; they made faces at each other in public, sometimes hilarious ones, a sisterly foolishness. The other people began staring. They were making me miserable, ruining the only drink I could afford. The embarrassment was Leigh's doing; the stranger had called my vocation 'poncing'.

'Telephone call for Bishop Bradley . . . Bishop Bradley . . .' The slow demanding announcement came over the loudspeaker in the lounge, a cloth-faced box on the wall above a slender palm in a copper pot. No one got up.

Two ladies looked at the loudspeaker.

It stopped, the voice and the hum behind it; there was an expectant pause in the lounge, everyone holding his breath, knowing the announcement would start again in a moment, which it did, monotonously.

'Bishop Bradley . . . Telephone call for Bishop Bradley . . .'

Now no one was looking at the loudspeaker.

I had fastened all the buttons on my black suit jacket. I stood up and turned an impatient face to the repeated summons coming from the cloth-faced box. I swigged the last of my gin and with the eyes of those people upon me strode out in my clerical-looking garb in the direction of the information desk. I knew I had made them sorry for staring at my sockless feet, for judging my action at the desk. 'There goes the bishop', they were saying.

Outside I walked up and down Orchard Road until Gunstone and Djamila appeared, all the while blaming Leigh for this new behaviour of mine, embarrassment and fumbling shame making me act strangely. His shadow obscured my way: I wanted him to go.

5

It was early lighted evening, that pleasant glareless time of day just before sunset; the moon showed in a blue sky – a pale gold sickle on its back – and it was possible to stroll through the mild air without hunching over and squinting away from the sun. It was the only hour when the foliage was not tinged with hues of sickly yellow; trees were denser, green and cool. All the two-storey Chinese houses set in courtyards along Cuppage Road had their doors and green shutters open for the breeze, and there was a sense of slowed activity, almost of languor, that the sight at dusk of men in pyjamas – the uniform of the peace-loving – produces in me.

A formation of swallows dived into view, pivoted sharply like bats, and then chased, lurching this way and that, towards the brightest part of the sky, where a reddening millrace of cloud poured this brightness into a subdued rosy wash. The palms towering above the Bandung did not sway – they never did in Singapore – but I could hear the papery rattle of the fronds shaking, hearing a coolness I couldn't feel. To me, a northern-born American, the palm-tree, when I was growing up, was a graceful symbol of wealth: it suggested lush Florida, sunny winter vacations, certain movie stars and long days of play, white stucco hotels and casinos on wide beaches, and fresh fruit all year round; fellers had fun under nature's parasol. I looked up at the Bandung's palms, trees I no longer associate with fun, so as to avoid looking at the top of the stockade wall enclosing the garden; on top of the wall glass shards were planted to discourage intruders and the sight of these bristling never failed to make my pecker ache.

I crunched down the cobblestone path, under the tunnel of

vines, in the comfortable damp of the freshly watered garden; the sun had dropped behind the roof of the Bandung and was now dazzling at the back door, shooting brilliant gold streaks through two rooms, along the ground floor, on the gleaming tiles. My jacket sat well on me for the first time that day, and with Gunstone's envelope of cash in my breast pocket I was cool and happy.

But I knew what I was in for. I quailed when I heard Yardley's angry whoop of abuse echo in the big room. I paused near the wicker chairs on the verandah, and for a hopeless fluid moment wished there was somewhere else I could go. It wasn't possible. A man my age, for whom a bar was a habit and a consolation – a reassurance of community that could be almost tender – a man my age didn't drink in strange bars; that meant an upsetting break in routine; my friends interpreted absence as desertion, and they did not forgive easily. It would have seemed especially suspicious if I had avoided the Bandung after being responsible for bringing Leigh there the previous evening. Leigh had intruded and disturbed Yardley – Yardley's last joke was proof of that. The blame was mine and an explanation was expected of me. I had come prepared to denounce Leigh.

Yardley saw me and stopped whooping. Frogget was beside him; Smale, Yates and Coony were at the bar, and over in an armchair drinking soy-bean milk and absorbed in the *Reader's Digest*, sat old Mr Tan Lim Hock. Mr Tan, a retired civil servant, helped the regulars at the Bandung with their income tax – 'he can skin a maggot,' Yardley said. He was a rather tense man whom I had seen smile only twice: once, when he saw what Hing paid me ('Is this *per mensem* or *per annum*?' he had asked), and once – that day in 1968 – when China exploded her H-bomb.

I crossed the tiles and ordered a gin. Yardley's defiant silence, and the sheepishness on the faces of the rest, told me what I had expected: that Leigh was the subject of the abusive shouts.

'What's cooking?' I said.

'Are you alone?' asked Yardley. Yates and Coony looked at him, as if they expected him to continue, but all he said, when I told him I was alone, was, 'Wally nearly got pranged this afternoon. Isn't that right, Wally? Got a damned great bruise on his arm. Show us your bruise again, Wally, come on.'

Wally, at the centre of attention, was uncomfortable. 'Not too bad,' he said, smiling at his bandaged elbow.

'That's not what you told me!' said Yardley. He turned to me. 'Poor little sod nearly got killed!' Ordinarily, Wally's injury would not have mattered to him – he might even have mocked it – but he was in a temper, and his anger about Leigh, which I had deflected by barging in, had become a general raging. It was at times like this that he called Frogget Desmond instead of Froggy (Frogget didn't object: he had attached himself to Yardley and like Wally simplified his loyalty by surrendering to abuse for praise); and it was only in anger that Yardley remembered I was an American.

'It's these bloody taxis,' said Yates – the 'bloody' was for Yardley's benefit. Yates was a quiet soul, the only one of us who did not work for a *towkay*. He got what were called 'perks', home leave every two years, education and family allowance, and could look forward to a golden handshake and one hundred cubic feet of sea-freight.

'No, it's not,' said Yardley. 'It's these jumped-up bastards who come here and act like they own the road.' He stared at me. 'You know the kind, don't you, Jack?'

'I see them now and again,' I said.

'Who was it, Wally? Was it a Chink that ran you down?'

Mr Tan Lim Hock was ten feet away; he chose not to hear.

'European,' said Wally, blinking and gasping at his own recklessness. 'He didn't hit me, I fell. Assident.'

'He *hit* you, you silly shit,' said Yardley. 'I knew it was a European, and I'll bet he doesn't live in Singapore either. No, sir, not *him*. Wouldn't dare. Take someone like that friend of yours, Jack –'

Yardley began blaming Leigh for Wally's bruise. Not so incredible: a month earlier, in a similar series of associations, after he had been overcharged by the Singapore Water Board on an item marked 'sewerfee' he flung the crumpled bill in Wally's face and said, 'There's no end to the incompetence of you fuckers.' Now, Yardley worked himself up into such a lather that soon he was saying, ignoring Wally and the bruise, 'That pal of yours, that shifty little bastard would run down the lot of us if we gave him half a chance, I can tell you that. If Jack keeps bringing him in here I'm going to stay home – nothing against you, Jack, but you should know better. Wally, for God's sake look alive and give me a double.'

'Let me explain,' I said. They didn't know the half of it; I could tell them Leigh's lie about his club, the airport story about 'What ship your flend flom?' and how he had suggested we go see Hing before having a drink ('Arse-licker!' Yardley would have cried). But I flubbed it before I began by saying, 'William arrived yesterday, and where else –'

'*William?*' Yardley looked at me. 'You call that little maggot *William*? Well, I'll be damned.' He shook his head. 'Jack, don't be a sucker. Even bloody Desmond can see that bugger's jumped-up, and he knows you're a Yank, so he can get away with telling you he's Governor-General – *you* won't know the difference. Listen to me. I'm telling you he's so shifty the light doesn't strike him.'

'I hear he's a nasty piece of work,' said Coony.

'He's all fart and no arse,' said Smale, who then mimicked Leigh saying, 'I haven't the remotest idea.'

'He'd try the patience of a bloody saint,' said Yardley.

'Why don't you lay off him?' I said, surprising myself with the objection.

'Jack likes him,' said Yardley. 'Don't he, Desmond?'

'Yeah,' said Frogget, turning away from me and rubbing his nose, which in profile was a snout. 'I fancy he does.'

'I don't,' I said, and although I had planned a moment earlier to denounce Leigh I hated myself for saying it. When I first saw Leigh at the airport I had an inkling – a tic of doubt that made me want to look into a mirror – of how other people saw me. Now I understand that tic, and whatever I might say about Leigh did not matter: I could prove my dislike to these fellers at the bar facing me, but there was no way I could make myself believe it. It was not very complicated. Middle age is a sense of slipping and decline, and I suppose I had my first glimpse of this frailty in Leigh, the feeling of the body growing unreliable, getting out of control in a mournfully private way – only the occupier of the body could know. Once *I* might have said, 'He's all fart and no arse,' but hearing it from Smale was a confirmation of my fear. The ridicule involved me – it was fear, and I was inclined now to defend the stranger, for hearing him ridiculed I knew how others ridiculed me; defending him was merciful, but it also answered a need in myself by providing me with a defence.

It was so simple. But the peril of being over fifty is, along with anger's quick ignition, the clinging to transparent deceptions. We let others confirm what we already know, and we get mad because they say it; what appears like revelation is the calling of a desperate bluff. The young wiseacre starting his story 'This feller was really old, about fifty or sixty –' drives every listener over fifty up the wall. We knew it before he said it. What is aggravating is not that the wiseacre knows, but that he thinks it's important and holds it against us. Our only defence is in refusing to laugh at his damned joke.

So 'He's not here,' I said, 'and it's not fair to talk behind his back.'

'Look who's talking about being fair!' said Yardley. He had overcome his colicky anger and was laughing at me. 'Who is it that imitates the maggot-skinner when his back is turned?'

It was true; I did. When Mr Tan left the bar I sometimes did an imitation of him with his *Reader's Digest* and bottle of Vimto soy-bean milk. I looked over and was glad to see that Mr Tan had gone home; Yardley's 'Chink' had done it. My other routines were Wally polishing glasses, Frogget's shambling and Yardley, drunk, forgetting the punch-line of a joke. My imitations were not very accurate, but my size and panting determination made the attempt funny. Mimicry reassures the weak, and the envious fool takes the risk as often as the visionary who mocks the error and leaves the man alone; I did not like to be reminded of my brand of mimicry.

'I'm turning over a new leaf,' I said.

'By wearing a suit?' Smale asked.

Of course: I had forgotten I was wearing a suit. That bothered them most of all. They were sensitive about fellers who dressed up and made a bluff of the success they felt was denied everyone because it was denied them.

'I had to go to a funeral,' I said. I took off my jacket and rolled up my shirt-sleeves. I knew instantly what Yardley's next words would be.

He said, 'Don't tell me your friend's packed it in!'

'That'd be a ruddy shame,' said Smale.

'Let's drop it, shall we?' I said. After all my indignant sympathy that was the only rebellion I could offer.

Then Leigh walked in.

I heard Gopi's characteristic trampling of the cobbled path in the garden, his whisper, and Leigh's, 'Ah, yes, here we are' and my heart quickened.

'Long time no see,' said Yardley.

Leigh brightened; but Yardley was beckoning to Gopi and ordering Gopi a drink. 'How you doing?' said Yardley, putting his arm around the *peon*.

'*There* you are,' said Leigh. I winced at the demonstration of pretended relief. Leigh glanced at the others and said, ''d evening' and 'M'ellew'.

'Go on,' said Yardley, 'drink up! There's a good chap.'

Gopi had a whisky in his hand. He drank it all and at once his eyes glazed, his face went ashen and matched his caste mark.

'Leave him alone,' I said. 'Gopi, don't drink if you're not in the mood.'

'He's going to be sick,' said Coony.

'I like this little chap's company,' said Yardley. It was his revenge on Leigh. 'Have another one?'

Gopi nodded, but he was not saying yes. He covered his face with a hanky and pedalled to the door. Outside, in the garden, he became loud, hawking and spitting.

'The call of the East,' said Smale.

Gopi groaned and dragged himself away.

'That was mighty nice of you,' I said to Yardley.

'He'll be all right,' Yardley muttered and turned away, saying, 'Now, where was I?' to Frogget and Smale.

'How are you doing?' asked Leigh.

'Anyone I can,' I said.

'That clerk of yours very kindly showed me the way here. Poor chap's got a sort of gammy leg, hasn't he, and I was a bit sorry he had to –' Leigh was still talking about Gopi's lameness, but he was not looking me in the eye. He stared at my tattoos, the ones on my left arm, and in particular at the long blue crucifix crowned with a circle of thorns dripping inverted commas of blood on to my wrist. I pressed my right to my side as soon as I saw him fasten on the left.

'He's a wonderful feller,' I said. 'Minds his own business.' I reached for my drink and when I raised it his gaze lifted until it met my own. He looked tired. He had been hard at work all day, probably sitting in that low chair in Hing's office, out of range of the fan's blowing, while Hing looked on and slapped at papers on his desk. His eyes were watery and his hair was stuck to his head with sweat; the floridness of his face, which had looked like ruddy good health the day before, was not a solid colour, but rather many little veins and splotches. I looked at him as at a picture in a newspaper that goes insubstantial with closeness, the face blurred to a snowfall of dots.

'How do the accounts look?' I asked, handing him a tumbler of gin.

'Bit ropy,' said Leigh. 'Any of the pink stuff?'

Wally shook some drops of Angostura into the gin.

'That'll put lead in your pencil,' I said.

'Best to put it in the glass before the gin and work it around the sides,' said Leigh. He wrapped the glass in his hanky, said, 'Cheers' and drank.

'I don't mind telling him to get knotted,' Yardley was saying.

'Bit ropy,' Leigh repeated, smacking his lips. 'We'll sort it out, though, if you ask me, your *towkay*'s missing a few beads from his abacus.'

'He'll drive you out of your gourd,' I said.

'Funny little thing, isn't he? I can't understand a word he says.'

'What about your *towkay* – in Hong-Kong?' I asked.

'Him!' Leigh gathered his features solemnly together and said, 'In actual fact . . . he's a cunt.'

Yardley heard and smiled, and I wondered for a moment whether the obscenity would redeem Leigh. It didn't. Yardley continued to talk to the fellers on my right, and sometimes to me; Leigh spoke only to me. I was, awkwardly, in the middle, a zone of good humour. There was no way out of it; to skip off with Leigh would mean the end of my drinking at the Bandung; the desertion would prohibit my return. Soon Yardley was saying less and less to me, and Leigh was growing quite talkative on his third drink.

'God, sometimes I hate it,' Leigh said. 'One thinks one is going to the tropics and one finds oneself in the Chinese version of Welwyn Garden City. The call of the East indeed – your friend over there was right. That fantastic hoicking puts me off my food, it really does. Still, it won't be much longer.'

'How long do you plan to stay in Hong-Kong?'

'My dear fellow,' said Leigh, 'not a moment longer than is absolutely necessary.'

In different words, for fourteen years I had said the same thing to myself; it was an ambiguous promise, and when I said it, it sounded like never. But Leigh's sounded like soon.

'Margaret – my wife – Margaret's got a magnificent cottage picked out. In Wiltshire – do you know it? Fantastic place. When

I go all broody about the Chinese, Margaret looks at me and says, "We're halfway to Elmview" – that's the name of the cottage. That cheers me up. And then I don't feel so bad about –'

The name depressed me; it sounded like the name of an old folks' home, and I imagined an overheated parlour, a radio playing too loud, an elderly inmate snoring in an armchair, another in a frilly apron busying himself with a dustpan and brush and a young heavy nurse patiently feeding a protesting crone wearing a blue plastic bib and batting the spoon away with her hand. Just saying the name lifted Leigh's spirits; he was still talking about the cottage.

'– thought of doing a little book about my experiences. Call it *Hong-Kong Jottings* and pack it with sampans and chatter from the club, that sort of thing. I see myself at Elmview on a spring morning, in the front room, sun splashing through the window, working on this book. In longhand, of course. Outside I can see masses of bluebells and a green meadow.' He sighed. 'An old horse out to pasture.'

'It sounds' – I could not think of another way of saying it – 'very agreeable.'

'You know,' he said, 'I've never set foot in that cottage. I saw it from a motorcar – Margaret pointed it out from the road. It was raining. We had a ploughman's lunch in the village – beautiful old pub – and went back to London that same afternoon. But it's as if I've been living there my whole life. I can tell you the position of every stick of furniture, every plate, how the sun strikes the carpet. I can see the tea things arranged on the table, and there's that' – he sniffed – 'curious stale smell of cold ashes in the grate.'

Yardley used to say, 'Everyone in the tropics has a funkhole,' and Leigh had told me his; his description had taken the curse off the name – the place was happy, a credible refuge. I had my own plans. I had never told a soul; I had kept my imaginings to myself and added little details now and then over the years. Maybe I had had one gin too many, or it might have been my triumphant feeling over that Bishop Bradley business. Whatever it was – it might have been Leigh's candour magnetizing mine – I drew very close to him and whispered, 'It's an odd thing, isn't it? Everyone imagines a different funkhole. Take mine, for example. You know what I want?'

'Tell me,' said Leigh, sympathetically.

'First, I want a lot of money – people don't laugh at a feller with dough. Then I want a yacht that you can sleep on and a huge mansion with a fence or a wall around it and maybe a peacock in the garden. I'd like to walk around all day in silk pyjamas, and take up golf and give up these stinking cheroots and start smoking real Havana cigars. And that's not all –'

Leigh gave me an awfully shocked look; it rattled me so badly I stuttered to a halt and finished my drink in a single gulp. He thought I was mocking him. The dream of mine, the little glimpse of fantasy that had widened into the whole possible picture I saw every day I spent on that island, saving my sanity as I obeyed Hing or turned my girls out or sorted pornographic pictures on the kitchen table in my house in Moulmein Green, hopeful and comforting in its detail, making me resourceful – that to him was mockery.

He said, 'Are you taking the mickey out of me?'

There was no way I could explain that I was perfectly serious. I saw it all coming to me quickly, like a jackpot. 'Just a minute,' I would say to the fellers at the bar, and while everyone watched I would put a coin – say my last – into a one-armed bandit, yank the lever and watch the whirr become a row of stars as the machine exploded and roared, disgorging a shower of silver dollars.

'An old horse out to pasture,' he had said; I had not giggled at that or the bluebells. I believed it because he did. But my version of Elmview, my own funkhole (deep-sea fishing in a silk robe and a velvet fedora, with a cigar in my teeth) made him mad. And what bothered me most was that I could not tell whether he felt mocked because my imaginings were grander than his or because they sounded absurd and he doubted them. I would not have minded his envy, but his doubt would have made my whole plan seem inaccessible to me by encouraging my own.

His grim expression made me say what I at once regretted: 'I guess it sounds pretty crazy.'

He did not hear me. Behind me, Yardley was horsing around, bawling a joke: '"*Organ*," she says. "*That's* no organ, breh-heh! Looks more like a *flute* to me!"'

'I take it Singapore's not a terribly expensive place to live,' said Leigh.

'That's a laugh,' I said. 'It's probably more expensive than Hong-Kong!'

'I'm quite surprised,' he said, lifting his eyebrows. He took a sip of his drink. 'Then the salaries here aren't very, um, realistic.'

'They're not too bad,' I said. I even laughed a little bit. But I stopped laughing when I saw what he was driving at. 'You mean Hing?'

He nodded and gave me the tight rewarded smile of a man who had just tasted something he likes. He said, 'You've got an *amah*'s salary.'

'You've got the wrong end of the stick,' I said. 'If you think I bank on –' But I was ashamed and flustered – and angry because he still wore that smile. He had spent the day in that upstairs cubicle examining my salary. What could I say? That Gunstone had a few hours before thanked me with an envelope of cash? That I was welcome in any club in Singapore, was snooker champion of one (unbeaten on the table at the Island Club), and knew a sultan who called me Jack and who had introduced me as his friend to Edmund de Rothschild at a party? That once, on Kampong Java Road, where I had had my own brothel, I had cleared a couple of thousand after pilferage and breakage was settled? That Edwin Shuck of the American Embassy had told me that if it had not been for me Singapore would never have been used as a base for the GIs' 'R and R' and Paradise Gardens would not have existed? That I had *plans*?

I hated him most when he said, with a concern that was contemptuous patronage, 'How do you manage?'

I put my elbows on the bar and my head in my hands. Far off on a green ocean I saw a yacht speeding towards me with its pennants snapping in the breeze. A man in a swivel chair on the afterdeck had his feet braced on the gunwales and was pulling at a bending rod. Just behind him a lovely girl in a swimsuit stood with a tray of drinks and – I knew – club sandwiches, fresh olives, dishes of rollmop herring and caviar spread on yellow crackers. The fish leaped, a tall silver thing turning in the sun, whipping the line out of the water. The yacht was close and I could see the man now. It was not me; it was no one I knew. I released my fingers from my eyes.

'Flowers,' said Leigh. Why was he smiling? 'How about a drink at the club?'

My girls were fairly well known at the Bandung – 'Jack's fruitflies,' Yardley called them – but no one there had any knowledge of my club work, and how I came straight from the Churchill Room or the Raffles Grill to the Bandung like an unfaithful husband home from his beguiling mistress's arms. I tried to whisper, 'Maybe later.'

Leigh looked beyond me to the others. 'Does this establishment,' he said, 'have a toilet?'

'In the kitchen,' said Coony, glad of a chance to say it.

Wally pointed the way.

'Does this establishment have a toilet?' said Smale. He guffawed. I wondered if Leigh could hear.

'Calls it a toilet,' said Yardley. 'He knows it's a crapper, but he calls it a toilet. That's breeding, you understand.'

Frogget went yuck-yuck.

'What's this club he's talking about?' asked Yardley suspiciously.

I said I didn't have the remotest idea.

'You sound more like him every day,' said Yardley.

'Knock it off,' I said.

'Don't be narked,' said Smale. 'He's your mate, ain't he?'

'He hasn't bought anyone a drink yet,' said Coony. 'I could tell he was a mean bastard.'

'Did you hear him rabbiting on?' asked Smale.

'I liked the part about him having tea in the pasture,' said Frogget. 'That shows he's round the twist.'

They had heard. They had been talking the whole time but they had caught what Leigh had said about Elmview – a distorted version of it. I had whispered, confiding my hopes; they could not have heard me. But why had I weakened and told Leigh? And who would *he* tell? He was out of the room; I wanted him to stay out, never to come back, for his engine to gripe and stop his mouth.

'He's a pain in the neck,' I said, at last.

'Been in the bog a little while,' said Smale. 'What do you suppose he's doing in there?'

'Probably tossing himself off,' said Frogget.

'You're a delicate little feller,' I said.

No one said anything for a little while, but it was not what I had said to Frogget that caused the silence. We were waiting for the flush, which you could hear in the bar. The only sounds were the fans on the ceiling and the murmuring of Wally's transistor. We were drinking without speaking and looking around in the way fellers do when they have just come into a bar; Leigh might have crept back without pulling the chain.

'So he's doing your *towkay*'s accounts,' said Yardley. It was a meaningless remark, but for Yardley an extraordinary tone of voice: he whispered it.

'It's a very fiddly sort of job,' said Yates after a moment. 'You really have to know what's what.'

'Takes ages to do those sums,' said Smale. 'Our accountant told me some days he looks at all those numbers and feels like cutting his throat.'

'You have to pass an exam,' said Coony, staring towards the kitchen, 'to be an accountant. It's a bugger to pass. I know a bloke who failed it five times. Bright bloke, too.'

Yardley called Wally, who was holding his radio to his ear the way a child holds a seashell for the sound. He ordered drinks and when Wally set them up Yardley handed me two gins and a bottle of tonic water. 'Pink one's for your pal,' he said. He glanced towards the kitchen.

'I wouldn't mind living in Wiltshire,' Smale said. He said it with reverent hope, and we continued talking like this, in whispers. I had not realized just how long Leigh had been gone until I saw that the ice in his pink gin had melted and my own glass was empty.

I climbed down from the bar-stool and hurried into the kitchen. The toilet door was ajar, but Leigh was not inside. He was sitting on a white kitchen chair, by the back door, with his head between his knees.

'William,' I said, 'are you okay?'

He shook his head from side to side without raising it.

'Get up and walk around a bit. It's cool out back. The fresh air – can you hear me? – the fresh air will do you a world of good. Can you get up?'

He groaned. The back of his neck was damp, the sick man's sweat made his hair prickle; his ears had gone white. I knew it was his engine.

'He sick-*lah*,' said Wally, appearing beside me with the radio squawking in his hand.

'Will you shut that fucking thing off!' I screamed. I do not know why I objected or swore. 'Get a doctor, and hurry!'

Wally jumped to the phone.

Yardley and the others came into the kitchen as I was helping Leigh up. Leigh's face had a white horror-struck expression – wide unmoving nose-holes – that of a man drowning slowly in many fathoms of water. I had seen these poor devils hoisted out of the drink: their mouths gaped open and they stared past you with anxious bulging eyes, as if they had acquired phenomenal sight, the ability to see far, and see at that great distance something looming, a throng of terrors. Leigh looked that way; he seemed about to whisper rather than scream. He was breathing: I saw a flutter in his throat and a movement like a low bubble rise and fall in the declivity of his shoulder.

We carried him into the lounge, stretched him out on the sofa and put pillows under his head. I took off his watch; it had made white roulettes on his wrist, perforations that wouldn't go away. He looked paler than ever, more frightening in the posture of a corpse. But the worst part was when his legs came alive – just his legs, like a man having a tantrum – and his kicking heels made an ungodly clatter on the bamboo arm-rest of the sofa.

'Christ,' said Coony, stepping back. Smale and Frogget clamped their hands on his ankles and held them down. The clattering stopped, but the silence after that weird noise was much worse.

I was conscious of standing there with my tattooed arms hanging at my sides, not doing a blessed thing, and I heard a voice, Yardley's, saying, 'See that tatty sofa over in the lounge near the piano? That's where Jack's mate from Hong-Kong packed it in. It was the damnedest thing –'

I turned to shut him up. But he was not talking; he was standing, expressionless, holding Leigh's drink, the pale pink gin in which all the ice had melted. He seemed to be offering it to Leigh and, though he held the tumbler in two hands, it was shaking.

Leigh stared past us, at that very far-off looming thing we could not see. I memorized his astonishment. It made us and the Bandung and everything on earth small and unimportant, not worth notice, and we were – for the time Leigh was on the sofa – as curious and baffled as those people on a city sidewalk who pass a man looking up at the sky and look up themselves but are made uneasy because they can't see the thing they know must be there.

6

That was how, in a manner of speaking, by the act of dying Leigh had the last word; though towards the end we tried to take back the things we had said. I have a memory of the six of us dancing around that green sofa in the badly lighted lounge, before the doctor came and took him away, frantically attempting ways to revive him, to coax him back to life so that we could have another chance to be kind to him – or perhaps so that he could amend his last words, which had been, 'Does this establishment have a toilet?' to something, if less memorable, more dignified.

Our reviving methods were the ineffectual kind we had learned from movies: lifting his eyelids (why? did we want to see the eye or not?); plumping his pillow; unbuttoning his shirt; pouring cold water over his face with the Johnnie Walker pitcher; fitting an ice-bag on his head like a tam-o'-shanter, and lightly slapping his cheeks while asking persistent questions – 'Where does it hurt?' and 'Can you hear me?' – to which there were no replies.

The doctor sensibly put a stop to this. 'How did he get so wet?' he asked as he knelt and swiftly tinkered with Leigh's chest and shone a light in his eyes. He held Leigh's wrist various ways and said, 'It's too late.' It sounded like a reproach for what I had whispered to Leigh: 'Maybe later.'

'A lot *he* cares,' said Smale, muffling what he had said with his hand and backing away from the doctor.

'Is it all right to smoke?' asked Coony. But he had already lit one, which was smouldering half-hidden in his cupped fingers.

'One of you will have to come along with me,' said the doctor, ignoring Coony's question. The doctor was Chinese, and I think what Smale held against him was his unclinical appearance; he was wearing a bright sports shirt and Italian sandals.

Yardley and the others turned to me and became very attentive and polite, as to the next-of-kin, offering me the considerate sympathy they had lavished on William, as they had started calling him when he was on the sofa and, most likely, dead. We wore long faces – not sad because we liked him, but mournful because we hated him. Coony put his hand on my shoulder and said, 'Are you okay, Jack?'

'I'll be fine in a minute,' I said, becoming the grieving person they wanted me to be.

'If there's anything we can do,' said Yates.

I put on my suit jacket and fixed my tie. I was dressed for a death, buttoning the black jacket over my stomach.

'What are you going to tell his wife?' asked Yardley.

I stopped buttoning. 'Won't the hospital tell her?' It had not occurred to me until Yardley mentioned it that I would have to break the news to Leigh's wife.

'They'll get it all wrong,' said Smale. He held my sleeve and confided, 'They'll make it sound bloody awful.'

'Don't tell her it happened here,' said Coony quickly. 'Say it happened somewhere else.'

'During the day,' said Smale. 'A sunny day.'

'But in the shade,' said Coony, 'of a big *angsana* tree. In the Botanical Gardens. While he was –' Coony hit his fist against his head.

'While he was having a good time with the rest of us,' said Yardley. He looked from face to face.

There was a long silence. The doctor was at the bar speaking on the telephone to the hospital.

'Near the bandstand,' said Frogget. 'Maybe he tried to climb that hill. And it was too hot. And his ticker gave out.'

'We told him to stop,' said Yardley, sounding convinced. 'But he wouldn't listen to us. "Have it your way," we said. So off he went –'

'I'll think of something,' I said, cutting Yardley off. I didn't like this.

It had all fallen to me. He was mine now, though I had tried several times to disown him. I had not wanted him; I had disliked him from the moment he asked, 'Flowers . . . are you a ponce?' And his triumphant contempt: 'How do you stand it?' and 'How do you manage?' It was as if he had come all that way to ask me those questions and to die before I could answer.

The doctor clicked Leigh's eyes shut, moving the lids down with his thumbs; but the lids refused to stick and sightless crescents of white appeared under the lashes. We carried him to the doctor's Volvo and folded him clumsily into the back seat. I sat beside him and put my arm around him to keep him from swaying. He nodded at every red light, and at the turning on River Valley Road his head rolled on to my shoulder.

'How long have you been in Singapore?' the doctor asked. It was a resident's question. I told him how long. He did not reply at once; I guessed I had been there longer than him. He drove for a while and then asked when I would be leaving.

'Eventually.' I said. 'Pretty soon.'

'Haven't I seen you at the Island Club?'

'Yes,' I said. 'I go there now and then, just to hack around.'

'What's your handicap?'

'My handicap,' I said. 'I wouldn't repeat it in public.'

The doctor laughed and kept driving. Leigh slumped against me.

In my locked bedroom on Moulmein Green, late at night and so dog-tired after driving one of my girls back to her house from a hotel that I had collapsed into bed without pulling my pants off or saying my prayers, I had imagined death differently – not the distant horror of the drowning man, but the sense of something very close, death crowding me in the dark: a thing stirring in a room that was supposed to be empty. The feeling I got on one of those nights was associated in my mind with the moment before death, the smothering sound of the cockroach. A glossy cockroach, motionless, gummed to the wall by the bright light, goes into action when the light is switched off. It is the female which flies and its sound is the Chinese paper fan rapidly opening and closing. This fluttering dungbeetle in the black room is circling, making for you. You listen in the dark and hear the stiff wings beating near your eyes. It is going to land on your face and kill you and there is nothing you can do about it.

I did not imagine a moment of vision before death, but quite the reverse, blindness and that fatal burr of wings. Leigh's eyes were not completely closed, the lids were ajar and the sulphurous streetlamps on Outram Road lit the gleaming whites. In the General Hospital Leigh peered past the orderly who pinned an admission ticket to his shirt – number eighty-six, a lottery number for Mr Khoo – and turned out his pockets: a few crumpled dollars, a withered chit, some loose change, a wallet containing calling cards, a picture of Margaret, a twenty-dollar Hong-Kong note and a folded receipt from the Chinese Emporium on Orchard Road. This went into a brown envelope.

'We'll need a deposit,' said the nurse.

I took out Gunstone's envelope, *Singapore Belvedere*, and handed over fifteen dollars. *How do you manage?*

'Please fill up this form,' she said.

The form was long and asked for information I could not provide without Leigh's passport. So with the matron's permission I went back to the Strand by taxi, told the desk clerk that Leigh was dead and picked up the passport. 'It seems like only yesterday that he checked in,' the desk clerk said; he assured me that he would take care of everything. By the time I was back at the hospital, copying Leigh's full name, home address, nearest relation, race and age – he was a year younger than me, the pen shook in my hand – Leigh was staring out of the chilly morgue drawer; after the autopsy he looked much the same, though, unzipped, he fixed on that distant thing with a single eye.

I had forgotten Leigh's suitcase. After the certificate of death had been made out I picked up the case at the Strand, and at my insistence the taxi-driver detoured past the Bandung. As we went past I could see lights burning and Yardley, Frogget, Smale and the others at the bar, like lost old men, vagrants huddled around a fire late at night, sharing a bottle, afraid to go to bed.

It was after midnight. I did not have the heart to wake up Leigh's wife and get her out of bed to tell her she was a widow. I locked my door, put a match to the mosquito coil and knelt beside it. The mosquito coil, lighted to suffocate the gnats and drive the cockroaches away, smoked like a joss-stick. I blinked in the fumes and tried to pray; the first words that came to me were, *Is this all?*

The next day I awoke as if after a binge, with that feeling of physical and mental fragility, exposure, distraction – the knowledge of having done something shameful which refuses to be summoned up: of having revealed my closest secret which now everyone knew except me! And then I remembered Leigh, not as a corpse; it was an uncharitable intrusive thought, something connected with the smile he wore when he had asked, 'How do you manage?' A picture of his dead face followed.

So, more as an act of penance than out of any curiosity, I opened his suitcase and picked through it. Each thing I found made me sad; nothing was concealed. There were tags and labels on the case, the traveller's campaign ribbons, 'Khao Yai Motor Lodge', 'Hotel Bel Vista – Macau', and the luggage tag from the airline with the destination lettered *Sin*. Here was a sock with a hole in the toe, a pathetic little sewing kit, some salt tablets, a packet of Daraprim, very wrinkled pyjamas with a white piping border, his human smell still upon them. In a paper bag from the Chinese Emporium there was a set of screwdrivers, a new shaving brush, some Lucky Brand razor-blades. There was a wrapped parcel of batik cloth from another shop, probably a present for his wife, and stuck to the parcel were two receipts for the cloth, but giving different prices, the lower faked price to fool the customs official in Hong-Kong and avoid a few dollars import duty. At the bottom of the case was a detective novel with a grisly title that described Leigh's own death, an eerie coincidence italicizing the improbable fraud of one, the pitiful condition of the other.

He was in the morgue drawer, and here was his poor bundle of effects: this was all.

I dressed, practising how to tell his wife what had happened. The suitcase caught my eye; I opened it again and sorted through it quickly, lifting everything out a second time and shaking the clothes. There was no money in it! I had told the desk clerk at the Strand he was dead, but only later picked up the suitcase. After I had left with the passport they had gone up to his room and robbed him.

The phone crackled; Hing fretted beside me; Gopi watched. I said, 'Listen carefully. Yesterday I was with your husband at the Botanical Gardens. Wait a minute – listen. It was a beautiful day –'

It was a suffocating day, producing the feverish symptoms of a fatal illness in me. I had picked up my car at the garage, we had all met at the mortuary, and we followed behind the hearse – polished and sculpted like an old piano – attempting funereal solemnity by keeping our faded elderly cars in file, my chugging Renault, Yardley's blue Anglia, Hing's Riley (he sat in the back seat with Little; a Malay drove), Mr Tan and Wallace Thumboo in an old Ford Consul, Yates in his boxy Austin and the others trailing, impossible to see in my rear-view mirror. We hit every red light, getting hotter and sicker at each stop, and we lost the hearse (I could see Yardley irritably pounding his palm against the steering wheel) at one junction when it speeded up and jumped the lights.

Gladys was with me. I had guessed in advance that only men would be there, and that didn't seem right. Also, I had to drop her off at a hotel immediately afterwards, an appointment of long standing I had only noticed that morning in my desk diary. Gladys was fanning herself, absentmindedly as I drove and quickly against her chin at traffic lights, making that fluttering I dreaded, the papery burr of beating cockroach wings. I told her to knock it off. That and the heat oppressed me. We were not in sunlight, but sweating in the mid-morning Singapore veil of dim steam that makes a grey tent of the slumping sky and nothing on the ground solid. There was nothing worse, I was thinking, than a cremation on a hot day in the tropics. It had all the inappropriateness of a man puffing on a pipe in a burning house. I vowed that I would spare myself that fate.

The crematorium off Upper Aljunied Road was a yellow building, with a chimney instead of a steeple, on a low hill, in a treeless Chinese cemetery, a rocky weedy meadow of narrow plots, with stone posts as gravemarkers, figured like milestones turned on a lathe, an occasional angel and worn cement vaults with peeling red doors set in scorched hillocks: a whole suburb of trolls' huts, clustered there in the kind of chaotic profusion that matched their lives, sleeping families on shop-house floors, and now, head to toe, beneath those posts and stones. Here and there was a high vault with a roof, fenced in from the others, the graveyard equivalent of a *towkay*'s mansion which might almost have borne a name-plate, 'The Wongs', 'Chee's Tower', or 'Dunroamin'. All this was hazy in the steamy air and, when I looked back, obscured by the dust-cloud our procession of cars was raising on the road that wound up to the crematorium. The chimney was not smoking. Some distance away, in the middle of the cemetery, a ghostly white-shirted party with umbrellas open stood slightly bowed before a vault-mound. They could have been praying, but they weren't. Stooping reverentially, they began to let off firecrackers.

'Can't they stop those little bastards?' said Yardley, rushing up to me after we parked. Our dust-cloud descended, sifting down on us. He looked at Gladys and suppressed another curse. 'We can't have that nonsense going on during the service.'

The Chinese mourners were lighting packets of fifty with the fuses knotted. The noise carried in steady burps; there were flashes and delayed bangs.

'Bloody –' Yardley turned and stalked away growling.

'To amaze the gods,' Gladys said. 'Very lucky to have big noise. Also can make devils piss off.'

The other fellers came over to us.

'Are you okay, Jack?' asked Coony.

'I hope it doesn't rain,' said Smale, leaning back and squinting at the sky.

We looked at him.

'It'd ruin it,' he said nervously. 'Wouldn't it?' Was he thinking of the fire that could be doused, or was it that fear of excessive gloom that fellers associate with rain at funerals?

'It won't rain until October,' said Yates.

The two Hings were in white, their terrifying colour of mourning, white cotton suits and straw hats, carrying umbrellas, looking wretched. Mr Tan wore a black tie. Because of the appointment, Gladys wore a bright green dress and carried a large handbag; her face was a white mask with wizard's eyes. Big Hing cracked his umbrella open, shook it and walked in oversized shoes towards the building, holding the umbrella upright, but bouncing it as he walked. The rest of the Chinese followed him.

I asked the hearse-driver what we were supposed to do. He said four of us were to carry the coffin into the chapel; the priest would take care of the rest. I objected to the word 'priest' to describe an effeminate Anglican cleric of perhaps thirty, blushing in the heat, his cheeks pink, and wringing his hands by the crematorium door; in his white smock-like surplice he eyed Gladys disapprovingly, like a spinsterish intern about to check her for the clap. I beckoned to Yardley and the others and said, 'Look alive.'

I had known most of them for fourteen years; I had drunk with them nearly every night at the Bandung. Only that. I had never seen them all together, assembled in daylight away from the Bandung. So I was seeing them for the first time. They were strangers who knew me. The bad light of the Bandung had been kind to Yardley's liverish pallor, a tropical sallowness in an unlined face; Frogget looked bigger and hairier, and his tie was frayed; Yates, I noticed, had freckles, and his glasses had slipped down his nose from his perspiring; Smale's hair was reddish – I had always thought of it as brown; Coony's hair was combed straight back, the shape of his head, and his lower lip, which always protruded when his mouth was shut, was dry for once. None of them was standing straight; they were self-conscious in their suits, in unfamiliar postures, and Yardley's leaning – one shoulder higher than the other – made him appear unwell.

It might have been the old-fashioned rumpled suits I had never seen them wear, dark grey or black, smelling of mothballs and spotted with mildew like soup-stains: an old ill-fitting suit makes the wearer seem shy. The wrinkles were not the consequence of sitting or reaching, but were in unlikely places, across the chest of the jacket, pinches on the back and sleeves, drawer folds, creases from storage, the cuffs bunched up; the trousers were more faded than the jackets and this mismatching together with the seediness of the suits reminded me of something Yates had once whispered at the Bandung. 'Tell me, Jack,' he had said. 'Don't we look like the legion of the lost?'

It seemed disrespectful to smoke near the crematorium, so we were all more edgy than usual. The hearse-driver and his assistant slid the coffin out and Yardley, Frogget, Smale and myself carried it across the dusty compound to the entrance where the rest stood behind the cleric. I thought I heard Yardley mutter, 'He's damned heavy', but he might have said, 'It's damned heavy'. It was. I was afraid we might drop it. The others had been up drinking the night before and I had not been able to sleep. I knew they were worried about dropping it too, because they were carrying it much too fast.

'Wally,' I said.

Wally stood blocking the door, looking inside, with his back to us.

'Wally!' I said again. He didn't hear. His square head was turned away. My hands were growing moist and slipping on the chrome fixture I was holding, and I snapped. 'Move it or lose it!'

He jumped out of the way, and we proceeded inside and unsteadily down the aisle, panting, the six busy overhead fans in the room of folding chairs mocking our forced solemnity with practical whirrs. We placed the coffin on a high wheeled frame at the front of the room and took our seats with the others.

After a few moments Yardley leaned over and asked, 'What's the drill?'

I shrugged. It was my first cremation, and in that bare room of steel chairs, the only ornaments the photographs of the President and his wife, I could not imagine what was going to happen. We sat expectantly, the chairs squeaking and clanking. Hing loudly cleared his throat, so loud it made me want to spit, and as one person's hacking inspires another's, particularly in a still room, soon Smale and Coony were at it, coughing in shallow growls. Outside, the poop-poop of firecrackers continued; and beside me Gladys began beating her fan, scraping it against her chin. The cleric walked up the aisle, his starched surplice rustling. The coughing stopped; now there were only the fans, the chair-squeaks and the distant firecrackers.

'Fellow brethren,' he said, looking at us with uncertainty and distaste; he clung to his Bible, holding it chest-high, and nodded at everyone individually with his pink flushed face – making suspense. He took a breath and began. His sermon was the usual one, but he was young enough and had delivered it few enough times to make it sound as if he believed it: life was short and difficult, a testing-time loaded with temptations; and he pictured God as the all-seeing bumptious neighbour, rocking irritably on his celestial porch and passing judgement. He talked about our weaknesses and then concentrated on Leigh's soul, which he addressed with great familiarity. The worst religions, I was thinking, rob you of your secrets by reminding you that you're all in the same sinking boat; harping on your sameness and denying you fancies and flesh and blood and visible hope, they reduce you to moaning galley slaves, manacled to a bloody oar, puking in a sunless passage and pulling blindly towards an undescribed destination; and constantly warning you that you might never arrive. 'Believe in God,' the cleric was saying, and I thought, Yes, that's easy, but does God believe in me? I liked my religion to be a private affair ashore, a fire by a stone, a smoky offering; one necessary at night, the light giving the heavens fraternal features to surprise me with the thrill of agreeable company. It was to make the authority of ghosts vanish by making holiness a friendly human act and defining virtue as joy and grace as permission granted.

'– to judgement,' the cleric was saying, and as he spoke he jerked around several times to nod at Leigh's coffin, as if Leigh was listening as long as his corpse was whole, and needed only combustion to get him to paradise. 'We are all of us sinners, wallowing in the flesh,' the cleric said. Gladys stopped fanning herself. She sniffed and began to cry; and I hoped she was not planning to repent and back out of the appointment at the Palm Grove. She was the only person weeping; the Hings were impassive and pale, Mr Tan and Wally limply crestfallen; Yardley and the others were sweating, but the sweat ran like tears and wet their faces and was almost like grief.

My face was streaming, too, but I wasn't crying; my thoughts were too confused for that. Leigh, alive, had reminded me of myself, and his death warned me about my own – a warning so strong it made me ignore his death for part of the time. But I was also thinking, Now he can't tell anyone about my plans, my silk pyjamas and cigars; and I felt childish relief mingled with adult sadness that he was out of the way. When the engines stop in mid-ocean the whole ship ceases to vibrate and it makes a silence so sudden after three weeks of continual noise that you think your heart has stopped and you wonder for seconds if you're dead. After those seconds you understand mortality and the silence that terrified you is a comfort. Leigh's death affected me that way, and at the cremation I felt peaceful. It seemed better that he was going to be reduced to ashes – a corpse made small and poured into a little pot was not a corpse; it was so tiny and altered you couldn't reasonably weep over it. Cremation simulated disappearance; it really was like flight, a movement I knew well. Bodies decaying underground made people cry, but a dozen pots on a shelf, a dead family, were uncharacteristic relics of the forgettable dead, who might have simply skipped off and left their urns behind, one apiece. Burning, as the cleric hinted – and here I agreed – was like deliverance; it was only bad on a hot day.

My thoughts stopped coming: the cleric had stopped talking. There was a clatter at the door; a scrape; a shuffle-thump, shuffle-thump. The cleric stared. We all turned. Gopi was cycling in, his shoulders heaving, making his sleeves flap. His eyes were big from the physical effort of his pedalling, and his shirt was stuck in a dark patch to his back. He took a seat at the front, alone, and he watched the coffin as if it was a magician's box.

The cleric, who might have thought Gopi was going to interrupt with Hindu wailing, quietly resumed. 'Let us pray.'

We knelt on the stone floor. Gopi had to look back to see how it was done. I was anxious for him, balanced on that wobbly knee; he managed by steadying himself on the chair next to him.

A sound of enormous wheezing filled the room as we stood; it was not ours. A clapped-out harmonium had begun asthmatically to breathe 'Jerusalem' at the back of the room. Yardley and the others seemed glad to have a chance to sing, and they did so with the hoarse gusto they gave the obscene songs Frogget started at the Bandung on Saturday nights. Frogget had a fine voice, higher than one would have expected from a feller his size and (Gopi and Gladys were both weeping for Leigh – why?) all the voices rang in the room, echoing on the yellow walls and drowning the fans, the firecrackers and even the woofing harmonium with the hymn:

> And did those feet in ancient time
> Walk upon England's mountains green?

We gave the lines in the last part – *Bring me my bow of burning gold, Bring me my arrows of desire* – the sahib's emphasis, trilling the *r* in the command resolutely.

The cleric walked over to the coffin and sprinkled it and prayed out loud. I started thinking of the man out back, stoking the fire like a fry-cook in clogs, stirring the coals in a black kitchen, sweating worse than we were and wiping his face on his shoulder, banging his poker on the furnace door to slam the hot ashes from the tip. What burial customs!

It was over. The cleric flung his arms into the sign of the cross, a novice's flourish of sleeves, and blessed us and said, 'Amen'. The coffin was rolled out of the room through a rear door and we all went out to our cars.

'You ready?' I asked Gladys.

Her tears had dried. She looked at me. 'This short-time or all day?'

Before I could answer Yardley was beside me asking, 'You coming along? We're going for a drink. The day's a dead loss – no sense going to work.'

'I'll be there in a little while,' I said and, seeing Hing leaving, smiled and waved him off. Hing's face was tight; he was unused to the lecturing at Christian services and might have expected the brass band, the busloads of relatives, the banners and pennants and cherry bombs that saw a Chinese corpse to the grave.

'Short-time,' said Gladys. 'Where I am dropping?'

I did not reply. Yardley and Frogget faced the sky behind me. I turned to look. Smoke had started from the chimney, a black puff and ripples of stringy heat, then a grey column, unimpeded by any breeze, shooting straight up and enlarging, becoming the steamy air that hung over the island. Despair is simple: fear without a voice, a sinking and a screamless fright. We watched in silence, all of us. Coony ground his cigarette out and gaped; then, conscious that we were all watching the smoke, we looked away.

'Who's paying for this?' Yardley asked.

'I am,' I said, and felt sad. But when I got into the little car with Gladys and started away, throwing the shift into second gear, I felt only relief, a springy lightness of acquittal that was like youth. I was allowed all my secrets again, and could keep them if I watched my step. It was like being proven stupid and then, miraculously, made wise.

PART TWO

7

For as long as I could remember I had wanted to be rich, famous if possible, and to live to the age of ninety-five; to eat huge meals and sleep late out of sheer sluttishness in a big soft bed; to take up an expensive but not strenuous sport, golf or deep-sea fishing in a fedora with a muscular and knowledgeable crew; to gamble with conviction instead of bitterness and haste; to have a pair of girl-friends who wanted me for my money – the security was appealing: why would they ever leave me? All this and a town house, an island villa, a light plane, a fancy car, a humidor full of fat fragrant cigars – you name it. I guessed it would come to me late: fifty-three is a convenient age for a tycoon; the middle-aged man turning cautious and wolflike knows the score, and if he has been around a bit he can take the gaff. It did not occur to me that it might never happen.

Being poor was the promise of success; the anticipation of fortune, a fine conscious postponement, made the romance, for to happen best it would have to come all at once, as a surprise, with the great thud a bag of gold makes when it's plopped on a table, or with the tumbling unexpectedness of thick doubloons spilling from the seams of an old wall you're tearing apart for the price of the used wood. One rather fanciful idea I'd had of success was that somehow through a fortuitous mix-up I would be mistaken for a person who resembled me and rewarded with a knighthood or a country estate; it was as good as admitting I did not deserve it, but that it was far-fetched made my receptive heart anticipate it as a possibility. It might, I thought, be a telephone call on a grey morning when, fearing bad news, I would hear a confident educated voice at the other end say, 'Brace yourself, Mr Flowers, I've got some wonderful news –'

Wonderful news in another fantasy was a letter. I composed many versions of these and recited them to myself walking to the 8-A bus out of Moulmein Green in the morning, or killing time in a hotel lobby when a girl was finishing a stunt upstairs, or dealing out the porno decks, or standing on the esplanade and staring at the ships in the harbour.

One started like this: 'Dear Mr Flowers, It gives me great pleasure to be writing to you today, and I know my news will please you as much . . .' Another was more direct: 'Dear Flowers, I've had my eye on you for a long time and I'm very happy to inform you of my decision concerning your future . . .' Another: 'Dear Jack, I am asking my lawyer to read you this letter after my death. You have been an excellent and loyal friend, the very best one could hope for. I have noted you in my will for a substantial portion of my estate as a token thanks for your good humour, charity and humanity. You will never again have to think of . . .' Another: 'Dear Sir, Every year one person is singled out by our Foundation to be the recipient of a large cash disbursement. You will see from the enclosed form that no strings whatever are attached . . .' Another: 'Dear Mr Flowers, The Academy has entrusted to me the joyful task of informing you of your election. This carries with it, as you know, the annual stipend of . . .' There were more; I composed as many as thirty in an afternoon, though usually I stuck to one and phrased it to perfection, working on it and reciting every altered declaration of the glorious news. The last was long and rambling; it was only incidentally about money, and it began, 'My darling . . .'

No man of fifty-three wants to look any more ridiculous than his uncertain age has already made him, and I am well aware that in disclosing this fantastic game I played with myself, the sentences above, which prior to a few moments ago had never been written anywhere but in my head, much less typed under the embossed letterheads I imagined and pushed through the mailslot of my semi-detached house on

Moulmein Green – I am well aware that in putting those eager ('Brace yourself') openings in black and white I seem to be practising satire or self-mockery. The difficulty is that unchallenged, squatting like trepanned demons in the padded privacy of an idle mind, one's lunatic thoughts seem tame and reasonable, while spoken aloud in broad daylight to a stranger or written before one's own eyes they are the extravagant ravings of a crackpot. 'You know what I want?' I said to Leigh, and told him and was made a fool by his look of shock; I should have kept my mouth shut, but how was I to know that he was not the stranger who would say, 'I've got some good news for you, Flowers.' He might have thought I was mad. Madness is not believing quietly that you're Napoleon; it is demonstrating it, slipping your hand inside your jacket and striking a military pose. He might have thought I was crude. But the beginner's utterance is always wrong: I used to stand in Singapore doorways and hiss, 'Hey, bud' at passers-by.

Crude I may have been, but mad never; and I would like to emphasize my sanity by stating that even though I dreamed of getting one of those letters ('It gives me great pleasure . . .') I could not understand how I would ever receive one, for I imagined thousands, paragraph by glorious paragraph, but I never mentally signed them, and none, not even the one beginning '*My darling*', bore a signature. Who was supposed to be writing me those letters? I hadn't the faintest idea.

The letters were fantasy, but the impulse was real: a visceral longing for success, comfort, renown, the gift that could be handled, tangible grace. That momentary daydream which flits into every reflective man's mind and makes him say his name with a title, *Sir* or *President* or *His Highness* – everyone does it sometimes: the clerk wants a kingship, it's only natural – this dubbing was a feature of my every waking moment. I wasn't kidding; even the most rational soul has at least one moment of pleasurable reflection when he hears a small voice addressing him as *Your Radiance*. I had a litany which began *Sir Jack*, *President Flowers*, *King John*, and so forth. And why stop at King? *Saint Jack!* It was my yearning, though success is nasty and spoils you, the successful say, and only failures listen, who know nastiness without the winch of money. If the rich were correct, I reasoned, what choice had they made? Really, was disappointment virtue and comfort vice and poverty like the medicine that was good because it stung? The President of the United States, in a sense the king of the world, said he had the loneliest job on earth; where did that leave a feller like me?

The theatrically convulsed agony of the successful is the failure's single comfort. 'Look how similar we are,' both will exclaim: 'We're each lonely!' But one is rich; he can choose his poison. So strictly off my own bat I gave myself a chance to choose – I would take the tycoon's agony and forgo the salesman's. I said I wanted to be rich, famous if possible, drink myself silly and sleep till noon. I might have put it more tactfully: I wanted the wealth to make a free choice. I was not pleading to be irresponsible; if I was rich and vicious I would have to accept blame. The poor were blameless; they could not help it, and if they were middle-aged they were doubly poor, for no one could see their aches and no one knew that the middle-aged man at that corner table, purple with indigestion, thought he was having a heart seizure. That man will not look back to reflect unless he has had a terrible fright that twists his head around. Characteristically, he will look back once, see nothing, and never look back again. But Leigh and his hopeless last words had given me such an awful shock that driving out of the crematorium with Gladys, I took a long look back – with the recent memory of imagining what my own last words might be: *Is this all?* mumbled in a hot room – and thought of nothing but what had brought me to Singapore, and the sinking ships I had boarded since then.

It was a bumboat. I had jumped off the *Allegro* and there I was, sitting at the stern of a chugging bumboat, making my way towards Collyer Quay. It might have been cowardice; in me, cowardice often looked like courage by worrying me into some panicky act. I ran, and it looked like pursuit; but it wasn't that – it was flight.

The bumboat touched the quay. The Chinese pilot pressed a finger in salute to the hanky that was knotted around his head like a tea-cosy.

Having learned the trick of survival and reached a ripe old age, most fellers can look back on their lives and explain the logic of everything they've done, show you the pattern of their movements, their circlings towards what they wanted and got. Justifying their condition, they can point without regret to the blunt old-type exclamation marks of their footprints, like frozen ones in snow, and make sense of them. If the footprints are a jumble and some are retreating the feller may say with a wild accompanying cackle that he had his shoes on backward and appeared to be walking away as he advanced. The explanation is irrefutable, for old age itself is a kind of arrival, but I could not say – being fifty-three in Singapore – that I had arrived anywhere. I was pausing, I thought, and there was no good reason for any of my movements except the truthful excuse that at the time of acting I saw no other choice. The absence of plot or design inspired my forlorn dream that magically, by letter, I would become a millionaire. My life was a pause; I lived in expectation of an angel.

My vision was explicit, and no guilt hampered it; I wished away the ego of my past – I would not be burdened by my history. But I had a fear: that I might turn out to be one of those travellers who, unnerved by the unconscious boldness of their distance – the flight that took them too far – believe themselves to be off course and head for anything that resembles a familiar landmark. Only, up close, they discover it to be a common feature of a foreign landscape on which identical landmarks lie in all directions. They chase these signs, their panic giving the wheeling chase some drama, and very soon they are nowhere, travellers who never arrive, who do not die but are lost and never found, like those unfortunate arctic explorers, or really any single middle-aged feller who dies in a tropical alien place, alone and among strangers who mock what they can't comprehend, the hopeful man with the perfect dream of magic, burned to ashes one hot day and negligently buried, who was lost long before he died.

8

The bumboat touched the quay. I vaulted to the stone steps and almost immediately, in a small but ingenious way, became a hustler. The word is unsuitable, but let it stand. It was an aspect of a business I understood well, for over the previous eleven months, soothed by Mothersill's pills, I had been crossing and recrossing the Indian Ocean in the *Allegro*, and at every port, from Mombasa to Penang, I had been appointed by the captain to perform a specific job for extra pay; that is, to take on supplies by contacting the ship chandler. I enjoyed doing this; it gained me admittance to a friendly family ashore, Ismailis in Mombasa, Portuguese in Beira, an Indo-French one in Port Louis, Parsees in Bombay. It was an entry into a world as mysterious for the sailor as the sea is for the landsman, the domestic life, the drama in dry rooms, that lay beyond the single street of seamen's bars, the frontier that barricades harbours from their cities. At each port the ship chandler was our grocer, butcher, *dhobi*, fishmonger, hardware man; he would supply anything at short notice, but I believe that at Hing's in Singapore – after I jumped ship – I could take credit for introducing a new wrinkle to one of the world's most versatile professions. Later it was taken up by other ship chandlers and Singapore became a port in which even a large vessel could make a turn-around in six hours without the crew mutinying.

I look back and see a wild August storm, known in Singapore as a 'Sumatra': a high wind blows suddenly from the west and the sky gathers into unaccountable blackness, a low heavy ceiling, night at noon, the cold rain sheeting horizontally into the surf. That day I was standing in the wheelhouse of a rocking launch. It was warm and sunny when we left the quay, but fifteen minutes out the sky darkened, the cabin door banged and rain began hitting the glass with a sound like sleet; we bolted the doors and breathed the engine fumes. Stone-like waves, each dark one with streaming ribbons of oil on its bumpy edges and topped with a torn cap of lacy froth, slammed into the starboard side of the launch, making the same boom as if we had run aground. I hung on to a canvas strap and, wiping the steam off the back window, put my nose to the moaning glass.

We were towing a forty-foot lighter, the sort used for transporting bales of raw rubber; Chinese decorations were painted on the bow, evil white and black eyes, green whiskers and a red dragon-fanged mouth. The painted face with its scabrous complexion of barnacles rose and fell, gulping ocean, and the canvas cover, a vast pup-tent pitched over the lighter, was being lashed by the wind; our tow-rope, now loose as the lighter leaped at us, now tight as it plunged and dragged, was periodically wrung of water, which shot out in a twist of bubbly spray as it stretched tight. A grommet on the corner of the canvas tarp tore free, and the tent-fly burst open, unveiling our cargo, twenty-three smartly dressed Chinese and Malay girls, their scared white faces almost luminous in the gloom of the quaking shelter; they were huddled on crates and kegs, their knees together, holding their plastic handbags on their heads.

The visibility, what with the fog and rain and steamed-up windows, was very poor, and I had the impression we were thrashing in the open ocean, for no ships and not even the harbourside could be made out. It was just after tiffin; no wharf lights were on. It was fearfully dark and cold, and I was dizzy from the cabin fumes. We might have been in the South China Sea.

'More to port,' I shouted to Mr Khoo, showing him a circle I had drawn on the Western Roads of my harbour chart.

'No,' he said, and spun the wheel starboard.

'Don't give me that!' I said and went for him. The launch bucked and threw me to the floor. I could feel the launch turning, slowed by the weight of the lighter, and just under the whistling wind the screams of my girls. Mr Khoo was taking us back.

I had seen seamen fight below decks during storms on the *Allegro*; it was something that made me want to strap on a life-jacket and hide near the bridge, like a child in a slum running from his quarrelling parents. My fear was of seeing people enclosed by a larger struggle swept away and dying in a hammerlock. The storms encouraged fighting, and the fighting seemed to intensify the storm.

'Give me the wheel like a good feller,' I said to Mr Khoo.

Mr Khoo threatened me with a sharp elbow and held tight to the wheel. The wipers were paralysed on the window; I swayed and tried to see.

'Do you know what this is costing me?' I shouted.

'Cannot,' said Mr Khoo, refusing to look at me.

'Drop the anchor, then,' I said. 'I'll do it.'

I unbolted the door and stepped into the wind. Up ahead, the rusty brown silo of a ship's stern loomed, a light flashed and I made out the name, *Richard Everett, Liverpool*.

'Oh boy, there it is!'

Mr Khoo gave a blast on the horn; he was crouched at the wheel. He looked up at the freighter, twisting his head. I stayed on deck, waving to faces framed by yellow bonnets. It was too rough to use the ladder; some men in slickers and boots were pushing a cargo net over the side.

The launch still pitched. Mr Khoo worked the lighter close by circling the launch around and nudging it against the side of the *Richard Everett*, and I had the satisfaction in a storm, during which other lightermen waited at the rivermouth by Cavanagh Bridge, of seeing my girls hoisted up, three at a time, in the hefty cargo net, all of them soaked to the skin, fumbling with collapsed umbrellas and shrieking at the gale. The crane swung them on board and lowered them into the hold. There was a cheer, audible over the storm and wind, as the cargo net descended.

I went up myself with the last load of girls and to the sound of steel doors slamming in the passageway had a brandy with the first mate and played a dozen hands of gin rummy; the light softened in the port-hole and then the sun came out. He paid me fifteen dollars a girl. He had asked for them on consignment, but I insisted on a flat rate. Two hours later, in sparkling sunshine, we were on our way. I rode in the lighter with the girls. We took down the canvas roof and May played a transistor radio one of the seamen had given her. Some of the girls put up their umbrellas, and they all sat as prim as schoolteachers on a Sunday outing. Junie wore a sailor hat. We cruised slowly back, enjoying the warmth and the light breeze, and docked at Pasir Panjang behind a palm grove – I could not risk arriving at Collyer Quay or Jardine Steps with that cargo.

It was not my first excursion. I had been doing it for several months, usually small loads, sometimes only two in a sampan rowed out from Collyer Quay to an old tanker, the girls disguised as scrub-women in faded *sam-foos*, with buckets and brushes and bundles of old rags, to fool the harbour police. I had always made it a practice – I was the first in Singapore, perhaps anywhere, to do so – to have a girl along with me when I delivered groceries and fresh meat and coils of rope, just in case. The girl was always welcome, and came back exhausted.

The storm made me; it became known that I was the enterprising swineherd who took a lighterful of girls out at the height of a Sumatra that swamped a dinghy of Danish seamen that same day. A week later a crewman on the *Miranda* buttonholed me: 'You the bloke that floated them pros out to the *Everett*?'

I told him I was, and stuck out my hand. 'Jack Flowers,' I said. 'Call me Jack. Anything I can do for you?'

'You're a lad, you are,' he said admiringly, and then over his shoulder, ''ey, Scrumpy, it's *'im*!'

I rocked back and forth, smiling, then took out my pencil, clownishly licked the lead, and winked, saying, 'Well, gentlemen, let's see what we can scare up for you today . . .'

The Sumatra had come sudden as a bomb, darkly filling the sky, outraging the sea, pimpling it with rain like lead shot, wrinkling it and snarling it into spiky heaves. I never let on that it hit us when we were halfway to the *Richard Everett* or that I had put my last dollar into releasing those girls and hiring the launch and lighter, and that to have turned back – no less perilous than going forward – would have disgraced me and ruined me irrecoverably. If we had sunk it would have been the end, for none of the twenty-three girls knew how to swim. I had not known the extent of the risk, but it was a venture – probably cowardly: I was afraid to lose my money and scared to turn back – that had tremendous consequences. The mates on the *Miranda* were the first of many who praised me and gave me commissions.

And Hing's business boomed.

I had known Hing long before I jumped ship. The *Allegro* was registered in Panama, but her home port was Hong-Kong. We were often in Singapore, and the only occasion in eleven months we left the Indian Ocean was to take a cargo of rubber to Vancouver. I thought of jumping ship there, and nearly did it, except that beyond Vancouver and the cold wastes of Canadian America I saw the United States, and that was the place I was fleeing.

Hing was the first person I thought of when I developed my plan for leaving the *Allegro*. At the time he seemed the kindest man. I always looked forward to our stops in Singapore, and Hing was glad of our business. Just a small-time provisioner, delivering cornflakes to housewives at the British bases and glad of the unexpected order of an extra pound of sausages, he worked out of his little shop on Beach Road; Gopi packed the cardboard cartons, and Little Hing took the groceries around in a beat-up van. We were not dealing with Hing then. Our ship chandler was a large firm, also on Beach Road, just down from Raffles Hotel. One day, checking over our crates of supplies I saw some second-hand valves wrapped in newspaper that I felt were being palmed off on me.

'We didn't order these,' I said.

The clerk took them out of the crate. He dropped them on the floor.

'Where are the ones we ordered?'

The clerk said nothing. The Chinese mouth is naturally grim; his was drawn down, his nether lip pouted; his head, too large for the rest of his body, had corners, and looked just like a skull, not a head fleshed out with an expression, but in contour and lightness, the sutures and jaw-hinges visible, a bone with a flat skeletal crown. This feller's head, ridiculously mounted on a scrawny neck, infuriated me.

'Where,' I repeated, 'are the ones we ordered?'

He swallowed, setting his adam's apple in motion. 'Out of stock.'

'I thought as much. So you gave us these. You're always doing that!' I almost blew a gasket. 'We're going to be at sea for the next ten days. What if a valve goes? They aren't going to be any good to us, are they?' I wanted him to reply. *'Are they?'*

Anger takes some responsive cooperation to fan blustering to rage. He would not play; the Chinese seldom did. Some fellers accused the Chinese of harbouring a motiveless evil, but it was not so. Their blank look was disturbing because it did nothing to discourage the feeling that they meant us harm. The blankness was blankness, a facial void reflecting a mental one: confusion. If I had to name the look I would call it fear, the kind that can make the Chinese cower or be wild. The clerk cowered, withdrawing behind the counter.

I kicked the crate and stamped out of the shop. Next door Hing was smiling in the doorway of his shop. I was immediately well disposed to him; he was reliably fat and calm, and he had the prosperous, satisfying bulk, the easy grace of a trader with many employees.

'Yes?'

Apart from a few wooden stools, a calendar, an abacus, bills withering on a spike and on the wall a red altar with a pot full of smouldering joss-sticks, the shop was empty of merchandise. Little Hing was carrying groceries from the back room, Gopi was ramming them into a crate.

'I need some valves,' I said. Then, 'Got?'

He thought I was saying 'bulbs', but we got that straight, and finally, after I described the size, he said, 'Can get.'

'When?'

'Now,' he said, calling Little over. 'You want tea? Cigarette? Here –' He shook a cigarette out of a tin. 'Plenty for you. Don't mention. Come, I light. Thank you.'

He had the valves for me in twenty minutes, and that was how we started doing business with Hing. The next time the *Allegro* called at Singapore, Hing had put up his ship chandler's sign. There was nothing he could not get; he had a genius for winkling out the scarcest supplies, confirming the claim he printed on his stationery: 'Provisions of Every Description Shall Be Supplied at Shortest Notice'. And every time I called on him with my shopping list he took me out to dinner, a roast beef and Yorkshire pudding feed at the Elizabethan Grill, or a twelve-course Chinese dinner with everything but bears' paws and fish-lips on the table.

It was simple business courtesy, the ritual meal. I was buying a thousand dollars' worth of provisions and supplies from him; for this he was paying for my dinner. I was an amateur. I thought I was doing very well, and always congratulated myself as, lamed by brandy, I staggered to the quay to catch a sampan back to the *Allegro*. I only understood the business logic of 'Have a cigar – take two', when it was too late; but, as I say, I started out hissing 'Hey, bud' from doorways along Robinson Road. I was old enough to know better.

During one of the large meals, Hing, who in the Chinese style watched me closely and heaped my plate with food every five minutes, leaned over and said, 'You . . . wucking . . . me.' His English failed him and he began gabbling in Cantonese. The waitress was boning an astonished steamed *garupa* that was stranded on a platter of vegetables. She translated shyly, without looking up.

'He say . . . he like you. He say . . . he want a young man . . .'

'*Ang moh*,' I heard Hing say. 'Red-head.'

The waitress removed the elaborate comb of the fish's spine

and softened Hing's slang to, 'European man . . . do very good business for European ship. European people . . . not speak awkward like Chinese people. And he say . . .'

Hing implored with his eyes and his whole smooth face.

I was thirty-nine. At thirty-nine you're in your thirties; at forty, or so I thought then, you're in the shadow of middle age. It was as if he had whispered, 'Brace yourself, Flowers. I've had my eye on you for a long time . . .' I was excited. The Chinese life in Singapore was mainly noodles and children in a single room, the noise of washing and hoicking. It could not have been duller, but because it was dull the Chinese had a gift for creating special occasions, a night out, a large banquet or festive gathering which sustained them through a year of yellow noodles. Hing communicated this festive singularity to me; I believed my magic had worked, my luck had changed with my age; not fortune, but the promise of it was spoken. I saw myself speeding forward in a wind like silk.

Three weeks later, I walked into Hing's shop. He shook my hand, offered the tin of cigarettes and began clacking his lighter, saying, 'Yes, Jack, yes.'

Little Hing came over and asked for the shopping list, the manifests and indents.

'No lists,' I said, and grinned. 'No ship, no list!' I had turned away to explain. 'From now on I'm working for the *towkay*.'

Behind me, Big Hing was screwing the lid back on to the tin of cigarettes, and that was the only sound; the lid caught and clicked and rasped in the metal grooves, and was finally silent.

Big Hing was grave, reflectively biting his upper lip with his lower teeth. He banged the cigarette-tin on the trestle table, making the beads on the abacus spin and tick. He became brisk. He led me to my cubicle, two beaverboard partitions without a ceiling, narrow as a urinal, and he shot the curtain along its rod, jangling the chrome hoops. I climbed on to the stool and put my head down. I did not turn around. I knew the *Allegro* had sailed without me.

9

The second time I met Hing, when I was still buying for the *Allegro* and thought of him as a friend, he took me to an opium parlour, a tiny smoke-smeared attic room off North Bridge Road. It was one of the stories I told later in hotel bars to loosen up nervous fellers whom I had spotted as possible clients. I had expected the opium parlour to be something like a wang-house filled with sleepy hookers relaxing on cushions; I was not prepared for the ghostly sight of five elderly addicts, dozing hollow-eyed in droopy wrinkled pyjamas, and two equally decrepit 'cooks' scraping dottle out of black pipes. The room was dark; a single shutter, half-open, gave the only light; the ceiling panels seemed kept in place by the cobwebs that were woven over the cracks between the panels and the beams they dangled from. The walls were marked with the cats'-paws of Chinese characters. There was some scarred wooden furniture, broken crates and stools and low cots and string beds with soiled pillows where the derelict men slept with their mouths open. A very old woman in wide silk trousers and red clogs drank coffee out of a condensed milk tin and watched me. It was an atmosphere only an opium trance could improve. I anxiously sucked one pipeful; none of the skinny dreamers acknowledged me, and we left. In front of the opium parlour, where Hing's Riley sat, a parking attendant, a round-faced girl in a straw hat and grey jacket, was writing out a ticket. Hing saw the joke immediately, and we both laughed: the parking ticket at the opium den. I embellished it as a story by increasing the over-time parking fine and glamourizing the dingy room, giving it silk pillows and the addicts youth.

The opium parlour was Hing's idea. He had convinced me that I could ask for anything of him; he said, 'Singapore have everything', and he wanted a chance to prove it. Faced by variety, my imagination was confounded; I chose simple pleasures, outings, walks, the Police Band concerts at the Botanical Gardens, fishing from the pier. Hing made suggestions. He introduced me to Madam Lum and her chief attraction, Mona, a girl with the oddest tastes whom I used to describe truthfully to fellers, saying, 'She's not fooling – she really likes her work, and everyone comes back singing her praises!' Hing took me to the 'Screw Inn', a little bungalow of teenage girls off Mountbatten Road, and he taught me that yellow-roofed taxis were the tip-off: more than two parked together in a residential area indicated a brothel close by. At Hing's urging I had my first taste of the good life: a morning shave flat on my back at the Indian barbershop on Orchard Road (Chinese barbers used dull razors – the sparse Chinese beard was easy to scrape off); a heavy lunch at the Great Shanghai, followed by a nap and a massage by a naked Chinese girl who sat astride me and kneaded my back and who afterwards invited another girl into the room so that the three of us could fool for the whole afternoon. After tea, both girls gave me a bath and we went for a stroll; I walked them to a bar, had a last drink, then early to bed with a novel – the sequence of a lovely exhausting day, which gave me a stomach full of honey and the feeling that the skin I wore was brand-new. Hing paid the bills. He had few pleasures himself, and he wasn't a drinker. What he liked were big Australian girls in night-clubs who stripped to the buff and then got down on all fours and shook and howled like cats. He understood food; he taught me the fine points of ordering Szechuan meals, the fried eels in sauce, the hot-sour soup, steamed pomfret and crisp duck skin that was eaten in a soft bun. He gave me bottles of ginseng wine, which he claimed was an aphrodisiac tonic, and on the appropriate festival a whole mooncake wrapped in red paper. He said he was glad I wasn't British, and why wasn't I married, and how did I like Singapore?

All this time I was his customer; the ritual friendship ended when I became his employee, and at six hundred Straits dollars a month I was treated as a difficult burden, crowding his shop with my bulk, wasting his time, eating his money. He stopped speaking to me directly, and if the two of us were in the shop alone he assumed a preoccupied busy air, rattling scraps of paper, pretending to look for things, banging doors, groaning, saying his commercial rosary on his abacus. He spoke to me through his dog; my mistakes and lapses got the dog a kick in the ribs. I thought I might be promoted, but I learned very early that no promotion would come my way. The job interested me enough so that I could do it without any encouragement from Hing. For Hing to thank me, something he never did, would have been an admission on his part of dependency, a loss of face: civility was a form of weakness for him. I understood this and took his rudeness to be the gratitude it was. We had no contract; after our verbal agreement Hing arranged a visa for me which allowed me to stay in Singapore as long as I worked for him. This was convenient (the bribe came out of his pocket), but limiting: if he fired me the visa would be cancelled and I would be deported. He needed me too much to fire me, but I knew that to remind him of this would be to ask for a sacking, for that was the only way he could demonstrate I wasn't needed.

But I was. A year on the *Allegro* and all the calls we had made at Singapore had acquainted me with most of the other vessels and skippers who called regularly, and I knew many of the fellers in the Maritime Building who managed the shipping lines. The advantage I had, which Hing had hinted at, only dawned on me later: I was white. The rest of the ship chandlers in Singapore were either Indian or Chinese. As a paleface in the late fifties in Singapore I drank in clubs and bars where 'Asians', as they were called, were not allowed. Largely, I drank in these places because I was not welcome in the Chinese clubs, and I didn't like the toddy in the Indian ones. It offended me that I was forced to drink with my own race – later, I would not do otherwise: I couldn't relax with fellers of other races – but in the end this simple fact of racial exclusiveness landed Hing with many contracts for supplying European ships. I was learning the ropes: Chinese and Indians transacted all their business in offices, Europeans did it in clubs and used their offices as phone-booths.

A club, even a so-called exclusive one, was easy to enter but hard to join. The doormen were Malays or Sikhs, and I had learned how to say, 'How's every little thing, brother?' in Malay and Punjabi. In any case, they would not have dared to turn an *ang moh* away; and as for signing the drink chits I had a number of match tricks and brain-twisters that I'd spring on anyone drinking alone. The loser had to sign for the drink. I never lost.

'Just in from Bangkok,' I'd say. 'Feller up there showed me a cute gimmick. You've probably seen it. No? Well, you put six matches down like this, make a little sort of circle with them. There. Now – I wonder if I've got that right? I'm a real jerk when it comes to these tricky things. What you're supposed to do is rearrange five matches without disturbing –'

After I had explained, I'd say, 'Loser signs, okay?' and the drink would be as good as mine. That was a British con. Americans were easier. 'Bet you can't name the twelve Apostles' or 'Whose picture's on the hundred-dollar bill?' or 'What's the capital of Maine?' secured my drinks with Americans, and with a drink in my hand I could stay in a club bar for hours, making up stories, chatting or telling jokes that appealed to the listener's prejudices by confirming them. There were not many Chinese jokes, apart from the funny names of which I had a long list culled from the Singapore Telephone Directory ('Pass me the phone-book, Ali; my friend here doesn't believe Fook Yew and Wun Fatt Joo really live in Singapore'). There were many good Indian jokes, and these always went down well. I told Englishmen the joke about the Texan who's accused of sodomizing animals. 'Cows, pigs, mules,' says his accuser, a girl he wants to take home. She goes on, 'Sheep, dogs, cats, chickens –' The Texan interrupts in annoyance: 'What do you mean, *chickens*?'

Americans were always bowled over by the story of the Englishman whose pecker is accidentally cut off. After a painful month he finally decides to see a doctor, who says he knows how to sew the thing back on. 'Just hand it over and I'll see to it straightaway.' The Englishman slaps his pockets, says, 'I've got the damned thing here somewhere' and gives the doctor a huge cigar. 'This is a cigar,' says the perplexed doctor, and 'My word,' says the Englishman, 'I must have smoked my cock!'

Sometimes I clowned around, like making a great show of ordering cherries in brandy, simply to say, 'To tell the truth, I hate these cherries, but I like the spirit in which they're given!' So, even without the match tricks and brain-twisters, someone was always buying me a drink and saying, 'You're a card.' And in clubs where I was not a member fellers said, 'We haven't seen you lately – missed you at the film show' and 'Don't forget the AGM next week, about time we tackled that gate-crashers' clause'. Eventually, a feller would ask, 'Say, Jack, what's your line of work?'

'Me? I'm in ship chandling.' I never said I was a water-clerk.

'Odd that,' would be the reply.

'I know exactly what you mean,' I'd say. 'But the way I figure it, this business could use a little streamlining. Methods haven't changed since Raffles' time, and, by God, neither have some of the groceries they're flogging, from the taste of them! Shops haven't been swept in years, bread's as hard as old Harry, weevils in the rice. Mind you, I've got nothing against our Asiatic brothers. It's just as you say, they work like dogs. On the other hand, your Indian is never really happy handling meat – but you can't hold their religion against them, can you?'

'One can't, I suppose. But still –'

'And your Chinese ship chandler – he'll give you a turd and tell you it's an orchid. Shall I tell you what I saw one day in a Chinese shop? This'll kill you –'

The feller would be agreeing with me and putting his oar in from time to time. I'd tell my valve story and he'd cap it with a better and terrifying one about defective life-jackets or wormy provisions, all the while working up the indignation to change ship chandlers.

My most effective selling ploy, which I used just before meal-times, when conversations always got around to food, was my English breakfast. This never failed. The English, I had discovered, had a weakness for large breakfasts; it might have had a literary source – a Dickens character having beefsteak with his tea – or the racial memory of cold mornings, or war-rationing. Whatever the reason, it was an inspired way of getting a contract.

I hit on this a few months after I began ship chandling in Singapore, with a feller from the Victoria Shipping Lines. It was on the verandah of the Singapore Cricket Club, on a Saturday just before tiffin. The feller was sitting beside me in a wicker chair and we were watching some ladies bowling on the grass. This form of bowling was exactly like the Italian game *bocce*, which my father played in an alley in the North End every Sunday afternoon. It was the only game I knew well, and I was commenting on the ladies' match to the feller on my right: 'Gotta have more left-hand side . . . Not enough legs on that one . . . Kissed it . . . Never make it . . . She's out for blood – it's going like a demon –' The ladies took a rest. I turned to the feller and said, 'Seems there was this Texan –'

'Very amusing,' he said when I finished, his understatement contradicting the honking laughter he couldn't suppress. 'Have a drink?'

'*Thank* you.'

'Actually, I'm hungry,' he said. 'No time for breakfast this morning. Ruins the day, don't you find?'

'Absolutely,' I said. 'That's what I try to tell these skippers I deal with. Give a seaman a slap-up breakfast and he'll do a fair day's work. Cut down on his lunch, but don't ever tamper with that breakfast of his!'

'My idea of a really top-notch breakfast is kippers, porridge, eggs and a pot of tea – hot and strong.' He smacked his lips.

'You're forgetting your fruit-juice – juices are *very* important. And choice of cereals, some bubble and squeak, huge rashers of bacon, or maybe a beefsteak and chips, a stack of toast, hot crumpets, marmalade. Boy!' The feller was nodding in agreement and swallowing. 'It's a funny thing, you know,' I went on. 'These ship chandlers don't supply fresh juice – oh, no! Course the fresh is cheaper and the fruit grows locally. They give you this tinned stuff.'

'You can taste the metal.'

'Sure you can!'

'Potatoes make a nice breakfast,' he said, still swallowing.

'Hash-browns – fry 'em up crisp and hot and serve them with gouts of H.P. Sauce.'

'I'm famished,' he said, and looked at his watch.

'Me too,' I said. 'I wouldn't mind a big English breakfast right this minute. I envy the seamen on some of the ships I supply.'

'All the same,' he said, 'it sounds an expensive meal.'

'Not on your nelly,' I said, and quoted some prices, adding, 'I buy in bulk, see, so I can pass the savings on to the customer. I still make a profit – everyone gains.'

'It sounds frightfully reasonable.'

'And that's not all –'

Our drinks arrived, and the ladies resumed their bowling. The feller said, 'I'm just the teeniest bit browned-off with my own chandler. What did you say was the name of your firm?'

I explained Hing's name on my card by saying he was a partner who came in handy when we were dealing with Chinese accounts – I'd known him for years. 'Like I say, we're an unusual firm.' I winked. 'Think about it. We'll see your men get a good breakfast. Oh, and if there's anything *else* you require – *anything at all* – just give me a tinkle and I'll see what I can scare up. Cheers.'

He rang the next day. He offered me a chandling contract for three freighters, a couple of tankers and two steamships of modest tonnage that did the Singapore–North Borneo run. At the end of the conversation he hesitated briefly and murmured, 'Yesterday, um, you said *anything*, didn't you?'

'You bet your boots I did.'

'Um, I was wondering if you could help me out with something that's just cropped up this morning. One of our freighters is in from Madras. Crew's feeling a bit bolshie about going off tomorrow to the Indonesian ports. We'd like to cheer them up a bit, um, give them a bit of fun without letting them ashore. Are you in the picture?'

'Leave it to me,' I said. 'How many guys are you trying to . . . amuse?'

'Well, it's the *Richard Everett*. She's got, say, twenty-three able seamen, and –'

'You've come to the right man,' I said. 'How about a coffee? I'll explain then.'

'*Lunch*,' he insisted, pleased. 'At the club. And thanks, thanks awfully.'

10

At that period in my life, my first years in Singapore, I enjoyed a rare kind of happiness, like the accidental discovery of renewal, singing in the heart and feet, that comes with infatuation. It was true power; mercy and boldness. I felt brave. I didn't belittle it or try to justify it, and I never wondered about its queer origin. I was converted to buoyancy, and, rising, understood survival: the surprise of the marooned man who has built his first fire. I had turned forty without pain, and until Desmond Frogget came I was the youngest drinker in the Bandung.

The Bandung was a lively place: freshly painted, always full, with free meat pies on Saturdays and curry tiffin on Sundays, and a ping-pong table which we hauled out to work up a thirst. A stubby feller named Ogham used to play the piano in the lounge, jazzy tunes until midnight finishing up with vulgar and patriotic songs. I can see it now on a Saturday night, the room lit by paper lanterns rocked by the fans, Wally in a short white jacket and black tie shaking a gin sling, the main bar heaving with drinkers, all of them regulars, and me in my white cotton suit and white shoes, wearing the flowered open-neck shirt that was my trademark, and Ogham in the lounge playing 'Twelfth Street Rag'. Some feller would lean over and say to me, 'Oggie could have been a professional, you know, but like he says, that's no life for a man with a family.'

Ogham pounded the piano at the Bandung and never introduced us to his family, and after he left Singapore there were various explanations of where he had gone. Some said to a London bank, but Yardley sneered, 'He was a lush. He got the sack and three months' *gadji* and now he's in Surrey, mending bicycles.' For Yardley no fate was worse. With Ogham gone I hacked around sometimes with 'The Warsaw Concerto', hitting a sour note at the end of an expertly played passage to be funny, but some fellers said I was being disrespectful to Ogham and I had to stop. Later, an old-timer wandering back through the lounge from the toilet in the kitchen would glance at the piano and say, 'Remember Oggie? I wonder what happened to him? Christ, he could have turned professional.'

'Oggie didn't know whether his arsehole was bored or punched,' Yardley would reply, believing Ogham to be a deserter. 'He got the sack and three months' *gadji* and now he's in –'

The day Ogham left he got very nostalgic about a particular towpath he had played on as a child; he bought us all a drink and reminisced. I had never seen him so happy. We listened at the bar as he took a box of matches and said, 'The gas-works was over here,' and put a match down, 'and the canal ran along what we used to call the cut – here. And –' The scene was repeated with the others, the memory of a picnic or tram-ride re-enacted at the bar before their ships sailed.

Many of the regulars at the Bandung started to leave. It was getting near to Independence, and, over a drink, when a feller said he was going home you knew he meant England and not his house in Bukit Timah. So the Bandung emptied. On a side-road at the city limit, it was too far off the beaten track for the average tourist to find it, and what tourists there were in those days came by ship. I spent most of my free time hustling in bars in the harbour area, places a tourist with a few hours ashore might wander into, or in the cut-price curio shops in Raffles Place. I had earned enough money in my first year to be considered a big spender in the Bandung and to rent a large yellow house on River Valley Road, with three bedrooms, a verandah supported by solid white pillars and shaded by chicks the size of sails on a Chinese junk. As a bachelor I lived in one room and allowed the other rooms to fall into disuse. I had two grey parrots who pecked the spines off all my books, a dozen cats and an old underemployed *amah* who played noisy games of mah-jong with her friends in the kitchen, often waking me at three in the morning as they shuffled, a process they called 'washing the tiles'. The *amah* had made the bed and fixed breakfast enough times to know that I was not practising celibacy, and she was continually saying that, as a 'black and white' she was trained to care for children, a hint that I should get married. She sized up the girls I took home and always said, 'Too skinny! You not like hayvie! Yek-yek!'

I believed that I would marry a tall young Chinese girl with a boy's hips and lank crow-black hair and a shining face and take her away, the hopeful mutual rescue that was the aim of every white bachelor then in the East. I did not give up the idea until later, when I saw one of these marriages, the radiant Chinese girl, shyly secretive, easily embarrassed, transformed into a crass suburban wife, nagging through her nose about prices in a monotonous voice, with thick unadventurous thighs, a complaining face, and at her most boring and suburban, saying to exhausted listeners in perfect English, 'Well, we Chinese –' I had the idea of marriage; as long as I postponed the action, romance was possible for me, and I was happy. Any day, I expected to get the letter beginning, 'Dear Mr Flowers, It gives me great pleasure to be writing to you today, and I know my news will please you –' Or perhaps the other one, starting, '*My darling* –'

My brief, unrewarding enterprises – evenings calling out 'Hey, bud' to startled residents walking their dogs, afternoons sailing two fruit-flies dressed as scrub-women (greasy overalls covering silk cheongsams) to rusty freighters – these were over. The *Richard Everett* episode and the notoriety that followed it singled me out. Fellers rang me up at all hours of the night, asking me to get them a girl, and one of my replies – delivered at four in the morning to an importuning caller who said he hoped he hadn't got me out of bed – became famous. 'No,' I had said, 'I was up combing my hair.' In the harbour bars I was 'Jack' to everyone, and I knew every confiding barman by name. What pleasure it gave me, after knocking off early at Hing's, to go home and put on my white shoes and a clean flowered shirt and then to make my rounds in a tri-shaw, a freshly lit cheroot in my teeth, dropping in on the girls, in bars or massage parlours, to see how many I could count on for the evening. The wiry tri-shaw driver pumped away; I sat comfortably in the seat with my feet up as we wound through the traffic. The sun at five o'clock was dazzling, but the bars I entered were dark and cool as caves. I would stick my head in and say in a jaunty greeting to the darkness, 'Hi, girls!'

'Jaaaack!' They would materialize out of booths, hobble over to me on high heels and, favouring their clawlike fingernails, hug my big belly and give me genial tickling pinches in the crotch. 'Come, Jack, I give you good time.' 'Me, Jack, you like?' 'Touch me, baby.'

'You're all flawless,' I'd say, and play a hand of cards, buy them all a drink and move on to a new bar. Many of the girls were independent, not paying any secret-society protection money. I called them 'floaters' because when they weren't floating around looking for a pick-up I was literally floating them by the dozen out to ships in the harbour. A great number of them who hung around the bars on Anson Road – the Gold Anchor, Big South Sea, Captain's Table, Champagne Club, Chang's – came to depend on me for customers. They were using me in the same way as Hing, to get Europeans, who didn't haggle and who would pay a few dollars more. The Chinese were after the *ang moh* trade, and it seemed as if I was the only supplier. I could get white tourists and sailors for the girls as easily as I got the club members who were in the shipping business for Hing. The floaters along Anson Road and the Hing brothers were not the only ones who depended on me; the British servicemen at Changi, the sailors from H.M.S. *Terror*, the club members and tourists did as well: the Chinese who sought the *ang mohs* were in turn being sought by the *ang mohs*, and both, ignorant of the others' hunting, came to me for introductions – finding me, they found each other.

But the girls in the wharf area bars forfeited all their Chinese trade when they were seen holding hands with a paleface. After that, they were tainted, and no Chinese would touch them or notice them except to bark a singular Cantonese or Hokkien obscenity, usually an exaggeration of my virility ('So the red-head's got a big doo-dah!'), meant as a slur on the girls for being lustful, and on me for possessing a deformity not in the least resembling the little dark bathplug most Chinese consider the size of the normal male organ.

I was resented by most of the Chinese men in the bars; they accused me, in the oblique way Hing had, of spoiling the girls. The occupation of a prostitute they saw as a customary traditional role, an essential skill. But pairing up with red-haired devils made the girls vicious – it was an abnormality, something perverse, and they considered these girls of mine as little better than the demon-women in folk stories who coupled with dogs and bore hairy babies. And that was not all. The men also had that little-country grievance, a point of view Yardley and the old-timers shared, about rich foreigners butting in and sending the prices up. Neither accusation was justified: the girls (who nearly always hated the men they slept with) were improved by their contact with Europeans, quiet undemanding men, unlike their sadistic woman-hating counterparts in the States. The men were instructive, curious and kind, and wanted little more than to sail home and boast that they had spent the night with a Chinese whore in Singapore. And as for the prices going up after a decade of inflation, when the cost of a haircut doubled, cigarettes increased five times, and some house-rents – my own, for example – went up by two hundred per cent, the price of a short-time with massage stayed the same, and an all-nighter cost only an extra three-fifty. Until Japanese cameras flooded the market, a night in bed with one of my girls was the only bargain a feller could find in Singapore.

The Chinese men would not listen to reason. '*Boochakong* just now cost twenty-over dollar-*lah*,' they complained. I felt loathed and large. Some simply didn't like my face or the fact that I was so pally with Chinese girls. I have already mentioned the secret-society member, the Three Dot in the Tai-Hwa who asked me threateningly, 'Where you does wuck?' Another brute, late one night, took a swing at me in the parking lot of the Prince's Hotel. He came at me from behind as I was unlocking my car – Providence made him stumble; and later the Prince's manager, who to a Chinese eye might have looked like me – they can't tell *ang mohs* apart, they say, and don't find it funny – was found in a back alley with his throat cut and his flowered shirt smeared with blood. Karim, the barman, said his eyes had been ritually gouged. I had to choose my bars carefully, and I made sure my tri-shaw driver was a big feller.

Still, I was making money, and it delighted me on sunny afternoons to have a cold shower, then make my rounds in a well-upholstered tri-shaw, chirping into dark interiors, 'Hi, girls!', and to say to a stranger in a confident whisper, 'If there's anything you want – *anything at all* –' and be perfectly certain I could supply whatever he named.

Being American was part of my uniqueness. There were few Americans in Singapore, and though the last thing I wanted to be – after all, I had left the place for a good reason – was the glad-hander, the ham with the loud jokes and big feet and flashy shirts saying, 'It figures' and 'Come off it' and 'Who's your friend?' and 'This I gotta see', it was the only role open to me because it was the only one the people I dealt with accepted. It alerted them when I behaved untypically; it looked as though I was concealing something and intended to defraud them by playing down the Yankee. In such a small place, an island with no natives, everyone a visitor, the foreigner made himself a resident by emphasizing his foreignness. Yardley, who was from Leeds, but had been in Singapore since the war – he married one of these sleek Chinese girls who turned into a suburban dragon named Mildred – had softened his accent by listening to the BBC Overseas Service. He put burnt matches back into the box (muttering, 'These are threepence in U.K.'), cigarette ash in his trouser-cuffs and poured milk in his cup before the tea. The one time I made a reference to the photograph in the Bandung of the Queen and Duke ('Liz and

Phil, I know them well – nice to see them around, broo-reh-ah!'), Yardley called Eisenhower – President at the time – 'a bald fucker, a stupid general who half the time doesn't know whether he wants a shit or a haircut'. Consequently, but against my will, I was made an American, or rather 'the Yank'. When America was mentioned, fellers said, 'Ask Jack'. I exaggerated my accent and dropped my *Allegro* pretence of being Italian. I tried to give the impression of a cheerful rascal, someone gently ignorant; I claimed I had no education and said, 'If you say so' or 'That's really interesting' to anything remotely intelligent.

It was awfully hard for me to be an American, but the hardest part was playing the dumb-cluck for a feller whose intelligence was inferior to mine. The fellers at the Bandung reckoned they had great natural gifts; Yates, in his own phrase 'an avaricious reader', would say, 'I'm reading Conrad' when he was stuck in the first chapter of a book he'd never finish; Yardley pointed to me one night and said, 'I wouldn't touch an American book with a barge-pole', and Smale ended every argument with, 'It all comes down to the same thing, then, don't it?' to which someone would add, 'Right. Six of one and half a dozen of the other'. They were always arguing, each argument illustrated by anecdotes from personal experience. That was the problem: they saved up stories to tell people back home; then, realizing with alarm that they probably weren't going home, wondered who to tell. They told each other. Stories were endlessly repeated, and the emphasis and phrasing never varied. The silent fellers in the Bandung were not listening; they were waiting for a chance to talk.

I was the only genuine listener – the inexperienced American, there to be instructed. But the funny thing was, I had a college education and almost a degree. It was no help in the Bandung to say a bright truth, for even if someone heard it he was incapable of verifying it; and on the job it created misunderstandings. I recall meeting an Irish seaman on one of my 'meat runs', as my ferrying of girls into the harbour was called. Hearing his brogue,

I said, 'I'm crazy about Joyce' and he replied, 'That the skinny one in the yellow dress?'

I said, 'You guessed it!' and he went over and pinched her sorry bottom through a fold in her frock. Later he thanked me for the tip-off. He was right and I was wrong: education is inappropriate to most jobs, and it was practically an impertinence to the enterprises of the feller whom the Indian ship chandler on Market Street described as 'having a finger in every tart'.

It was on the G.I. Bill; I was thirty-five, a freshman. I always seemed to be the wrong age for whatever I was doing, and because of that paying dearly for it. But I was not alone. Older students were a common sight in every university in the late forties and fifties, army veterans from the Second World War and then Korea, wearing faded khaki jackets with the chevrons torn off, the stitch-marks showing, and shoes with highly polished toes. My inglorious war – a punctured eardrum put me behind a desk in Oklahoma – ended in 1945. I came home expecting a miracle letter ('Dear Jack, It's good to hear you're home and I have some fabulous news for you . . .'), but nothing happened. I helped my father in the tailor shop, blocking hats and putting tickets on the dry cleaning and sometimes doing deliveries. My uncle said, 'There's good money in printing,' so I joined a linotype school, which I quit soon after. 'They're crying out for draughtsmen' and 'A good short-order cook can name his salary' sent me in other directions.

I was reading a great deal – the serious paperback was having its vogue in the early fifties (they were thought to be somewhat salacious: 'He's just reading a paperback' was considered mockery) – and I was encouraged by the biographical notes, less frequent today, which listed the previous occupations of the author on the back cover. 'Jim Smith has had a varied career', they'd begin, and go on to list twenty back-breaking jobs. I imagined my own biographical note: 'After his discharge from the U.S. Army, where he reached the rank of corporal, John ('Jack') Fiori worked as a hat-blocker in his father's tailor shop, and then, in succession, as a printer, draughtsman, short-order cook, bartender, dishwasher, life-guard, baker and fruit-seller. He has always considered fiction to be his chief aim, and has this to say about the present novel: "I believe that mankind struggled from the sea to –"' It was a good biographical note, enhanced by an imagined photograph of me smoking a cigarette over a typewriter. I smoked. I bought a typewriter and learned to use it. I typed my biographical note. But that was all: there was no book. I had nothing to write. I knew nothing beyond my name and the face I practised. I didn't understand danger or regret; a book was an extensive biographical note.

Twenty years later William Leigh turned up and asked me urgent questions and died with a foolish sentence on his lips before I could reply; and I burned him to dust. So this memoir was provoked. Writing a book is a splendid idea, but it was not mine. My notion was simpler, just a picture of my experienced face and the list of jobs that made the face that way. This memoir is not the book or the work I imagined; it was urged upon me, like a complicated, necessary enchantment I did little to inspire, made mostly of terror, which forced me to learn, laboriously, to conjure: an imprecise trick, half accident, half design, begun as a deliberate memory ('Mister Hing vaunting Mister Jack . . .') and completed by a kind of magic that to discover thoroughly is to fail at.

I thought I could learn at college. It was my only reason for going. I found myself among a few earnest veterans and many fresh-faced kids. The older fellers never flunked out, but at the same time never excelled, resenting being lectured to and corrected by educated fellers the same age or younger, draftdodgers or fairies with leather elbow-patches, whom they could only nag with the reply, 'I'll bet you don't even know how to clean a gun!' The ones on the G.I. Bill lived with their harassed wives and children in grey Nissen huts, referred to as 'married quarters'. Most of the older fellers were economics majors or engineers (the pocketful of pens, the slide-rule in a scabbard) and had too much homework on their hands to take an interest in the college routine. Besides, they had problems at home, and so they treated their education as a job, being punctual and tidy, carrying creased lunch-bags and keeping regular hours. I saw them in the Students' Union salting a hard-boiled egg and underlining a physics book.

Some, of whom I was one, because I was unmarried and majoring in English, were accommodated by the fringe people, the art majors, would-be poets, weekend winos, hangers-on and hitch-hikers. That was the enterprise then, saying, 'Aw shit, I gotta bust out' and hitch-hiking in sweat-shirts across the country, aiming for California or Mexico and staying drunk the whole way by gagging down bottles of Tokay or Muscatel. These fellers would show up with stories of their travels ('I met this beautiful sad old man in Denver, and he says to me . . .') and some poems about America which they'd shout, taking swigs out of a can of beer. The writers they respected had all been deck-hands on freighters, and going to sea was the height of their ambition. Some hung around the Seafarers' International Union in Brooklyn, hoping for a job, but few of them succeeded – they were too young and not strong enough for the work. They talked about Zen Buddhism, Ezra Pound, the atom bomb, mystical experiences. There was a little marijuana around, but the big kicks were in drinking three bottles of terpin hydrate cough syrup, or washing down a can of nutmeg with a glass of milk, or getting drunk like Dylan Thomas, or trying to grow a beard.

It was my beard that gained me entry. I had stopped shaving when I worked the night-shift at the bakery and still had it the day I shambled in to register for classes. It was bright red, cut square across the bottom. They complimented me on it and I explained its redness by saying that Vivaldi's hair was the same colour.

I suppose I should have kept to myself, but I had been doing that joylessly for ten years and I liked the company, the spirit of careless romance in the younger kids. People called them 'beatniks', already a dated word then, but they thought of themselves as 'the folk'. I moved into the top floor of a coffee-shop, and generally I stuck close to them, proving my friendship the only way I knew, buying beer for them, lending them money, trying to set them straight on Ezra Pound, who was a fake poet but a genuine fascist; and I kept my hot eyes on the long-haired girls who strummed guitars and wrote poems in black sweaters and dancers' tights. I wrote poems, too, unfashionable rhyming ones:

> Is that the wind, I asked my friend,
> That shakes the trees and makes them bend?

In a group of six or seven grim-looking undergraduates I was the big bearded one in army fatigues, older than the others and trying to look inconspicuous; and more than likely there would be a small pale girl next to me, who couldn't stand her parents. 'When you were my age,' she would say, and go on cracking my heart, bending my ear.

It did not last long. My reading only trained me to read better. What I wrote sounded like what I read. 'A cold dark November in my soul,' I'd write, and then furiously cross it out, or again and again, 'I was born in the year 1918, in the North End of the city of Boston, the second child of two transplanted Italians –' Then half a chapter about childhood fears – not the informed apprehension of the adult, but the impatient uncertainty of the little boy who was always made to wait, who thought he might die in his bed if the lamp was switched off and whose pleasures were his thumb and the minutes after Confession and the time spent in a slate urinal, pissing with one hand and eating an ice-cream sandwich with the other. To sit down and write *Chapter One – Childhood* was to begin a book rather than a story, a bold guarantee against ever finishing it. My character's name was Jack Flowers, not John Fiori. A first-love chapter and an army chapter loomed, and Jack was going to discover the simplicity of love and the surprise of wealth. If the book succeeded I would write another about success; if it failed, one about failure. The fellers in the coffee-shop asked me what my book was about. I said, 'It's about this guy who's trying to write a book –'

Writing bored me, and it sickened me in my attic to be staring at a white sheet of paper ('Chapter One') while the sun was shining outside and everyone else was at play, for every word I wrote seemed a denial of the complex uniqueness I could see just outside the window. My descriptions reduced what lacy trees and grass I could see to sorry props on the page, and my characters were either brutes or angels, too extreme and simple to be human. Still, fiction seemed to give me the second chances life denied me.

But there were other difficulties. In my short time as a student the artistic fringe people switched from getting drunk to getting high. I could cope with alcohol, but drugs baffled me, and I didn't even know that the pills I was taking to get my weight down, little heart-shaped orange tablets, were a kind of pep pill.

'John,' a girl said, seeing me swallow one. 'What's that?'

I was too embarrassed to explain that they had been prescribed to reduce my waist-line. They killed my appetite: skinny fellers had more girl-friends. I said, 'It's just a tablet. I don't even know the name –'

'Dexedrine,' she said. 'Fantastic.'

'You want one? Here, take a dozen.'

'Cool.' She swallowed three.

'You won't want any lunch,' I said.

'Crazy.' She shuddered.

That amused me. Handing out these reducing tablets won me the girl-friends I had hoped to get by being thin. Briefly, I was happy. But happiness is a blurred memory of sensational lightness; fear and boredom leave me with a remembrance of particular details. I recall the discomfort: squatting or sitting cross-legged on the floor, listening to long poems by nineteen-year-olds beginning, *I have seen* . . . – getting cramps behind my knees, my back aching – *And I have seen* . . . I made myself sick on that sweet wine ('Look out, John's barfing!') and they talked about Zen, rejection slips from quarterlies with names like *The Goatsfoot*, banning the Bomb, Ezra P. I would be dying for a hot bath. I admired their resilience; they could stay up all night gabbing, eating nothing but dexedrines and cough syrup. I'd say, 'Hell, I hate to be a party-pooper, but –' and crawl off to bed, hearing, *And I have seen* – all the way to my room. The next morning I'd see them stretched out on the floor, paired up but still chastely in their clothes, all of them sleeping in their shoes.

They invented a past for me. I deserved it; I had not told them a thing about myself. They intended flattery, but the stories were truly monstrous. 'You've got a wife and kids somewhere, haven't you?' a girl whispered to me in my attic, candid in the dark after love. Another, rolling over, said, 'Do anything you want to me – I know you're a switch-hitter.' I was a genius; I was a deserter; I was shell-shocked; I was a refugee; I sometimes took a knife to bed; the Germans had tortured me. The stories were too ridiculous to deny, the truth too boring to repeat. I had grown to like the kids: I did not want to disappoint them.

It ended badly. The coffee-shop was in a residential area, and the late nights the kids spent discussing music and poetry were interpreted by the neighbours as sex orgies. We got strange phone calls, and visits at odd hours from well-dressed men. Then the police raided us. I say 'raided'. Two cops opened the door and said, 'We've had a complaint about you.'

'Let's see your search warrant,' I said. It seemed a good gambit, but they weren't buying it.

'Out of the way, fatso,' they said, pushing past me. They went upstairs, rousing people and saying, 'Nothing here' and 'Okay in here'. Soon they were back in the hall, surrounded by angry poets and pretty girls.

One cop showed me his white glove. The palm was filled with dexedrines. 'Whose are these?'

They weren't mine. I had stopped taking them, though I still passed them around. I said, 'Mine.'

'No, they're not,' said a girl named Rita. 'Those are mine.'

'They're his,' said the cop, 'so shut up.'

'Anyway, what's the problem?' I said. 'I take these things to kill my appetite. I got a weight problem.'

'You got a problem, fella,' the cop said, 'but it ain't no weight problem. Better come along with us.'

Rita screamed at him.

In the squad car the cop driving said, 'We know all about you and those kids. You should be ashamed of yourself.'

I was charged with possessing drugs without a prescription, procuring drugs for a minor, and, on hearsay, with fornication, bigamy, homosexuality and petty theft. My trial would be in three weeks. Bail was steep, but the coffee-shop fellers and some sympathetic faculty members started a fund and bailed me out; they told me I was being victimized.

Jumping bail was easy; the only loss was the money. I took a Greyhound bus to Los Angeles and, leaving everything including my name, flew to Hong-Kong and signed on on the *Allegro*. It was not despair; it was the convenience of flight, an expensive exit that was possible because it was final. I had no intention of going back. It would have been bad for my heart, and I'm using that word in its older sense.

And: 'Flowers,' said the skipper of the *Allegro*, reading my name from the crew list. He made a mark on the paper. 'Age – thirty-eight. Single. No identifying marks or scars.' He looked up. 'Your first contract, I see. Know anything about oiling?'

'No,' I said, 'but I don't think it would take me long to learn.'

'What *can* you do?'

'Anything,' I said. 'I suppose you've heard this one before, but what I really wanted to do was write.'

'Take that pencil,' the skipper said.

'This one?' I selected one from a pewter mug on his desk.

'And that pad of paper.'

The letterhead said, *Four Star Shipping Lines*.

'Write,' he said.

'Shoot,' I said.

'Carrots, eighty pounds,' he said. 'White flour, two hundred pounds. Fresh eggs –'

II

A year later, nimble in my soft white shoes, I was guiding a deeply tanned cruise passenger in his club blazer through the low sidewalk corridors of Singapore back-lanes. It was night, dark and smelly in the tunnel-like passageways, and quiet except for the occasional snap of mah-jong tiles and the rattling of abacus beads coming from the bright cracks in burglar doors on shop-house fronts. Some shops, caged by protective steel grates, showed Chinese families sitting at empty tables under glaring bulbs and the gazes from the walls of old relations with small shoulders and lumpy heads in blurred brown photograph ovals – the lighted barred room like an American museum-case tableau of life-size wax figures depicting Chinese at night, the seated mother and father, ancestral relics, and three children's little heads in a coconut row at the far edge of the table. Sikh watchmen huddled, hugging themselves in bloomers and undershirts, on string beds outside dark shops; we squeezed past them and past the unsleeping Tamil news vendors playing poker in lotus postures next to their shuttered goods cupboards. Here was a Chinese man in his pyjamas, crouching on a stool, smoking, clearing his throat, watching the cars pass. Farther along, four children were playing tag, chasing each other and shrieking in the dark; and under a street-corner lamp a lone child tugged at an odd flying toy, a live beetle, captive on a yard of thread – he flung it at us as we passed and then pulled it away, laughing in a shy little snort.

'Atmosphere,' murmured the feller.

'You said it.' There was a quicker way to Muscat Lane, but that took you over uncovered sidewalks, past new shops, on a well-lighted street. The 'atmosphere' was an easy detour.

'It's like something out of a myth.'

'Too bad the shops are closed,' I said. 'One down this way has bottles filled with dead frogs and snakes – right in the window. Frog syrup. Sort of medicine. The mixture – two spoonfuls three times daily. Hnyeh!'

'You seem to know your way around.'

'Well, I live here, you see.'

'Funny, meeting someone who actually *lives* in a place like this,' said the feller. 'I'm glad I ran into you.'

'Always glad to help out. You looked a bit lost,' I said. I had met him in the Big South Sea, and all I had said – it was my new opening – was, 'Kinda hot'. 'By the way, it's not very far from here.'

'Wait,' he said, and touched my arm. 'Is that a rat?'

A smooth dark shape, flat as a shadow, crept out of the monsoon drain and hopped near a bursting barrel.

'Just a cat,' I said. 'Millions of them around here.' I stamped my foot; the rat turned swiftly and dived back into the drain. 'A small pussy cat.'

'I've got a thing about rats.' There was a child's fearful quaver in his voice.

'So do I!' I said, so he would not be embarrassed. 'They scare the living daylights out of me. Feller I know has dozens of them in the walls of his house. They scratch around at night –'

'Please.'

'Oh, sorry,' I said. 'Not to worry. Take a left – mind your head.'

We passed under a low black archway into Sultana Street – a darkened shop-house smelling gloriously of cinnamon made me slow down to take a good whiff of the sweet dust in the air – then we turned again into an alley of wet cobblestones where there was no sidewalk, Muscat Lane.

'I never would have found this place alone,' the feller said behind me, and I could tell by his voice that he had turned to look back. He was nervous.

'That's what I'm here for!' I said, trying to calm him with heartiness. 'I just hope they're not all asleep.' I stopped at an iron gate, the only opening in a high cement wall, burglar-proofed with rows of sharp iron crescents instead of broken glass bristles. The house had once belonged to a wealthy Muslim, and the iron gate was worked in an Islamic design. Across the alley, four yellow window-squares in the back of a shop-house illustrated the night: a Chinese man and wife faced each other in chairs at one; above them a schoolboy, holding a fistful of his hair, wrote at a desk; next to him, an old man looked into a mirror, scraping his tongue with a stick; and in the yellow window under the old man's an old lady nuzzled an infant.

'It's night,' said the feller, 'but it's so hot! It's like an oven.'

A padlock chained to the bars held the gate shut. I was rapping the lock against a bar.

'Yes?' A dim face and a bright flashlight appeared at the side of the gate.

'Mr Sim, is that you?'

'Jack,' said Mr Sim.

'Yeah, how are they treating you? I thought you might be in the sack. Look, have you got a girl you can spare?'

'Got,' said Mr Sim.

'Good, I knew I could count on you. But the thing is, we're in kind of a rush. My friend's ship is leaving in the morning –'

'Six-twenty,' said the feller anxiously, still glancing around.

'– and he doesn't want one too old,' I said. The feller's instruction meant he wanted one younger than himself; that was simple – he was over sixty, and no hooker downtown was over thirty. I went on to Mr Sim, 'And she has to be nice and clean. They're clean, aren't they? The feller was asking about that.'

'Clean,' said Mr Sim.

'Fine,' I said. 'So can we come in and have a look-see?'

'Can,' he said. He undid the chain and swung the gate open. 'Come in, please.'

'A red light,' said the feller. 'Appropriate.'

'Yes, sir, appropriate all right!' I said, stepping back. 'After you.'

He was mistaken, but so pleased there was no point in correcting him. The red light was set in a little roofed box next to the door. It was a Chinese altar; there was a gold-leaf picture inside, a bald, fanged warrior-god, grinning in a billowing costume, wearing a halo of red thunderbolts. He carried a sword – a saint's sword, clean and jewelled. A plate of fresh oranges, a dish of oil and a brass jar holding some smoking joss-sticks had been set before him on a shelf. The feller had seen the light but not the altar. It was just as well: it might have alarmed him to know that the girls prayed and made offerings to that fierce god.

'Cigarette?' asked Mr Sim, briskly offering a can of them. 'Tea? Beer? Wireless?' He flicked on the radio, tuned it to the English station and got waltz music. 'I buy that wireless set – two week. Fifty-over dollar. Too much-*lah*. But!' He clapped his hands and laughed, becoming hospitable. 'Sit! Two beers, yes? Jack! Excuse me.' He disappeared through a door.

'So far, so good,' said the feller, fastidiously examining the sofa cushion for germs before he sat down and looked around.

He seemed satisfied. It was what he expected, obviously the parlour of a brothel, large, with too much furniture, smelling of sharp perfume and the dust of heavy curtains, and even empty, holding many boisterous ghosts and having a distinct shabbiness without there being anything nameably shabby in it. The light bulb was too small for the room; the uncarpeted floor was clean in the unfinished way that suggested it was often very dirty and swept in sections. It was a room which many people used and anyone might claim, but in which no one lived. The calendar and clock were the practical oversized ones you find in shops; the landscape print on the wall and the beaded doilies on the side tables looked as if they had been left behind rather than arranged there, and they emphasized rather than relieved the bareness. The room was a good indicator of the size and feel of the whole house, a massive barge-like structure moored at Muscat Lane. Outside, the date 1910 was chiselled into a stone shield above the door; the second-floor verandah had a balcony of plump glazed posts – green ones, like urns; the tiled roof had a border of carved wooden lace and barbed wire – antique enough to look decorative – was coiled around the drainpipes and all the supporting columns of the verandah.

The feller sniffed: he knew where he was. In the room, as in all brothel rooms, a carnal aroma hung in the air, as fundamental as sweat, the exposed odour from the body's most private seams.

'Ordinarily,' I said, 'Mr Sim wouldn't have opened up for just anyone. Like I say, he knows me. They all do. Not that I'm bragging. But it's the convenience of it.'

'I'm very grateful to you,' he said. He was sincere. The house on Muscat Lane was a classic Asian massage parlour and brothel. If it had been a new semi-detached house on a suburban street he would not have stayed. But when he spoke there was the same nervous quaver in his voice as when he had spied the rat. He was trembling, massaging his knees.

That made half the excitement for a feller, the belief that it was dangerous, illegal, secretive; the bewildering wait in a musky anteroom, swallowing fear in little gulps. A feller's fear was very good for me and the girls: it made the feller quick; he'd pay without a quibble and take any girl that was offered; he'd fumble and hurry, not bothering to take his socks off or get under the sheet. Fifteen minutes later he'd be out of the room, grinning sheepishly, patting his belt buckle, glancing sideways into a mirror to see whether he was scratched or bitten – and I'd be home early. I disliked the fellers who had no nervous enthusiasm, who sat sulkily in chairs nursing a small Anchor, as gloom-struck and slow as if they were at the dentists, and saying, 'She's too old' or 'Got anything a little less pricy?'

'I wonder what's keeping your friend?' said the feller, leaning over to look through the door. The movement made him release one knee; that leg panicked and jumped.

'He'll be along in a jiffy,' I said. 'He's probably getting one all dolled-up for you.'

'I was going to ask you something,' the feller said. 'The purser on the ship said there were pickpockets here. People in Singapore are supposed to be very light-fingered.'

'You don't have to worry about that,' I said.

'I was just asking,' he said. 'The purser lost a month's salary that way.'

'It happens, sure,' I said. 'But no one can take that fat pigskin thing you cart around.'

'How did you –?' He hitched forward and slapped his backside. 'It's *gone*!'

I pulled his wallet out of my pocket and threw it over to him. 'Don't get excited. I pinched it when we saw the rat. It was hanging out a mile – I figured you might lose it.'

The explanation upset him. He checked to see that all the money was there, then tucked the wallet inside his blazer. 'So it *was* a rat.'

'Well –' I started, and tried to laugh, but at that moment Mr Sim came through the door with Betty, who was carrying a tray with two beers and some cold towels on it.

'Hi, sugar,' I said.

The nut-cracker, I called her, because her legs were shaped exactly like that instrument; she was not simply bow-legged – her legs had an extraordinary curvature and the way they angled into the hem of her skirt gave no clue to how they could possibly be hinged. Her legs were the kind a child draws on the sketch of a girl, a stave at each side of a flat skirt.

Betty poured the beers and handed us each a cold towel with a pair of tongs. She took a seat next to the feller and waited for him to wipe his face with the towel and have a sip of the beer before she put her brave hand casually into his lap. The feller clutched his blazer, where he had stuck the wallet.

'You like *boochakong*?' asked Betty.

The feller looked at me. 'They understand that my ship is leaving at six-twenty?'

'She know,' said Mr Sim. 'I tell her. Betty very nice girl. She . . . *good*.'

'She's a sweetheart. She'll really go to town on you,' I said to the feller; and to Betty, 'You take good care of him – he's an old pal of mine.' I stood up. 'Well, nice meeting you.'

'You're not going, are you?' said the feller. He plucked Betty's hand out of his lap and stood up.

'Things to do,' I said, burying my face in the cold towel. 'I've got to get some rest – the fleet's in this week. Those fellers run me ragged.'

'I'll never find my way back.'

'Can ring for a taxi,' said Mr Sim. 'Where you are dropping?'

The feller was beside me. 'Stay,' he whispered, 'please. I'll pay for your trouble.'

'No trouble at all,' I said. 'I just wanted to help you out. You looked lost.'

'I'll treat you to one,' he said confidentially.

'It doesn't cost me anything,' I said.

'I thought maybe you were doing this for the money.'

'I get my share from Mr Sim,' I said. 'Don't worry about that.'

'So there's no way I can get you to stay?'

'You can ask.'

'I'm *asking*, for Pete's sake!'

'Okay, I'll hang on here,' I said. 'Take your time.'

'Thanks a million,' he said, and nodded in gratitude.

'What your name?' asked Betty, steering him out of the room, carrying his glass of beer.

'Oh, no you don't!' I heard the feller say to her on the stairs.

'He'll be back in ten minutes,' I said to Mr Sim.

'No, no!' said Mr Sim. 'Rich fella – old man. Half-hour or more-*lah*.'

'Bet you a fiver.'

'Bet,' said Mr Sim, eager to gamble.

We put our money on the table and checked our watches.

'Quiet tonight,' I said.

'Last night! English ship! Fifty fella!' He shook his head. 'All the girls asleeping now. Tired! You like my new wireless set?'

'Nifty,' I said. 'Nice tone. It's a good make.'

'The fella come back, he want me to eat a mice?'

It was Mr Sim's party trick. He ate live ones whole to astonish and mortify rowdy seamen; he appeared beside a feller who was getting loud and offered a handful of them. When they were refused, Mr Sim would dangle one before his mouth, allowing it to struggle, and then pop it in like a peanut, saying, 'Yum, yum!' It was a shrewd sort of clowning, and it never failed to quiet a customer.

'I don't think so,' I said. 'Might give him a fright. He's scared of rats.'

'Rats.' Mr Sim laughed. 'During Japanese occupation we eating them.'

'Rat *foo yong*,' I said. 'Yech.'

'No,' Mr Sim said, seriously. 'Egg very scarce. We make with *tow foo*, little bit chillies and *choy-choy*.' He wrinkled his nose. 'We hungry-*lah*.'

'I'm not scared of rats,' I said. 'But I really hate cockroaches. I suppose you could say I'm scared of them.' And what else? I thought – odd combinations: locked rooms, poverty, embarrassment, torture, secret societies, someone in a club asking me 'Who are you?', death.

'Aren't you scared of anything, Mr Sim?'

'No,' he said firmly, and he looked handsome.

'What about the police?'

'These Malay boys? I not scared. But they making trouble on me.'

'Buy them off,' I said.

'I buy-*lah*,' he said. 'I give *kopi*-money. Weekly!'

'So what's the problem?'

'These politics,' said Mr Sim. 'The other year some fella in here shopping votes – "Okay, Sim *Xiensheng*, vote for me-*lah*" – and now they wanting close up house. Pleh!' He laughed – the insincere, unmodulated Chinese cackle, the mirthless snort of a feller surprised by a strong dig in the ribs. It was brief, it had no echo. He said, 'They close up house – where can we go? What we can do?'

'Go some place where they can't find you,' I said. 'I know a few.

I've been playing with the idea of starting up on my own, something really fancy.' Mine would be at the edge of town, a large house with stained-glass windows – dolphins, lilies and white horses – to keep the sun out; an orchestra in the parlour – six black South Indians with brilliantined hair, wearing tuxedos, playing violins; silk cushions on the divans, gin drinks and sweet sherbets. 'Jack's place', they'd call it.

Mr Sim laughed again, the same reluctant honking. 'You not start a house. You get trouble.'

'Well, no more than you.'

'More,' said Mr Sim, and he showed me his face, the Hakka mask of a tough pug, the broad bony forehead, no eyebrows, just a fold, the swollen eyes and lower lip thrust out and the hard angular jaw. He said again, 'More.'

The door opened.

'Hi there,' said the feller, moving quickly towards us. 'Sorry to keep you waiting.'

Mr Sim looked at his watch and grunted.

'That's mine, I believe,' I said, and scooped up the ten dollars from the table.

The feller sat down. Betty brought him a glass of tea and a hot towel. The feller wiped his hands thoroughly, then started on his chin, but thought better of it and made a face; he dropped the towel on the tin tray. 'Shall we go?'

'I'll just knock this back,' I said, showing him my glass of beer. 'Won't be a minute.'

He had crossed his legs and was kicking one up and down and attempting to whistle. What looked like impatience was shame.

'Betty . . . *good*,' said Mr Sim.

'Very pleasant,' said the feller. But he avoided looking at Betty as he said so. To me, he said, 'You must find Singapore a fascinating place. I wish we had more time here. We've got three days in Colombo, then off to Mombasa – a day there – then –'

'Nice watch,' said Mr Sim. 'Omega. How much?'

'Thank you,' said the feller, and pulled his sleeve down to cover it. 'Er, shouldn't we be going?'

'Plenty of time,' I said. 'It's only a little after eleven. Say, how'd it go inside?'

'Not, um, too bad,' he said, still kicking his leg. 'Say, I really think we must –'

'Jack,' said Betty.

'Yoh?'

'He got one *this big*!' She measured eight inches with her hands. It was a vulgar gesture – the feller winced – but her hands were so small and white, the bones so delicate, they made it graceful, turning the coarseness into a dancer's movement. Only her open mouth betrayed the vulgarity. I saw a tattoo on her arm and reached over to touch it.

'That's pretty,' I said. 'Where'd you get it?'

'No,' she said. She covered it.

The feller coughed, stood up and started for the door.

'See you next time,' said Mr Sim.

'Thanks a lot,' I said.

'Don't mention. Bye-bye, mister,' he called to the feller. Then Mr Sim drew me aside. 'You taking girls out to ships, some people they don't like this, but I say forget it. Everybody know you a good fella and I say Jack my friend. No trouble from Jack. Two hand clap, one hand no clap. But you listen. You don't pay *kopi*-money. You don't start up a house, or –' He rubbed his nose with the knuckles of his fist and looked at the floor, saying softly, 'Chinese fella sometime very awkward.'

'Don't worry about me,' I said.

'Would it be safe to take a taxi?' the feller asked when we got to the corner of Sultana Street.

'Oh, sure,' I said, and flagged one down.

On the way to the pier I said, 'It's rather late for intros, but anyway. My name's Jack Flowers – what's yours?'

'Milton,' he said quickly. 'George Milton. If you're ever in

Philadelphia it'd be swell to see you. I wish I had one of my business cards to give you, but I'm fresh out.'

'That's all right,' I said. He was lying about his name, which on the I.D. card in his wallet was W. M. Griswold; and his address was in Baltimore. It might have been an innocent lie, but it hurt my feelings: he didn't want to know me. I had rescued him, and now he was going away.

'The first thing I'm going to do when I get down to my cabin is brush my teeth,' he said. The taxi stopped.

'I don't blame you, George,' I said.

'Will you take twenty bucks?'

'Now?' I said. 'Yes.'

'Be good,' he said, handing it over.

It was still early and I was within walking distance of the sea-front bars. I strolled along the pier, stepping carefully so I wouldn't get my shoes dirty on the greasy rope that lay in coils between the parked cars and taxis. At Prince Edward Road, near the bus depot, two fellers were standing under a streetlamp trying to read what looked like a guidebook. They were certainly tourists and probably from Griswold's liner; both wore the kind of broad-brimmed hat strangers imagine required headgear in the tropics. It gave them away instantly: no one in Singapore wore a hat, except the Chinese at funerals.

I walked over to them and stopped, rattling coins in my pocket with my fist and negligently whistling, as if waiting for a bus. Their new shoes confirmed they were strangers. I could tell a person's nationality by his shoes. Their half-inch soles said they were Americans.

'Kinda hot.'

They turned and enthusiastically agreed. Then they asked their reckless question in a mild way. I nodded, I whistled, I shook my jingling coins; I was the feller they wanted.

It was so easy I could not stop. I hustled at a dead run until the streets were empty and the bars closed. New to the enterprise, I had the beginner's stamina. It wasn't the money that drove me; I can't call it holy charity, but it was as close to a Christian act as that sort of friendly commerce could be, keeping those already astray happy and from harm, within caution's limits. I raided my humanity to console them with reminders of safety, while reminding myself of the dangers. I was dealing with the very innocent, blind men holding helpless sticks; their passions were guesses. It especially wounded me that Griswold had lied about his name: in my conscientious shepherding I believed I was doing him, and everyone, a favour.

Guiding rather than urging, I paid close attention to a feller's need and was protective, adaptable and well known for being discreet. In those days it mattered, and though I acted this way out of kindness, not to impress anyone as a smoothie, it won me customers. There were so many then, and they were so grateful. I shouldn't remember Griswold among them, for he was so typical as to be unmemorable – something about the very desire for sex or the illicit made a feller anonymous without trying. But Griswold had lied; the lie marked him and identified his otherwise nameless face and brought back that evening. His distrust made me relax my normally cautious discretion, and for years afterward if a feller said he was from Baltimore I replied, 'Know a feller named Griswold there?' Some knew him, or said they did, and one night a feller said, 'Yes, we were great friends. That was such a damned shame, wasn't it?' And I never mentioned him again, this man who had refused my grace.

12

The house on Muscat Lane was one of several in Singapore that did business in the old way. Any port is bound to cater for the sexually famished, but the age and wealth of a city, until recently, could be determined by how central the brothels were. Once, in old and great cities, they were always convenient, off shady boulevards, a stone's throw from the state house; in the post-war boom they went suburban to avoid politicians and high rents; then they moved back to the centre – Madam Lum's place was near a supermarket – and it was no longer possible to tell from their location the city's age, though prosperity could still be measured by the number of whores in a place: the poorest and most primitive, having none, made do with forced labour, blackmail or unsatisfying casual arrangements in ditches and alleyways and in the rear seats of cars.

Singapore was very old then, not in years but in attitude and design because of the way the immigrants had transplanted and continued their Chinese cities, duplicating Foochow in one district, Fukien in another. As a feller who had seen Naples and Palermo duplicated in the North End of Boston, down to building styles, hawkers' cries, gangster practices and patron saints, I understood that traditional instinct to preserve. The completely Chinese flavour of vice in Singapore made it attractive to a curious outsider, at the same time releasing him from guilt and doubt, for its queer differences (Joyce Li-ho had the tattoo of a panther leaping up her inner thigh) made it a respectable diversion, like the erotic art anthropologists solemnly photograph, maharani and maharajah depicted as fellatrix and bugger on the Indian temple. The sequence of activities in a Chinese brothel parodied oriental hospitality: the warm welcome – the host bowing from the waist – the smoke, the chat, the cold towel, then the girl – usually the feller chose from one in a parade; money changed hands in the bedroom when the feller was naked and excited; then the stunt itself, and afterwards a hot towel and a glass of cold tea on the verandah while some old *amahs* ironed bedsheets and yapped beyond the rail.

It was the Chinese host's puritanism, his ability to make pleasure into a ritual, that added so much enjoyable delay to it. And though the Chinese customers, with a hare-like speed, treated the whole affair with no more concern than we would in popping out for a quick hamburger, the fellers I took along, mainly gawking travellers bent on carrying away an armload of souvenirs, welcomed the chance to enter, and more than enter – participate in – a cultural secret, to be alone with the exotic oriental girl in a ceremonial state of undress, and later to have that unusual act of love to report upon. It was much appreciated because it was perfect candour, private discovery, the enactment of the white bachelor's fantasy, the next best thing to marrying a sweet obedient Chinese girl. I could provide, without danger, the ultimate souvenir: the experience, in the flesh, of fantasy.

By never putting a price on my services, and by joking about the enterprise the feller would take so seriously – Americans treating it, they'd say, as part of their education, continentals looking on it as a kind of critical therapy, the English preferring not to discuss it – I always came out better. I was prompt and responsive; I didn't insist on my presence; and I had a sense of humour.

'That was quite an experience,' the feller would say, his face flushed.

'Glad you approved,' I'd say, hailing my tri-shaw for the ride home.

'You've been a great help. Really, I –'

'Don't mention it. It's just a question of mind over matter, ain't it?'

'How's that?'

'I don't mind and you don't matter – hyah!'

My dedication to these souls, whom anyone else would call suckers, was so complete it made me unselfish in a way that calmed and rewarded me, for paradoxically it was this unselfish dedication that was commercially useful – I was making money. I was not so much a fool as to think that the money had been virtuously earned – there was no brotherhood in a cash transaction; my small virtue was a fidelity to other people's passion, but I would not martyr myself for it, I expected some payment. I was not a pimp with a heart of gold; however, I knew and could prove that I had saved many fellers from harm and many girls from brutes – not only from greedy cabbies, but from the curfew districts controlled by the secret societies, the streets where all the pretty girls were men with *kukris* in their handbags, the girls with pox, the sadists, the clip-joints, the houses you came away from with the fungus on your pecker known as 'Rangoon itch'. 'I've saved a lot of fellers from Rangoon itch in my time' is hardly a saintly testimony, but it might be the epitaph of a practical man who gave relief the only way he could, trusting instinct and operating in the dark. I took blame, I risked damnation, I didn't cheat: *A Useful Man*, my tombstone motto would go. I was a knowledgeable friend in a remote place, able to read obscure and desperate verbal signals; with a deliberate corny sense of humour – the undemanding comedy that relaxed the fellers by avoiding all off-colour or doubtful jokes, specifically the ones relating to lechery, which in the circumstances could only annoy the fellers by mocking or challenging their heat.

And Singapore helped. It was that atmosphere that had been exported with the immigrants from China and the olde-worlde style of the city's subdivision into districts. To say that there was only one street in Singapore where you could buy a mattress is to describe the rigidness of the pattern; ship chandlers occupied one street, coffin-makers another, banks another, printeries another. Brothels took up a whole block, mixed higgledy-piggledy with Chinese hotels, from Muscat Lane to Malacca

Street, and the area was self-contained, bordered on one side by bars and noodle shops and on the other by laundries and pox doctors.

'It's like something out of a myth,' Griswold had said. Without fuss, the excesses of Shanghai were available in the dream district – opium dens here, brothels and massage parlours and cockfights there – constructed by the wishful immigrant who in his homesick fantasy remembered a childhood longing for wealth and provided for his pleasure with the tourists' subsidy. An American appropriately complimented the unreality of it by saying, 'It's just like a movie!'

'Jack, I want to tell you I feel very lucky,' the same feller went on. 'Give them a few years and they'll pull this all down and build over it – apartment houses, car parks, pizza joints, every lousy thing they can think of. Tokyo's already getting commercialized.'

We were on Sago Lane, near Loon's Tip-Top; through the upstairs window of Loon's we could see two Chinese girls in red dresses, one smoking and looking out at the sky, the other combing her long hair.

'They'll put a gas station there or some dumb thing. It gives me the creeps to think about it,' he said. 'It'll just ruin it.'

'It makes my blood boil,' I said. But I could not match his anger.

Then he said something I have thought of many times since. 'I feel damned lucky,' he said. 'At least I can say I knew what it was like in the old days.'

Nineteen fifty-nine! The old days!

But he was right; it *was* pleasant then, and it changed. Answering the squalor of the city were the girls; noiseless and glittering and narrow as snakes, they looked like anyone's idea of the oriental concubine. That was theatrical, a kind of costuming: the whore's mask depicted the client's sexual ideal – they were expected to pose that way, as in white shoes I was expected to look like a pimp. It was the nearest word, but it didn't describe me: I was too gentle. The girls were practical and businesslike.

Their obsession was with good health, and they treated their tasks like ritual medicine or minor surgery, assisting like sexy nurses, those dentist's helpers who work on complicated extractions, bending over a feller's open mouth, making him comfortable and being quick when he grunted unusually. They believed in ghosts and had a horror of hair and kissing and stinks and dirt, and complained we smelled like cheese. Some didn't feel a thing, but just lay there, sacrificed and spread, and might say, 'You are finished, yes?' before a feller had hardly started. Most had the useful skill of the reliable worker, the knack of being able to do their job convincingly and well without having the slightest interest in it, and all had the genius to be remote at the moment of greatest intimacy, a contemplative gift. They were sensationally foul-mouthed, but they swore in English – I was certain from the soft way they spoke to each other in Chinese that they seldom swore in their own language – and had that learner's curious habit of finding it easy to say 'fuck' in another tongue, for a foreign swear-word is practically inoffensive except to the person who has learned it early in life and knows its social limits.

Dirty talk stimulated a lot of fellers, but left others cold. I remember a feller demanding to leave the Honey Bar, and as we left saying disgustedly, 'I could never screw a girl that said "bullshit". Bullshit this, bullshit that. I'm not a machine. I like a girl I can talk to, a little human warmth.'

Many of the girls were modest in a conventional way, which even as a pretence was compellingly sexy in a whore. 'I couldn't get the little doll to take her dress off' was a frequent comment from the fellers, and as no tipping was allowed in the houses no amount of money could persuade the girls to disrobe. Yet far from diminishing their effectiveness it made them sought-after; any variation increased desire and the silk dresses gave these cold quick girls an accidental allure, titillating by flouncy mystification, partly concealing the act in the dark, keeping enough of it quaintly secret for a feller's interest to be provoked. A girl stark naked was not sexy. Hing was driven wild by even a clothed woman on all fours – as long as she was Australian and large; Ogham said the finest pleasure was to stick an ice-pick into a woman's bloomered bottom; and once in the Bandung, when we were on the subject, Yardley said with awful sincerity, 'Jesus, I love to see a woman with her mouth hanging open.'

I knew the girls too well to think of them as kindly and cheerful, but they understood their cues and were dependable. Observe what virtue was in them: obedience, usefulness, reliability, economy – not mortification and solitary prayer. On one occasion, boarding a launch for a run out to a ship, Doris Goh (never absent, never late) stumbled and fell into the water at the quayside. She could not swim and went rigid as soon as she was under. I hauled her out; she was soaking wet, her dress stuck to her, her make-up was streaked and her nice hair-do a heavy rope of loose braid. I told her she could go home if she wanted to, but she said no and soldiered on, earning forty dollars in the wheelhouse while her dress dried on a hanger in the engine room. They were unambitious in some ways, but not at all lazy and didn't steal.

So it surprised me – my amusement crept up on by an old slow fear – when I opened the *Straits Times* and saw, under *Island-Wide Vice Ring Broken – Joo Chiat Raid Nets 35*, a photograph of five girls being dragged by the arms towards a police van while grim Malay policemen watched, sturdily planted on widely spread bandy legs, holding truncheons and riot shields. The girls' faces were very white from the flashbulb's brightness and their astonished eyebrows were high and black, their objecting mouths in the attitude of shouting. That they were objecting did not surprise me – they were indignant, an emotion as understandable in them as in any harmless lathe-operator yanked from his machine. But that particular raid was a great surprise: the Joo Chiat house was thought to be safe, with a Chinese clientele, protected by the fierce Green Triangle secret society whose spider-like and pock-marked members could be seen at any time of the day or night playing cards by the back entrance, their knives and bearing-scrapers close to hand. The article in the paper said this was 'the first raid in an all-out campaign launched by the P.A.P. to rid the island of so-called massage parlours'.

There were two raids the following day. One at an opium den resulted in the arrests of seven elderly men, six of whose worried, sunken-eyed faces appeared in the paper; the seventh was pictured on a stretcher with his hands clasped – he had broken his leg when he slipped trying to escape across a steep tile roof. The second was at a massage parlour very close to Muscat Lane where all the girls, and the décor, were Thai. The raids disturbed me, but the picture I had of it in my mind was not of the girls – it was the terrifying vision of the old addict being hounded in his pyjamas across a clattering rooftop.

I decided to lie low that night at the Bandung. 'You don't understand the political background, Jack,' Yates said. 'I'd steer clear of Chinatown if I were you.'

'Don't say we didn't warn you,' said Yardley.

'I never go to Chinatown,' said Frogget. 'Bloody waste of time.'

'Harry Lee's putting the boot in,' said Smale. 'I hate that little sod.'

'I was just wondering what was going on,' I said.

'Nothing that concerns you,' said Yardley. 'So keep out of it.'

The next morning I went to see Mr Sim. He seemed suspicious at my arriving so early, and reluctantly let me in. I asked him about the raids.

'Must be careful,' he said. 'How Kheng Fatt is keeping, okay?'

'Hing? He's doing all right. I'm only putting in a couple of hours a day, unless I've got business on a ship.'

'So what you are worried? You got a job, neh?'

'If you want to call it that. Look, I earn peanuts there – little-little money. I can't bank on it. If they go on closing the houses down and arresting the girls I'm going to be out of luck. And so are you!'

'Better than in jail.'

'What are you going to do?'

He didn't look at me, but he showed me his face. He said, 'Funny thing. You know new wireless I got? Yes? It don't work now. I *enjoy* that wireless set, but it need repair.'

'Where are you planning to go?' I asked.

He discovered his shirt and smoothed the pockets.

'They say a lot of the cops are plain-clothesmen – you know, Special Branch fellers wearing shirts like mine and plain old pants, pretending they want a girl. They pay up and just before they get into the saddle they say, "Okay, put your clothes on – you're under arrest." I think that's terrible, don't you?'

Mr Sim twisted the tail of his shirt, and he worked his jaw back and forth as he twisted.

'I'll level with you, Mr Sim. The reason I came over is I've got a plan. We know they're trying to close things up – they've already nabbed about a hundred people. So why wait? Why not just put our heads together and set up somewhere safe? Like I was telling you. We'll go where they least expect us, rent a big house up on Thomson Road or near a cemetery, get about ten girls or so and run a real quiet place. Put up a sign in front saying "The Wongs" or "Hillcrest" or "Dunroamin". What do you say to that?'

'It is a very hot day.' He went imbecilic.

'Come on, we haven't got much time. Are you interested or not?'

'It is a hot day,' said Mr Sim. 'I am expecting my auntie.'

'No taxis allowed, only private cars, no *syces*. Girls by appointment. If you think the Dunroamin idea is silly we can put up a sign saying "Secretarial School – Typing and Shorthand Lessons". No one'll know the difference.'

He had twisted his shirt-tail into a hank of rope and now he was knotting it. 'My auntie is very old. I tell her to stop so much smoking – forty-over sticks a day! But old peoples. Kss!'

'Okay, forget it.' I stood up.

Mr Sim let go of his shirt and leaped to the door. 'Bye-bye, Jack. See you next time. Don't mention.'

That night I brought a feller to Muscat Lane. I had met him in a bar on Stamford Road, he had asked me if I knew a good 'cat-house' and I told him to follow me. But the house was in darkness, the shutters were closed and the red light over the altar was turned off. I rapped the lock against the gate-bar, but no one stirred. Mr Sim had run out on me.

'This looks like a wash-out,' the feller said. 'I'm not even in the mood now.'

'They're worried about the cops. There's a political party here that's putting the heat on – trying to close down the whole district. They've got everyone scared. It didn't use to be this way, but maybe if we walk over –'

'I don't know why it is,' said the feller, 'but people are always saying to me, "You should have been here last year." It really burns me up.'

'That's natural,' I said. 'But you gotta understand the political background, you see.'

'Political background is crap,' he said. 'I'm going back to the ship.'

'If there's anything *else* you want, anything at all,' I said. 'I could find you a gal easy enough. Fix you up in a hotel. Bed and breakfast.'

He shook his head. 'I had my heart set on a cat-house.'

'We could try another one,' I said. 'But I don't want you to get in dutch. How would it look if you got your picture in the papers – cripe!'

'Makes you stop and think, don't it?' he said.

'Sure does,' I said. 'But if there's anything else –'

'Naw,' he said, but saying so, he laughed and said again, 'Naw', as if he was trying to discourage a thought. I was hoping he didn't want a transvestite – it would be hours before they'd be on Bugis Street.

'What is it?' I asked in a whisper. 'Go ahead, try me. God, you don't want to leave empty-handed, do you?'

'Naw, I was just kicking around an idea that popped up,' he said, laughing down his nose. 'I don't know, I've never seen one.'

'Seen what?'

He stopped laughing and said gravely, 'Back home they call them skin flicks.'

The room was stifling, with all the shades drawn, and the screen was a bedsheet, which struck me as uniquely repellent. We sat, six of us, wordlessly fixed on the blue squares jumping and flickering on the screen while the rattling projector whirred: the countdown – a few numbers were missing; the title – something about a brush salesman; the opening shot – a man knocking at a door. We fidgeted when the man knocked; no knock was heard; it was a silent film.

The absence of a sound-track necessitated many close-ups of facial expressions; and a story was attempted, for both characters – salesman and housewife – were clothed, implying a seduction, the classic plot of conquest with a natural climax – an older concept of pornography. The salesman wore a tweed double-breasted suit and his hair was slick and wavy. I guessed it was late forties, but what country? The housewife wore a long bathrobe trimmed with white fur, and when she sat down the front flapped open. She laughed and tucked it back together. The salesman sat beside her and rolled his eyes. He took out a pack of cigarettes and offered one, a Camel. So it was America.

He opened his case of samples and pulled out a limp contraceptive and made a face ('Oh gosh!') and shoved it back. Then there was an elaborate business with the brushes, various shapes and sizes. He demonstrated each one by tickling the housewife in different places, starting on the sole of her foot. Soon he was pushing a feather duster under her loosening bathrobe. The housewife was laughing and trying to hold her robe shut, but the horseplay went on, the robe slipped off her shoulders.

I recognized the sofa, a large pre-war clawfoot model with thick velvet cushions, and just above it on the wall a picture of a stag feeding at a mountain pool. The man took off his shoes. This was interesting: he wore a suit but these were workman's shoes, heavy-soled ones with high counters and large bulbous toes – the steel-toed shoes a man who does heavy work might wear. His argyle socks had holes in them and he had a chain around his neck with a religious medal on it. His muscled arms and broad shoulders confirmed he was a labourer; he also wore a wedding ring. I guessed he had lost his job; as a Catholic he would not have acted in a blue movie on a Sunday, and if it was a weekday and he had a job he would not have acted in the movie at all. Through the apartment window the sun shone on rooftops, but I noticed he did not take his socks off. Perhaps it was cold in the apartment. Afterwards he walked back to his wife through some wintry American city and said, 'Hey honey, look what I won – twenty clams!'

The housewife was more complicated. Judging from her breasts she had had more than one child. I wondered where they were. There was a detailed shot of her moving her hand – long perfect fingernails: she didn't do housework. Who looked after her kids? From the way she sat on the sofa, on the edge, not using the pillows, I knew it was not her apartment. She took off the fancy bathrobe with great care – either it was not hers (it was rather big) or she was poor enough to value it. She had a very bad bruise on the top of her thigh; someone had recently thumped her; and now I could see the man's appendix scar, a vivid one.

Two details hinted that the housewife wasn't American: her legs and armpits were not shaved, and she was not speaking. The man talked, but her replies were exaggerated faces: awe, interest, lust, hilarity, pleasure, surprise. She kissed the man's lips and then her head slid down his chest, past the appendix scar – it was fresh, the reason he was out of a job: he had to wait until it healed before he could go back to heavy work. The housewife opened her mouth; she had excellent teeth and pierced ears – a war-bride, maybe Italian, deserted by her G.I. husband (he thumped her and took the children). The camera stayed on her face for a long time, her profile moved back and forth, and even though it was impossible now for her mouth to show any expression, as soon as she closed her eyes abstraction was on her face – she was tense, her eyes were shut tight, a moment of dramatic meditation on unwilling surrender: she wasn't acting.

Mercifully, the camera moved to a full view of the room. On the left there was a wing-chair with a torn seat, a coffee table holding a glass ashtray with cigarette butts in it (they had talked it over – *Are you sure you don't mind?* – perhaps rehearsed it), and on the right the face of a waterstain on the wall, a fake fireplace with a half-filled bottle on the mantelpiece – the Catholic labourer had needed a drink to go through with it. There had been a scene. *If you're not interested we'll find someone else*. And: *Okay, let's get it over with*. It was breaking my heart.

There was a shot of the front door. It flew open and a large naked woman stood grinning at the pair on the floor – this certainly was the owner of the fancy bathrobe (the cameraman's girl-friend?). She joined them, vigorously, but I was so engrossed in the tragic suggestion I saw in their nakedness that I had not questioned the door. It was a silent movie, but the door had opened with a bang and a clatter. The feller beside me had turned around and was saying, 'What do we do now?'

13

With some kidding fictor's touches, by changing the time of day and my tone of voice to make the story truer, by intensifying it to the point of comedy where it was a bearable memory, my escape from the blue movie raid became part of my repertoire and within a year I was telling it at the bar of my own place, Dunroamin: '– Then the Chief Inspector, a Scotty, says to me, "Have I not seen you somewhere before?" and I says, "Not the club, by any chance?" and he says, "Jack, I'll be jiggered – fancy finding you in a place like this!" "I can explain everything," I says. "Confidentially, I thought they were showing *Gone With the Wind*," and he laughs like hell. "Look," he says in a whisper, "I'm a bit short-staffed. Give me a hand rounding up some of this kit and we'll say no more about it." So I unplugged the projector and carried it out to the police van and later we all joked about it over a beer. And, to top it off, I still haven't found out which club he had in mind!'

I walked through the bar at Dunroamin all night, chatting fellers up, introducing the girls and settling arguments.

'If you've got a certain attitude towards cats, you're queer they say. Ain't that right, Jack?'

'Sure. If you want to bugger a male cat, that means you're queer, prih-hih!'

As always, my clowning went over well, but like my new version of the blue movie story it was the clowning that worried me – the comedy struck unexpected notes of despair. I turned my worst pains into jokes to make myself small and to obscure my sick aches; it was my fear of being known well and pitied – my humour was motivated by humility. I sang songs like 'What Did Robinson Crusoe Do with Friday on a Saturday Night?' and, saying

'I wouldn't have anyone here that I wouldn't invite into my own home', I treated Dunroamin – where I had moved in with my *amah* and pets – as another joke. But it was no laughing matter. I had ploughed my whole savings into it. My refusal to admit I took it seriously was my way of guarding against anyone feeling sorry for me if it failed.

It didn't fail; and the feature of it that I had conceived as a joke of last desperation was what saved the house from collapse. The house itself was not large, but it was walled-in and set back from the road. I picked it for its high wall and rented it cheap from a superstitious *towkay*: it was on Kampong Java Road and the rear opened on to the Lower Bukit Timah Road cemetery. Those several acres of tombstones and the fact of the house being associated with some Japanese atrocities accounted for the low rent, but gave me headaches when it came to getting girls to live in. The joke was the Palm Court orchestra: fellers often came and paid my slightly higher bar prices to sit and listen.

Finding girls who didn't believe in ghosts was very difficult – the house was haunted; finding South Indian violinists was easy – many were looking for work. Mr Weerakoon was my first violinist; he was backed up by Mr ('Manny') Manickawasagam and Mr Das. Albert Ratnam played the piano, Mr ('Subra') Subramaniam the 'cello, Mr Pillay the clarinet. Manny, an impressive baritone, sometimes sang, and Subra switched to the accordion for the faster numbers. They turned up punctually at six every evening in their old-fashioned tuxedos and bow-ties, smelling of Indian talcum, breathless after their hike from Serangoon Road. Their hair was neatly parted in the middle, making two patches of brilliantined waves which shook free to glistening black springs as soon as they began playing. Weerakoon, who had a severely large handlebar moustache, made them practise until seven, and he interrupted them constantly, saying, 'No, no, no! – take that from the top again', while looking at me out of the corner of his eye.

He refused praise. I would say, 'A very nice rendition of "Roses from the South".'

'Hopeless. But what to do? Ratnam can't read music.'

'It was very bouncy. I've never heard it played bouncy before.'

'Fast tempo – I think it suits your house. But Pillay was dragging his feet. We need much practice.' And pinching the waxy tails of his moustache, he'd add, 'We shall have umple of trouble with more tricky numbers.'

Weerakoon persuaded me to redecorate the front lounge and turn it into a music room. He had me print a concert card with the selections and intervals listed on it, menu-fashion: he propped this on a music-stand at the door. The orchestra had the effect Mr Sim obtained by swallowing live mice – it fixed restless seamen into postures of calm (later they told me Dunroamin had class). I could see them from the bar, where I stood to greet fellers arriving: a row of rough-looking men with sunburned arms, sitting and listening attentively on the folding chairs. And all night the *scree-scree* from the music room took the curse off the banging bedroom doors and the noisy plumbing, the creaky bedsprings and quacking fans, and that loud way the girls had of washing, sluicing themselves with dippers and gargling at the same time.

The Singapore residents, clubbable ones especially, flattered themselves that the Palm Court orchestra was for them, though some complained, calling Weerakoon and the others 'greasy babu fiddlers'. Some said I should sack them and get a couple of girls to put on a show. But I resisted these suggestions – sex exhibitions saddened me nearly as much as blue movies: this panicky nakedness was desire's dead-end. The Palm Court orchestra, central to what I came to think of as my little mission-station – a necessary comfortable house on the island outpost – was for the seamen. I had discovered something about them that I had been too obtuse or distracted to grasp on the *Allegro*: most men who go to sea are quiet and conservative by nature, an attitude that is fostered by the small protected community on a ship where the slightest disorder can be fatal; even the youngest have elderly cautious tastes – pipe-smoking and hobbies – and few read newspapers; most are anxious in the company of women and very shy on land, natural drunkards and rather unsociable. It was for them that Mr Weerakoon practised the waltz from *Swan Lake*, and he encouraged them to make requests after he had finished the selections listed on the concert card. Then a seaman with a ruined face would lean over, making his wooden chair squawk, and in a gravelly voice ask for 'Brightly Shines Our Wedding Day' or 'Time On My Hands'.

My girls passed out cold towels from trays or leaned against the walls with their thin pale arms folded, or scuffed back and forth in the flapping broken slippers they always wore. In many ways, though it was not my wish – I was still groping to understand my job – Dunroamin was a traditional establishment, with cold towels, hot towels, glasses of tea, offering a massage at five dollars extra and all drinks more expensive than in a downtown bar; the oldest and frailest *amahs* did the heaviest work – yoked themselves to buckets of water and tottered upstairs to fill the huge stone shower jars, scrubbed sheets on the washboards out back, or boiled linen, which they stirred with wooden paddles, in frothy basins of hot evil-smelling water on the kitchen stove. In those same basins, after a quick rinse, they made *mee-hoon* soup and ladled it out to the customers who demanded 'real Chinese food'.

Dunroamin worked smoothly, but it was older than my devising. The system of payment – the chit-pads in the bar, the shakedown in the bedroom – Ganapaty, the *jaga* at the front gate who said, 'I am a dog, only here to bark'; the thickly waxed oxblood-coloured floors in the graceful white house camouflaged by vast *angsana* trees that dripped tiny yellow blossoms and flanked by servants' quarters and a carriage shed, sloping rattan chairs with leg-rests on the top-floor verandah, the light knock on my back room and (though I insisted they call me Jack) the soft cry of '*Tuan*' with the morning tea, the skill of the Indian musicians and Weerakoon's habit of saying 'Blast' when he played a wrong note – it was all a colonial inheritance, and it had fallen to me. But if my whorehouse was a scale model of the imperial dream, I justified my exploitation by adding to it humour and generous charity, and by making everyone welcome.

What Chinese fellers visited us, mostly embarrassed businessmen with names like Elliot Ching and Larry Woo, did so for the same reason the rest of the Chinese stayed away – because my girls made love to red-heads. I watched from my corner of the long bar, near the telephone and Ganapaty's emergency buzzer, greeting arrivals with 'Glad you could make it – what can I do you for?' and later saw them go down the gravel drive, each one depleted, rumpled from having dressed hurriedly – their ties and sometimes their socks stuffed in their back pockets – and wearing the pink face people associate with outrage but which I knew to be the meekness that comes after spending energy in a harmless way. It was pleasant to see them leave with new faces and I was flattered and reassured by their promises of generosity: 'If there's ever anything I can do for you, Jack –'

But I was the host. 'Just settle your bar-bill at the end of the month, thank you, and a very good night to you all.'

I got up early. In my pyjamas at a sunny desk I totalled the previous night's receipts and checked to see that the bar was well stocked and the rooms were clean – in each room a girl would be brushing her hair before a mirror, a houseful of girls brushing: it cheered me. It was a strenuous round of ordering and overseeing, making sure the laundry was done, the pilferage recorded, the grass cut, the house presentable; then I took my shower, cut across the cemetery to Lower Bukit Timah Road, caught the Number 4 Green Line Bus to Beach Road and climbed on to the stool in my little cubicle and took orders from Hing.

In the days when I had hustled on the street and in bars, saying 'Kinda hot' to likely strangers, I had been glad of the safety of Hing's. I knew my job as a water-clerk well enough to be able to do it easily. And though the money was nothing (any of my girls earned more in a week), the stool where I hooked my heels and pored over the shipping pages of the *Straits Times* was important. It was the basis for my visa, a perfect alibi and a place to roost. But the success of Dunroamin made me consider quitting Hing's.

I continued to get friendly promises of attention from the fellers who came to Dunroamin, yet my relationship with them remained a hustler–client one. I was a regular visitor to the clubs and knew most of the members; in the shipping offices of the Asia Insurance Building and in the Maritime Building fellers called me by my first name and said how nice it was to see me. But they never stopped to pass the time of day. The talks I had with them took place at prearranged times and for a specific purpose, and I was seldom introduced to their friends. I was careful not to remind them that I knew more about them than their wives, and seeing them with their wives – by chance after a movie or at a cricket match at the Padang – it amazed me that the fellers came to Dunroamin: their wives were beautiful smiling girls (it was about this time that I had my fling with the Tanglin Club wife whom I reported as being 'ever so nice'). My quickness might have disturbed the fellers. My attention to detail in arranging for girls to be sent out to ships or for club members to make a discreet visit in a tri-shaw for a tumble at Dunroamin could have been interpreted as somewhat suspicious, a kind of criminal promptitude, the blackmailer's dogged precision. Still, most of the fellers insisted I should get in touch if I ever had a problem.

Once, I had one. It was a simple matter. Mr Weerakoon said he needed new violin strings and could not find any in the shops. I knew the importer; I had fixed him up on several occasions. I gave him a telephone call.

'Hi, this is Jack Flowers. Say, I've got a little problem here –'

'I'll ring you back,' he said quickly, and the line went dead.

That was the last I heard from him. I asked about him at his club.

'Why don't you leave the poor chap alone?' one of his pals – also a customer of mine – said. 'You've got him scared rigid. He's trying to make a decent living. If you start interfering it'll all be up the spout.'

That was the last I heard from the pal, too. I got the message and never again asked for a favour. But favours continued to be offered. They sounded sincere. Late at night, after the larking, the contented pink-faced fellers were full of gratitude and goodwill. I had made them that way: I was the kind of angel I expected to visit me. They said I should look them up in Hong-Kong; I should stop over some day and see their ships or factories; I should have lunch with them one day – or the noncommittal, 'Jack, we must really meet for a drink soon'. The invitations came to nothing; after the business about the violin strings I never pursued them. So I stayed at Hing's, as his water-clerk, both for safety and reassurance: it was the only job I could legally admit to having – and soon I was to be glad I had it.

A young Chinese feller came in one evening. It was before six, the place was empty, and I was sitting at the bar having a coffee and reading the *Malay Mail*.

'Brandy,' he said, snapping his fingers at Yusof. 'One cup.'

Yusof poured a tot of brandy into a snifter and went back to chipping ice in the sink.

I knew from his physique that the Chinese feller did not speak much English. The English-educated were plump from milk-drinking, the Chinese-educated stuck to a traditional diet, bean curd and meat scraps – they were thin, weedy, like this feller, short, girlish, bony-faced. His hair was long and pushed back. His light silk sports-shirt fitted snugly to the knobs of his shoulders, and his wrists were so small his heavy watch slipped back and forth on his forearm like a bracelet. He kept looking around – not turning his head, but lowering it and twisting it sideways to glance across his arm.

'Bit early,' I said.

He looked into his drink, then raised it and gulped it all. It was a stagey gesture, well executed, but made him cough and gag, and as soon as he put the snifter back on the bar he went red-faced and breathless. He snapped his fingers again and said, '*Kopi.*'

'No coffee. Cold drink only,' said Yusof.

The feller frowned at my cup. Yusof reached for the empty snifter. The feller snatched it up and held it.

I heard footsteps on the verandah and went to the door, thinking it might be Mr Weerakoon. I faced three Chinese who resembled the feller at the bar – short-sleeved shirts, long hair, sun-glasses, skinny pinched faces. One was small enough to qualify as a dwarf. He swaggered over to a bar-stool and had difficulty hoisting himself up. Now the four sat in a row; they exchanged a few words and the one who had come in first asked for a coffee again.

Yusof shook his head. He looked at me.

'We don't serve coffee here,' I said.

'That is *kopi*,' the feller said slowly. The others glared at me.

'So it is,' I said. 'Yusof, give the gentlemen what they want.'

At once the four Chinese raised their voices, and, getting courage from the little victory, one laughed out loud. The dwarf hopped off his stool and came over to me.

'You wants book?' he asked.

'What kind?'

'Special.' He unbuttoned his shirt and took out a flat plastic bag with some pamphlets inside.

'Don't bother,' I said. 'Finish your coffee and hop it.'

'Swedish,' he said, dangling the plastic bag.

'Sorry,' I said. 'I can't read Swedish.'

'Is not necessary. Look.' He undid the bag and pulled one out. He held it up for me to see, a garish cover. I could not make it out at first, then I saw hair, mouths, bums, arms.

'No thanks,' I said.

'Look.' He turned the page. It was like a photograph of an atrocity, a mass killing – naked people knotted on a floor.

'I don't need them,' I said. He shook the picture in my face. 'No – I don't want it. Yusof, tell this creep I don't want his pictures.'

'*Tuan* –' Yusof started, but the dwarf cut him off.

'You buy,' said the dwarf.

'I *not* buy.'

Now I looked at the three fellers near the bar. The first had swivelled around on his stool. He held the brandy snifter out at arm's length and dropped it. It crashed. Upstairs, a giggle from a girl in a beaverboard cubicle.

'How much?' I asked.

'Cheap.'

'Okay, I'll take a dozen. Now get out of here.'

The dwarf buttoned the pamphlets into his shirt and said, 'You come outside. Plenty in car. You choose. Very nice.'

I shook my head. 'I not choose. I stay right here.'

Glass breaks with a liquid sound, like the instantaneous threat of flood. One feller shouted, *'Yoop!'* I saw Yusof jump. The mirror behind him shattered, and huge pieces dropped to the floor and broke a second time.

'Tell them to stop it!' I said, and went to the door. 'Where's your lousy car?'

A black Nissan Cedric was parked on Kampong Java Road, just beyond the sentry-box where Ganapaty was hunched over a bowl of rice. He was busily pawing at it with his fingers.

'In there,' said the dwarf, opening the trunk.

There were torn newspapers inside. I turned to object. My voice would not work, my eyes went bright red and a blood-trickle burned my neck; I seemed to be squashed inside my eyeballs, breathing exhaust fumes and being bounced.

Believe any feller who, captive for a few days, claims he has been a prisoner for months. My body's clock stopped with the first sharp pain in my head, then time was elastic and a day was the unverifiable period of wakefulness between frequent naps. Time, like pain, had washed over me and flooded my usual ticking rhythm. I swam in it badly, I felt myself sinking; pain became the passage of time, pulsing as I drowned, smothering me in a hurtful sea of days. But it might have been minutes. I ached everywhere.

For a long time after I woke they kept me roped to a bed in a hut room smelling of dust and chickens and with a corrugated iron roof that baked my broken eyes. This gave my captors problems: they had to feed me with a spoon and hold my cup while I drank. They took turns doing this. They untied me, removing everything from the room but a bucket and mattress, and they brought me noodles at regular intervals. My one comfort was that obviously they did not plan to kill me. They could have done that easily enough at Dunroamin. No Chinese will feed a man he intends to kill. Anyway, murder was too simple: they didn't want a corpse, they wanted a victim.

'Money? You want money? I get you *big* money!' I shouted at the walls. The men never replied. Their silence finally killed my timid heckling.

Grudgingly saying 'noodoos', banging the tin bowls down, they continued to feed me. Now and then they opened the shutters on the back window to let me empty my bucket. They didn't manhandle me – they didn't touch me. But they gave me no clue as to why they were holding me.

Confinement wasn't revenge for fellers who lingered at a murder to dig out the corpse's eyes or cut his pecker off and, risking arrest by wasting getaway time, dance triumphantly with it. I guessed they had kidnapped me, but if so – time and pain was shrouding me in the wadded gauze of sleep – something had gone wrong. Often I heard the Cedric start up and drive away, and each time it came back they conversed in mumbles. The Singapore police were poor at locating kidnappers. Even if the police succeeded, what rescue would that be? It would mean my arrest on a charge of living off immoral earnings. Some friend would have to ransom me. In those days wealthy *towkays* and their children lived in fear of kidnappers; they were often hustled away at knife-point, but they were always released unharmed after a heavy payment. Who in the world would pay for my life?

A memory ambushed my hopes. On the *Allegro* a feller had told me a story I remembered in the hut. A loan-shark had worked on a freighter with him. He called him a loan-shark, but his description of the feller's loans made them sound like charity of the most generous and reckless kind, and eventually everyone on the ship owed him money, including the skipper. One day at sea the loan-shark disappeared, just like that. 'We never found him,' said the feller on the *Allegro*, and his wink told me no one had ever looked.

The remembrance scared me and made me desolate, and I believed I would stay that way, in the misery that squeezes out holy promises. But that loneliness was electrified to terror the day my Chinese captors had a loud argument outside my hut. I had felt some safety in their mutters, in the regular arrivals of meals and in the comings and goings of the Cedric; and I had begun to pass the time by reciting my letters of glad news and my litany, *Sir Jack*, *President Flowers*, *King John*, *Bishop Flowers*. I drew comfort from the predictable noises of my captors and their car. My comfort ended with the arguing – that day they didn't bring me food.

I heard it all. The dwarf's name was Toh. He fretted in a high childish voice; the others bow-wowed monotonously. I listened at a crack in the wall, as my empty stomach scolded me and the argument outside grew into a fight. It had to concern my fate – those whinnyings of incredulity and snuffling grunts, smashings and bangings, and Toh's querulousness rising to an impressively sustained screeching. Then it was over.

That night they put the bed back into my room, but I was so hungry and disturbed I couldn't sleep. I was drowsy hours later when I heard the door being unlocked. The morning dazzle of the sun through the door warmed my face. I started to rise, to swing my feet off the bed.

'You stay,' said Toh.

Two fellers began tying me up.

'What's the big idea?' I said. 'You want money? I get you money. Hey, not so tight!'

I considered a fist-fight, working myself into a fury sufficient to beat them off and then making a run for it. I decided against it. Any rashness would be fatal for me. They were small, but there were four of them, and now I looked up and saw a fifth. I had survived so far by staying passive; I was sensible enough to prefer prison to death – to surrender anything but my life. Something else stopped me: I was in my underwear and socks – they had taken my shoes. I wouldn't get far. If I had been dressed I might have taken a chance, but semi-naked I felt particularly vulnerable. I let them go on tying me.

They roped my ankles to the end of the bed and then put ropes around my wrists and made me fold my arms across my chest. I was in a mummy posture, bound tightly to the bed. The fifth man was behind me. I rolled my eyes back and saw that he was stropping a straight razor, whipping it up and down on a smacking tongue of leather.

'Who's he?' Numbness throttled my pecker.

Toh was checking the knots, hooking a finger on them and pulling. Smick-smack went the razor on the strop. Toh pushed at my arms and, satisfied they were tight, said, 'That Ho Khan.'

'Just tell me one thing,' I said in a pitifully unfamiliar voice. 'Are you going to kill me? Tell me – please.'

Toh looked surprised. 'No,' he said, 'we not kill you.'

'Why the razor?'

'Shave,' he said.

The other fellers erupted into yakking laughter. I tried to shift on the bed to see them. It was impossible. I couldn't move.

'You're trying to scare me, aren't you?' I heard smick-smack-smuck.

Toh leaned over and nodded, smiling. His dwarf's face made the smile impish. 'Scare you,' he said, 'and scare udda peoples, too.'

'What do you mean by that?' Smuck-smuck. 'Come on, this is silly. I'm an American, you know. I am! The American Consulate is looking for me!'

'*Mei-guo ren*,' someone said. 'An American.' Another replied in Chinese, and there was laughter.

'Now I give you but,' said Toh. He scrubbed the backs of my arms with a soapy cloth. The others leaned over for a good look. One was holding a bowl, eating noodles as he watched, gobbling them in an impatient greedy way, smacking his lips and snapping at them like a cat, not chewing. He peered at me over the rim of his bowl. He gave me hope. No one would eat that way in the presence of a person about to be slashed.

Ho Khan fussed with the razor. He braced his elbows, one against my throat, one on my stomach, and then, scraping slowly, shaved the hairy parts of my arms that Toh had soaped, from my elbow to the rope at my wrists. To my relief he put the razor aside.

My relief lasted seconds. Ho Khan fitted a pair of wire glasses over his eyes and took a dart-shaped silver tool which he dipped into a bottle of blue liquid. He leaned on me again and with the speed of a sewing machine began jabbing the needle into the fleshy part of my arm. He was tattooing me – biting on his tongue in concentration – and behind him the others shouted bursts of Chinese, seeming to tell him what to write in the punctures.

14

At Newton Circus, by the canal, they pushed me out of the car and sped away, yelling. I found a few wrinkled dollars in the clothes they had handed over, enough for a pack of cheroots and a meal of mutton-chops at a Malay gag-stand on the corner. I was grateful for the night, and glad too for the incuriousness of the Chinese who wolfed food noisily at tables all around me and didn't once look at me. My arms appalled me; I examined them in the light of the stall's hissing pressure-lamp. The shaven backs of my arms were swollen and raw, the fresh punctures tracking up and down from elbow to wrist, the small half-exploded squares of Chinese characters, perhaps fifty boxes, puffed-up and blue and some still leaking blood. I felt better after a meal and a smoke, and left swinging my arms so that no one could see their disfigurement, down the canal path, past the orphanage, in the direction of Dunroamin.

I smelled the acrid wood-smoke, the stink of violence, before I saw the damage; the strength of it, at that distance, telegraphed destruction. The house was gutted. The tile roof had fallen in and the moon lighted the two stucco roof-peaks, the gaping windows, the broken and burned verandah chicks. The abandoned black house looked like an old deserted factory; the fire had silenced the insects and killed the perfume of my flowering trees. No crickets chirped in the compound, a smell of burning hung in the still air. Torn mattresses were twisted and humped all over the driveway and lawn. I was about to go away when, feeling the fatigue and pause of melancholy, I decided that I would enter the house, to try to find something in the ruins that belonged to me, anything portable I could recognize to claim as a souvenir, maybe a scorched clock or the German metronome Mr Weerakoon kept in a cupboard drawer: *There's an interesting story behind this little thing . . .*

I stumbled in the driveway, and stumbling felt like an intruder. Stepping over the splintered front door, I passed through the bar. Broken glass littered the floor. I balanced on fallen timbers, tiptoed into the music room, and there I stood in the decay the fire had made, not wanting to go upstairs to see what had happened to my cats. The staring shadows of the overturned chairs stopped me. I could feel the tattoos aching on my arms.

Then I saw the candle burning in the kitchen, and near it a crouching man, his face lighted by the yellow flame.

The eeriest thing about him, this old scarecrow in the burned-out house, was that he was imperturbably reading a folded newspaper. I would leave him in peace. I started towards the front door and kicked a loose board with my first step. *Bang*. The candle-flame flickered and went out.

'Don't worry,' I called to him. 'I'm not going to hurt you.'

I made my way into the kitchen, found the candle and lit it. The old man had run to the wall where a blanket was spread. He was Chinese and had the look of a tri-shaw-driver, the black sinewy legs and arms, close-cropped hair, a small dark reptile's face. He wore a blue jacket and shorts, and on his feet were rubber clogs cut from tyres.

'You know me, eh? Me Jack.' I laughed. 'This my house!' In that dark, smelly place every sound was weird and my laugh was ghoulish. 'You want smoke?' I threw him a cheroot. He cowered when I brought the candle over for him to light it.

'Me Jack,' I said. 'This my house – Dunroamin.'

He blinked. 'You house?'

'Yeah,' I said. 'All finished now.'

He cackled and said something I couldn't make out.

'You live here now?' I asked. 'Sleep here, eat here – *makan* here, eh?'

'*Makan, makan*,' he said, and picked up a small bowl. He offered it to me. 'You *makan*.'

There were lumps of rice inside, with two yellow pork rinds on top. I took it and thanked him and choked back one of the rinds. It was a sharing gesture and it worked. The poor man was calmed. He went to a tin lunch-pail and spooned some more rice into the bowl.

'No,' I said.

'*Makan*,' he said, and smiled.

I took the bowl and ate a few grains, chewing slowly. I pointed to the newspaper. 'You read, eh? *Sin Chew Jit Poh*?' Naming the paper was like conversation. I thought of another. '*Nanyang Siang Pau*, eh?'

He nodded eagerly and handed me the paper.

I put the bowl down and unfolded the paper, looked at it, said, 'Yes, yes', and gave it back.

He didn't respond. He was looking at my arms. He put a skinny finger on one row of tattoos and, tapping each character, worked his way down, tracing the vertical column. He frowned and tapped at another column, but faster now.

'Chinese,' I said. 'Chinese tattoo.' I grinned.

He backed away, holding an outstretched palm up to ward me off; he groaned distinctly, and he ran, kicking over the tin lunch-pail and tramping the broken boards of the music room and howling down the drive.

That night I slept on the old man's blanket and breathed the fumes from his crudded lunch-pail.

'"Curse of Dogshit",' said Mr Tan, translating in the Bandung the next day. He read my left arm. '"Beware Devil", "Whore's Boy", "Mouth Full of Lies", "Remove This and Die". Very nasty,' said Mr Tan. 'Let me see your other arm.' The right said, 'Red Goat-face', 'Forbidden Ape', 'Ten Devils in One', 'I am Poison and Death', 'Remove This and Die'.

After that, Mr Tan was included in the conversations Yardley had with the others when my tattoos were mentioned. For years Mr Tan had sat every afternoon alone with his bottle of soybean milk. Now he was welcome. Yardley couldn't remember all the curses and he called upon Mr Tan to repeat them.

'Incredible,' Yardley said. 'There, what about that one?'

'"Forbidden Ape",' said Mr Tan promptly.

'Can you imagine,' said Yardley. 'And that one – "Monkey's Arse" or something like that?'

'"Dogshit",' said Mr Tan.

'All right,' I said. 'That's enough.'

'Remember old Baldwin, the chap that worked for Jardine?' asked Smale. 'He had tattoos all over the place. Birds and that.'

'You going to keep them, Jack?' asked Coony. 'Souvenir of Singapore. Show 'em to your mum.'

'You think it's a joke,' I said. 'These things *hurt*. And the doctor says I have to wait till they heal before I can get them off.'

'You'll never get them buggers off,' said Yardley.

'The doctor says –'

'They can graft them,' said Smale.

'Acid,' said Yates. They burn them off with acid. I read about it somewhere. It leaves scars – that's the only snag. But scars are infinitely preferable to what you've got there, if you ask me.'

'Maybe they used some kind of Chinese ink,' said Coony. 'You know, the kind that never comes off.'

'Balls!' said Smale. 'If it was Chinese ink he'd be able to wash the flaming things off with soap and water. No, that there's your regular tattooing ink. You can tell.'

'"Monkey's Arse",' said Yardley, laughing. 'Christ, be glad it's not in English! What if it was and Jack was in London, on a bus or something? "Fares please," the conductor says and looks over and sees "Monkey's Arse", "Pig Shit" and all that on Jack's arm.'

'He'd probably ride free,' said Frogget.

'No, I've got a better one,' said Smale. 'Let's say Jack's in church and the vicar's just given a little sermon on foul language. The lady next to Jack looks down and –'

'Lay off,' I said, rolling down my sleeves to cover the scabrous notations. 'How would you like it if they did it to you?'

'No bloody fear,' said Coony. 'If one of them little bastards –'

'Shut up,' said Yardley. 'They'd tattoo the same thing on your knackers before you could say boo.' Yardley turned to me and said, 'Don't get upset, Jacko. They got ways of getting that stuff off. But I'll tell you one thing – you'd be a fool to try it again.'

'What are you talking about?'

'That whorehouse of yours,' said Yardley. 'You were asking for it. Any of us could have told you that. Right, Smelly?'

'Right,' said Smale.

'So you're saying I deserved it.'

'What do *you* think?'

I said, 'I was making a few bucks.'

'Where is it now?' Yardley nudged Frogget.

'None of your business,' I said.

'Jack thinks he's different,' Yardley said. 'But the trouble is, he's just the same as us, living in this piss-hole, sweating in a *towkay*'s shop. Face facts, Jack, you're the bleeding same.'

'Really?' I said, wondering myself if it was true and deciding it was not.

'Except for that writing on his arms,' said Coony.

Macpherson, an occasional drinker at the Bandung, came through the door. He said, 'Good evening.'

'Hey, Mac, look at this,' Yardley said. He grabbed my arm and spoke confidentially. 'This is nothing compared to what they do to some blokes. You learned your lesson. From now on, stick with us – we'll stand by you, Jack. And just to show you I mean what I say, the first thing we'll do is get that put right.'

'What's it supposed to say?' asked Macpherson.

Mr Tan cleared his throat.

Weeks later, Yardley found a Chinese tattooist who said he knew how to remove them. We met at the Bandung one evening and he looked as if he meant business. He was carrying a doctor's black valise. But he never opened it; he took one look at the tattoos, read a few columns, and was out of the door.

'Look at him go,' said Smale. 'Like a shot off a shovel.'

'A Chink won't touch that,' said Coony.

'So we'll find a Malay,' said Yardley.

The Malay's name was Pinky, and his tattoo parlour was in a *kampong* out near the airport. He was not hopeful about removing them, though he said he knew the acid treatment. But no matter how much acid he rubbed in, he said, I would still be left with a faint but legible impression. And grafting took years.

'Why don't you just cut your arms off and make the best of a bad job?' said Smale.

'Isn't there anything you can do?' I asked Pinky.

'Can make into something else,' said Pinky. 'Fella come in. He tattoo say "I Love Mary" but he no like. So I put a little this and that, sails, what. Make a ship, for a sample.'

'I get it,' I said. He could obliterate the curse but not remove it.

'He puts a different tattoo over it, apparently,' said Yates.

'Only the one on the bottom stays the same,' said Frogget.

'It's better than leaving them like they are,' said Yardley.

The walls of Pinky's parlour were covered with sample tattoos. Many were the same design in various sizes, 'Death Before Dishonour', Indian chiefs, skulls, eagles and horses, 'Sweet-Sour', 'Cut Here', tigers and crucifixes, 'Mother', blue-birds, American flags and Union Jacks. Behind Pinky, on a shelf, were many bottles of antiseptic, Dettol, gauze, aspirin, and rows and rows of needles.

'You'll have a hard job making those into ships,' said Yates, tapping my blue curses.

'Do you fancy a dagger?' asked Smale. 'Or what about the old Stars and Stripes?'

'That's right,' said Coony. 'Jack's a Yank. He should have an American flag on his arm.'

'Fifty American flags is more like it,' said Smale.

'Hey, Yatesie,' said Coony, pointing to the design reading 'Mother', 'here's one for you.'

My arms were on Pinky's table. 'Chinese crackter,' he said. 'I make into flowers.'

So I agreed. But on each wrist the wide single column – 'Remove This and Die' – was too closely printed to make into separate flowers. Pinky suggested stalks for the blossoms on my forearms. I had a better idea. I selected from the convenient symbology on the wall: a dripping dagger on my left wrist, a crucifix on my right.

I went back to Hing's. I was thankful to climb on to my stool and pick up where I left off: vegetables for the *Vidia*, stirrup-pumps for the *Joseph B. Watson*, new cargo nets for the *Peshawar*. It was as if I had never been away. But what counted as an event for the fellers at the Bandung and gave the year I was tattooed the same importance they had attached to the year Ogham left and the year the bees flew through the windows – an importance overshadowing race riots, bombings, Kennedy's death and the threat of an Indonesian invasion – went uncommented upon by Hing. Gopi said, 'Sorry, mister.'

Hing's lack of interest in anything but his unvarying business made him doubt the remarkable. He refused to be amazed by my survival or by the motley blue pictures that now covered my arms. He did not greet me when I came back. He refused to see me as I passed through the doorway. It was his way of not recognizing my long absence: no explanation was necessary. Though he was my own age, his years were circular, ending where they began. He turned the tissue leaves of a calendar that could have been blank. His was the Chinese mastery of disappointment: he wouldn't be woken to taste it, he wouldn't be hurt. Some days I envied him.

I moved into the low sooty semi-detached house on Moulmein Green, an uninteresting affair which the washing on the line in front gave the appearance of an old becalmed boat. My aged *amah* found me and turned up with a bundle of my clothes and two of the cats. She wouldn't say what had happened to the others; she reported that no one had been injured in the fire at Dunroamin. My tattoos intrigued her and when her mah-jong partners came over she asked me if they could have a look. My kidnapping and tattoos raised her status in the neighbourhood. Now and then, for pleasure, I had a flutter at the Turf Club and it was about this time that I persuaded Gopi to be fitted for the brace, but that came to nothing. I slept much more, and on weekends sometimes slept throughout the day, waking occasionally in a sweat and saying out loud, 'It's still Sunday' and then dozing and waking and saying it again.

I did no hustling. Every evening I drank at the Bandung and I became as predictable in my reminiscences as the other fellers; the re-creation of what had gone, a continual rehearsal of the past in anecdotes, old tales sometimes falsified to make the listener relax, made the present bearable. I told delighted strangers about 'Kinda hot', the *Richard Everett*, Dunroamin and my tattooing. 'And if you don't believe it, look at this –'

My fortunes were back to zero, but, as I have said, it was desolation of this sort that gave me more hope than little spurts of success. However uncongenial poverty was, to my mind it was like the explicit promise of a tremendous ripening. I hadn't regretted a thing. But there was something that mattered more than this, to which I was the only witness. My stories glamourized the terror and often I brooded over my capture to look for errors or omissions. I had proved my resoluteness by surviving the torment without denying what I had done – my house, my girls – and at no moment had I gone down on my knees and said a prayer. It wasn't that I didn't think I ought to be forgiven. Forgiveness wasn't necessary. I had nothing to live down. The charitable loan-shark, pitched overboard by his furious debtors, had swum to shore.

15

'You don't know me,' said the foxy voice at the other end of the phone. 'But I met a good pal of yours in Honolulu and he – well –'

'What's the feller's name?' I asked.

He told me.

'Never heard of him,' I said. 'He's supposed to be a friend of mine?'

'Right. He was in Singapore a few years ago.'

'You don't say! His name doesn't ring a bell,' I said. 'What business was he in? Where did he live?'

'I can't talk here,' he said. 'I'm in an office. There's some people.'

'Wait,' I said. 'What about this feller that knows me? Did he have a message for me or something like that?' *Brace yourself. I've got some fantastic news for you. Ready? Here goes* . . . I braced myself.

'Maybe you don't remember him,' he said. 'I guess he was only in Singapore one night.'

'Oh.'

'But that was enough. You know?'

'Look –'

'He, um, *recommended* you. Highly. You get what I'm driving at?'

'What's on your mind?'

'I can't talk here,' he said. 'What are you doing for lunch?'

'Sorry. I can't talk here either,' I said. How did *he* like it?

'A drink then, around six. Say yes.'

'You're wasting your time,' I said.

'Don't worry,' he said. 'Let's have a drink. What do you say?'

'Where are you staying?'

'Something called the Cockpit Hotel.'

'I know where it is,' I said. 'I'll be over at six. For a drink, okay? See you in the bar.'

'How will I recognize you?'

I almost laughed.

'So-and-so told me to look you up.' He was the first of many. He didn't want much, only to buy me a drink and ask me vulgarly sincere questions, 'What's it really like?' and 'Do you think you'll ever go back?' I used to say anything that came into my head, like 'I love lunchmeat' or 'Sell me your shoes.'

'What made you stop pimping?' a feller would ask.

'I ran out of string,' I'd say.

'How long are you going to stay in Singapore?'

'As long as my citronella holds out.'

'What do you do for kicks?'

'That reminds me of a story. Seems there was this feller –'

In previous years the same fellers would have wanted to visit a Chinese massage parlour; now they wanted to see me. The motive had not changed: just for the experience. And evidently stories circulated about me on the tourist grapevine: I had been deported from the States; I was a pederast; I had a wife and kids somewhere; I was working on a book; I was a top-level spy, a hunted man, a rubber planter, an informer, a nut-case. The fellers guilelessly confided this gossip and promised they wouldn't tell a soul. And one feller said he had looked me up because 'Let's face it, Flowers, you're an institution.'

I didn't encourage them. If they wanted a girl I suggested a social escort who, after a tour of the city – harbour sights, Mount Faber, Tiger Balm Gardens, Chinese temples, War Memorial, St Andrew's Cathedral – would amateurishly offer 'intimacy', as they called it. Politics hadn't stopped prostitution; it had complicated it, taken the fun out of it and made it assume disguises. The houses had moved to the suburbs – Mr Sim operated on Tanjong Rhu, in an innocuous-looking bungalow near the Swimming

Club – many had gone to Jahore Bahru, over the Causeway, and all paid heavily for secret-society protection. There were two brothels in town, Madam Lum's, behind the supermarket, and Joe's in Bristol Chambers, across from the Gurkha's sentry-box on Oxley Rise: they were characterless apartments, unpersuasively decorated and they relied on taxi-drivers to bring them fellers.

Oddly enough, the fellers who looked me up were seldom interested in girls. They were tourists who fancied themselves adventurers, bold explorers, and they had two opposing wishes: to be the very first persons to reach that far-away place, and to be seen arriving. They thought it was quite a feat to fly to Singapore, but they needed a reliable native witness to verify their arrival. I was that witness, and the routine was always the same – a drink, a stroll around the seedier parts of town, then a picture, posed with me and snapped by the Indian with the box camera on the esplanade. All these fellers did in Singapore was talk, remarking on the discomfort of their hotels, the heat, the smells, their fear of contracting malaria. And when I told my heavily embroidered tales they said, 'Flowers, you're as bad as me!' Sometimes, with wealthy ones, I wanted to lean across the table and plead, '*Get me out of here!*' But that was the voice of idleness, the one that screamed prayers at the Turf Club and hectored the fruit-machines for a jackpot. I did my best to suppress it and listened to the travellers chuntering on about their experiences. I wish I had a nickel for every feller who told me the story about how he had picked up a pretty girl and taken her back to his hotel, only to find ('I was flabbergasted') that she was really a feller in a swishy dress; or the story, favourite of the fantasist, beginning, 'I used to know this nympho –'

For me these were not productive years. The longer I stayed at Hing's the more I had in common with the fellers at the Bandung: 'My *towkay* says –'. The Sunday curry was the only event in the week I viewed with any pleasure. Though Singapore was awash with tourists and, for the first time, American soldiers on leave from Vietnam, I did very little hustling. The attitude towards sex was changing in the States and I found it hard in Singapore to keep pace with the changes; the new attitudes arrived with the tourists. Fellers were interested in exhibitions of one sort or another, Cantonese girls hanging in back rooms like fruit-bats and squealing 'Fucky, fucky' to each other; sullen displays of grey anatomy on trestle-tables; off the Rochmore Canal Road there were squalid rooms where a dozen tourists sat around a double bed, like interns in a clinic, and applauded cucumber buggeries. The feller who said he was in love with a slip of a girl meant just that; and one joker implored me to get a young Chinese boy to (I think I've got this right) stand over him and, as he put it, 'do number two – oh lots of it – all over me.'

'Now, you're going to think I'm old-fashioned,' I said to this dink. 'And I know nobody's perfect. But –'

I could see nothing voluptuous about being recumbent under a Chinese and shat upon, something I went through, in a sense, every day at Hing's. I would fall into conversation with a tourist and hear myself saying, 'That's where I draw the line.' My notion of sex, call me old-fashioned, was a satisfying and slightly masked and moist surprise, unhurried, private, imaginative and inexpensive, as close to passion as possible, neither businesslike nor over-coy, maintaining the illusion of desire with groans of proof, celebrating fantasy, a happy act the price kept in perspective: give and take, no lies about love.

The anonymous savagery of the new pornography might have had something to do with the change in the tourists' attitude. I had always considered myself a reasonable judge of pornography, but I was out of my depth with the stuff that came in on the freighters and was good-naturedly handed over to me by the mates responsible for the provisioning. It was as unappealing as a pair of empty rubber gloves. I refused to sell it, though I still sold decks of pornographic playing cards. I didn't know what to do with the new cruel sort; I had too much of it to burn discreetly, and someone would have found it if I had thrown it in a trash barrel. I kept it at the Bandung, behind the bar. At the Bandung I was able to confirm that I was not alone in finding it grotesque.

'It's useless,' said Yardley. 'They don't have expressions on their faces.'

'She got *something* on her face,' said Frogget. 'Sickening, ain't it?'

'That's what I always look at first,' said Smale. 'Their faces.'

'Do you suppose,' said Yates, selecting a picture, 'that she expects that bulb to light up if she does that with it?'

'Maybe she blew a fuse,' said Frogget.

'Yeah,' said Smale, 'here she is blowing a fuse.'

''orrible,' said Coony. 'A girl and a mule. Look at that.'

'Let's see,' said Yates. 'No, that's no mule. It's a donkey, what you call an ass.'

'Oh, that's an ass,' I said. 'Oh, yes. Broo-hoo-hoo!'

'Do herself a damage,' said Smale.

''orrible,' said Coony.

'This one's all blokes,' said Yardley. 'All sort of connected-up. I wonder why that one's wearing red socks.'

'Are there names for this sort of thing?' asked Yates.

'I'd call that one "the Bowling Grip",' said Frogget.

'Hey, Wally, come here,' said Yardley.

'Leave him alone,' I said.

'See what he does,' said Yardley.

Wallace Thumboo came over, grinning; he glanced down at the pictures, then looked away, into space.

'What do you think of that, Wally, old boy?'

'Nice,' said Wally. He looked at the ceiling.

'Cut it out,' I said. 'He doesn't like them. I don't blame you, Wally. They're awful, aren't they?'

'Little bit,' he said and screwed up his face, making it plead.

'You said they were *nice*, you lying sod!' Yardley shouted. Wally wrung his hands. Yardley turned to me. 'You're a bloody hypocrite, Jack.'

'These photographs are shocking,' said Yates. 'What kind of people –'

'And he's the one who sells this rubbish!' said Yardley.

'Not this stuff,' I said. 'The other stuff, but only if they ask.'

Edwin Shuck asked. He phoned me one morning at Hing's and said, 'You don't know me –'

'Yes, I do,' I said snappishly. I had wanted for a long time to put one of these yo-yo's in his place, and this was the day to do it. Out in the van a consignment of frozen meat for the *Strode* was going soft in the sun. Little Hing was double-parked on Beach Road and beeping the horn. The *Strode* had a right to refuse the meat if it wasn't frozen solid, which meant we would have to sell it cheap to a hotel kitchen. 'You met a horny feller somewhere who said he was a pal of mine, right?' I accused. 'And he told you to look me up, right? You don't want to take too much of my time, just have a drink, right? And after that –'

'Not so fast,' he said.

'Friend,' I said, 'the only thing I don't know about you is your name.'

'Why don't we have lunch? Then I can tell you my name.'

'I'm busy.'

'After work.'

'For Christ's sake, don't you understand? My meat's getting all thawed out!'

'What's *that* supposed to mean?'

'My meat's in the van,' I said.

'I won't argue about it,' he said.

'So long, then,' I said.

'Give me a chance,' he said. 'Surely the Bandung can spare you for one night?'

The Bandung was my private funk-hole. 'What *is* your name, friend?'

And: 'Eddie Shuck, pleased to meet you,' he said that evening in the floodlit garden of the Adelphi. I had just come from the

Strode where I had spent the whole afternoon on a shady part of the breezy deck playing gin rummy with the chief steward.

'Hope I haven't kept you waiting,' I said.

'Not at all,' said Shuck. 'What'll you have?'

'I usually have a pink gin about this time of day.'

'That's a good Navy drink,' he said, and he called out 'Boy!' to the waiter.

I found that objectionable, but something interested me about this Edwin Shuck. It was his lisp – not an ordinary lisp, the tongue lodged between the teeth, that gives the point to the joke about the doctor who examines the teenage girl with a stethoscope and says, 'Big breaths'; Shuck's was the parted fishmouth: his folded tongue softened and wetted every sibilant into a spongy drunken buzz. He prolonged 'Flowers' with the buzz, and what was endearing was that his lisp prevented him from saying his own name correctly.

'Got some homework, I see.'

'This?' I had a thick envelope on my lap, pornography from the *Strode*, a parting gift from the friendly steward. I said, 'Filthy pictures.'

'Seriously?' Buzz, buzz; he lisped companionably.

'The real McCoy,' I said.

'Can I have a look?'

We were the only ones in the garden. I put the envelope on the table and pulled out the pictures. I said, 'If anyone comes out here, turn them over, quick. We could be put in the cooler for these.'

'You've sure got enough of them!'

'They're in sets. Get them in sequence. Ah, there we are. Starts off nice, all the folks in their skivvies having a cosy drink in the living-room.'

'What's the next one?' Shuck was impatient.

'Now we're in the bedroom. A few preliminaries, I guess you could call that.'

'Kind of a group thing, huh? That gal –'

The waiter came over with our drinks. I flipped the large envelope over the pictures. I wasn't afraid of being arrested for them, but the thought of that old polite Chinese waiter seeing them embarrassed me. Pornography affected me that way: I could not help thinking that whoever looked at the stuff was responsible for what was happening in the picture. That girl, that dog; those kneeling men and vaulting women; those flying bums. A single look included you in the act and completed it. Until you looked it was unfinished.

'Down the old canal,' said Shuck, guzzling his fresh lime. 'Hey, is that the guy's arm or what?'

'No, that's his bugle.'

'His *what*?'

'Pecker, I think.' I turned it over. 'Here are your Japanese ones.'

'You can't see their faces,' he said. 'How do you know they're Japs?'

'By their feet. See? That's your Japanese foot.'

'It's in a damned strange position.'

'This one's blurry. Can't make head or tail of it.'

'Wise guy.' Shuck laughed. 'What else have you got?'

'I've seen this bunch before,' I said. 'From some hamlet in Denmark.'

'I wonder why that guy's wearing red socks.'

'Search me,' I said. 'Got some more – here we are. God, I hate these. I really pity those poor animals.'

'Labrador retriever,' said Shuck.

'Poor bugger,' I said. 'Well, that's the lot.'

'Huh?' Shuck was surprised. He didn't speak at once. He frowned and said thoughtfully, 'Haven't you got any where the guy's on top and the girl's on the bottom, and they're – well, you know, *screwing*?'

'Funnily enough,' I said, 'no. Not the missionary position.'

'That's a riot,' said Shuck.

'It's pitiful,' I said. 'There's not much call for that kind. Here, you can have these if you want. My compliments. Strictly for horror interest.'

'That's mighty neighbourly,' said Shuck. 'Shall we eat here?'

'Up to you,' I said. 'What time is your plane leaving?'

'I'm not taking any plane,' said Shuck. 'I live here.'

'What business are you in? I've never seen you around town.'

'This and that,' he said. 'I do a lot of travelling.'

'Where to?'

'K.L., Bangkok, Vientiane,' he said. 'Sometimes Saigon. How about you? How long do you aim to stay in Singapore?'

'As long as my citronella holds out,' I said. 'What's Saigon like?'

'Not much,' said Shuck. 'I was there when the balloon went up.'

I didn't press him. He was either a spy and wouldn't admit to it, of course, or he was a businessman who was ashamed to say so and took pleasure in trying to give me the impression he was a spy. In any case, hemming and hawing, a mediocre adventurer.

We had a meal at the Sikh restaurant on St Gregory's Place and then went on to a nightclub, the Eastern Palace, where Hing had taken me in my *Allegro* days. Shuck fed me questions – about hustling, the fantastic rumours (a new one: was I the feller who appeared in Whatshisname's novel?), the 'meat-run', Dunroamin, short-time rates, all-nighters. It was the same interview I got from other fellers, the gabbing that was like a substitute for the real thing.

The Eastern Palace had changed. 'Years ago, this place had a bunch of Korean chorus girls and a little Chinese orchestra. It wasn't as noisy as this. There was even a dance-floor.'

'Tell me a little bit more about this Madam Lum,' said Shuck. 'How does she get away with it in town?'

'Good question. She –' But I could not be heard over the roaring of a machine offstage. The curtains parted and in the centre of the stage a girl crouched on a black motorcycle. The back wall slipped sideways – it was a moving landscape, a film of trees and telephone poles shooting past. By concentrating I could imagine that stationary girl actually speeding along a country road.

She flung off her goggles and helmet. A fan in the wings

started up and blew her long hair straight back. She wriggled out of her leather jacket and let that fly. The music became louder, a pumping rhythm that emphasized the motorcycle roar.

'I don't like this,' I said.

Shuck frowned, as he had when he had said, 'Haven't you got any where the guy's on top –?'

The girl stood up on the saddle and kicked off her boots and tore off her breeches. She was buffeted by the wind from the fan; she undid her bra and squirmed out of her pants – they sailed away. Then she hopped back on to the seat, naked, and pretended to ride, bobbing up and down, chafing herself on the saddle.

'I'm shocked,' said Shuck.

I liked him for that. I said, 'Isn't that a Harley-Davidson?'

The film landscape was moving faster now, the music was frenzied, the engine screamed. The girl started doing little stunts, horsing around, lifting her legs, throwing her head back. She bugged out her eyes and shrieked; she covered her face with her hands. There was a terrific crash. The landscape halted, the motorcycle tipped over, the naked girl took a spill and sprawled across the machine in the posture of an injured rider, her legs spread, her head awry, her arms tangled in the wheels.

Around us, Chinese businessmen, *towkays* in immaculate suits, applauded wildly and shouted, '*Hen hao!*', which meant 'Very good' and sounded like 'And how!'

'This is where I draw the line,' I said. 'Let's get out of here.' The act had disturbed me – what fantasy did such violence promote? – and I avoided mentioning it to Shuck. Walking down Orchard Road, past Tang's, and confounded by what to say, I asked him again about his business.

'You might say "Asian affairs",' said Shuck.

'Well,' I said, 'how do you expect to know anything about Asian affairs if you've never had one?'

Madam Lum greeted me as an old friend, with an affectionate bear-hug, and with her arms around me she turned to Shuck and said, 'Mister Jack a very nice boy and he my best brother, no, Jack?'

'She's a real sweetie,' I said.

'You want Mona?' asked Madam Lum. 'She free in a coupla minutes – hee-hee!'

'Who's Mona?' asked Shuck.

'One of the fruit-flies,' I said. 'Rather athletic. She's got a nine-inch tongue and can breathe through her ears.'

'Just my type,' said Shuck, looking around. 'Cripe, look at all the broads.'

Over by the window, three girls were seated on a sofa, languidly reading Chinese comic books; one in a chair was buffing her fingernails, and another was eating pink prawns off a square of newspaper. No towels, no tea. It would never have happened at Dunroamin: no girls sat down if two fellers had just come through the door. 'This is your newer sort of wang-house,' I said to Shuck. 'Not my style at all.' One of the girls put down her comic and sauntered over to Shuck, smoothing her dress.

'What your name?' she asked.

'Shuck.'

'Twenty-over dollar.'

'No, no,' said Shuck, wincing, setting his mouth so as not to lisp. '*Me* Shuck.'

'*Me* shuck you,' said the girl, pointing.

'Forget it,' I said. But I had recorded the exchange; it was 'material', and it bothered me to acknowledge the suspicion that very soon, chewing the fat with an admiring stranger who had looked me up, I would be saying, 'Funny thing happened the other day. I know a feller with the unfortunate name of Shuck, and we were goofing off in –'

'Mona coming,' said Madam Lum.

'Not tonight,' I said. 'But my buddy here might be interested. What do you say, Ed?'

'I'm just window-shopping,' he said. Buzz, buzz. 'What was the name of that other place you mentioned?'

'Bristol Chambers,' I said. 'But, look, they don't like people barging in and out if they're not serious about it.'

'You're a funny guy,' said Shuck. 'I used to know a guy just like you.'

That annoyed me. It was presumptuous; he didn't know me at all. I could not be mistaken for anyone else. The half-baked whoremonger in the flowered shirt, with the tattoos on his arms, hamming it up on Orchard Road ('How do you expect to know anything about Asian affairs if you've never had one?') – that was all he saw. I resented comparisons, I hated the fellers who said, 'Flowers, you're as bad as me!' They looked at me and saw a pimp, a pornocrat, an unassertive rascal marooned on a tropical island, but having the time of his life: a character. I said, 'I don't want to hurt their feelings.'

'That's what I mean,' said Shuck.

'Well, what the heck's wrong with that?'

'The next thing you'll be telling me is that they've got hearts of gold, like these strippers that say they do algebra in their dressing-rooms. They're better than we are or something.'

'Not on your life,' I said and, feeling the prickly sensation that his judgement on them was a judgement on me, added, 'But they're no worse.'

'I guess you're right. We're all whores one way or another,' said Shuck, with a hint of self-pity. 'I mean, we all sell ourselves, don't we?'

'Do we?'

'Yeah. We all sell our souls.'

'Those girls don't sell their souls, pal. There's no future in that.'

'You know what I mean. Holding a job, people climbing all over you. It's a kind of screw. I do it for fifteen grand.'

'Madam Lum does it for fifty,' I said, trying to wound him. 'Tax-free.'

Walking down Mount Elizabeth, I said, 'Years ago, it was better, with the massage parlours and all that. There are still some in

Johore Bahru. Madam Lum's place always reminds me of a doctor's office. Did you notice the potted plants and magazines? The only good thing about it is that it's convenient. The number twelve bus stops here and that supermarket over there is very good, probably cheaper than Cold Storage. I usually pick up half a pound of hamburg and some frozen peas before I nip over to Madam Lum's. You can't beat it for convenience.'

'You really are a funny guy,' said Shuck.

'Thanks,' I said.

'I mean it in the good sense,' he said.

'I'll take you to the Bristol,' I said. 'It's not far. But you can't go inside unless you want some action.'

'If I must,' said Shuck, buzzing. 'What's the attraction?'

'The guy that runs it isn't very friendly,' I said. 'And the girls are nothing to write home about. It's a pretty run-of-the-mill sort of place, except for one thing.'

'Spit it out.'

'One of the bedrooms – the air-conditioned one – faces the Prime Minister's house. Some afternoons you can see him on his putting green. At night, around this time, you can get a look at him through the window. While you're in the saddle, you know? Strictly for laughs. But since you're interested in Asian affairs –'

'I think I saw him,' Shuck said later at the Pavilion where we had agreed to meet for a drink. 'He was talking to a guy with a goatee and a shirt like yours. That takes the cake,' he said, smiling to himself. 'But the hooker kept telling me to hurry up. Is that the usual thing? God, it put me off.'

'It's a popular room,' I said.

'Vientiane,' said Shuck, using the monotone of reminiscence. 'That's a wide-open place. Lu-Lu's, the White Rose. First-class hookers. They do tricks with cigarettes. "Hey, Joe, you wanna see me smoke?" I had the strangest experience with a broad there – at least I *thought* it was a broad.'

'But it wasn't.'

'No, but that's not the whole story,' said Shuck.

'I have to go,' I said.

'Wait a minute,' said Shuck. 'I'm not finished.'

'I've heard it before.'

'No, you haven't.'

'About the bare-assed waitresses in the White Rose in Vientiane, and the girl that was really a feller, and the nympho you used to know. I've heard it before. Now, if you'll pipe down and excuse me –'

'Jack,' said Shuck, 'sit yourself down. I've got some good news for you.' Buzz, buzz.

16

Sex I had seen as a form of exalted impatience, trembling as near to hilarity as to despair – just like love – but so swift, and unlike love, it happily avoided both; that was a relief, grace after risk. And the strangest part of the sex-wish was that you wore all of it on your face. This assumption had been the basis of my whole enterprise. Paradise Gardens, Shuck's good news, made me change my mind about this.

'Here she comes,' I said, and Ganapaty scrambled to his feet. I was standing in bright sunshine at the end of the cinder drive by his sentry-box, squinting down Adam Road where, at the junction, the shiny bus had stopped at the lights. I folded my arms. The first fellers were arriving. Behind me, glittering, was Paradise Gardens, known in District Ten as a private hotel.

It was a new three-storey building, long and narrow, white stucco trimmed with blue, and with a blue square balcony and a roaring air-conditioner attached to every room. The usual high whorehouse fence, this one strung with morning-glories and supporting a hedge of pong-pong trees, concealed it from Dr B. K. Lim's bungalow on one side and a row of semi-detached houses (each with a barbed-wire fence and a starved whimpering guard-dog) on Jalan Kembang Melati on the other side. On our cool lawn there were mimosas and jasmine and the splendid upright fans of three mature traveller palms. In the secluded patio out back we had a small swimming pool.

The idea of Paradise Gardens was Shuck's, or perhaps that of the United States Army, who employed him and now me. The design was my own; I had supervised the construction. The catering contract was Hing's and the glass-fronted shops in the arcade – the entire ground floor – were run by Hing's relations: a tailor

(I was wearing one of his white linen suits that first day), a photographer, a curio-seller (elongated Balinese carvings, *wayang* puppets and a selection of Chinese bronzes ingeniously faked in Taiwan), a druggist with a *Rubber Goods* sign taped to his window, a barber and a newsagent. My orders had been to design a place that guests – Shuck told me ours would be G.I.s when it was done – would check into and stay for five days without having to leave the grounds. It was an early version of the tropical tourist hotel which, more than a place to sleep, contains the country, a matter of size, food, décor and entertainment. I had a vision of luxury hotels underpinning the rarest and most exotic features of a people's culture, the arts and crafts surviving in the Hilton long after they had ceased to be practised in the villages. Tourism's demand for atmosphere and authentic folklore would force the hotel to be the country. So I made it happen. We had Malay and Chinese dances every night and traditional food, and we were scrupulous about observing festivals. It took two days for our Mr Loy to cook a duck; outside Serene House the Chinese ate hamburgers standing up at lunch counters or in their parked cars at the A & W Drive-In. Once a week we put on a mock-wedding in the Malay style. It had been years since anyone had seen something like that in Singapore.

'The bus coming,' said Ganapaty.

'She's full up,' I said.

Ganapaty came to attention, a crooked derelict figure with a beautiful white caste-mark, a finger's width of ashes between his eyes. It pleased me that at Paradise Gardens I was able to employ everyone I owed a favour to: Yusof tended the big bar, Karim the smaller one; the room Shuck called 'your theaterette' was run by Henry Chow, a blue-movie projectionist who had been out of work since the raids; Mr Khoo, my old boatman, I employed as a mechanic; Gopi picked up the mail – though the post office was only across the street, his limp made what I intended as a sinecure for him a tedious and exhausting job. And the girls; the girls were no problem – fruit-flies from Anson Road, floaters and athletes from the shut-down massage parlours, the sweet dozen from Dunroamin, and Betty from Muscat Lane; all my quick and limber daughters.

Shuck wanted to see their papers: 'We're not taking any chances'. He made me fire three who had been born in China, one with a sore on her nose and a Javanese girl, a willowy fellatrix with gold teeth, reputedly a mistress of the late Bung Sukarno.

Every five days, as on that first day, the bus swayed into the driveway and I could see the young faces at the green-tinted windows. I waved. They did not wave back. They stared. I learned that unimpatient stare. It was a look of pure exhaustion focusing on the immediate, fastening to it, not glancing beyond it. It was new to me. Once, I had been able to spot a likely client thirty yards off by the way he watched girls pass him, the face of a feller running a temperature, wearing helpless lechery on his kisser, with that telling restive alertness as, turning around with tensed arms and eager hands, sipping air through the crack of a smile starting to be hearty, he looks as if he is going to say something out loud. Each fidget was worth ten dollars. But the faces of the boys on the buses that deposited them for what Shuck called 'your R and R' were expressionless and kept that bombed uncritical stare until they boarded the same bus five days later. The boys sat well back in their seats; they didn't hitch forward like tourists, and they didn't chatter.

I expected uniforms the first day. Shuck hadn't mentioned that they would be wearing Hawaiian shirts, but here they were getting off the bus with crew-cuts, bright shirts, the white socks that give every American away, and staring with tanned sleepy faces.

'Jack Flowers,' I said, stepping forward. 'Glad you could make it, fellers.'

'It's sure as hell –' a feller began slowly.

'Excuse me, sir,' another butted in. 'Are those girls –'

'The girls,' I said, raising my voice, 'are right over there and dying to get acquainted!'

Florence, May, Soo-hin, Annapurna and nut-cracker Betty,

hearing me, responded by ambling into the sunlight on the arcade's verandah. The other girls moved behind them. The fellers carried their duffel bags and handgrips over to the verandah and dropped them, and almost shyly walked over to the girls and began pairing off.

'We're in business,' said Shuck.

Later they walked in the gardens, holding hands.

The soldiers' five-day romance was a rehearsal of innocence, and then they went back to Vietnam. This all-purpose house was the only gentle shelter, halfway down the warpath, with me at the front gate saying, 'Is there anything –?' My mutters made me remember: in the passion that caged us the issue was not escape – it was learning gentleness to survive in the cage, and never loutishly rolling against the bars.

'For some of these guys it's their first time with a whore,' said Shuck. 'What do you tell them?'

'Don't smoke in bed.'

Was I serving torturers? I didn't feel I had a right to ask. I believed in justice. The torturer slept with harm and stink, the pox would eat him up, his memory would claw him. I wanted the others to wrestle in their rooms until they were exhausted beyond sorrow – a happy bed wasn't everything, but it was more than most worthy fellers got.

I write what I never spoke. Conversation is hectic prayer; it deprived me of subtlety and indicated time passing. It didn't help much. At Paradise Gardens, by the bar, showing my tattoos and joshing the girls and soldiers, I was a noisy cheerful creature. But the mutters in my mind told me I was Saint Jack. Edwin Shuck saying so casually, 'We're all whores one way or another' was parodying an enormous possibility that could never be disproved until we had rid ourselves of the habit of slang, the whore's own evasive language, a hard way to be honest and always a mockery of my mutters. I simplified. I used slang, I was known as a pimp, the girls as whores, the fellers as soldiers: none of the names fit.

I kept Paradise Gardens running smoothly, and what made me move was what had stirred me for years, my priestly vocation, my nursing instinct, my speedy hunger and curiosity, my wish to head off any cruelty, my singular ache to be lucky. I had seen a lot of fellers come over the hill, and, as I say, the drift then was away from all my old notions of sex. In Singapore my suggestions had long since been overtaken by wilder ideas, pictures, movies, potions, acrobatics or complete reticence; my vocabulary was obsolete and words like 'torrid', 'fast', 'daring' and 'spicy' meant nothing at all. What had once seemed to me as simple as a kind of ritual corkage became a spectator-sport or else an activity of nightmarish athleticism. It made me doubly glad for Paradise Gardens. The soldiers were happy with a cold beer and the motions of a five-day romance. I made sure the beer was so cold their tonsils froze and had Karim put four inches of ice in every drink. All afternoon we showed old cowboy movies in the theaterette. Some of the fellers taught the girls to swim. Every five days the bus came, and for five days most of the fellers stayed inside the gates. When they wandered it was up to the university, close by, to try out their cameras.

One group of G.I.s bought me a pair of binoculars, expensive ones with my initials lettered in gold on the leather case, and a little greeting card saying, *To a swell guy*.

'Now I can see what goes on in your rooms,' I said.

They laughed. What went on in those rooms, anyway? *Aw, honey*, the purest cuddlings of romance, pillow fights; they tickled the girls silly, and they never broke or pilfered a thing.

'You won't see much in Buster's,' one said.

I turned to Buster. 'That right? Not interested in poontang?'

'I can't use it,' Buster said, with a lubberly movement of his jaw.

'Buster's married.' The feller looked at me. 'You married, Jack?'

'Naw, never got the bug – ruins your sense of humour,' I said.

'Marriage – I've got nothing against it, but personally speaking I'd feel a bit overexposed.'

'Where's your old lady, Buster?' the feller asked.

'Denver,' said Buster, shyly, 'goin' ape-shit. How about a hand of cards?'

'Later,' a tall feller said. 'My girl wants a camera.'

My girl. That was Mei-lin. They all wanted cameras; they knew the brands, they picked out the fanciest ones. When the fellers boarded the bus for the ride back to the war the girls rushed to Sung's Photo in the arcade and sold them for half-price.

'Used camera,' said Jimmy Sung, when I challenged him.

'Cut the crap,' I said. It was a shakedown. From a two-hundred-dollar camera Sung made a hundred and the girl made a hundred; the soldier paid. But Sung ended up with the camera, to sell again.

'Full prices for the cameras,' I said to Sung, 'or I'll toss you out on your ear.'

In the kitchen Hing made up huge deceitful grocery lists which he passed to Shuck without letting me see, and he got cheques for items he never bought. The arcade prices were extortionate, the girls were grasping. No one complained. On the contrary, the fellers often said they wanted to marry my girls and take them back to the States, 'the world', as they called it.

I did what I could to reduce the swindling. The arcade shop-keepers saw it my way. 'Sure, sure', they'd say, and claw at their stiff hair-bristles with their fingers when I threatened.

In Sung's, on the counter, there was an album of photographs, a record of Paradise Gardens which thickened by the week. Many were posed shots Sung had snapped, tall fellers embracing short dark girls, fellers around a table drinking beer, muscle-flexers by the pool, group shots on the verandah, candid shots – fellers fooling with girls in the garden. There were many of me, but the one I liked showed me in my linen suit, having my late-afternoon gin, alone in a wicker chair under a traveller palm, with a cigar in my mouth; I was haloed in gold and green, and dusty beams of sunlight slanted through the hedge.

Shuck was right: the news was good, almost the glory I had imagined. I was surprised to reflect that what I wanted had taken a war to provide. But I hadn't made the war, and I would have been happier without the catastrophe. In every picture in Sung's album the war existed in a detail as tiny and momentous as a famous signature or a brace of well-known initials at the corner of a painting: the dog-tag, the socks, the military haircut, the inappropriate black shoes the fellers wore with their tropical clothes, a bandage or scar, a particular kind of sun-glasses, or just the fact of a farmboy's jowl by the pouting rabbit's cheek of a Chinese girl. In the house it was a smell, leather and starch and after-shave lotion, and a nameless apprehension like the memory of panic in a room with a crack on the ceiling that grows significant to the insomniac towards morning. 'Saigon, Saigon,' the girls said; we didn't talk about it, but the fellers left whispers and faces behind we could never shoo away.

And Sung's photograph album, the size of a family Bible and bound with a steel coil, was our history.

A sky of dazzling asterisks: the Fourth of July. The fellers set off rockets and roman candles in the garden with chilly expertness, a sequence of rippling blasts that had Dr B. K. Lim screaming over the hedge and all the guard-dogs in the neighbourhood howling. The fellers ate weiners and sauerkraut, had a rough touch-football game; that night everyone jumped into the pool with his clothes on.

Mr Loy Hock Yin holding a huge Thanksgiving turkey on a platter. Fellers with napkins tucked in at the throats of their shirts. I was at the head of the table, and the feller next to me said, 'How'd you get all those tattoos, Jack?' The fans were going, the table was covered with food, I had a bottle of gin and a bucket of ice beside my glass. 'What I'm going to tell you is the absolute truth,' I said, and held them spellbound for an hour. At the end I showed my arm to Betty.

'What's underneath that flower?' I asked.

She squinted. '"Whore's Boy".'

Me as Santa Claus, with a sack. Late Christmas afternoon we ran out of ice. I drove downtown in Shuck's Toyota with four uproarious soldiers and some squealing girls. I was still wearing my red suit, perspiring in my cotton beard, as we went from shop to shop saying, 'Ice for Santy!' On the way back, in traffic, we sang Christmas carols.

Gopi with an armful of mail. He said, 'Nice post for you.' Postcards of Saigon I taped to my office wall. Messages: 'It's pretty rough here all around –' 'When I get back to the world –' 'Tell Florence my folks don't care, and I'll be down in September –' 'We could use a guy like you, Jack, for a few laughs. This is a really shitty platoon –' 'The VC were shelling us for two days but we couldn't even see them –' 'Richards got it in Danang, but better not tell his girl –' 'What's the name of that meat on sticks Mr Loy made – ?' 'I had a real neat time at Paradise Gardens. How's Jenny?' 'It's fucken gastly or however you write it – I know my spelling is beyond the pail –'

A Malay orderly in a white smock tipping a sheeted stretcher into the back of an ambulance.

'Fella in de barfroom no come out.'

I knocked. No answer. We got a crowbar and prised the lock apart. The feller had hanged himself on the shower-spout with a cord from the venetian blind. A whisky bottle, half full, stood on the floor. He was nineteen years old, not a wrinkle on his face.

'It was bound to happen,' said Shuck. What certainty! 'But if it happens again we'll have to close this joint.'

No one would use the room after that, and later the door

grew dusty. All the girls played that room number in the National Lottery.

Flood. When a strong rain coincided with high tide the canal swelled and Bukit Timah Road flooded; muddy water lapped against the verandah. The photograph was of three girls wading to Paradise Gardens with their shoes in one hand and an umbrella in the other, and the fellers whistling and cheering in the driveway.

The theaterette. Audie Murphy in a cowboy movie. 'He's a game little guy,' I said. 'He won the Medal of Honor.' A feller to my right: 'Fuck that.'

A group photograph: Roger Lefever, second from the left, top row.

'What's the big idea, Roger?'

'I didn't mean it.'

'She came down crying and said you slugged her.'

'It wasn't hard. Anyway, she pissed me off.'

'I got no time for bullies. I think I could bust you in the mouth for that, Roger. And I've got a good mind to write to your C.O. You wouldn't do that back home, would you?'

'How do you know?'

I slapped his face.

'Smarten up. You're on my shit-list until you apologize.'

A group photograph: Jerry Waters, on the end of the middle row, scowling.

'You're lucky, Jack. You were fighting the Nazis.'

'I didn't see any Nazis in Oklahoma.'

'You know what I mean. It helps if the enemy's a bastard. But sometimes we're shooting the bull at night, tired as shit, and a guy comes out and says, "If I was a Vietnamese I'd support the VC", and someone else says, "So would I", and I say, "That's for sure." It's unbelievable.'

*

The curio shop. After a while the carvings changed. Once there had been ivory oxen and elephants, teakwood deer, jade eggs and lacquer jewellery boxes. Then we got bad replicas, and finally obscene ones – squatting girls, heavy wooden nudes, carvings of eight-inch fists with a raised middle finger, hands making the *cornuto*.

The Black Table.

'I'd like to help you, George, but it's against the rules to have segregated facilities.'

'We don't want no segregated facilities *as such*, but what we want's a table to sit at so we don't have to look at no charlies. And the brothers they asked me to spearhead this here thing.'

'I don't think it's a good idea,' I said.

'I ain't asking you if you think it's a good idea. I'm telling you to get us a table or we'll waste this house.'

'You only have three more days here. Is it too much to ask you to simmer down and make friends?'

'We got all the friends we want. There's more brothers coming next week, so if you say no you'll have to negotiate the demand with a real bad ass, Baraka Johnson.'

'*Haraka-haraka, haina baraka*,' I said. 'Swahili. My ship used to stop in Mombasa. *Nataka* Tusker beer *kubwa sana na beridi sana*.'

'Cut the jive, we want a table.'

'What if everybody wanted a table?'

'That's the nitty-gritty, man. Every mother *got* a table except us. You think them charlies over in the corner of the big bar want us to sit with them? You ever see any brothers sitting along the wall?'

'Maybe you don't want to.'

'Maybe we don't, and maybe them charlies and peckerwoods don't want us to. Ever think of that?'

'What you're saying is there are already white tables, so why not have a table for the coloured fellers?'

'What *coloured fellers*?'

'Years ago –'

'We are *black* brothers and we wants a *black* table!'

'The point is I didn't know there were white tables. I would have put my foot down.'

'Go ahead, mother, put your foot down, you think I care? I'm just saying we want a table – *now* – and if we don't get it we'll waste you. Dig?'

It was true. Yusof said so: we had a wall of 'white' tables. I gave in. Sung's photograph showed smiling and frowning faces, all black, and long-haired Tamil girls – the only ones they would touch, because they were black, too.

'Give them what they want,' said Shuck.

'Up to a point,' I said; 'that's my philosophy.'

Me in my flowered shirt, having a beer with three fellers. A middle-aged sentence recurred in my talk, 'That was a lot of money in those days –'

A group photograph; Bert Hodder, fifth from the end, middle row. He got tanked up one night and stood on his chair and sang:

'East Toledo High School,
The best high school in the world!
We love East Toledo,
Our colours are blue and gold.'

Neighbourhood kids from the block of shop-houses around the corner. They were posed with their arms around each other. They lingered by the gate, calling out, 'Hey, Joe!' Ganapaty chased them with an iron pipe. The fellers chatted with them and gave them errands to run. They came to my office door.

'Ten cents, mister.' This from one in a clean white shirt.

'Buzz off, kid, can't you see I'm busy?'

'Five cents.'

'Hop it!'

*

Edwin Shuck. His blue short-sleeved shirt, freckled arms and narrow neck-tie; clip-on sun-glasses, sweat-socks and loafers.

'Got a minute?' he asked.

I was with Karim. 'The cooler's kaput. I'll be with you in a little while.'

'That can wait,' he said. 'I've got to see you in your office.'

'Okay,' I said, and wiped my greasy hands on a rag.

Shuck poured himself a drink at my liquor cabinet. He closed the door after me.

'I spent yesterday afternoon with the Ambassador.'

'How's his golf game?' I took a cigar out of the pocket of my silk shirt.

'He spent yesterday morning with the Army.'

'So?'

'I've got some bad news for you.'

'Spill it,' I said. But I had an inkling of what it would be. A week before, a Chinese feller named Lau had come to me with a proposition. He was from Penang and had twenty-eight girls up there he wanted to send down. He expected a finder's fee, busfare for all of them and a job for himself. He said he knew how to do accounts; he also knew where I could get some pinball machines, American sports equipment, a film projector and fittings for a swimming pool, including a new diving board. I told him I wasn't interested.

'They're closing you up,' said Shuck.

'That's one way of putting it,' I said. 'Who's *they*?'

'U.S. Government.'

'They're closing *me* up?' I snorted. 'What *is* this?'

'It's nothing personal –'

'You can say that again,' I said. 'This isn't my place – it's *theirs*! So I suppose you mean they're closing themselves up.'

'In a manner of speaking,' said Shuck. 'Officially the U.S. Army doesn't operate cat-houses.'

'If you think this is a cat-house you don't know a hell of a lot about cat-houses!'

'Don't get excited,' said Shuck, and now I began to hate his lisp. 'It wasn't my decision. The Army's been kicking this idea around for ages. I've got my orders. I'm only sorry I couldn't let you know sooner.'

'Do me a favour, Ed. Go down the hall and find Mr Khoo. He's just bought the first car he's ever owned – on the strength of this job. He's got about ninety-two more payments to make on it. Go tell him the Pentagon wants him to sell it and buy a bike. See what he says.'

'I didn't think you'd take it so hard,' said Shuck. 'You're really bitter.'

'Go find Jimmy Sung. He's paying through the nose for a new shipment of Jap cameras. Tell him the Ambassador says he's sorry.'

'Sung's a crook, you said so yourself.'

'He knew what he was doing,' I said. 'I shouldn't have stopped him. I was getting bent out of shape trying to keep this place honest, and then you come along and piss down everyone's shoulder-blades.'

'Everyone's going to be compensated.'

'What about Penang? You screwed them there.'

'That's classified – who told you about Penang?'

'I've got information,' I said. 'You're ending the R and R programme there. They're all looking for jobs, and you know as well as I do they're not going to find them. It's not fair.'

'Jack, be reasonable,' said Shuck. 'We can't keep half of Southeast Asia on the payroll indefinitely.'

'Why put them on the payroll in the first place?'

'I suppose it seemed like a good idea at the time,' Shuck said. 'I don't know. I don't make policy.'

'I can't figure you out,' I said. 'You're like these fellers from the cruise ships that used to come to Singapore years ago, dying to get laid. Money was no object, they said. Then when I found them a girl they'd say, "Got anything a little less pricy?" And you! You come in here with an army, making promises, throwing money around, hiring people, building things, and – I don't know – *invading* the frigging place and paying everyone to sing *God Bless America*. And then you call it off. Forget it, you say, just like that.'

'Maybe it got too expensive,' said Shuck. 'It costs –'

But I was still fulminating. 'Play ball, you say, then you call off the game! You call that fair?'

'I never figured you for a hawk.'

'I'm not a hawk, you silly bastard!'

'Okay, okay,' said Shuck. 'I apologize. What do you want me to say? We'll do the best we can for the people here – compensate them, whatever they want. You're the boss.'

'Oh, yeah, I'm the boss.' I was sitting behind my desk, puffing on the cigar, blowing smoke at Shuck. Briefly, it had all seemed real. I had a notebook full of calculations: in five years I would have saved enough to get myself out, quietly to withdraw. But it was over, I was woken.

Shuck said, 'You don't have anything to worry about.'

'You're darned *tootin* I don't,' I said. 'I had a good job before you hired me. A house, plenty of friends.' Hing's, my semi-detached house on Moulmein Green, the Bandung. *There's Always Someone You Know at the Bandung*.

'I mean, I've got a proposition for you.'

'Well, you can roll your proposition into a cone and shove it. I'm not interested.'

'You haven't even heard it.'

'I don't want to.'

'It means money,' said Shuck.

'I've seen your money,' I said. 'I don't need it.'

'You're not crapping out on us, are you?'

'I like that,' I said. 'Ever hear the one about the feller with the rash on his arm? No? He goes to this skin specialist who says, "That's a really nasty rash! Better try this powder." The powder doesn't work. He tries ointment, cream, injections, everything you can name, but still the rash doesn't clear up. Weeks go by, the rash gets worse. "It's a pretty stubborn rash – resisting treatment," says the doc. "Any idea how you got it?" The feller says he doesn't have the foggiest. "Maybe you caught it at work," the doc says, "and by the way where *do* you work?" "Me?" the feller says, "I work at the circus. With the elephants." "Very interesting," says the doctor. "What exactly do you do?" "I give them enemas – but the thing is, to give an elephant an enema you have to stick your arm up its ass." "Eureka!" says the doc. "Give up your job and I guarantee the rash on your arm will clear up." "Don't be ridiculous," says the feller, "I'll never give up show-biz".'

Shuck pursed his lips. I didn't blame him: I had told the joke too aggressively for it to raise a laugh.

'Do you know the one about Grandma's Wang-house? Seems there was this feller –'

'I've heard it,' said Shuck. '"You've just been screwed by Grandma".'

'That's how I feel,' I said. I split a matchstick with my thumbnail and began picking my teeth.

'Just listen to my proposition, then say yes or no.'

'No,' I said. 'Like the feller says, it's a question of mind over matter. You don't mind and I don't matter. Get it?'

'You're being difficult.'

'Not difficult – impossible,' I said, and added, 'Mister Shuck,' lisping it with the same fishmouth buzz that he gave his name. I regretted that, and to cover it up, went on, 'Now, if you'll excuse me, I think I'll go break the news to Hing. I get the feeling Hing and I are on our way back to Beach Road. I'm not really a pimp, you know. That's just talk.' I puffed the cigar and grinned at him. 'I'm a ship chandler by profession, and it's said that at ship chandling I'm a crackerjack.'

I winked.

Shuck glumly zipped his briefcase. 'If you ever change your mind –'

'Never!'

At lunch-time it rained and the rain quickly developed into a proper storm, a Sumatra of the same velocity I had weathered in the harbour on Mr Khoo's launch when we towed that lighterful of girls to the *Richard Everett*. Ever since then storms had excited me: I could not read or write during a storm, and for the duration of the rain and wind my voice was louder; I found it easy to laugh, and I drank more quickly, standing up, peering out the window. I couldn't turn my back on a storm. I switched off the radio and watched this one from my office at Paradise Gardens. It grew as dark at half-past twelve as it was at nightfall – not sunset, but after that, dark sunless evening. I threw the windows open to hear the storm; it was cool, not raining yet, but very dark, with leaves turning over and stiff branches blowing like hair.

The lower part of the sky was lighted dully and all the pale green grass and the palm-leaves turned olive, and tree-trunks blackened. The birds disappeared: a last blown one straggled over Dr Lim's hedge. The fronds of the traveller palms parted and the larger trees swayed, and in the darkness the widely spaced drops began, as big as half-dollars, staining the driveway. There was a rumble of far-away thunder. At the beginning it was still dark, but with the torrent it grew silvery, the air brightened as the rain came down, and softened to daylight as the larger clouds collapsed into the dense glassy streaks of the downpour flooding the garden. Soon it was all revolving sound and water and light; the trees that had thrashed grew heavy, the drooping leaves seeming to force the branches downwards. Water foamed and bubbled down the rooftiles and flooded the gutters of Dr Lim's bungalow.

It continued for less than an hour, and before it was over the sun came out and made the last falling drops and the mist from the hot street shine brilliantly. Everything the rain touched glistened and dripped, and afterwards all the houses and trees and pushcart awnings and bamboo fences were changed. The wetness gave everything in the sun the look of having swelled and, just perceptibly, buckled.

Some months later, in the old shop on Beach Road, Gopi the *peon* sidled into my cubicle, showed me two large damp palms and two discoloured eyes and said, 'Mister Hing vaunting Mister Jack in a hurry-*lah*.' You know what for.

PART THREE

17

The smoke behind me – Leigh combusted – as I drove from the crematorium with Gladys, was the same pale colour as the mid-morning Singapore cloud that sinks in a steamy mass over the island and grows yellow and suffocating throughout the afternoon, making the night air an inky cool surprise. I felt relief, a springy lightness of acquittal that was like youth. I was allowed all my secrets again, and could keep them if I watched my step. It was like being proven stupid and then, miraculously, made wise: a change of air.

Leaving, I was reminded of the chase of my past, my season of flights and reverses; and I began to understand why I had never risen. The novelist's gimmick, the dying man seeing his life flash before him, is a convenient device but probably dishonest. I had once been clobbered on the head: my vision was an unglued network of blood canals at the back of my eyes and the feeble sight of the sausage I'd had for breakfast. Pain made my memory small, and Leigh had looked so numb and haunted I doubt that he had remembered his lunch. A life? Well, the dying man risks pain's abbreviations or death's halting the recollection at a misleading moment. The live glad soul I was, bumping away from the crematorium, had access to the past and could pause to dwell on the taste of an ambiguity or to relish an irony. 'Let's face it, Flowers,' the feller had said, 'you're an institution!' I was rueful: feeling chummy, I had helped so many, stretching myself willingly supine on the rack of their fickleness – any service short of martyrdom, and what snatchings had been repeated on me! But, ah, I wasn't dead.

Leigh was dead. He had told me his plans, everything he wanted. It amounted to very little, a quiet cottage on that rainy island, a few flowers, some peace – an inexpensive fantasy. He had got nothing. His example unsettled me; and as death rephrases the life of everyone who's near, I felt I was reading something new in my mind, an altered rendering of a previous hope. It was a correction, needling me to act. It worried me. My resolution, inspired by his death, was also mocked by his death, which appeared like an urging to hope at the same moment as it demonstrated the futility of all hope. His life said: *Act soon*. His death said: *Expect nothing*. My annoyance with him as a rude stranger who had messed up my plans was small compared to my frustration at seeing him dead – there was no way to reply. And worse, his staring astonished look had suggested the unexpected, the onset of a new vision irritatingly coupled with an end to speech. Behind me, clouding Upper Aljunied Road, was the smoke of that dumb prophet, made private by death, who had stared at an unshareable revelation, which might have been nothing at all.

'Where I am dropping?' Gladys's voice ended my reverie.

'Palm Grove.'

'Air-con?'

'I wouldn't be a bit surprised.'

'I *like* Palm Grove.' Gladys hugged herself.

'Good for you,' I muttered.

'You sad, Jack. I know. You friend dead,' said Gladys. 'He was a nice man, I think.'

'He wasn't,' I said. 'But that's the point, isn't it?'

'Marry with a wife?'

'Yeah,' I said. 'In Hong-Kong. The cremation was her idea. She chose the hymn. The ashes go off to Hong-Kong in the morning, by registered mail. She thought it would be better that way.' I could see the mailman climbing off his bike and pulling a brown paper parcel out of his knapsack. Your husband, one pound, eight ounces; customs declaration and so forth. *Sign here, missy*.

'Why you not marry?'

'That's all I need.' Marriage! Any mention of the Chinese gave me a memory-picture of a caged shop near Muscat Lane, the family seated grumbling around a table (Junior doing his homework), beneath an unshaded bulb of uselessly distracting brightness; I couldn't think of the Chinese singly – they lived in gangs and family clans, their yelling a simulation of speech. The word marriage gave me another picture, a clinical American bathroom, locked for the enactment of marriage: Dad shaving, Mom on the hopper with her knees pressed together, the kids splashing in the tub, all of them naked and yakking at once. It was unholy, safety's wedded agony; I had been tempted, but I had never sinned that way. I said to Gladys, 'What about you?'

'Me? Sure, I get marry every night!' She cackled. My girls were always asked the same questions – name, age, status – and they built a fund of stock replies. It was possible for me to tell by the speed and ingenuity of the reply how long a girl had been in the business. *I get marry every night*: Gladys was an old-timer.

In the lobby of the Palm Grove Hotel a huddle of tourists gave us the eye as we walked towards the elevator. If I needed any proof that there was no future in hustling for tourists there it was: two wizened fellers gasping on a sofa, another propped on crutches, a vacant wheelchair, a white-haired man asleep or dead in the embrace of a large armchair. Struldbrugs. Like the joke about the old duffer who says he has sex fifty weeks a year with his young wife. 'Amazing,' says a youngster, 'but what about the other two weeks?' The old duffer says, 'Oh, that's when the feller that lifts me on and off goes on vacation.'

Gladys was no beauty, I wasn't young; the tourists were watching, trying to determine the relationship between the red-faced American and the skinny Chinese girl. I hooked my arm on hers like a stiff old-fashioned lover and began remarking loudly on the tasteful décor of the lobby and the thick carpet, pleased that the suit I was wearing would deflect some of the scorn. *Who does that jackass think he is?*

Upstairs, the feller answered the door in his bathrobe.

'My name is Flowers.'

He looked at Gladys, then at me.

'We spoke on the telephone about a month back, when you were passing through on the *Empress*.'

'That's right,' he said. 'I thought maybe you'd forgotten.'

'I made a note of it here,' I said, tapping my desk diary. 'Anyway, here she is, skipper.'

Now he leered. Gladys nodded and looked beyond him into the cool shadowy room.

'Thanks very much,' he said. He opened the door for her, then fished five dollars out of his pocket and handed the money to me.

'What's this?'

'For your trouble.'

'That doesn't exactly cover it,' I said.

'It'll have to.'

'Hold your horses,' I said. 'How long do you want her for?'

'We'll see,' he said.

Gladys was in the room, looking out the window.

'Gladys, don't let –'

'Leave her out of this,' the feller said.

I wanted to sock him. I said, 'Until tomorrow morning is a hundred and twenty bucks, or Sterling equivalent, payable in advance.'

'I told you *we'll see*,' he said. 'Now bugger off.'

'I'll be downstairs.'

'That won't be necessary.'

'It's my usual practice,' I said. 'Just so there's no funny business.'

'Suit yourself,' he said, and slammed the door.

At half-past three Gladys was nowhere in sight. I was standing by the elevator, afraid to sit in the main lobby and get stared at by the struldbrugs who would know what I was up to as soon as they saw me alone. Until Leigh came I had never found that embarrassing.

Next to the elevator there was a blue Chinese vase filled with sand, and bristling from the sand were cigarette ends, crumpled butts and two inches of what looked to me like a good cigar. I was anxious, and I quickly realized that the source of my anxiety was a longing to snatch up that cigar, dust it off and light it. What troubled me was that only the thought that I would be seen prevented me from doing it.

A fifty-three-year-old grubber in ashtrays, standing in the shadows of the Palm Grove lobby. Downtown, on Beach Road, a *towkay* hoicked my name and kicked his dog and demanded to know where I was. Between the cremation of a stranger and the session of hard drinking that was to come, I had obliged a feller with a Chinese girl and been handed five bucks and told to bugger off. I had kept the five bucks. I waited, dog-like but without a woof, and went on swallowing self-pity, hugging my tattoos and watching Chinese hurry through air remarkably like the smoke their own ashes would make. I knew mortality, its human smell and hopeless fancies. What was I waiting for?

'She's not down here, skipper,' I said over the room-phone. 'You're overtime.'

'You're telling me!'

'Where is she?'

'Take a wild guess.'

'I'll inform the management,' I said. 'You leave me no other choice.'

'I'll inform the management about *you*. Moo-wah!'

'Be reasonable, skipper. I don't find that funny.'

'Stop pestering me. You her father or something?'

'Guardian you might say.'

'Is *that* what they call it these days!'

'I've just done you a big favour, pal!' I shouted. 'And this is what I get for it, a lot of sass!'

'I don't owe you a thing.'

'You owe me,' I said, 'a great deal, and you owe Gladys –'

'Go away.'

'I'm staying put.'

'You should be ashamed of yourself,' the feller said, and hung up.

In the basement corridor I passed a fire-alarm; the red spur of a switch behind glass, with a handy steel mallet hanging next to it on a hook. The directions shouted to me. I waited until the corridor was empty, then sprang to it and followed the clear directions printed on the black label riveted to the wall. I smashed, I pulled. A bell above my head rapped and rang and lifted to a scream.

18

An hour later in a phone-booth that alarm was still screaming in my ears, turning my recklessness into courage as I dialled the American Embassy. I held the receiver to my mouth like an oxygen mask; I was out of breath and, panting, felt incomplete – rushed and unimaginative. The phrases I was prepared to use, urgent offers of service my canny justifications you might say had once mercifully blessed, struck me as whorish. They had not troubled me before – 'Anything I can do –', 'Just name it –', 'Leave it to me –', 'An excellent choice: couldn't have done better myself –', 'No trouble at all –', 'It was a pleasure –', 'That's what I'm here for –', 'What are friends for –?'. But that was when I had a choice. This phone-call was no decision. It was hardly my choice; it was the last plea possible. I was on my back. I needed a favour. *Is there anything – anything at all – you can do for me?*

'Ed, remember –'

'Flowers, is that you?' It was a relief to hear Shuck's jaws, the familiar and endearing buzz as he casually moistened my name with the kiss of his fishy lisp. 'Where have you been hiding yourself?'

'Had my hands full,' I said.

'It's good to be busy.'

'It was driving me bananas,' I said.

'Nice to hear your voice.'

'Same here,' I said. 'I thought I might drop around sometime. Chew the fat. Maybe this afternoon if it's okay with you. Things are pretty quiet at the office. I could hop in a taxi and be over in a few minutes, or –'

'I'd really like that,' Shuck said. 'But I'm tied up at the moment.'

For pity's sake, I was going to say. I resisted. 'Some other time then. It's just that I'm free this afternoon, and, ah, I don't know whether you remember, but we've got some unfinished business.'

Shuck hummed. He said, 'Jack, to tell the honest truth I didn't think I'd hear from you again. You know?'

'That's what I want to explain.'

'Don't get me wrong, I'm glad you called,' he said. 'I'm *damned* glad you called.'

'How about a drink?'

'Sorry,' he said.

'What about after work? What time do you knock off?'

'I'll write you a letter,' Shuck said quickly.

'A *letter*? What if it gets lost in the mail?'

'You're a card,' said Shuck. 'Hey, heard any good ones lately?'

'Gags? No, nothing.' But I thought of Leigh, the hilarity and malice he had provoked, the embarrassment of his presence which was the embarrassment of a comic routine ('Does this establishment –?'), fumblings which circumstances twisted into laughless gestures of despair, the alien clown killed by tomfoolery. At a distance, as a story – with death absent – it was a joke I could enter into. But death turned the shaggy-dog story into tragedy by making it final. If Leigh had survived I would have found it all screamingly funny; I could have kicked his memory with a mocking story at the Bandung. But it was different, I was on the phone; the memory of smoke stopped my mouth.

'You'll get the letter tomorrow,' said Shuck. 'Stay loose.'

It was delivered to Hing's by an embassy *peon*. I signed for it and took it into my cubicle to open. It was a limp envelope of the sort that, just squeezing it in my fingers, I knew contained nothing important. I slit it open and shook out a brown coupon and a small memo. The coupon said, *Harbour Tour – Admit One Adult $3.50*; the memo specified a day and time, and bore Edwin Shuck's squinting initials.

'We can talk better here,' said Shuck on the launch *Kachang*. We climbed the ladder to the cabin roof and took up positions some distance from the tourists. Shuck looked back and said, 'Hold the phone.'

A feller in a straw hat had crawled up behind us. He said, 'Hi! Do me a favour? Take a picture of me and my wife? That's her down there, with the hat. All you have to do is look through here and snap. I've set the light-meter. Swell.'

'It's not usually this crowded,' said Shuck, aiming the camera at the man and wife on the afterdeck.

'Thanks a lot,' said the feller, retrieving his camera. 'How about a snap of you two? I'll send you a print when we get back to the States.'

'No,' said Shuck sharply, and turned away and closed his eyes in an infantile gesture of refusal.

The *Kachang*'s engine whirred and pumped, and she leaned away from the quay steps. All around us a logjam of bumboats and sampans began to chug and break up, bobbing across our bow. Waiting behind a misshapen barricade of duffel bags and cardboard suitcases at the top of the stairs were six sun-burned Russians, two stocky women with headscarves and cotton dresses, four men with slavic lips, blond crewcuts, transparent nylon shirts and string vests. One smoked a tube-like cigarette.

'Russkies,' I said.

'What do *they* want?' muttered Shuck.

'Going out to their ship,' I said. 'Next stop Bloodyvostok, heh.'

Grey sluggish waves, streaked with garter snakes of oil slick, sloshed at the cement stairs, lapped at an upper step, then subsided into rolling froth, depositing a crushed plastic bottle on a step halfway down. A new wave a second later lifted the bottle a step higher. I watched the progress of this piece of flotsam travelling up and down the stairs – the stairs where smalltoothed Doris Goh had stumbled and soaked herself, where my handsome girls had boarded sampans in old pyjamas and overalls and giggled all the way to the freighters.

It was late afternoon; the sun behind the Customs House and Maritime Building put us in shadow that made the inner harbour all greasy water and dark vessels. But farther out, where the water was lit, purest at the greatest distance, ships gleamed and made true reflections in the sky-blue sea mirror.

'See that little jetty?' I said. 'Years ago, I used to take gals out from it in little boats. There, where that old feller's in the sampan.'

The old man in flapping black pyjamas, his foot braced against a plank seat, stirred his long oar-pole back and forth on its crutch, rocking the sampan through the continual swell.

'I used to worry. What if a storm comes up and blows us out to sea? We're set adrift or shipwrecked. Makes you stop and think. You'd probably say, "Great, alone with some hookers on a desert island." But it would be fatal – you'd croak or turn cannibal. You'd be better off alone.'

'You'd still croak,' said Shuck.

'But you wouldn't turn cannibal,' I said.

'I'm glad you made it today,' said Shuck.

'So am I,' I said. 'God, I'm tickled to death.'

Shuck pulled a sour face. 'The way you talk,' he said. 'I can never make out if you're putting me on.'

'Cut it out,' I said. 'I wouldn't do that.'

'At Paradise Gardens I used to see you rushing around, getting into a flap and think, *Can he be serious?*'

'I worried about those fellers,' I said. The *Kachang* was a hundred yards out; the tour-guide had started his spiel. 'That grey stone building over there is the General Post Office. One Christmas eve, about eleven o'clock, I stopped in to send a telegram for Hing. There were three Marines in there sending telegrams – to their folks, I suppose. I followed them out, and down the street. They headed over Cavanagh Bridge at a pretty good clip and I went after them. At Empress Place I was going to say something, wish them a merry Christmas, offer them a drink or take them around. I had some dough then – I could have shown them a real good time. But I didn't do a thing. They went off with their hands in their pockets. I felt like crying. I'd give anything to have that chance again.'

The story made Shuck uneasy. 'I thought you were telling a joke,' he said. 'Don't sweat it, Jack. The military take good care of themselves.'

'It wasn't that they were soldiers,' I said. 'They were strangers. I had the feeling that after they turned the corner something awful happened to them. For no good reason.'

'You would have made a good – what's the word I'm looking for?'

'I know what you mean,' I said. 'There isn't one. Anyway, what's on your mind?'

'Hey, *you* called *me*, remember?'

'This Harbour Tour wasn't my idea,' I said. 'I just wanted to shoot the bull in your office.'

'You said we had some unfinished business.'

'Did I? Oh, yeah, I guess I did.' I tried to laugh. Shuck's silence prompted me. I said, 'I'm looking for work.'

'What makes you think I can help you?'

'You said you had a proposition. I told you I wasn't interested. Now I am.'

'I remember,' said Shuck. 'You told me to roll it into a cone and shove it.'

'A figure of speech,' I said. 'I got a little hot under the collar – can you blame me?' I leaned close. 'Ed, I don't know what you had in mind, but I could be very useful to you.'

If he laughs I'll push him overboard, I thought.

Shuck said faintly, 'Try me.'

I was trembling. I was prepared to do anything, say anything. 'See that channel?' I said. 'Well, follow it far enough and you come to Raffles Lighthouse. Go a little beyond it and you're in international waters. You don't know what goes on there. I do.'

'What does that prove?'

'Listen,' I said, 'smugglers from Indonesia sink huge bales of heroin in that water and then go away. Skin-divers from Singapore go over and dredge it up. That's how the stuff's transferred – underwater. You didn't know that.'

'That's the narcotics division. Not my bag.'

'Commies your bag? How about the Goldsmiths and Silversmiths Union on Bras Basah Road – what do you know about them?'

'We've got a file on them.'

'I know a feller who's a member – pal of mine, calls me Jack. He makes teeth for my girls. I could show you the teeth.'

'Making gold teeth doesn't count as subversion, Jack.'

'He's a Maoist,' I said. 'They all are. What I'm trying to say is I'm welcome in that place any time. I could get you names, addresses, anything.'

'That stuff's no good to us.'

'I'll buy that – I'm just using it as an example,' I said. 'Don't forget, I've been hustling in Singapore for fourteen years. What I don't know about the secret societies isn't worth knowing. See those tattoos? I've learned a trick or two.'

Shuck smiled.

'You look suspicious,' I said.

'You're too eager,' said Shuck. 'We get guys coming into the embassy every day with stories like that. They think we'll be interested. Lots of whispering, et cetera. The funny thing is, we know most of it already.'

I tried a new tack. 'Tell me frankly, what's the worst job you can imagine?'

'Frankly yours,' said Shuck. 'I think hustling is about as low as you can go.'

'Fair enough,' I said. 'Now, who's the straightest feller you know?'

'I used to think it was you.'

'Why don't you think so now?'

'You're coming on pretty strong, Jack.'

'I'm looking for work,' I said. I was getting impatient. 'You told me you had a proposition. All I want to know is – is it still on? Because if it is, I'm your man.'

The *Kachang* was speeding alongside a wharf where a high

black tanker was tethered. The tour-guide was saying, '– fourth largest port in the world –'

'It was just an idea,' said Shuck finally. 'And the whole thing's pretty unofficial. I mean, it's *my* baby, not Uncle Sam's.'

'All the better,' I said. 'So it's just between us two.'

'There's someone else,' said Shuck. 'But he doesn't know a thing.' Shuck spoke slowly, teasing me with lisps and pauses. 'Let's call this guy Andy Gump. He comes to Singapore now and then. From Saigon. Is there anyone behind me? No? Andy Gump doesn't do much here – probably picks up a hooker and rips off a piece of ass. That's not news to you. In Saigon, though, it's a little bit different. He makes policy there.'

'How high up is he?'

'High,' said Shuck. 'Now this is the crazy thing. No one finds fault with what he does there, but they'd shit if they knew what he did here. I'm talking about pictures and evidence.'

'Can we be a little bit more concrete?'

'I'm just sketching this thing out,' said Shuck. 'Take a guy that's got the power to keep a whole army in Vietnam. He says he's idealistic and so forth. Everyone believes him, and why shouldn't they? He's got some shady sidelines, but he's a family man, he's fair to his troops – more than fair, he covers up for them when they kill civilians. He does his reports on time and flies to Washington every so often to explain the military position. So far, so good. Now, let's say we know this guy is screwing Chinese whores – maybe slapping them around, who knows? Ever hear of the credibility gap?'

Even in the stiff sea-breeze my hands were slippery. I said, 'For a minute I thought you were going to ask me to kill him.'

'You're not *that* desperate for work,' said Shuck, 'are you?'

'In despair some fellers contemplate suicide,' I said. 'I'm different. I contemplate murder.'

'From what we hear, the same might be true of Andy Gump.'

I said, 'You want something on him?'

'That would be nice,' said Shuck, squashing 'nice' with a buzz.

'A few years ago,' I said, 'you would have been pimping for him. With a smile.'

'That was a few years ago,' said Shuck. 'Now *you're* going to pimp for him. You know all the girls, you've got friends in the hotels. It should be easy.'

'I don't monkey around with a feller's confidence,' I said. 'This is pretty nasty.'

'It *stinks*,' said Shuck. 'I wouldn't do it myself. But you might think it over and if it interests you – you say you're looking for work – maybe we can talk about the details.'

'There's only one detail I'm concerned about,' I said. 'Money.'

'You'll be paid.'

'Who names the price?'

'Good question,' said Shuck. 'Tell me, in your business who does that?'

'With hustling?' I said. 'The gal does.'

'The whore?'

'Yeah,' I said. 'The one that does the work.'

'So what's your price?'

I scratched my tattoos; the tourists hooted in the cabin below; the breeze on my face was so warm it made me gasp, and when I looked at the *kampong* on stilts we were passing I saw some children swimming near the hairy bobbing lump of a dead dog. I said, 'I won't lift a finger for less than five grand.'

Shuck didn't flinch.

'And another five when I finish the job.'

'Okay,' said Shuck. Was he smiling, or just making another fish-mouth?

'Plus expenses,' I said.

'That goes without saying.'

'I could use a drink.'

'They pass out Green Spot when we get to the model shipyard in Kallang Basin,' Shuck said. 'What's wrong?'

'I was just thinking about Andy Gump,' I said. 'How old would you say he is?'

'Mid-fifties.'

I shook my head. 'I might have known.'

'I'll tell you a couple of stories,' said Shuck, 'just so you don't go and get a conscience about him.'

19

'And get this –' Shuck rattled on, itemizing Andy Gump's waywardness with such gloating and sanctimonious fluency he could have been lying in his teeth. Still, the image of the man, whose proper name was Andrew Maddox, rank Major-General, was a familiar one to me – so familiar that twice I told Shuck I had heard enough to antagonize me: it was not the man I was after, but the job. I did not need convincing; my mind was made up. This effort of mine, a last chance to convert my fortunes in a kind of thrusting, mindless betrayal, had required a number of wilful deletions in my heart.

But Shuck was unstoppable. He ranted, pretending disgust, though the man he described was of a size that every detail, however villainous, enhanced. Shuck's accusations were spoken with the kind of envious praise with which someone in a bar retails the story of a resourceful poisoner.

'You name a way to make a fast buck, and he's tried it,' said Shuck. And he added in the same tone of admiring outrage that General Maddox had a yacht, smoked plump cigars, sported silk shirts, went deep-sea fishing off Cap St Jacques and stayed in expensive hotels.

'I know the type,' I said.

The stories were not new – the fellers at Paradise Gardens had told me most of them without naming the villain, and Shuck had alluded to him before. But while I had taken all of it seriously, none of it had given me pause. I had lived long enough to know how to translate this bewilderment. I heard it as I heard most human sounds – Leigh's pastoral retirement plans, Yardley's jokes, Gunstone's war stories, my old openers (*Years ago* – and *I once knew a feller* –), and especially the exultant woman's moan of pleasure and pain, half sigh, half scream, while I knelt furiously reverent between her haunches – all this I heard as a form of prayer.

Vietnam stories throbbed with contradiction, but were as prayerful and pious as any oratorio. Like the tales of murder and incest associated with Borgia popes – horror stories to compliment the faith by supposing to prove the durable virtue of the Church – the song and dance about corruption in Vietnam never intended to belittle the bombings and torturings or the fact of an army's oafish occupation (the colonial set-up, with Maddox as viceroy), but were meant as a curious sidelight on a justly fought war in which Shuck maintained, and so did some of the fellers, we had already been rightfully victorious: 'But human nature being what it is –'

'I'll tell you another thing about him,' said Shuck. He screwed up his face. 'He's got a finger in the B-girl rackets.'

'So he can't be all bad,' I said. The *Kachang*, turning to port, pitched me close to Shuck's face. 'Ed, I've got a whole *arm* in those!'

'He's a general in the U.S. Army,' said Shuck. 'You're not.'

Shuck then set out to describe what he took to be the darkest side of General Maddox, his operating a chain of Saigon brothels and his involvement with the less profitable skin-trade sidelines – which I knew to be inescapable – wholesaling massages, pornography, exhibitions, forging passports, nodding to conmen and smuggling warm bodies over frontiers for the servicemen. Without wishing to, Shuck convinced me that, murder apart, this general was a more successful version of myself, his charitable carnal felony a fancier and better-executed business than 'Kinda hot', the meat-run or Dunroamin. I hadn't bargained on this; warm wretchedness thawed my resolve.

'I don't get it,' I said. 'Your objection to this feller is that he's ungallant.'

'He's a creep,' said Shuck. 'A disgrace.'

'Tut-tut, you're flattering yourself,' I said, and went on, 'Still, he's no stranger to me. If you called him a hero I'd find him ten times harder to understand.'

'That's what *you* say.'

'Heroes aren't my department,' I said. 'You want to end the war, so you try to unmask the villain. Me, I'd unmask the hero – he's your feller. Especially war heroes. If I was in charge I'd have them shot.'

'You've got some screwy ideas,' said Shuck.

'I haven't had your advantages,' I said. 'See, I don't know very much about virtue.'

'*I* do,' said Shuck.

'Good for you,' I said. 'Virtue is the distance that separates you from your favourite villain, right? It's an annual affair – every year there's a new American villain. Ever notice that? Virtuous people like you elect him, and then stone him to death. It's a sign of something.'

'Maybe it's because we're puritanical,' said Shuck.

'I was going to say bankrupt, and pretty fickle.'

Shuck gave me a sour laugh. 'So Maddox is an angel.'

'Maddox is a hood, obviously,' I said. 'But you think he has a complicated motive. I know lots of fellers like him who behave that way because they're middle-aged and have bad teeth.'

'Suppose he really *is* evil,' said Shuck. 'Think what a service you'll be doing by nailing his ass to the wall.'

'Don't give me that,' I said.

'You know what I think?' said Shuck. 'I think you don't want to do this.'

'I don't always want what I need,' I said. 'Why else would I have so little?'

'You're losing your nerve.'

'Only when you try to justify this lousy scheme.'

'Who's justifying? I told you the whole thing stinks.'

'Now you're talking!' I said.

*

Not a job – an exploit, blackmail, an irrational crime with an apt rotten name; it was what I needed, the guarantee of some evil magic I didn't want to understand. Like a casual flutter at the Turf Club on an unpromising pony, and then a big pay-off; the single coin in the fruit machine for the bonus jackpot; anything for astonishment, no questions asked. Then I understood my fantasies – they were a handy preparation for making me bold; little suggestions made my tattooed bulk jump to oblige. As a young man I had often dreamed of a black sedan pulling up beside me as I sauntered down an empty street, the door swinging open and the exquisite lady at the wheel saying softly, 'Get in.'

My fantasies provided something else: method, and a means of expression.

So: *'Follow that car,'* I said to the taxi-driver at the airport. The fantasy command, immediately suspicious to any native English-speaker, I could use in Singapore. I had wormed a copy of the passenger list from May Lim, a fruit-fly turned ground hostess. From behind a pillar near the Customs and Immigration section, not far from the spot where I had first recognized Leigh, I watched the general arrive – a tanned, well-shod, barrel-chested man who walked with the easy responsible swing of a man accustomed to empty hands. He strode past me, followed by a laden porter, and got into a waiting taxi. Now, in my own taxi, I was saying, 'Don't lose him – *keep on his tail.*'

At the Belvedere I stood next to him while he checked in. He signed the register with a flourish, then straightened up. He untangled the springy wire bows of his military sun-glasses from his ears and glanced around the lobby: that look of lust, the prompt glee of the man about to deliver a speech. I caught his eye.

'Kinda hot.'

He agreed. 'Muggy.'

'This way, sir,' said a costumed porter to him. He said, 'See you around,' and overtook the porter with long scissor steps.

I scribbled my name in the register, noting that Maddox had

omitted his rank, that he was in room 913 and was staying for a week.

'Here I am again,' I said to the Chinese clerk. 'Remember me?'

'Oh, yes,' he said, without looking up. He was scribbling on a pad. 'So you like Singapore? Clean and green.'

'A great little place,' I said.

'Don't mention,' he said, still scribbling.

'And this is a mighty fine hotel,' I said. 'I wouldn't stay anywhere else. I got sorta attached to that room you gave me before – nine-fifteen. Can you put me in the same one?'

'If it is empty.'

'I'll make it worth your while,' I said softly.

'Can,' he said, glancing at the pigeon-holes behind him.

I congratulated myself on knowing that odd-numbered rooms were on one side of the corridor, evens on the other. After all, it had only been a matter of weeks since I had fixed up Gunstone with Djamila here; over there, in the bar lounge, I had pretended to be Bishop Bradley.

'This way, sir,' said the porter at the door of the elevator.

'Put my suitcase in the room,' I said, when we got to the ninth floor. 'I'm just going to have a word with my friend here.'

The elevator operator's face creased with terror. He shut his mouth.

'You look like a smart feller,' I said. 'Do you know how to keep your eyes open?'

'Do,' he said, and widened his eyes.

'That's it,' I said. 'You're destined for big things. If you want to make a little extra money, just listen –'

After an hour my buzzer rang.

'Yoh?'

It was the elevator operator, grinning. 'I take him down to lobby. He walk outside. I come straight back.'

'Beautiful,' I said, handing him five dollars. 'Keep up the good work.'

*

'Okay, boys, this is it,' I said into the phone, and five minutes later, Mr Khoo, Jimmy Sung and Henry Chow were in my room, sitting on the edge of the bed, straining to understand the plan. *The boys, the room, the plan*: the labels had an appealing sound.

What was most touching was the way the patient fellers listened, gaunt, threadbare, unblinking: my shabby gang of Chinese commandos. It was pleasing to conspire with a makeshift army, skinny sharpshooters in cast-off clothes. I had always served the rich by depending on such people, putting trust in the only helpers I could afford, the irregulars, the destitute, the socially famished – silent Karim, crooked Ganapaty, limping Gopi, the whispering urchins who stood sentry-duty outside the blue-film sheds off Rochore Road, my girls. Poverty made them invisible, and I saw how much their devious skills resembled mine. I picked them for cunning and loyalty. I liked the drama: the rumpled middle-aged blackmailer in the elegant but smoke-fouled hotel room, saying, 'Okay, boys –' to his team of ragged disciples.

In his lap, Mr Khoo cradled an electric drill, like a nickelplated tommy-gun; Jimmy Sung held a tape-recorder, Henry Chow a camera. They hadn't asked why, and wouldn't – Chinese: the people with no questions.

'You know what you're supposed to do,' I said. 'Let's get moving.'

Henry Chow flipped the lever on the camera; he had removed the ratchet from the spools: it wound noiselessly. Mr Khoo speedily drilled and reamed a hole through the skirting-board into the next room, just under the general's bed. We took the additional precaution of disguising the microphone as a light-socket. The positioning of the camera was next. Henry took a bucket and a window-washer's squeegee, crawled from my balcony to the general's and, giving the glass doors a good splash, estimated the angle for a shot at the bed. He returned, white-faced and shuddering, heaving himself slowly over the parapet, holding tightly to the balcony rail.

'Can we sling a camera up?'

'Can,' he said, 'but curtains –'

'It's no good,' I said. 'If he goes out to the balcony he'll see it and the jig's up. We can't do it that way.' I was stumped. How *did* you take pictures in a feller's room without his knowing it? After I had spoken to Shuck I imagined myself, tape-recorder slung over one shoulder, camera over the other, in a blackmailer's crouch, by a keyhole or window, listening, watching, pressing buttons and then hopping away on tip-toe with the damning evidence.

The simplicity of that had struck me as cruel, but it wasn't so simple. This was a technical problem, a dilemma which in the solving made the cruelty slight, and as an executioner might think of himself as an electrician, absorbed in the study of watts and volts, a brainwasher a man concerned with candlepower, my sense of being a betrayer was soon forgotten in my handyman's huffing and puffing over the matter of wires, lenses, drilling and testing – so complicated that the general no longer seemed vulnerable. He was safe; I was the victim.

'Now, let's see here,' I said. 'We can't put the camera on the balcony. What about in his air-conditioner? Make it look like a fuse-box.' My boys were silent. I replied to my own question: 'That means we have to get into the room.'

'Get a key,' said Jimmy Sung.

'If only the bed was on the other side of the room,' I said. 'Then we could cut a hole up there, stick the camera through, and bingo.'

'Move the bed,' said Henry.

'He'll see the mike if we do that,' I said. 'Gee, this your original sticky wicket.'

Jimmy Sung suggested an alternative. He had once been hired to spy on a *towkay*'s wife, to get evidence of adultery. He had followed the wife and her lover to a hotel, bribed the cleaning woman to give him a key and had simply burst through the door at an opportune moment, taken a lightning shot of the copulating pair and run.

'That's okay if you want one picture,' I said. 'But one's not enough. There must be another way.'

I paced the room. 'Henry says the general's room is just like this one, right? Bed here, chair there' – the three men looked from object to object as I named them – 'bureau there, desk over there – *wait*!'

Over the desk was a large rectangular mirror, reflecting the room, Mr Khoo, Jimmy Sung, Henry Chow, seated uneasily on the bed. A mirror, distracting for anyone using the desk, made it useful as a woman's dressing table.

'We can't photograph the bed,' I said, 'but we can make a small hole in the wall and aim the camera at that mirror. It's right across.'

'Wide-angle lens,' said Jimmy.

Henry Chow smiled.

This time Mr Khoo used his drill like a chisel, to loosen plaster and scoop out brick from our side of the wall. He made a niche for the camera and punched a small lens-hole through to the other side. Jimmy Sung fitted the camera with a plunger on a long cable, and fixed the camera against the hole, bandaging it into the niche with adhesive tape.

'I guess that wraps it up,' I said.

Mr Khoo wiped his drill with a rag.

'This calls for a drink.'

Henry said no. Mr Khoo shook his head. Jimmy Sung scratched his head nervously and said he had to take his wife shopping.

'Come on, I'll treat you,' I said. 'They've got everything at this hotel. We could have lunch sent up. Anything – you name it. No charge!'

Mr Khoo muttered something in Chinese. Henry looked embarrassed. Jimmy said, 'Seng Ho want money,' and winced.

'Anything you say.' I paid them off, and when I did they edged towards the door. I said, 'What's the rush? It's early. Stick around.'

There is a Chinese laugh that means 'Yes, of course!' and another that means 'No, never!' The first is full of sympathy, the second is a low mirthless rattle in the throat. They gave me the second and were gone.

'So long, boys.' I was alone. It was bright and noisy outside, but waiting I felt caged in the dim cold room of the Belvedere's ninth floor. On the far wall was the print of an old water-colour, Fort Canning, ladies with parasols, children rolling hoops, the harbour in the distance. I became aware of the air-conditioner's roar, and shortly it deafened me and gave me gooseflesh. In my bedroom in Moulmein Green I had a friendly fan that went *plunk-a-plunk-a* and a scented mosquito coil; a fig-tree grew against the window. An old phrase came to me, my summing-up: *Is this all?* I looked at the completed handiwork and hated it. The problem of eavesdropping had been complicated and nearly innocent. The solution was simple and terrible: the sticky tape, the wires, the mirror, the black contraptions, the violated wall.

20

Crash, bang. The general went to his room after lunch, and my tape-recorder amplified the racket of his entry to a hurried blundering. The door banged, the fumbled bolt was shot. Footsteps and belches and undressing noises, the flip-flap and yawn of a shirt being stripped off, coins jingling in lowered trousers, the bumps of two discarded shoes. Then bedsprings lurching, sighs, yawps. I stood on a chair and peeked through the camera's view-finder. No girl; he napped alone, his arms surrendering on his pillow. He slept, snorting and shifting, for over an hour, awoke, changed into a green bathing suit, scratched his chest, made a face at me in the mirror and went out in clunking clogs, with a towel scarf-like around his neck – I guessed he was going to the swimming pool on the roof.

He needed tempting. But I had a sprat to catch this mackerel.

'Madam Lum? Jack here. Thelma busy? Yeah, right away. You're a peach –'

Thelma Tay goggled at the room. 'Smart,' she said, pronouncing it *smut*. She tossed her ditty-bag on the bed and went over to the window. She worked the venetian blinds and said, 'Cute.'

'It's great to see you,' I said, giving her cheek a pinch. 'I've been going out of my gourd.'

She glided up and down, sniffing, touched the ashtray, turned on the bedside lamp, felt the curtains. She was no beauty, but I knew she was capable and had the right enthusiasm. Her glossy black hair was carefully set in ringlets and long curls and crowned with a small basket of woven plaits; she had the lovely hollows in her face that indicate in a Chinese girl small high breasts. She kicked off her shoes and smoothed her shiny belted dress. She posed and said, 'Wet look.'

'It's catching on,' I said. 'Very classy.'

She undid the belt and pulled the dress over her head, and then, in her red bra and red half-slip, walked over to me and leaned her soft stomach into my face. 'You ready?'

'Wait a sec, Thelma,' I said, looking up. 'It's next door.'

She stepped back. 'You not want?'

'Not me – the feller in there,' I said, pointing to the broken wall. 'He just stepped out, but he'll be back pretty soon.'

'Oh,' she said. She sat on the edge of the bed and found something on her elbow to pick.

'How's Madam Lum?'

'Is okay. Not so busy.'

'It's hard all around,' I said. 'Not like it used to be. These people from the package tours – they're all ninety years old. God knows why they come here.'

Thelma wasn't listening. She made a miaowing sound in her nose – a Chinese pop song.

'Seen any good films lately?'

'*Dracula*,' she said. 'At Cathay.'

'How was it?'

'I was scared-*lah*!' She laughed.

I poured myself a neat gin. 'You want one?'

'Soft drink,' she said. 'Got Green Spot?'

'Thelma, anything you want –'

Crash, bang.

'It's him,' I whispered. 'Wait here. The lift-boy's going to introduce you.' I tip-toed over to the chair and looked through the view-finder.

A dark Chinese girl in a frilly bikini walked past the mirror. The door banged, and my tape-recorder spoke: *No, really, I think you were getting the hang of it. You've just got to remember to keep your legs straight and kicking and paddle like this –*

'You dirty devil,' I mumbled, fiddling with the volume knob.

'I go now?' asked Thelma. She held her shiny dress up.

I drew her over to the bed. 'Apparently,' I said, 'it's all been fixed.'

– no, keep your fingers together. That's right. Here, hop on the bed and I'll show you –

'I'm sorry about this,' I said. 'Wait a minute. I'll explain.' I grasped the plunger and snapped a picture, then went back and sat on the bed next to Thelma. 'It looks like I got you up here for nothing.'

'You no want fuck?'

'I've got my hands full,' I said. 'Don't worry, I'll pay you just the same. In the meantime let's watch our language.'

'Mushudge?'

'Oh, I don't know,' I said.

– lift those arms up! Like this – keep kicking! Sort of move your head –

Thelma started kneading my shoulders, working her way down, and then pinching my backbone. It was soothing. I got down on the bed and she took my shirt off and straddled me, hacking at my shoulders and back with the side of her hands, rubbing, clapping, like someone preparing a pizza.

'Gosh, that feels good.' I closed my eyes, enjoying it, feeling my muscles unknot.

– breath control's very important. Take a deep breath – way down. Beautiful. Now let it out real slow, and twist –

'Hop off, Thelma,' I said. I went over and looked through the view-finder. The general crouched next to the girl in the bikini who was stretched out and making loud sounds of breathing. I snapped two pictures.

Thelma had stripped and, bare, seemed serious and businesslike, her nakedness like a uniform. She straddled herself on the small of my back and dug her knuckles against my ribs, and then went through the kneading and pinching routine again, neck, shoulders, and spine, warming me all the way down to my kidneys.

'Gorgeous,' I said. Her knees were tight against my ribs, and still she rode me, jogging slightly as she massaged.

– that's what we call the crawl. Now let me show you the breast-stroke. This is a very useful one. All you have to do –

'Picture,' I said, and Thelma slid off. I wound the film and shot.

'Turn over,' said Thelma when I crept on to the bed again.

'Hey, wait a minute –'

But she had already unbuckled my belt and, laughing softly, was exploring me as she shoved my trousers down to my ankles.

– push those hands all the way out –

'You say no, but he say yes.'

'He? Who's *he*?' I looked at the tape-recorder.

'This one,' said Thelma. She gave my pecker a squeeze and made it look at me with the single slit eye on its rosy dome.

'Oh, I see,' I said. 'Our friend here.'

– pretend you're flying. That's it –

I disengaged myself and hopped to the wall to take another picture.

'You very sexy, mister,' said Thelma. 'Look!'

'That's right,' I said, 'broadcast it.'

'He *like* me, mister.'

'Not so loud,' I hissed.

'What style you wants?' She lay flat and put her hands behind her head, as if responding to the swimming lesson coming over the tape-recorder's speaker; *Floating on your back is easy if you know how –*. Then Thelma did an extraordinary thing; she knelt in a salaaming position, an expressive and dainty obedience, and put her face against the pillow, and raised her buttocks into the air. She laughed and said what sounded like, 'Woof, woof.'

'Let's keep it simple,' I said. I stood thoughtfully between the camera and the bed, holding my pecker the way a patient fisherman holds his pole. 'And don't be surprised if I hop up in the middle of it. I've got a job to do, Thelma.' I shuffled over to the bed, muttering, 'And honestly it's a very ticklish business.'

Sexual desire, a molehill for a boy of twenty, gets steeper with age, and at fifty-three it is a mountain. You pant up slowly at a tricky angle; but pause once and you slide back to where you started and have to begin all over again. *You're learning real quick*, the general said, and *Try it this way – don't be shy*, and *Let me hold you*. The interruptions of these three pictures almost undid me, and at the end Thelma said '*Ai-yah!* Like Mister Frank!'

'You've got the wrong end of the stick there, sugar,' I said. Frank, one of the balding 'eggs' from the Cricket Club, supported his love-making with an assortment of Swedish apparatus. The pesky things were always slipping or jamming and needed constant adjustment. One day I met the old feller on Bencoolen Street. He was smiling. He took an ugly little cellophane-wrapped snorkel out of his briefcase and said proudly, 'I think this is the answer, Jack. She runs on batteries.'

Thelma shook her head. She was amused but nevertheless disgusted.

'This is official business,' I whispered. 'You wouldn't laugh if you knew what.'

'Like Mister Frank!'

'Have it your way,' I said, and paid her. 'Feel like sticking around?'

She counted the money and put it into her purse. 'Madam Lum say come back with legs on. If I late she scold-*lah*.'

'Stay till six,' I said. 'For old times' sake.'

She smiled. 'For twenty-over dollar.'

I considered this.

She said, 'For twenty, can.'

'Never mind,' I said. I opened the door for her, and then I had the same feeling that worried me when the boys left: with no one else in the room I didn't exist, like an unwitnessed thunderclap in the desert. I sat down with a gin and read through the Belvedere brochures. They offered room-service – 'full-course dinners or snacks served piping hot in the traditional Malay style'. Also: 'Relax at our poolside bar – or have a refreshing dip', 'Your chance to try our newly installed sauna' and 'It's happening at our discotheque – the "right-now" sounds of The Chopsticks!' Another bar promised 'alluring hostesses who will serve your every need'.

There was a 24-hour coffee-shop, a secretarial service, French, Chinese and Japanese restaurants, and a nightclub 'featuring the Freddy Low Dancers', a Japanese kick-line and an Australian stripper. And mawkish suggestions: *No visit to Singapore is complete without* – and *You will also want to try* –

This 'you' they kept addressing, was it me? I looked at the nightclub brochure again. The stripper was waving from the seat of a motorcycle. That finished me. I changed into my flowered shirt and started lacing my shoes.

– You're sure I'm not hurting you?

– Sure.

I wound the film. I closed my eyes. I snapped and, securing my room with a *Do Not Disturb* sign, fled down the fire-stairs.

They were on the verandah of the Bandung, in the low wicker chairs with the swing-out extensions on the arms, all of them with their feet up, their heels hooked, as if they were about to be shaved. Yardley was reading the *Straits Times* to Frogget, who listened with a pint of beer resting on his stomach.

'That ghastly old sod got an O.B.E.,' said Yardley. 'Would you believe it? And guess who got an M.B.E.? This is ridiculous –'

'What's cooking?' I said, pulling out the arm extensions on a chair next to Yates and settling in. I put my legs up and was restored.

'Honours List just published,' said Yates. 'Yardley's rather cross. He wasn't knighted.'

'I'd send the bloody thing back,' said Yardley. 'I wouldn't be caught dead on the same list with that abortionist. Christ, why don't they give these things to people who deserve them?'

'Like Jack,' said Frogget.

'Maybe Jack got an O.B.E.,' said Smale.

'Very funny,' I said.

'Let's have a look,' said Yardley. He rattled the paper.

'Don't bother,' I said. 'Pass me the shipping pages.'

'Aw, that's a shame,' said Yardley. 'They missed you out again.'

'Where's Wally?' I asked.

'*Wally!*' shouted Smale. Once a feller came to the Bandung and did that very same thing, shouted Wally's name from the verandah, and Smale said, 'If you do that again I'll boot your rude arse.' The feller was an occasional drinker; no one had ever spoken to him, and after Smale said that he never came again. Soon each of us had a story, a reminiscence of his behaviour, and Yardley finally arrived at the view that the feller was crazy.

Wally appeared at my elbow.

'A double pink gin with a squirt of soda,' I said. 'And ask these gentlemen what they'd like.'

'Telephone for you, today morning,' said Wally. 'Mister Gunstone.'

It passed without a remark. I had just bought everyone a drink.

'What about you, Yatesie?' asked Smale. 'When's your M.B.E. coming around?'

'It's just a piece of paper,' said Yates.

'Listen to him,' said Yardley. His legs clattered on the wooden rests as he guffawed. 'When I came in here at half-five he was reading the paper, looking for his name.'

'That is untrue,' said Yates with a note of hurt in his voice that contradicted his words.

'He'd give his knackers for an M.B.E.,' said Yardley, 'and even the flaming Beatles got *that*.'

'I wouldn't mind,' said Smale, and cursed under his breath. 'I wouldn't complain if I got one of those things. Face it, none of you would.'

There was a moment of silence then, the silence a bubble of sheepishness, as mentally we tried on a title. Viscount Smale. Lord Yardley. Sir Desmond. Lord Flowers, I was thinking, Saint Jack.

'Who's on the list?' I asked. 'Anyone I know?'

'Apart from Wally, who got a knighthood – right, Wally? Sure you did – only Evans, the twit that works in the Hong-Kong and Shanghai Bank. M.B.E.'

'Evans? Oh, yeah,' I said. 'I know him. He's in the Cricket Club.'

'I wouldn't know about that,' said Yardley.

'Or so I heard,' I said.

'He makes a good screw,' said Smale. 'Him a banker.'

'Rubbish,' said Yardley. 'Not more than three or four thousand quid.'

'Call it four,' I said. 'It's ten thousand U.S. That's pretty good money.'

'Pretty good money,' said Yardley, mocking me. 'Four thousand quid! That's not money.'

'Ten thousand bucks would take you pretty far,' I said.

Frogget laughed uncertainly and looked at Yardley.

Yardley shifted in his chair. He said, 'That's not money.'

'No,' said Smale. 'Not *real* money.'

'I suppose not,' I said.

We stared into the garden. It was darkening; the garden became simple and orderly in the twilight, the elastic fig and the palm it strangled were one. The mosquitoes were waking, gathering at the verandah light and biting our exposed ankles. Frogget slapped at his bare arm.

'Say fifty or sixty thousand quid,' said Yardley. 'That's money.'

Someone's wicker chair creaked.

'Or maybe a hundred,' said Frogget.

'You could live on that,' said Yardley.

'You certainly could,' said Yates.

'Imagine,' said Smale.

'Funnily enough,' I said, 'I can.'

'So can I,' said Frogget.

'The last time I was on leave,' said Smale, 'I took a taxi from Waterloo to King's Cross. Had a lot of baggage. I paid the fare and told the driver to keep the change. "A bob," he says, and hands it back to me. "Fit it up your arse."'

'That rosebush wants pruning,' said Yates.

'"Fit it up your arse",' said Smale. 'A shilling!'

'It wouldn't fit,' said Frogget.

'That reminds me,' said Yardley. 'The funniest thing happened today. It was at Robinson's. Jack, you're not listening.'

'I'm all ears,' I said.

21

My week was over, though it had seemed like more than a week: it was very hard for me to tell how fast the time went with my eyes shut. It was the suspenseful captivity I had known with Toh's gang, the time no one ransomed me. I sat blinded by resolution in my luxurious armchair – luxury at that price now something like a penalty – and I recorded the general confirming his plane ticket, packing his bags, phoning for a taxi; I knew that I was listening to the end. Mr Khoo came up and filled the holes in the wall. I checked out quietly and went back to Moulmein Green. It was three in the afternoon. I slept under the fan and woke up the next day to the squeals of children playing outside my window. They were comparing paper lanterns they had obviously just bought: squarish roosters in red cellophane, airplanes and box-like fish.

A few days later, at Hing's, I was standing in the shade of the portico, watching the traffic on Beach Road, my hands in my pockets.

'Sorry,' said a voice behind me. I turned and saw Jimmy Sung unzipping a briefcase. 'The pictures,' he said, laughing, 'no good, myah!' He passed me a thick envelope of pictures.

'If they're duds it's not your fault,' I said. I flicked through the envelope and saw rippling waterstains on an opaque background; some were totally black, others smirched and blurred. No human form was apparent. I was off the hook.

'Wrong esposure,' he said.

'That's how it goes,' I said. I wanted to hug him.

'And these,' he said. He gave me a smaller envelope.

'What's this?'

'Some good ones.'

'You said they were all dark.'

'Not all.' He nodded. 'I make some extra print. Okay, Jack, I see you.'

'Be good,' I said. I took the envelope into my cubicle to open it, and with fingers slowed by dread I started shuffling. The swimming lesson was first, and though 'swimming lesson' sounds like a euphemism for a pervert's crimp, this one looked genuine enough: the girl thrashed, the general stood at the end of the bed and coached, and in one he appeared to be giving the girl artificial respiration. Some showed the girl alone, or the general alone, and at the side of the picture the arm or leg of the other. Two I liked. In the first the general was wagging his finger at the grinning girl; in the second they were staring in different directions, the general vacantly at his watch, the girl at her splayed-out fingers. It was always the swimmer. One I treasured: the general's arms were folded around the dark girl, who sat in his lap and held his head in her hands. He was a big man, his embrace was protective, and her posture replied to this. If the photograph of a posture could prove anything, this proved fondness, even if it was a hopeless adventure like his own war.

As blackmail they were of no value – the opposite of incriminating. It might have been different; in the Belvedere that week a crime fantasy had sustained me. The blackmailer photographing what he thinks is an infidelity discovers that he is witnessing a murder; he hears the threats, he sees the violence, he springs into the room, a nimble rescuer in the nick of time. It would have made a good story. Mine was not so neat, but there in my cubicle I had my first insight into the whole business: betrayal may damn, or it may vindicate. It was, after all, revelation. I had spied on the general to find him guilty; I came away with proof of something ordinary enough to be blameless. I was as relieved as if it was an affirmation of whatever well-intentioned gesture I had made: that impulsive embrace when one can believe for a full minute that one is not alone. So I was saved, and I thought, Might not some chilly grey intriguer, hard by an enemy window, watch sadness or love rehearsed and change his mind? Shuck held him responsible for a war. I could not speak for that outrage, but in one respect, the only one I had seen, the man was gentle. I had spied on innocence.

'You look pleased with yourself,' said Shuck in the Pavilion. Shuck had taken a corner table, and he looked around the bar as he spoke to me.

'I've got them.' I patted my breast pocket. 'He's in here.'

'How about a drink first?' said Shuck. 'I'm just having a Coke.'

'Gin for me,' I said. 'Well, here they are.'

We were beside a ship's clock, under a long shelf of brassware, old pistols, sabres and muskets. Shuck looked closely at the clock before he opened the envelope. He kept his poker face while he examined each picture, and when he finished and put them back he said, 'Any others?'

'Nope.'

He creased the envelope. 'He's no Casanova, that's for sure. I wouldn't have believed it. But these'll be useful. I mean, he's with a Chinese girl, loving her up and so forth. He'll have a hard time explaining that to the Pentagon. You know the girl?'

'Swimming lessons,' I said. 'Can I see them a minute?'

Shuck palmed them and put them into my hand. I slipped the envelope into my pocket.

'What are you doing?'

'Keeping them.'

'Maybe it's better that way, for the time being.' Shuck was still looking around the bar, half covering his mouth when he spoke, though with his lisp I doubted whether anyone could have understood a word he said.

'For good,' I said. 'Until I burn them.'

'Hey, not so fast,' he said. 'Those pictures are mine.'

'I took them,' I said. 'They're mine.'

Shuck laughed uncertainly. 'I know your game,' he said. 'You want more money. Okay, I'll give you more – in addition to the ten grand we agreed on.'

'It's not enough.'

Shuck gripped his Coke; his face was malevolent. 'Another five.'

'No.'

'Jack –'

'It's not enough.'

'Six,' he lisped and his expression changed from malevolence to concern. 'I understand. You're holding out for more and you think I have to give it to you because you've got something on me – because I put you up to this. I've got news for you – it won't wash. Now hand over the goods.'

'It's not enough money, one,' I said. 'And, two, you're not getting them anyway.'

'It figures,' said Shuck. His smile was grim. 'This happens with nationals all the time. Thais, say, or Cambodians. They agree on a price, usually peanuts – but they're Thais, so how do they know how much to ask? They deal in small figures, then later they want more. It always gets bigger. And then they really get expensive.'

'So you tell them to get lost.'

'Sometimes,' said Shuck. 'Anyway, as soon as you told me how much you wanted I knew you'd been out of the States for a long time. You really belong here. Ten grand! I couldn't believe it.'

'I know,' I said. 'That's not money. I'm glad you didn't ask me to shoot him. I might have done that for fifteen.'

'So what's your price?'

'No price.'

'You're putting me on again, aren't you?'

'I'm not,' I said. 'No price, no pictures. I'm giving you back the five grand. No sale.'

'You *did* lose your nerve after all,' said Shuck.

'Not on your life,' I said. 'I've even got tapes of the guy – more graphic than the pictures in a way, but harder to visualize. Muffled noises, very touching really.'

'Jack,' said Shuck, 'are you going to the other side with them?'

'You're a tricky feller,' I said. 'Do you know that until now that possibility hadn't even occurred to me?'

'You're playing with dynamite.'

'Dynamite,' I said. 'A feller kissing a girl. A girl saying "fuck". A feller in bed. A girl doing the breast-stroke. Dynamite!'

'He's a general!' said Shuck.

'He was out of uniform,' I said. 'I want to change the subject.'

'I know you're going to the Russians,' said Shuck. 'Or is it the Chinese?'

'Neither.'

'I'll tell you something,' said Shuck. 'They're not even good pictures. They're very amateurish.'

'To me they're hopeful,' I said. 'I'd give them to you – for nothing – but you'd do the wrong things with them. You'd misuse them.'

'Jack, I promise –'

'You'd put the wrong interpretation on them,' I said. 'That would kill me.' And I wanted to say, but I couldn't phrase it, that the honour he talked about was a very arbitrary notion, as temporary as power, and would be out of fashion tomorrow, when the sides changed. I wanted no part of the graceless distortion. I was a person of small virtue; virtue wasn't salvation, but knowing that might be.

'I don't believe he's guilty,' I said at last.

'How do you know?'

'Because *I*'m not.'

'If you don't hand those over, you are.'

'If I give you these,' I said, 'I'm sunk.'

'So you're trying to save yourself!'

'And you, too,' I said.

Shuck appealed, but I was scarcely listening: 'You'd never have to worry . . . I'm not talking about nickels and dimes . . . Blow the lid off this thing . . . only the beginning . . . everything you always wanted . . . *famous*.'

I was looking at the old waiter with the lucky moles on his face, the dusty sabres, the pots of beer; and I was thinking, *What a pleasant bar this is, what happy people.*

And I walked, alone, leaving Shuck and my untouched gin, out the swinging doors, stumping regally down Orchard Road, which was choked with traffic and the night-time bustle of shoppers and late eaters, past the car dealers and the Istana gardens, to Dhoby Ghaut, where a gigantic blood-flecked poster of a fanged and green-faced Dracula was suspended, garishly lit, over the Cathay marquee, past the second-hand bookshops on Bras Basah Road ('*Ksst.* Mistah, something special?'). I had panicked and acted. I shouldn't have panicked; but the act had released me. I was a lucky feller.

'Hey, Jack!' A nasal Chinese yell, the man's shyness causing him to scream. I saw a white shirt in a doorway, not a zombie – a friend with no face.

I waved to him and kept walking, cutting through the noise that was crowding me, liking the night air. I had had my nose pressed against two fellers, one dead, one alive. I knew them, and my betrayal, begun exclusively as a crime – I had insisted on that – had ended as an act of faith, the conjuring trick that fails you when you understand it. The Oriental Bookstore, Convent of the Holy Infant Jesus, Bamboo Bar, Goldsmiths and Silversmiths Union – mottled and beflagged – and down Victoria Street I could see children ducking into alleys, carrying flimsy red lanterns for the moon festival: coloured lights jostling in the dark, illuminating shirt-fronts and faces. I walked across the grassy *maidan*, past the War Memorial to civilians which looks like four flood-lit chopsticks, and, dodging traffic – pretty nimble for a feller my age – bounded to the steel rail on the harbour promenade. Out there, ship lights twinkled. This was the very edge of the island, on the thickest part of the world.

Not one life – I had had many. A memoir selects from the

interruption of different fears. There had been others; I expected more, and I was calm, for I had had a death as well. But all the actions I thought of as preparations for flight had readied me for staying, a belonging the opposite of what I wanted: familiar, yes, and yet who would willingly die here? I was no exile. There were fast planes west, and I knew the cosiest ships. Being away can make you a stranger in two places, I thought; but it wasn't a country I needed, and not money, though I knew some cash would improve my backward heart. I had a ten-dollar win-ticket on *Major-General* in the fourth race on Saturday, and a lottery ticket – Toto Number 915. Fortune might be denied me, but that denial still held a promise like postponement. No drums, no trumpets; a love-gallop thundered in my head, and the random sea-splash quickened below me, signals of danger very much like the sounds of rescue.

I was tranquil enough at last to kill myself – to toss myself into the harbour; but I changed my mind and decided to live for a hundred years. So my life was only half gone. I would celebrate the coming glory with an expensive drink at Raffles, down the road, and, time permitting, do a spot of work before I put in an appearance at the Bandung. Children with bright lanterns moved along the promenade towards me, swinging their blobs of light. I blessed them simply, wishing them well with a nod.

There was another admirer. A woman in a white dress, with a camera slung over her shoulder, leaned against the sea-rail twenty feet away. When the children passed by, she approached me, smiling.

'What beautiful children,' she said. 'Are they Chinese?'

'Yeah,' I said. 'But they should be in bed at this hour.'

'So should I,' said the woman, and she laughed gently. She was a corker. She looked across the street and held her fingers to her mouth and kissed them in concentration. 'Oh, hell,' she said, 'I'm lost.'

'No, you're not,' I said.

'Hey, you're an American, too,' she said. 'Do you have a minute?'

'Lady, I've got all the time in the world,' I said, and a high funny note of joy, recovered hope, warbled in my ears as I pronounced this adventurous sentence.

He just wanted a decent book to read ...

Not too much to ask, is it? It was in 1935 when Allen Lane, Managing Director of Bodley Head Publishers, stood on a platform at Exeter railway station looking for something good to read on his journey back to London. His choice was limited to popular magazines and poor-quality paperbacks – the same choice faced every day by the vast majority of readers, few of whom could afford hardbacks. Lane's disappointment and subsequent anger at the range of books generally available led him to found a company – and change the world.

'We believed in the existence in this country of a vast reading public for intelligent books at a low price, and staked everything on it'
Sir Allen Lane, 1902–1970, founder of Penguin Books

The quality paperback had arrived – and not just in bookshops. Lane was adamant that his Penguins should appear in chain stores and tobacconists, and should cost no more than a packet of cigarettes.

Reading habits (and cigarette prices) have changed since 1935, but Penguin still believes in publishing the best books for everybody to enjoy. We still believe that good design costs no more than bad design, and we still believe that quality books published passionately and responsibly make the world a better place.

So wherever you see the little bird – whether it's on a piece of prize-winning literary fiction or a celebrity autobiography, political tour de force or historical masterpiece, a serial-killer thriller, reference book, world classic or a piece of pure escapism – you can bet that it represents the very best that the genre has to offer.

Whatever you like to read – trust Penguin.